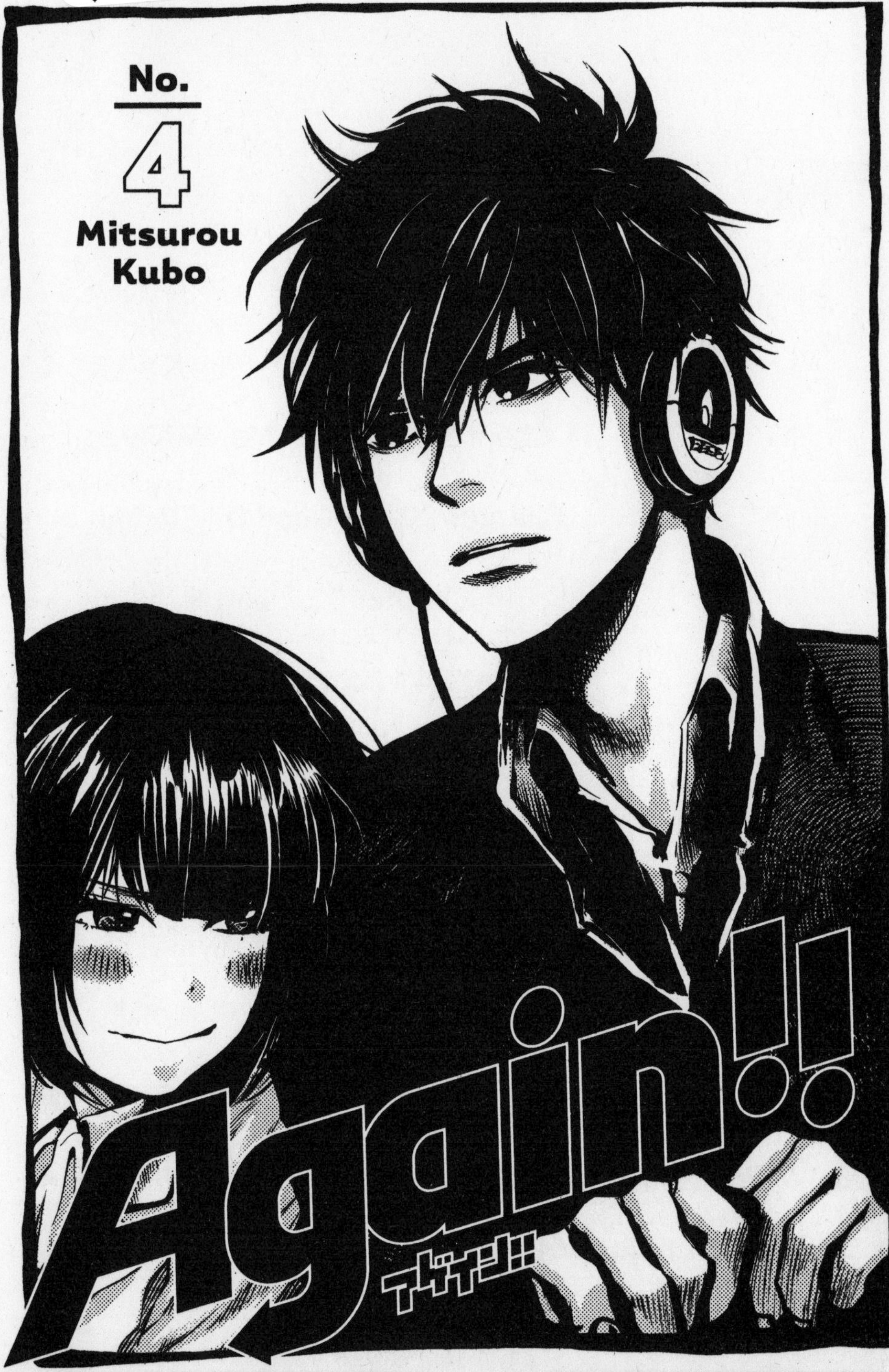
No.
4
Mitsurou Kubo
Again!!
アゲイン!!

contents

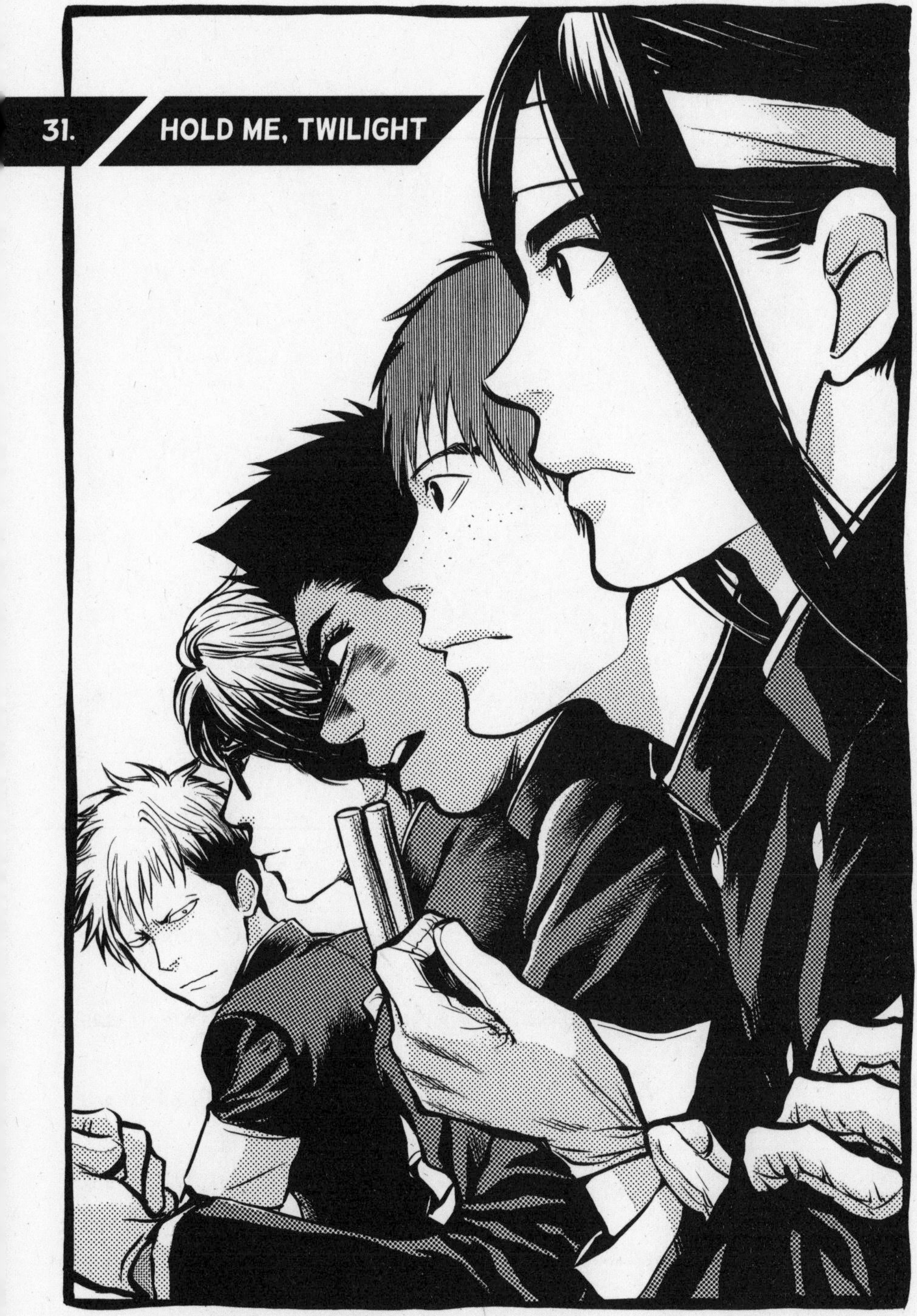
31. HOLD ME, TWILIGHT

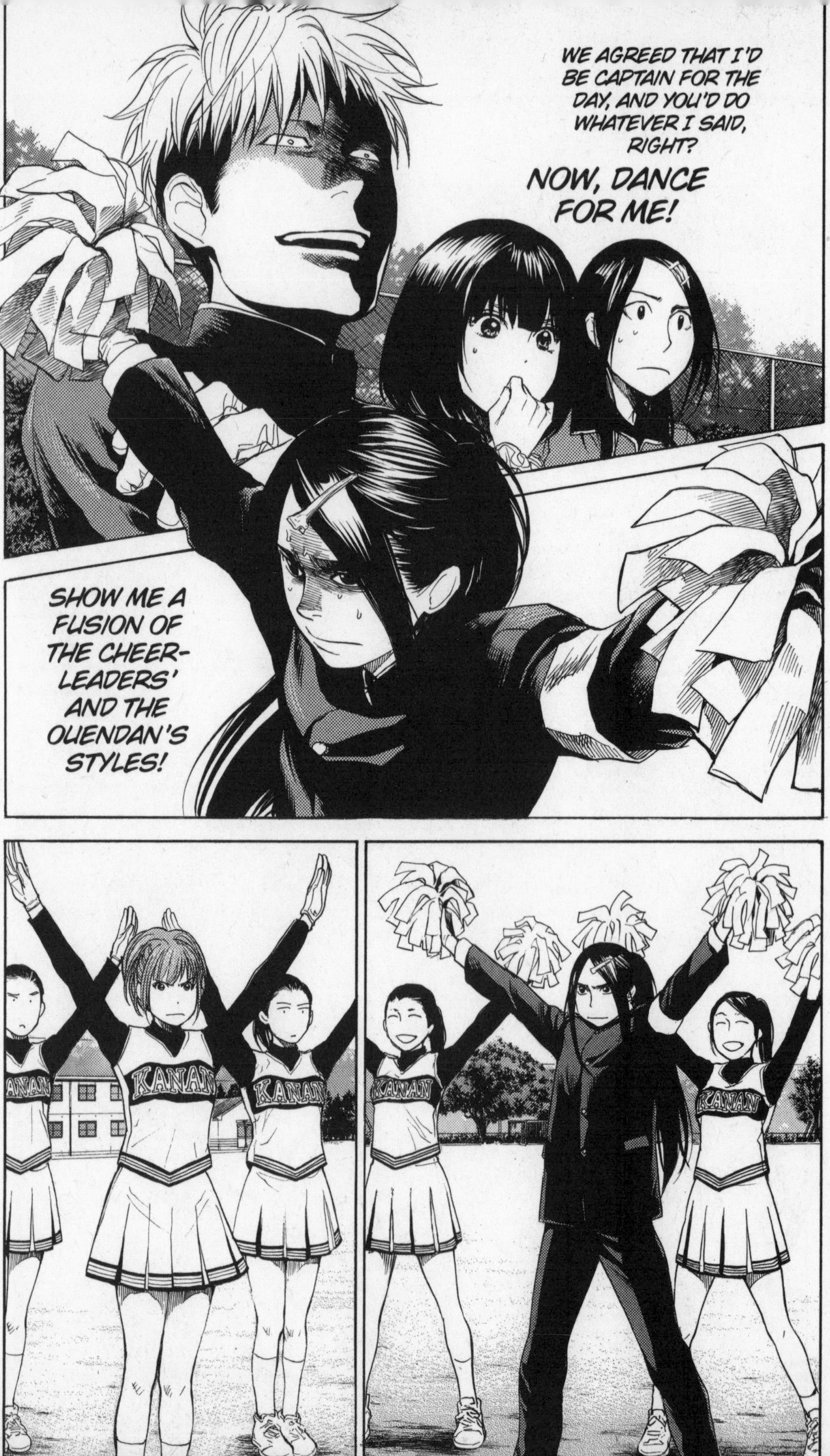
WE AGREED THAT I'D BE CAPTAIN FOR THE DAY, AND YOU'D DO WHATEVER I SAID, RIGHT?
NOW, DANCE FOR ME!
SHOW ME A FUSION OF THE CHEER-LEADERS' AND THE OUENDAN'S STYLES!
KANAN
KANAN
KANAN
KANAN

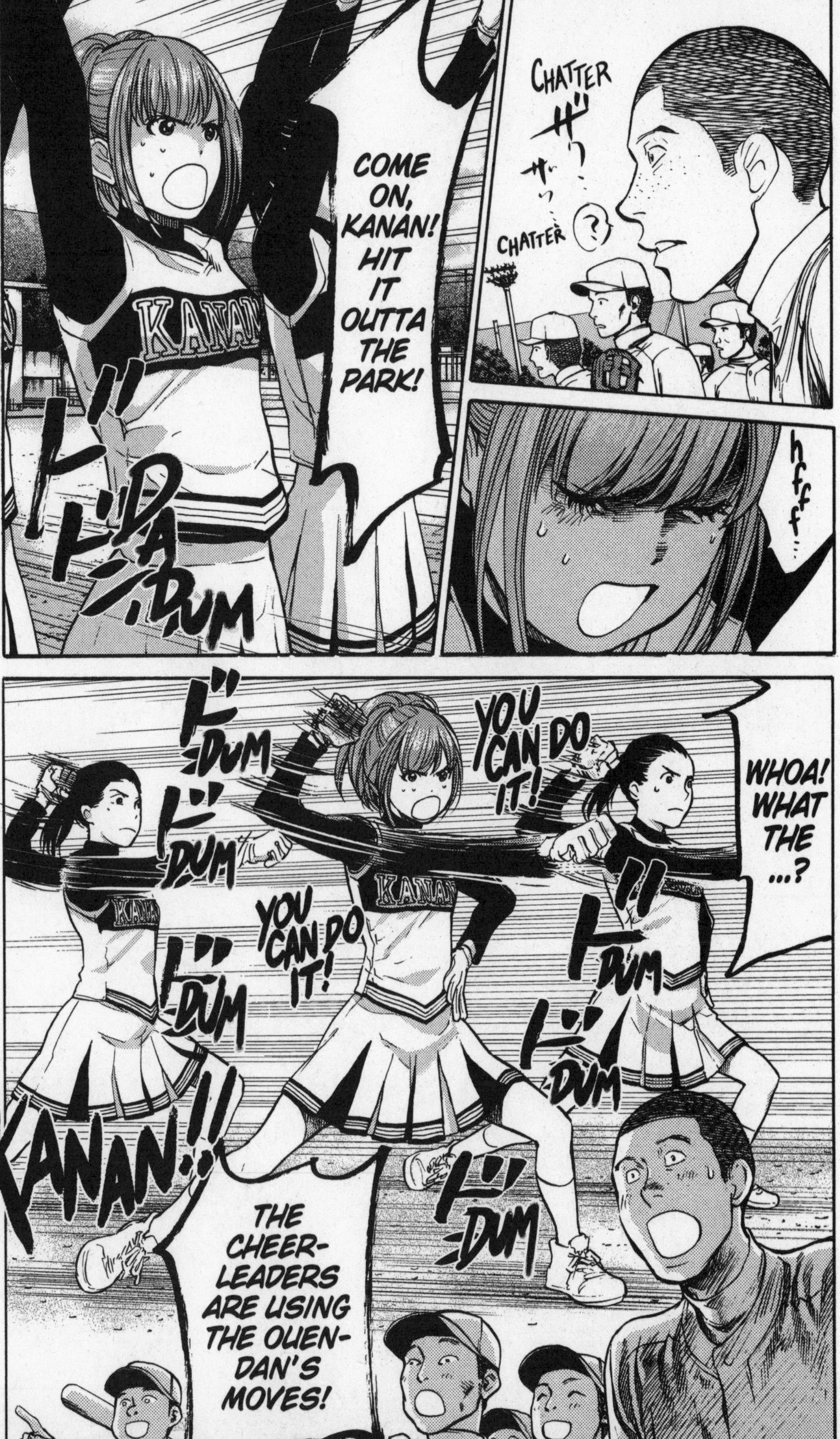
CHATTER
CHATTER
?
hfff...
COME ON, KANAN! HIT IT OUTTA THE PARK!
DA
DUM
WHOA! WHAT THE ...?
YOU CAN DO IT!
DUM
DUM
DUM
DUM
YOU CAN DO IT!
DUM
DUM
DUM
KANAN!!
THE CHEER-LEADERS ARE USING THE OUEN-DAN'S MOVES!

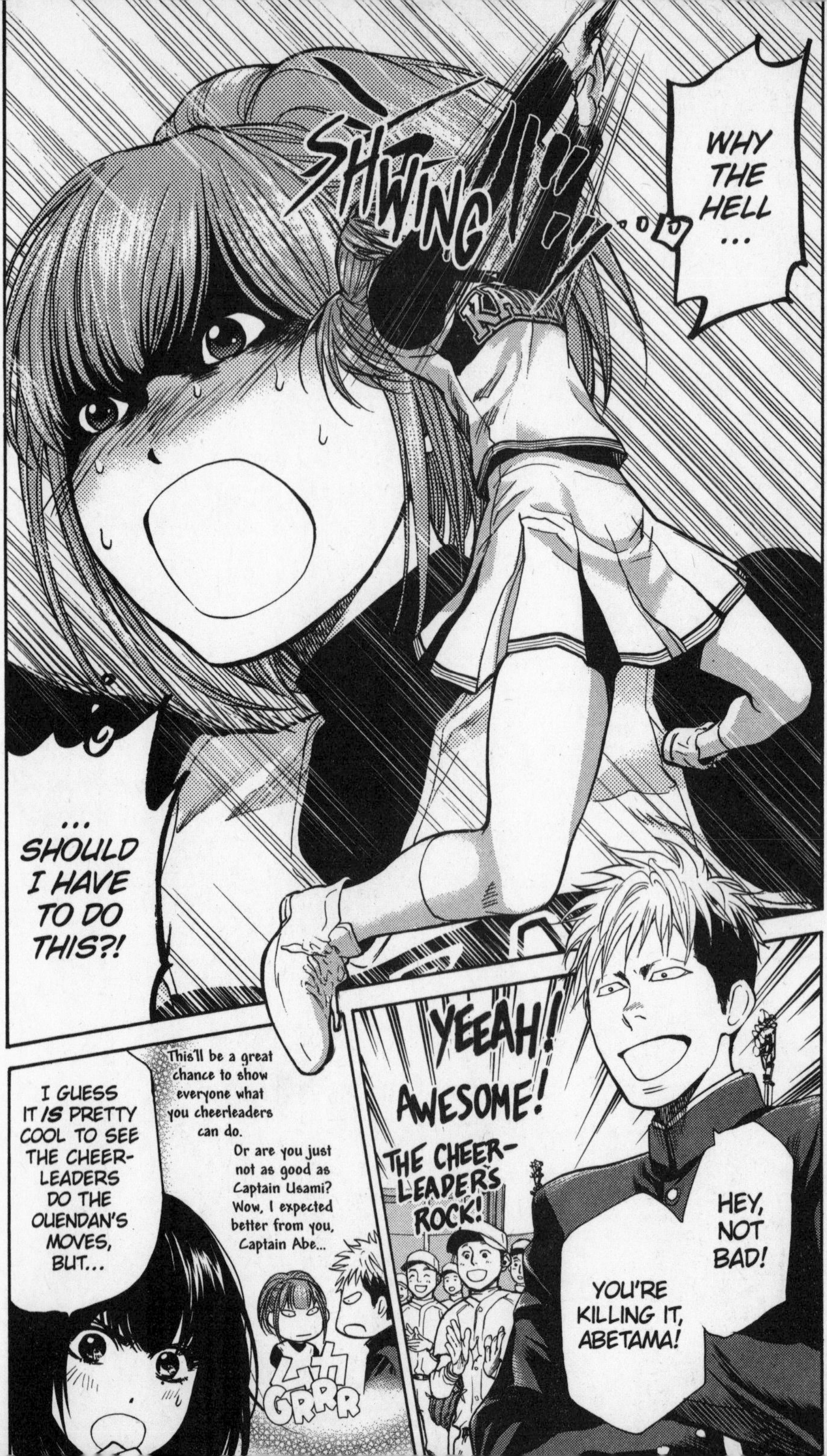
SHWING!!
WHY THE HELL ...
... SHOULD I HAVE TO DO THIS?!
YEEAH!
AWESOME!
THE CHEER-LEADERS ROCK!
HEY, NOT BAD!
YOU'RE KILLING IT, ABETAMA!
I GUESS IT *IS* PRETTY COOL TO SEE THE CHEER-LEADERS DO THE OUENDAN'S MOVES, BUT...
This'll be a great chance to show everyone what you cheerleaders can do.
Or are you just not as good as Captain Usami? Wow, I expected better from you, Captain Abe...
GRRR

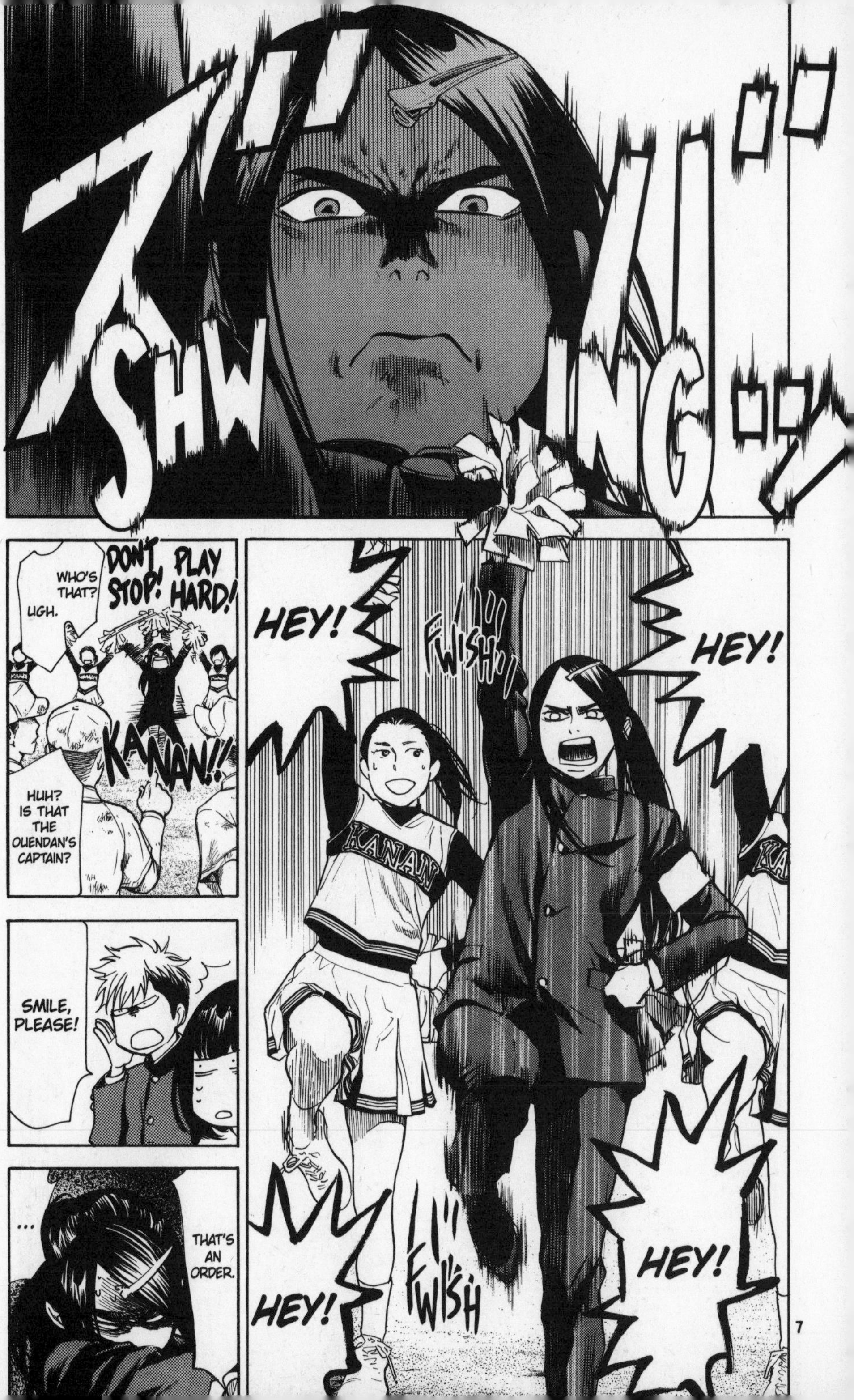
SHWING
HEY!
HEY!
FWISH
HEY!
FWISH
HEY!
DON'T STOP! PLAY HARD!
WHO'S THAT?
UGH.
KANAN!!
HUH? IS THAT THE OUENDAN'S CAPTAIN?
SMILE, PLEASE!
THAT'S AN ORDER.
...

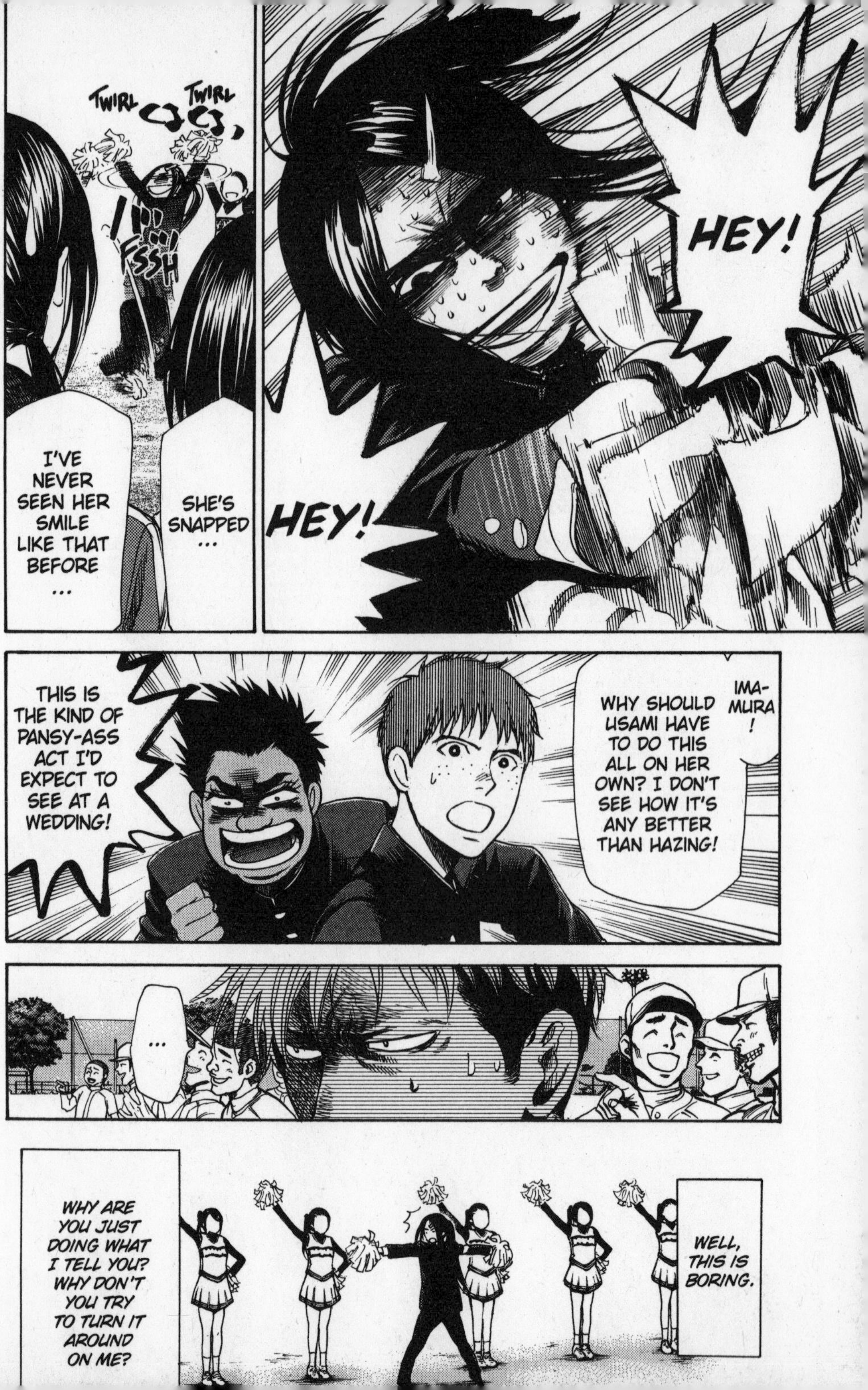
HEY!
HEY!
TWIRL TWIRL
FSSH
SHE'S SNAPPED ...
I'VE NEVER SEEN HER SMILE LIKE THAT BEFORE ...
IMA-MURA!
WHY SHOULD USAMI HAVE TO DO THIS ALL ON HER OWN? I DON'T SEE HOW IT'S ANY BETTER THAN HAZING!
THIS IS THE KIND OF PANSY-ASS ACT I'D EXPECT TO SEE AT A WEDDING!
...
WELL, THIS IS BORING.
WHY ARE YOU JUST DOING WHAT I TELL YOU? WHY DON'T YOU TRY TO TURN IT AROUND ON ME?

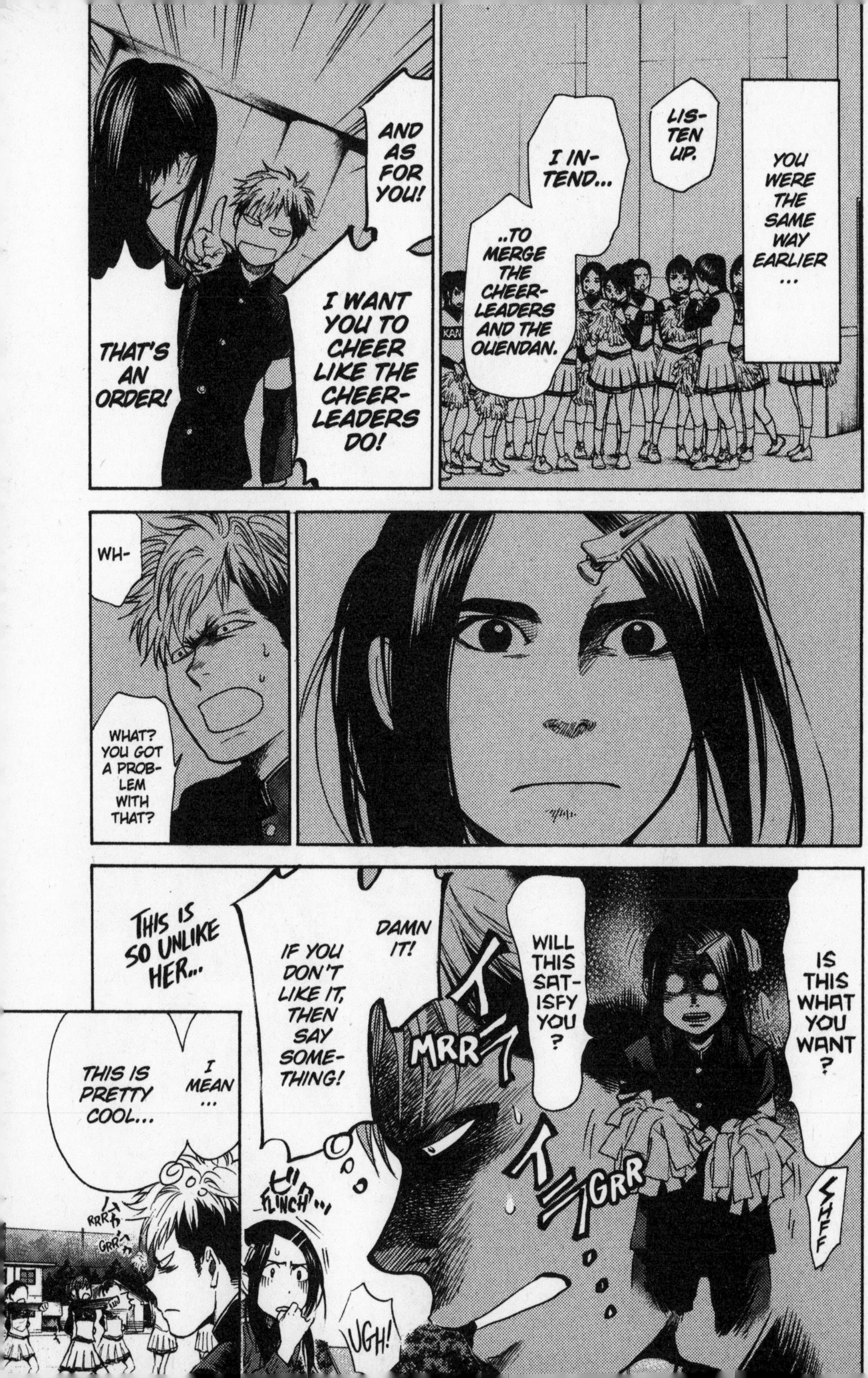
YOU WERE THE SAME WAY EARLIER...
LIS-TEN UP.
I IN-TEND...
..TO MERGE THE CHEER-LEADERS AND THE OUENDAN.
AND AS FOR YOU!
I WANT YOU TO CHEER LIKE THE CHEER-LEADERS DO!
THAT'S AN ORDER!
WH-
WHAT? YOU GOT A PROB-LEM WITH THAT?
IS THIS WHAT YOU WANT?
SHFF
WILL THIS SAT-ISFY YOU?
DAMN IT!
IF YOU DON'T LIKE IT, THEN SAY SOME-THING!
MRR
GRR
THIS IS SO UNLIKE HER...
UGH!
I MEAN...
THIS IS PRETTY COOL...
FLINCH
RRR
GRR

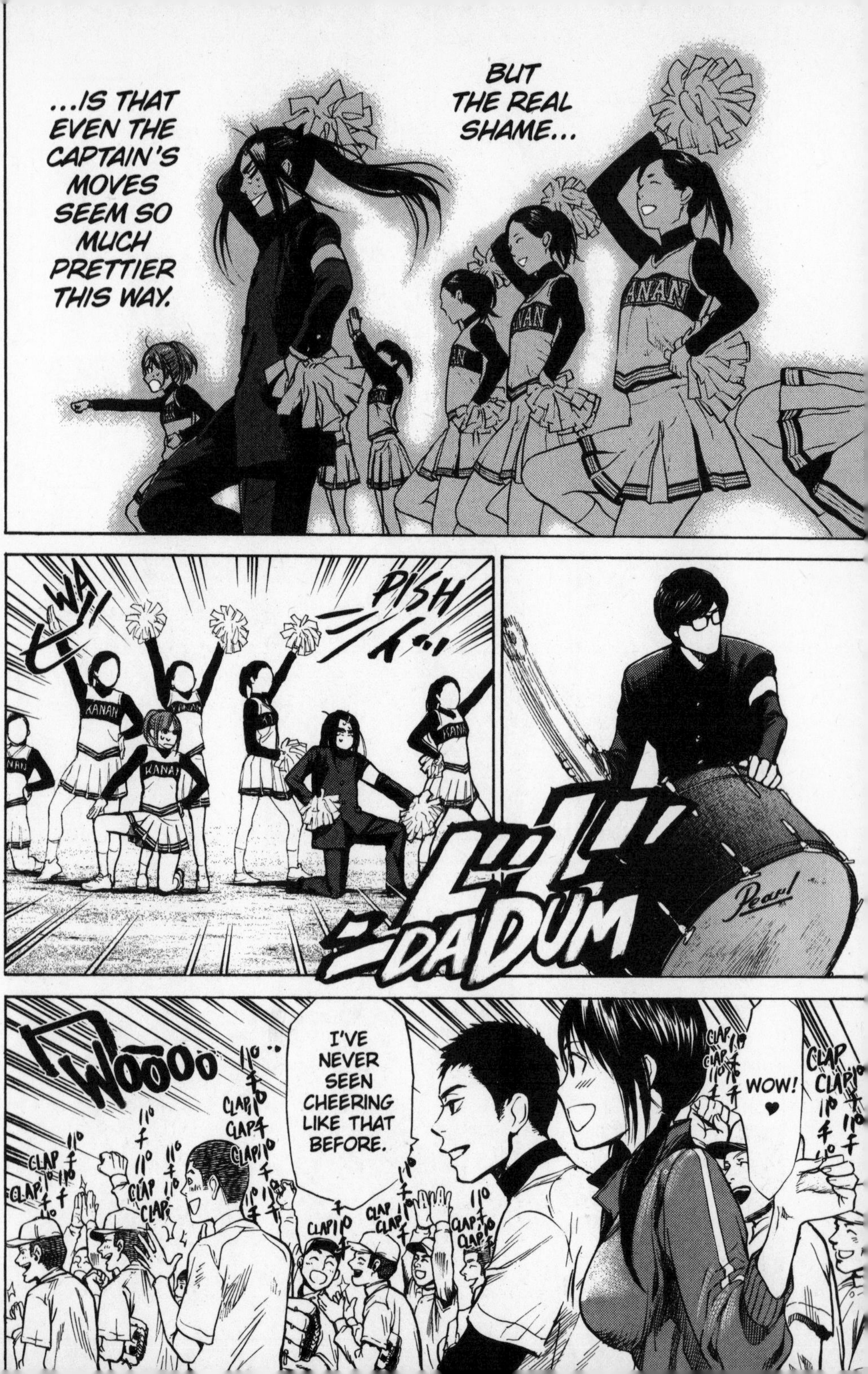
BUT THE REAL SHAME...
...IS THAT EVEN THE CAPTAIN'S MOVES SEEM SO MUCH PRETTIER THIS WAY.
DADUM
PISH
WAI
WOW!
CLAP CLAP
I'VE NEVER SEEN CHEERING LIKE THAT BEFORE.
WOOOO
CLAP CLAP
CLAP CLAP
CLAP CLAP
CLAP CLAP
CLAP CLAP
CLAP CLAP
CLAP CLAP

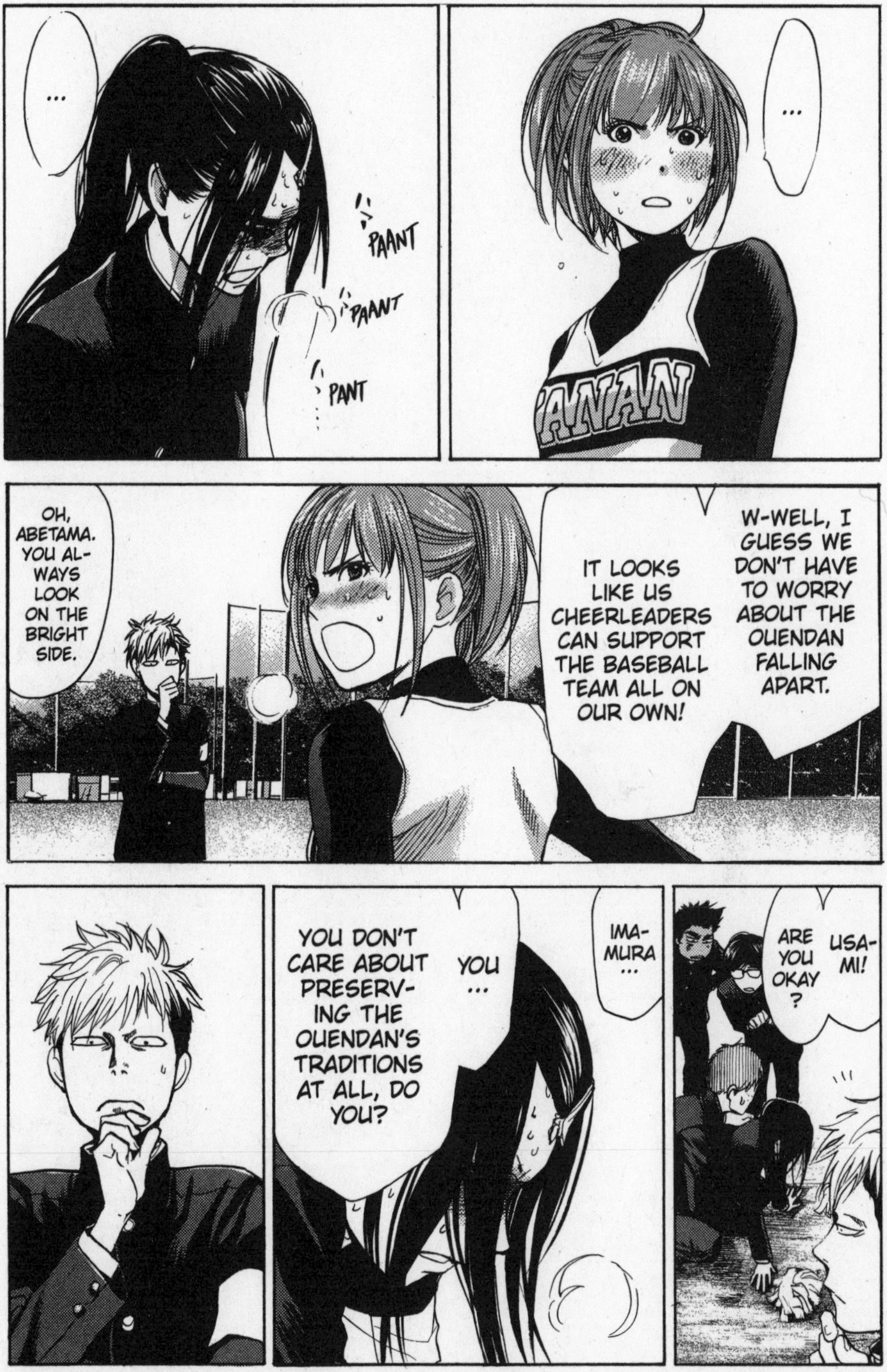
...
...
PAANT
PAANT
PANT
W-WELL, I GUESS WE DON'T HAVE TO WORRY ABOUT THE OUENDAN FALLING APART.
IT LOOKS LIKE US CHEERLEADERS CAN SUPPORT THE BASEBALL TEAM ALL ON OUR OWN!
OH, ABETAMA. YOU AL-WAYS LOOK ON THE BRIGHT SIDE.
USA-MI!
ARE YOU OKAY?
IMA-MURA ...
YOU ...
YOU DON'T CARE ABOUT PRESERV-ING THE OUENDAN'S TRADITIONS AT ALL, DO YOU?

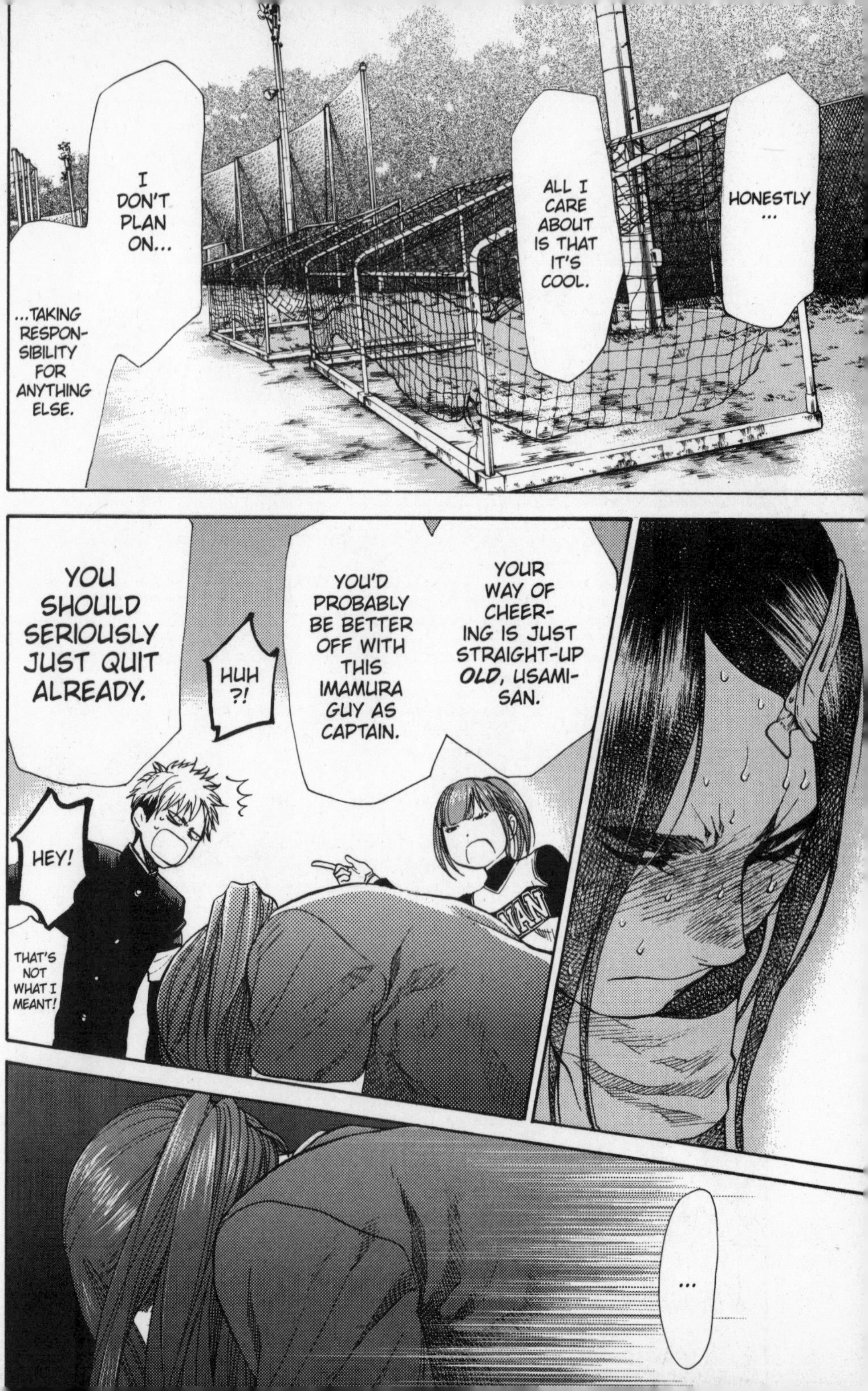
HONESTLY...
ALL I CARE ABOUT IS THAT IT'S COOL.
I DON'T PLAN ON...
...TAKING RESPONSIBILITY FOR ANYTHING ELSE.
YOUR WAY OF CHEERING IS JUST STRAIGHT-UP *OLD*, USAMI-SAN.
YOU'D PROBABLY BE BETTER OFF WITH THIS IMAMURA GUY AS CAPTAIN.
HUH?!
YOU SHOULD SERIOUSLY JUST QUIT ALREADY.
HEY!
THAT'S NOT WHAT I MEANT!
...

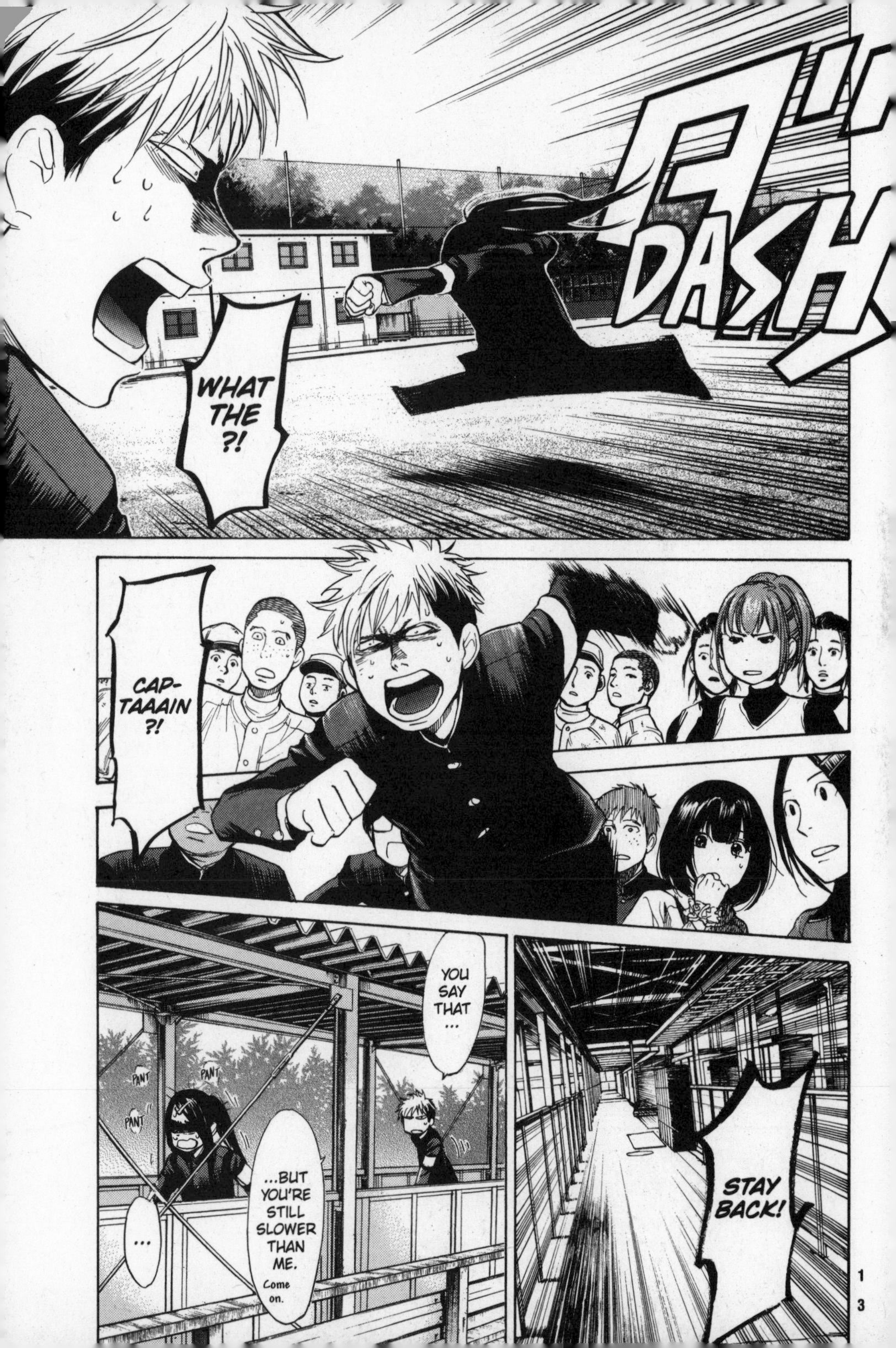
DASH
WHAT THE ?!
CAP-TAAAIN ?!
STAY BACK!
YOU SAY THAT ...
...BUT YOU'RE STILL SLOWER THAN ME.
Come on.
PANT
PANT
PANT
...

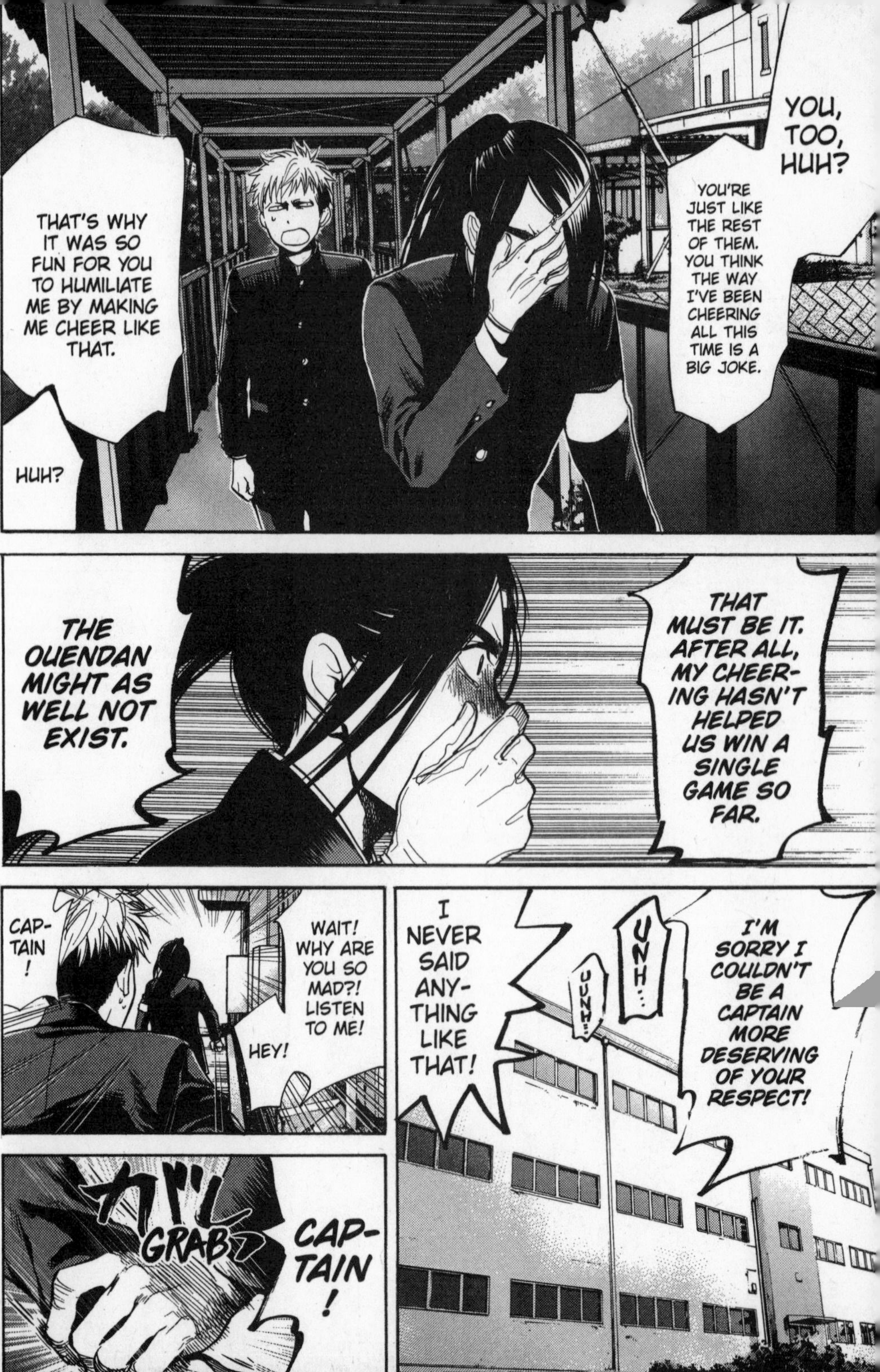
YOU, TOO, HUH?
YOU'RE JUST LIKE THE REST OF THEM. YOU THINK THE WAY I'VE BEEN CHEERING ALL THIS TIME IS A BIG JOKE.
THAT'S WHY IT WAS SO FUN FOR YOU TO HUMILIATE ME BY MAKING ME CHEER LIKE THAT.
HUH?
THAT MUST BE IT. AFTER ALL, MY CHEER-ING HASN'T HELPED US WIN A SINGLE GAME SO FAR.
THE OUENDAN MIGHT AS WELL NOT EXIST.
I'M SORRY I COULDN'T BE A CAPTAIN MORE DESERVING OF YOUR RESPECT!
UNH...
UUNH...
I NEVER SAID ANY-THING LIKE THAT!
WAIT! WHY ARE YOU SO MAD?! LISTEN TO ME!
HEY!
CAP-TAIN!
GRAB
CAP-TAIN!

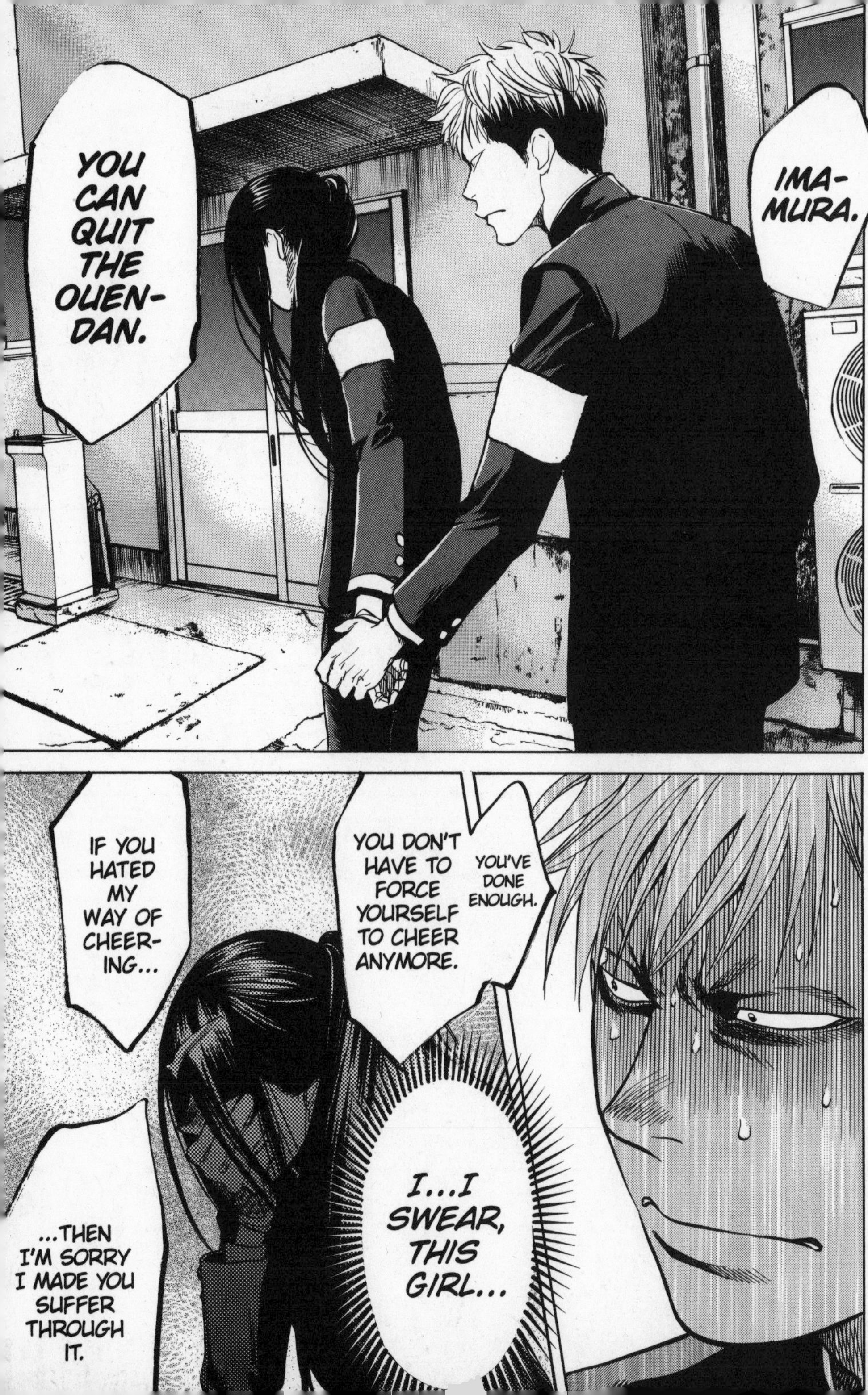
IMA-
MURA.
YOU CAN QUIT THE OUEN-DAN.
YOU'VE DONE ENOUGH.
YOU DON'T HAVE TO FORCE YOURSELF TO CHEER ANYMORE.
IF YOU HATED MY WAY OF CHEER-ING...
I...I SWEAR, THIS GIRL...
...THEN I'M SORRY I MADE YOU SUFFER THROUGH IT.

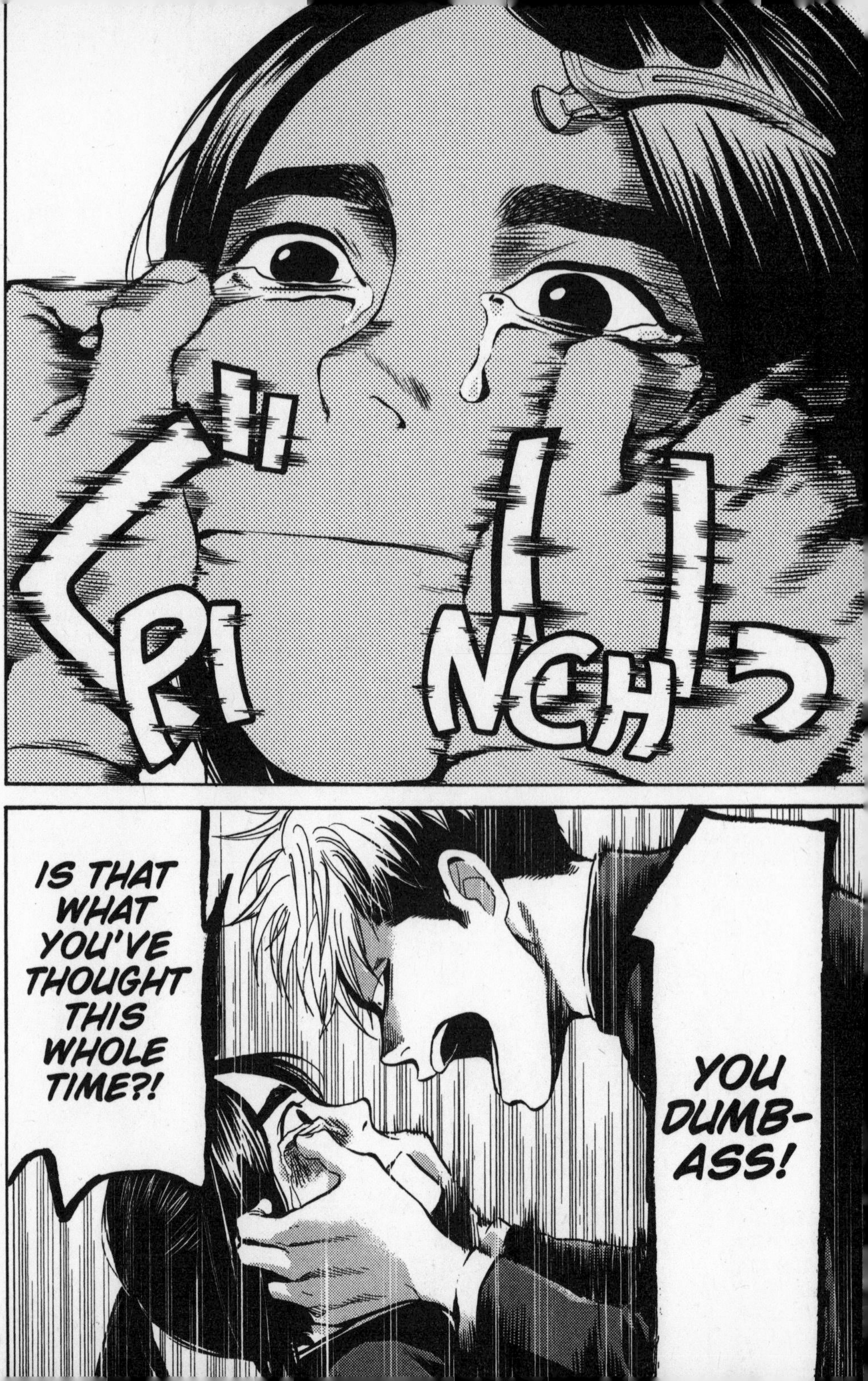
PINCH
YOU DUMB-ASS!
IS THAT WHAT YOU'VE THOUGHT THIS WHOLE TIME?!

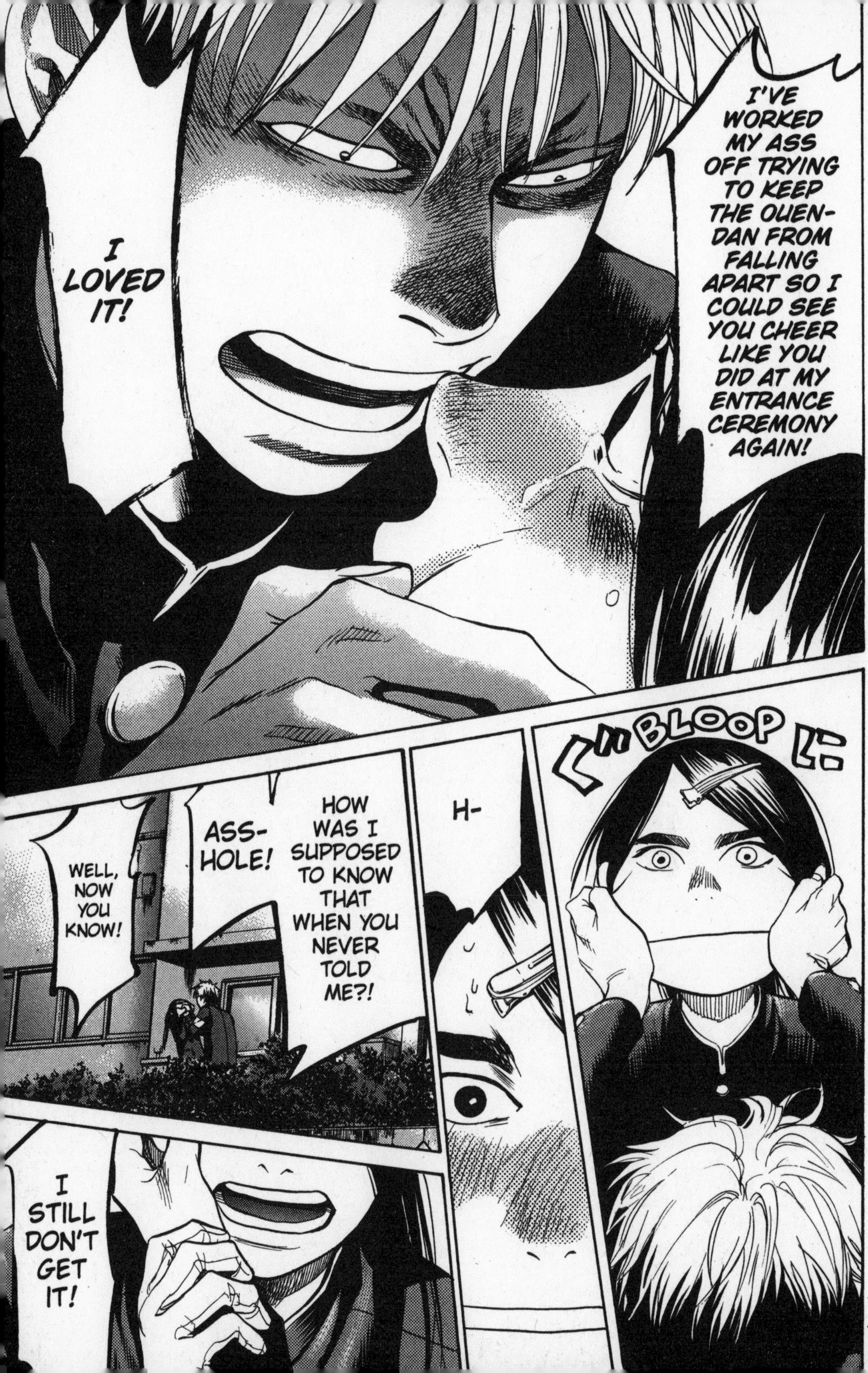
I'VE WORKED MY ASS OFF TRYING TO KEEP THE OUEN-DAN FROM FALLING APART SO I COULD SEE YOU CHEER LIKE YOU DID AT MY ENTRANCE CEREMONY AGAIN!
I LOVED IT!
BLOOP
H-
HOW WAS I SUPPOSED TO KNOW THAT WHEN YOU NEVER TOLD ME?!
ASS-HOLE!
WELL, NOW YOU KNOW!
I STILL DON'T GET IT!

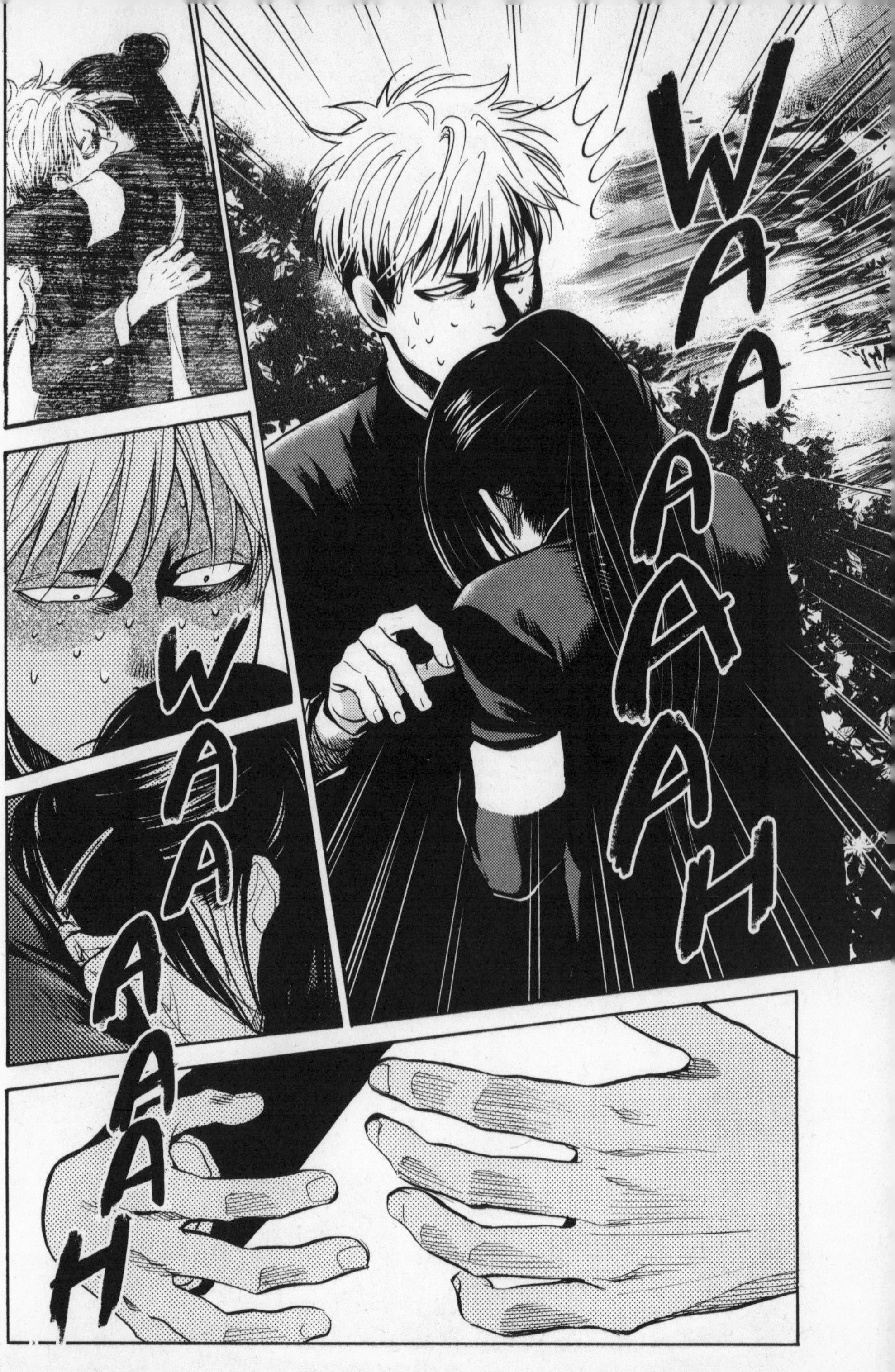
WAAAAAAH
WAAAAAAH

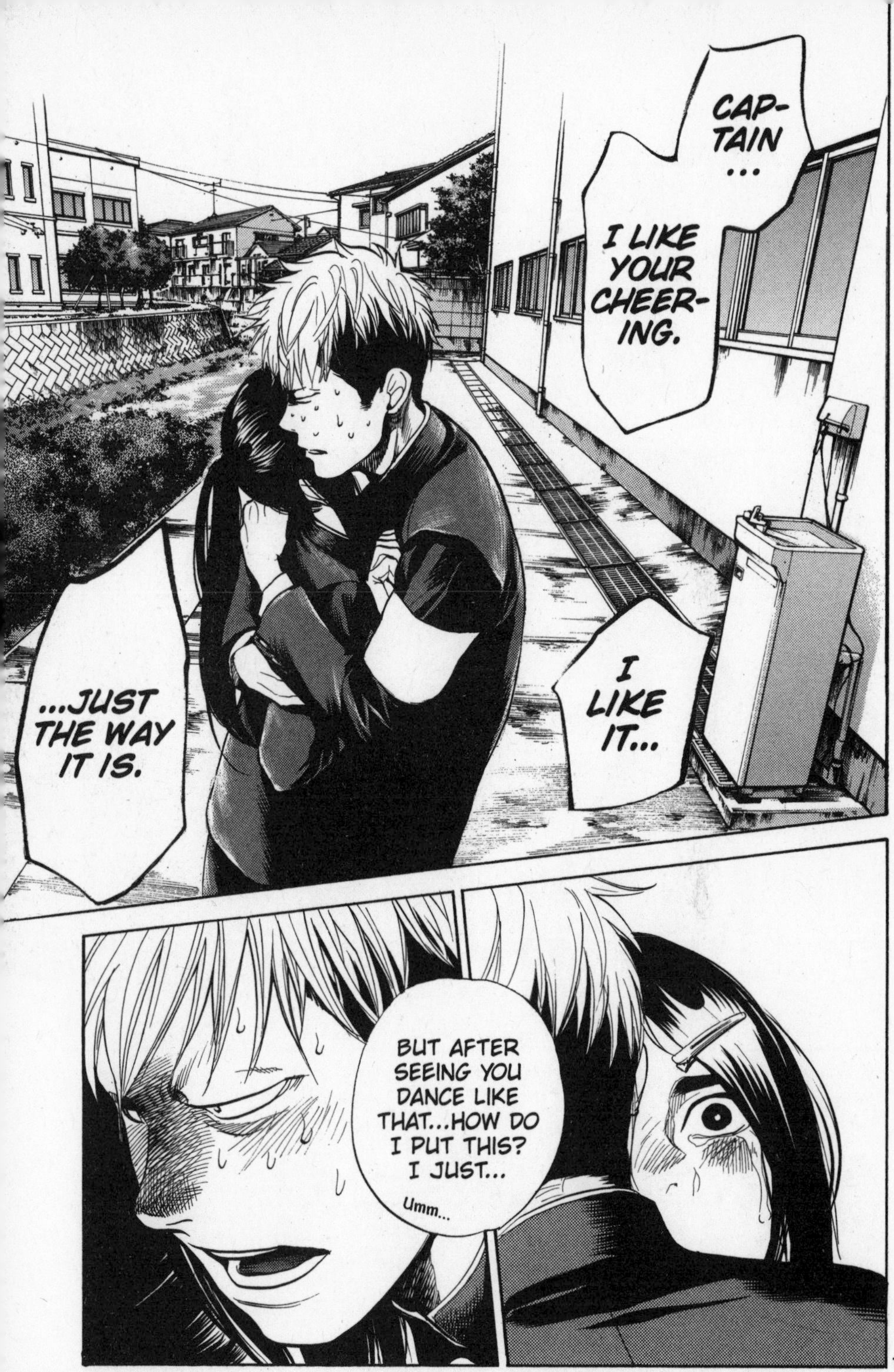
CAP-TAIN...
I LIKE YOUR CHEER-ING.
I LIKE IT...
...JUST THE WAY IT IS.
BUT AFTER SEEING YOU DANCE LIKE THAT...HOW DO I PUT THIS? I JUST...
Umm...

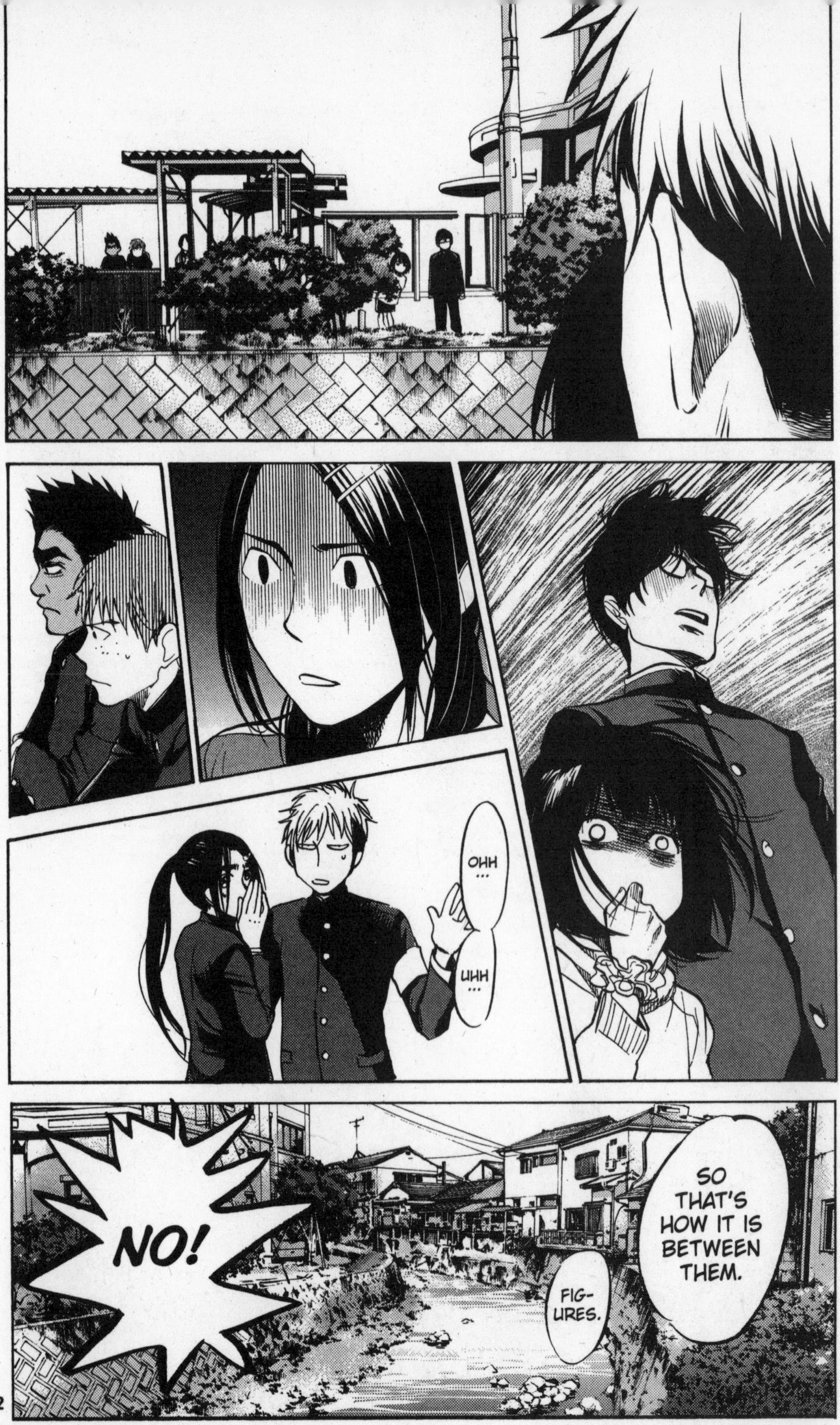
OHH...
UHH...
SO THAT'S HOW IT IS BETWEEN THEM.
FIG-URES.
NO!

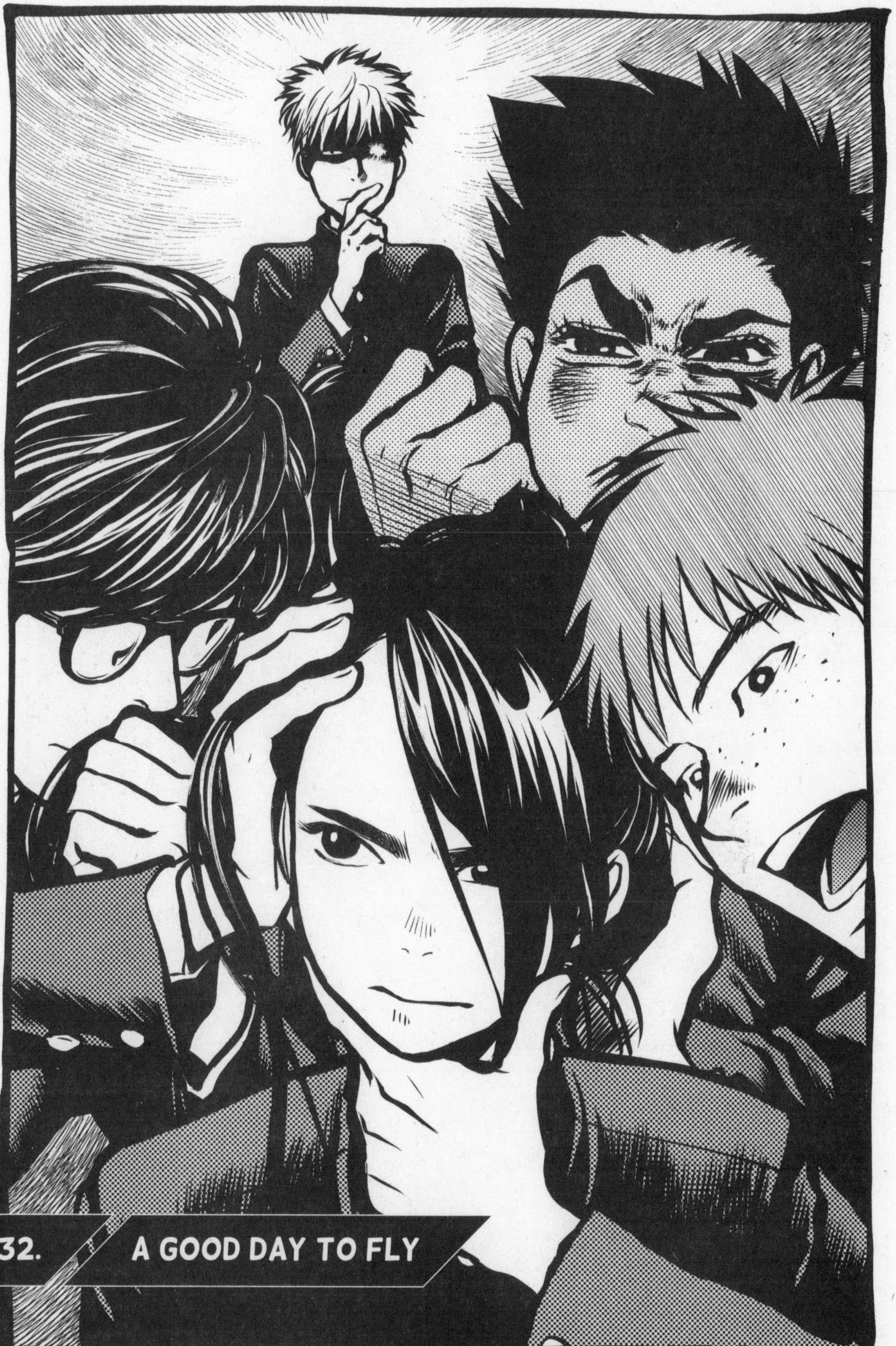
32.
A GOOD DAY TO FLY

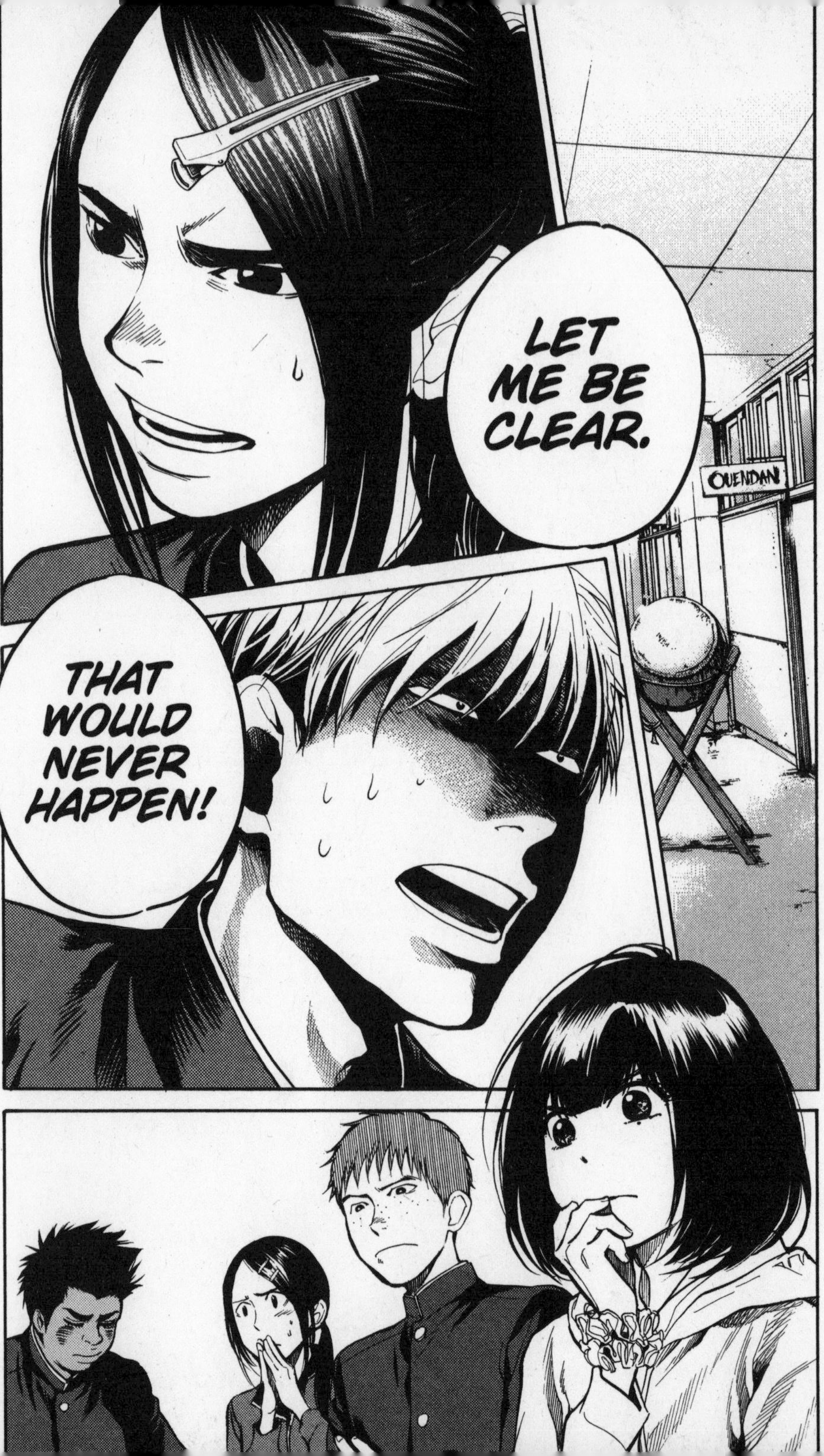
LET ME BE CLEAR.
OUENDAN
THAT WOULD NEVER HAPPEN!

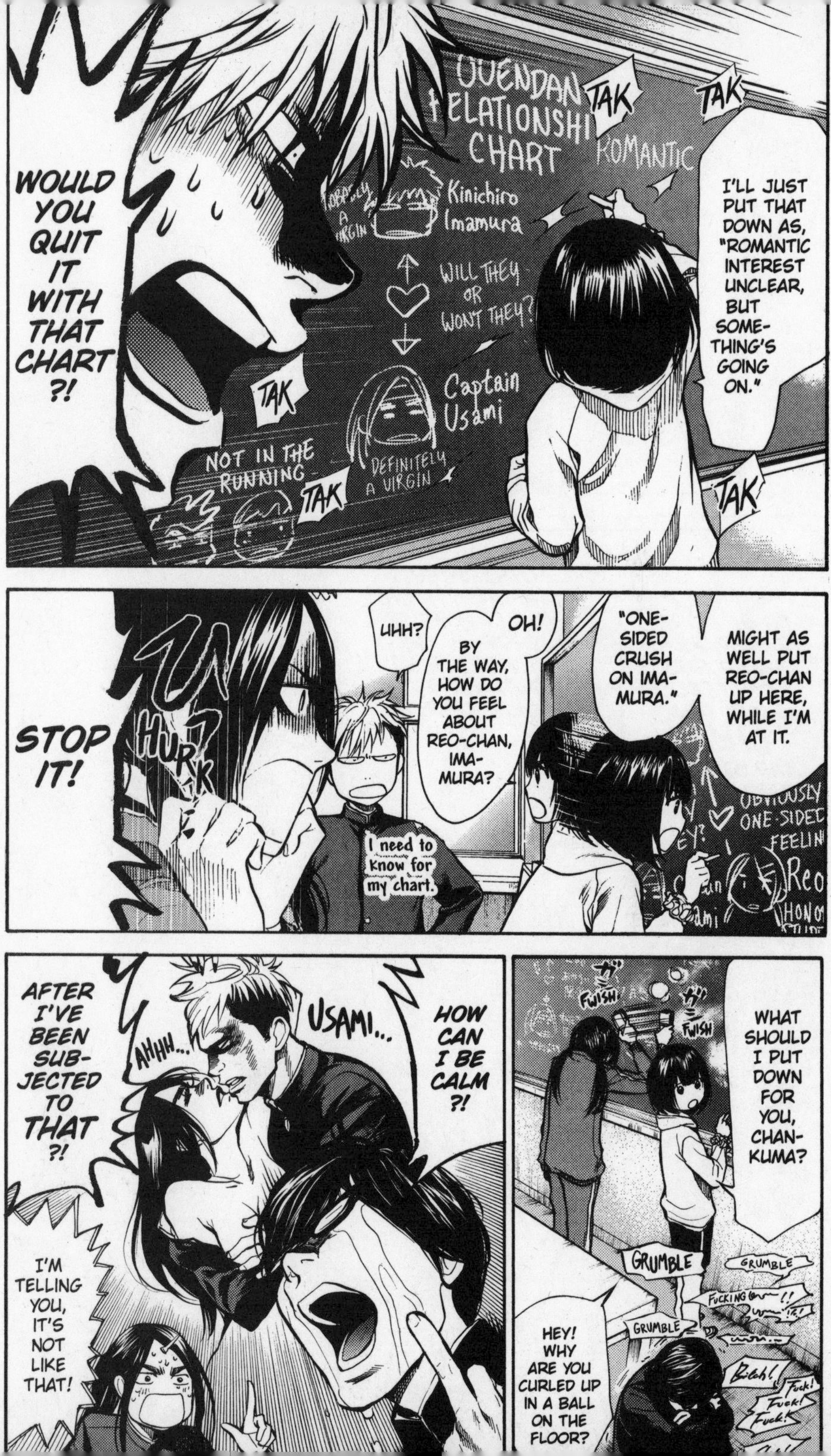
I'LL JUST PUT THAT DOWN AS, "ROMANTIC INTEREST UNCLEAR, BUT SOME-THING'S GOING ON."
TAK
TAK
OUENDAN RELATIONSHI CHART
ROMANTIC
Kinichiro Imamura
WILL THEY OR WONT THEY?
Captain Usami
DEFINITELY A VIRGIN
NOT IN THE RUNNING
TAK
TAK
TAK
WOULD YOU QUIT IT WITH THAT CHART?!
MIGHT AS WELL PUT REO-CHAN UP HERE, WHILE I'M AT IT.
"ONE-SIDED CRUSH ON IMA-MURA."
OBVIOUSLY ONE-SIDED FEELIN
Reo
OH!
BY THE WAY, HOW DO YOU FEEL ABOUT REO-CHAN, IMA-MURA?
UHH?
I need to know for my chart.
HURK
STOP IT!
WHAT SHOULD I PUT DOWN FOR YOU, CHAN-KUMA?
FWISH
FWISH
GRUMBLE
GRUMBLE
GRUMBLE
FUCKING
Bitch!
Fuck! Fuck! Fuck!
HEY! WHY ARE YOU CURLED UP IN A BALL ON THE FLOOR?
HOW CAN I BE CALM?!
USAMI...
AFTER I'VE BEEN SUB-JECTED TO THAT?!
AHHH...
I'M TELLING YOU, IT'S NOT LIKE THAT!

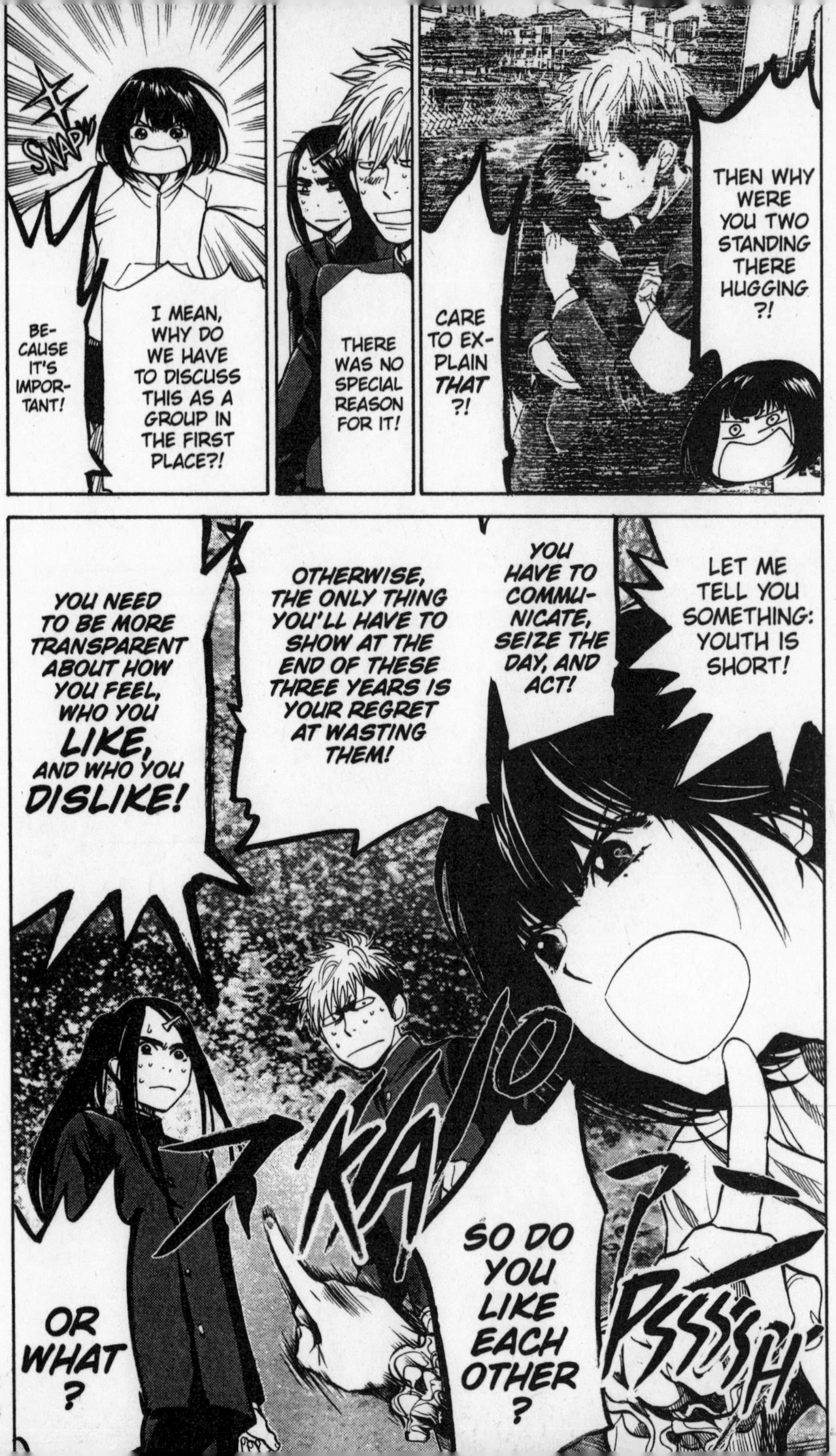

THEN WHY WERE YOU TWO STANDING THERE HUGGING?!
CARE TO EXPLAIN *THAT*?!
THERE WAS NO SPECIAL REASON FOR IT!
SNAP
I MEAN, WHY DO WE HAVE TO DISCUSS THIS AS A GROUP IN THE FIRST PLACE?!
BECAUSE IT'S IMPORTANT!
LET ME TELL YOU SOMETHING: YOUTH IS SHORT!
YOU HAVE TO COMMUNICATE, SEIZE THE DAY, AND ACT!
OTHERWISE, THE ONLY THING YOU'LL HAVE TO SHOW AT THE END OF THESE THREE YEARS IS YOUR REGRET AT WASTING THEM!
YOU NEED TO BE MORE TRANSPARENT ABOUT HOW YOU FEEL, WHO YOU **LIKE,** AND WHO YOU **DISLIKE!**
PSSSSH
SO DO YOU LIKE EACH OTHER?
KA
OR WHAT?

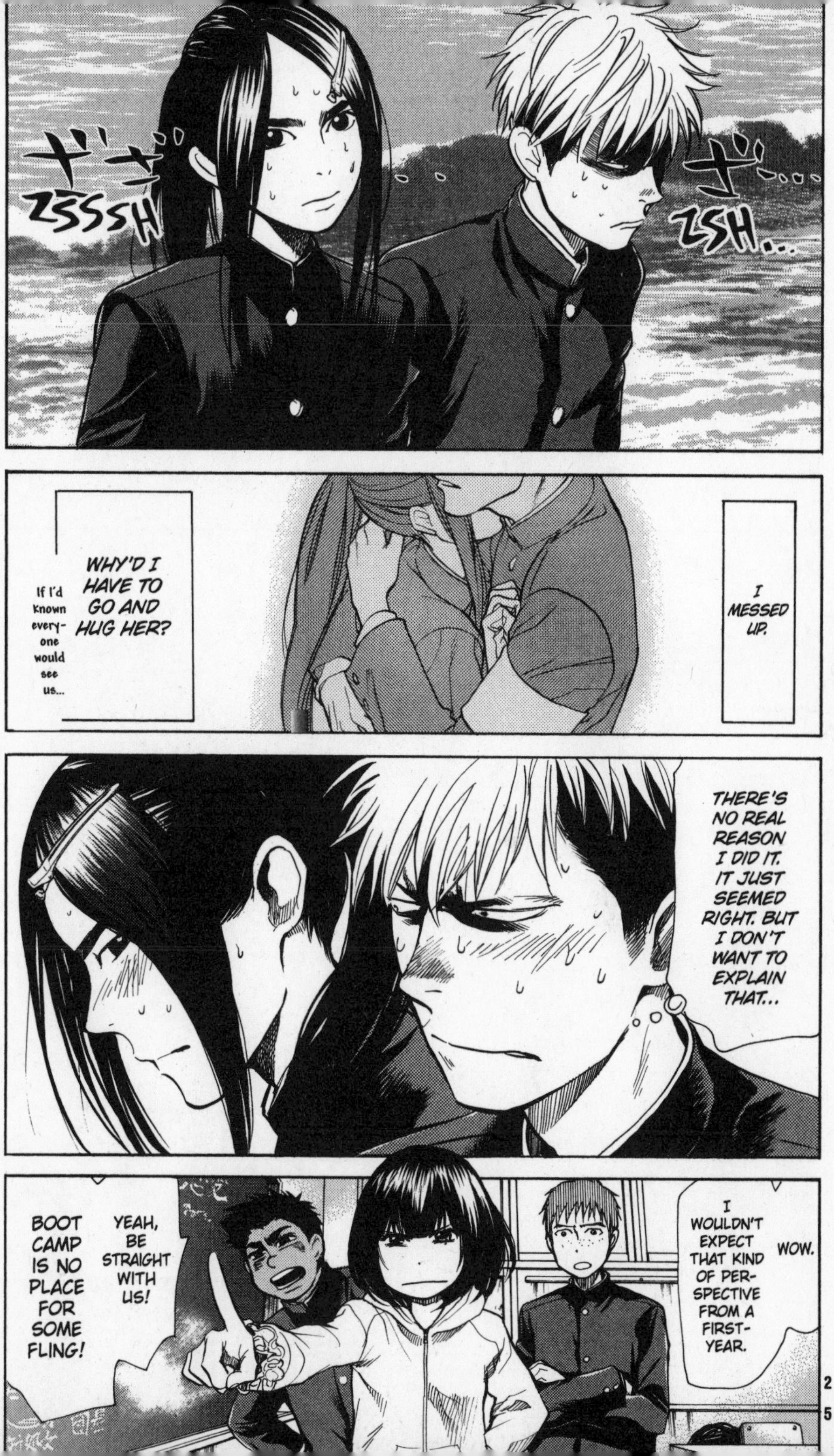
ZSH...
ZSSSH
I MESSED UP.
WHY'D I HAVE TO GO AND HUG HER?
If I'd known every-one would see us...
THERE'S NO REAL REASON I DID IT. IT JUST SEEMED RIGHT. BUT I DON'T WANT TO EXPLAIN THAT...
WOW.
I WOULDN'T EXPECT THAT KIND OF PER-SPECTIVE FROM A FIRST-YEAR.
YEAH, BE STRAIGHT WITH US!
BOOT CAMP IS NO PLACE FOR SOME FLING!

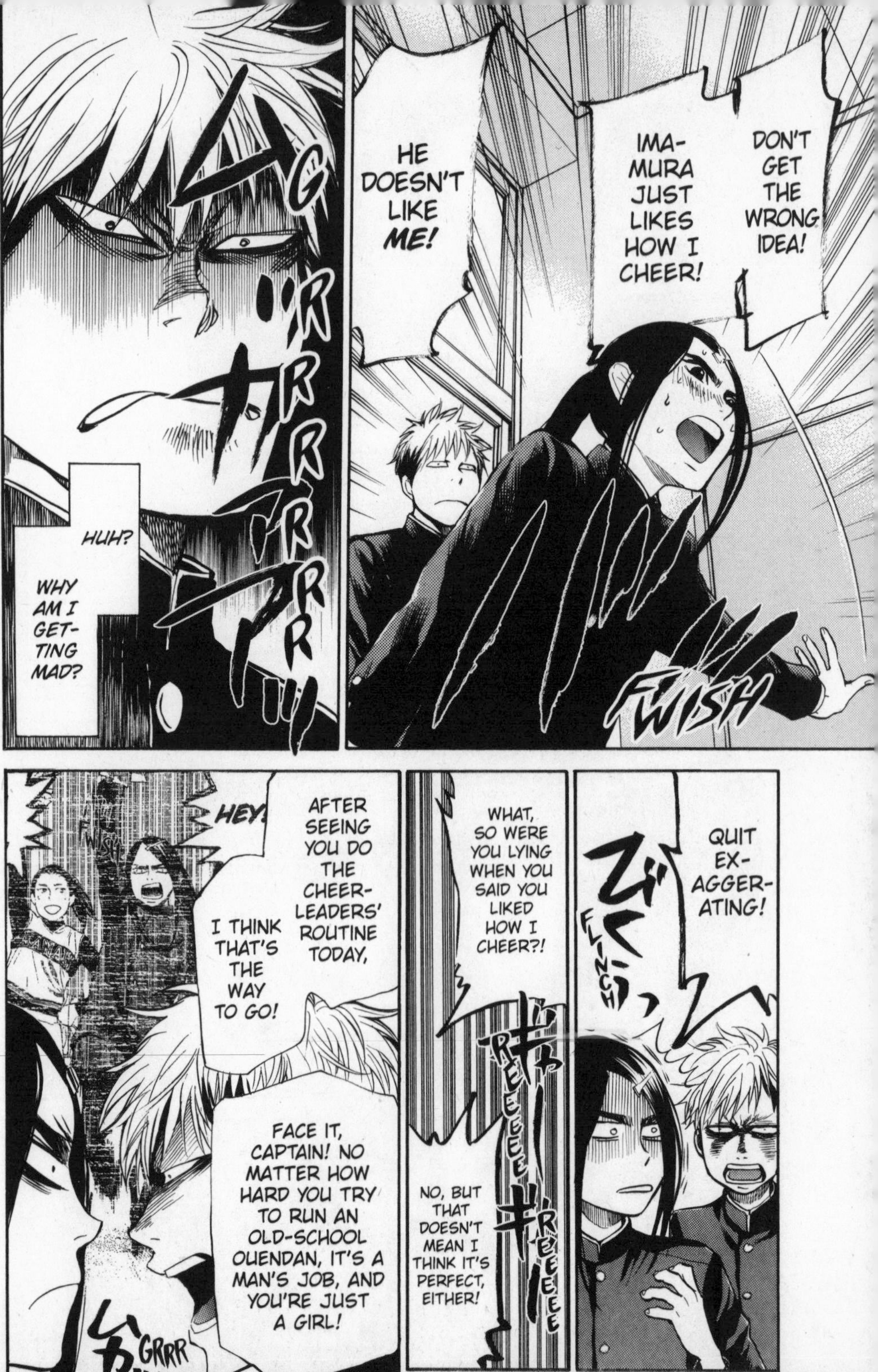
DON'T GET THE WRONG IDEA!
IMAMURA JUST LIKES HOW I CHEER!
HE DOESN'T LIKE ME!
FWISH
GRRRRRRRR
HUH?
WHY AM I GETTING MAD?
QUIT EXAGGERATING!
FLINCH
WHAT, SO WERE YOU LYING WHEN YOU SAID YOU LIKED HOW I CHEER?!
REEEEE
REEEEE
NO, BUT THAT DOESN'T MEAN I THINK IT'S PERFECT, EITHER!
AFTER SEEING YOU DO THE CHEERLEADERS' ROUTINE TODAY,
I THINK THAT'S THE WAY TO GO!
HEY!
FWISH
FACE IT, CAPTAIN! NO MATTER HOW HARD YOU TRY TO RUN AN OLD-SCHOOL OUENDAN, IT'S A MAN'S JOB, AND YOU'RE JUST A GIRL!
GRRR

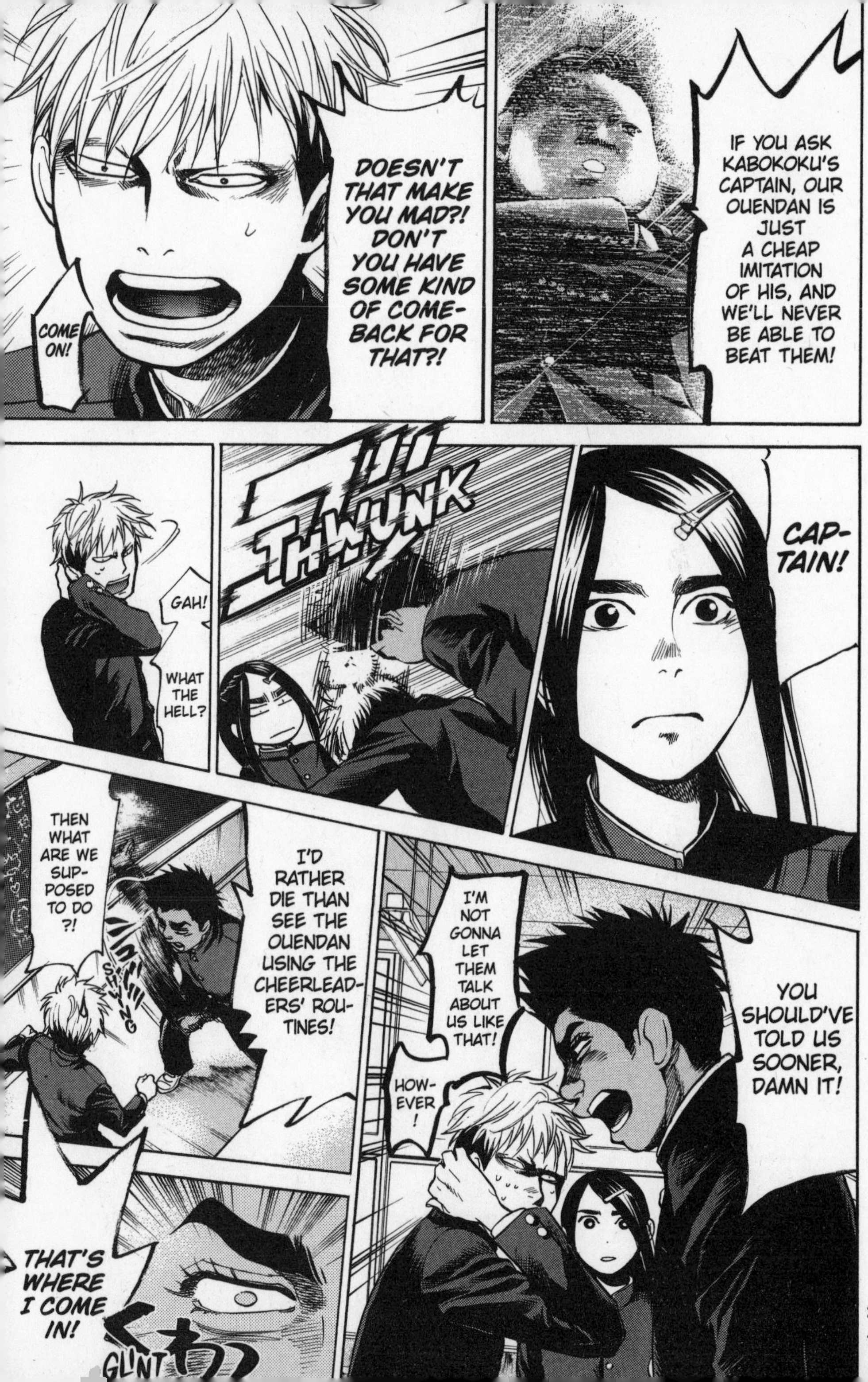
IF YOU ASK KABOKOKU'S CAPTAIN, OUR OUENDAN IS JUST A CHEAP IMITATION OF HIS, AND WE'LL NEVER BE ABLE TO BEAT THEM!
DOESN'T THAT MAKE YOU MAD?! DON'T YOU HAVE SOME KIND OF COME-BACK FOR THAT?!
COME ON!
CAP-TAIN!
THWUNK
GAH!
WHAT THE HELL?
YOU SHOULD'VE TOLD US SOONER, DAMN IT!
I'M NOT GONNA LET THEM TALK ABOUT US LIKE THAT!
HOW-EVER!
I'D RATHER DIE THAN SEE THE OUENDAN USING THE CHEERLEADERS' ROUTINES!
THEN WHAT ARE WE SUP-POSED TO DO?!
SHWING
THAT'S WHERE I COME IN!
GLINT

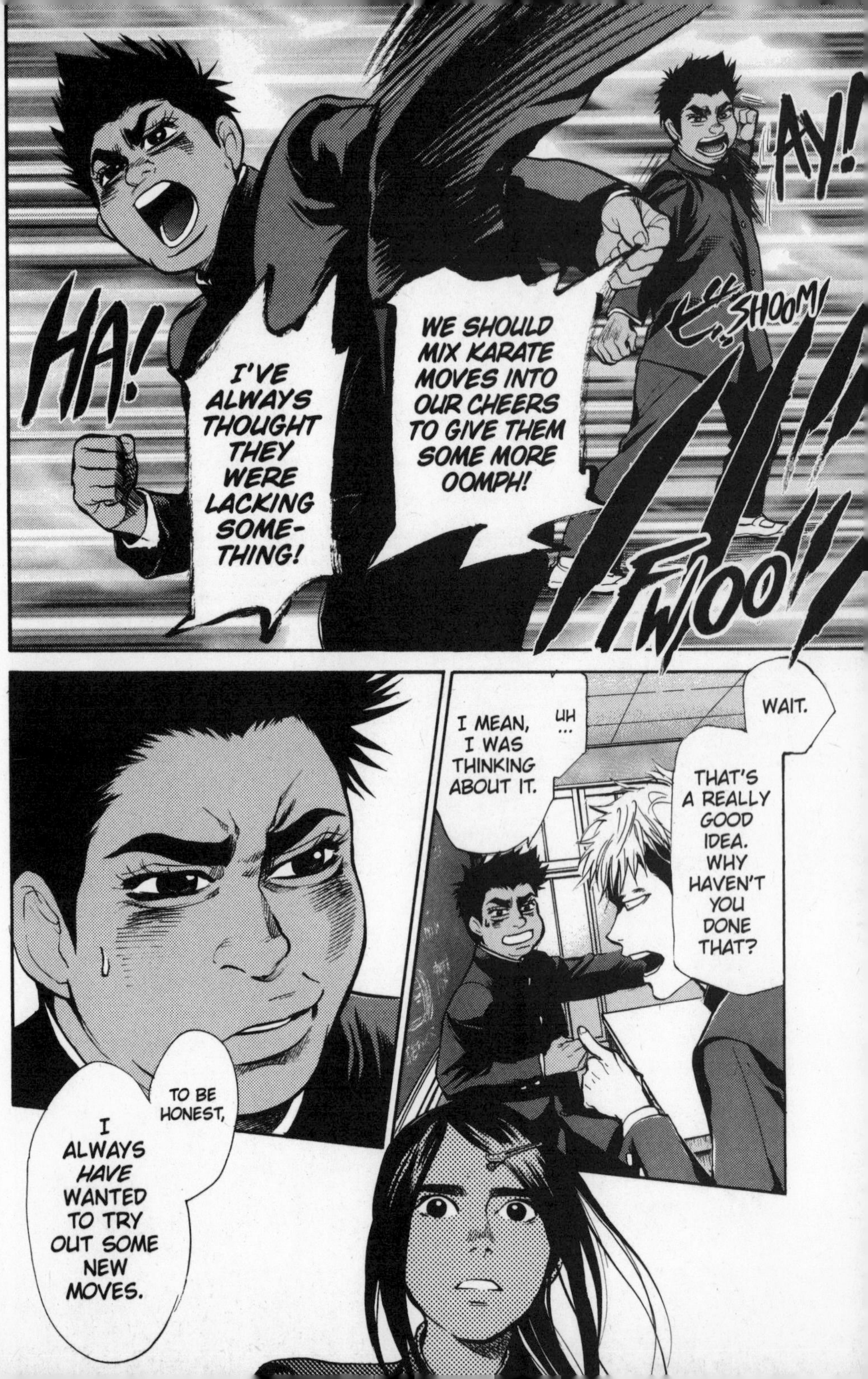
AY!!
SHOOM
WE SHOULD MIX KARATE MOVES INTO OUR CHEERS TO GIVE THEM SOME MORE OOMPH!
I'VE ALWAYS THOUGHT THEY WERE LACKING SOME-THING!
HA!
FWOO
WAIT.
THAT'S A REALLY GOOD IDEA. WHY HAVEN'T YOU DONE THAT?
UH...
I MEAN, I WAS THINKING ABOUT IT.
TO BE HONEST,
I ALWAYS *HAVE* WANTED TO TRY OUT SOME NEW MOVES.

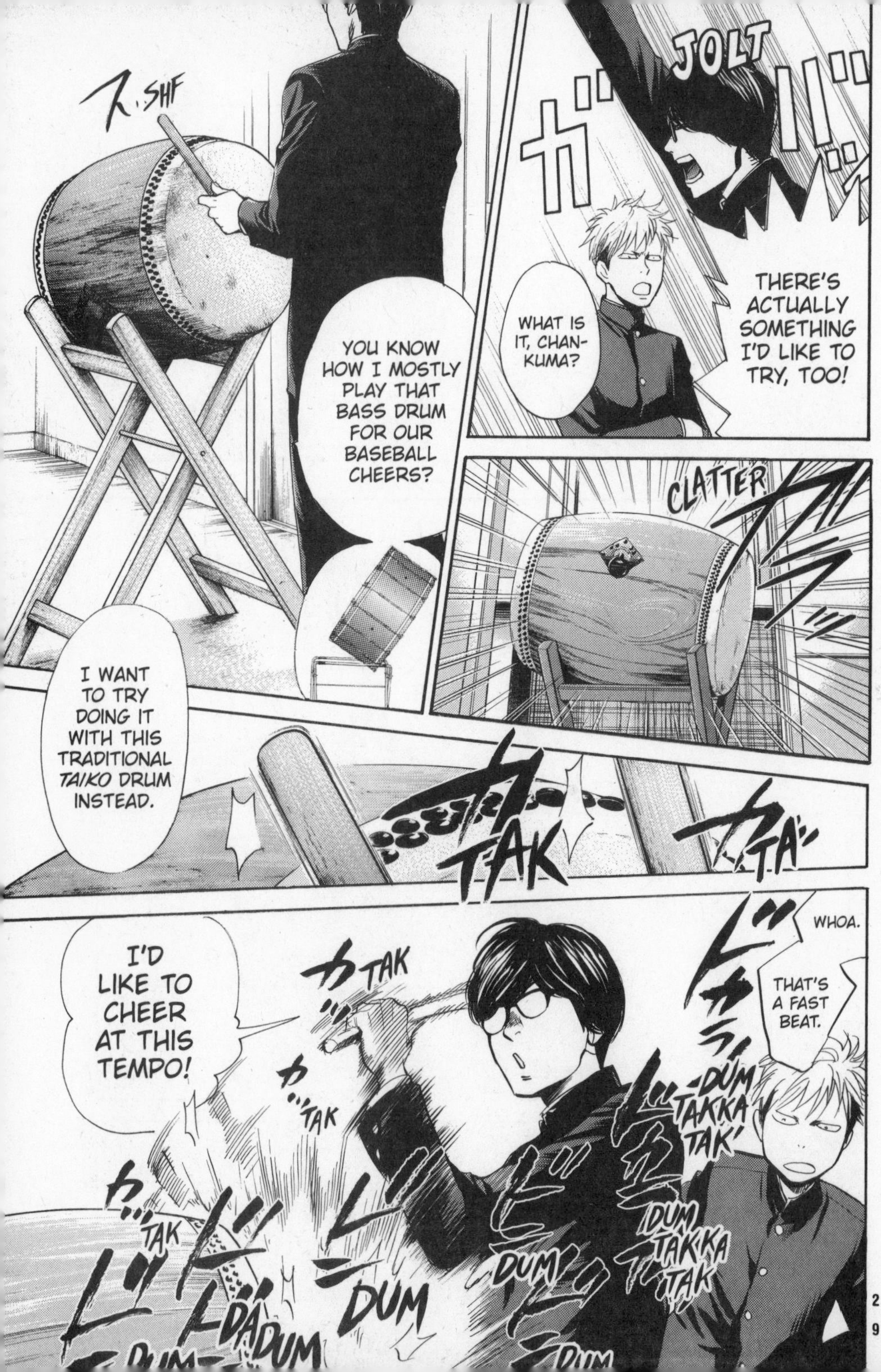
JOLT
THERE'S ACTUALLY SOMETHING I'D LIKE TO TRY, TOO!
WHAT IS IT, CHAN-KUMA?
CLATTER
SHF
YOU KNOW HOW I MOSTLY PLAY THAT BASS DRUM FOR OUR BASEBALL CHEERS?
I WANT TO TRY DOING IT WITH THIS TRADITIONAL *TAIKO* DRUM INSTEAD.
TA
TAK
WHOA.
THAT'S A FAST BEAT.
DUM TAKKA TAK
DUM TAK KA TAK
TAK
I'D LIKE TO CHEER AT THIS TEMPO!
TAK
DUM
TAK
DUM
DADUM

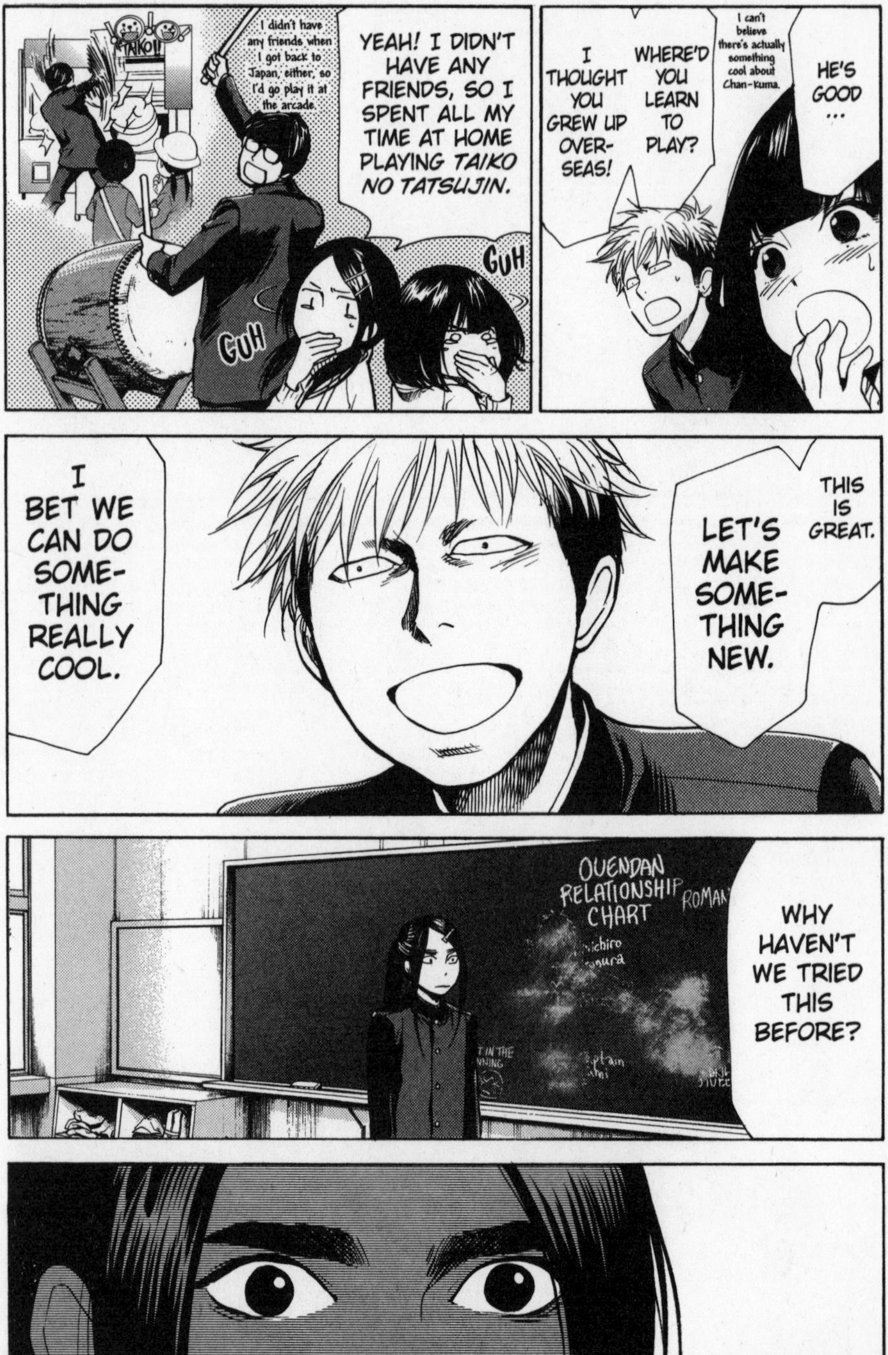
HE'S GOOD ...
I can't believe there's actually something cool about Chan-kuma.
WHERE'D YOU LEARN TO PLAY?
I THOUGHT YOU GREW UP OVER-SEAS!
YEAH! I DIDN'T HAVE ANY FRIENDS, SO I SPENT ALL MY TIME AT HOME PLAYING *TAIKO NO TATSUJIN.*
I didn't have any friends when I got back to Japan, either, so I'd go play it at the arcade.
TAIKO!!
GUH
GUH
THIS IS GREAT.
LET'S MAKE SOME-THING NEW.
I BET WE CAN DO SOME-THING REALLY COOL.
WHY HAVEN'T WE TRIED THIS BEFORE?
OUENDAN RELATIONSHIP CHART

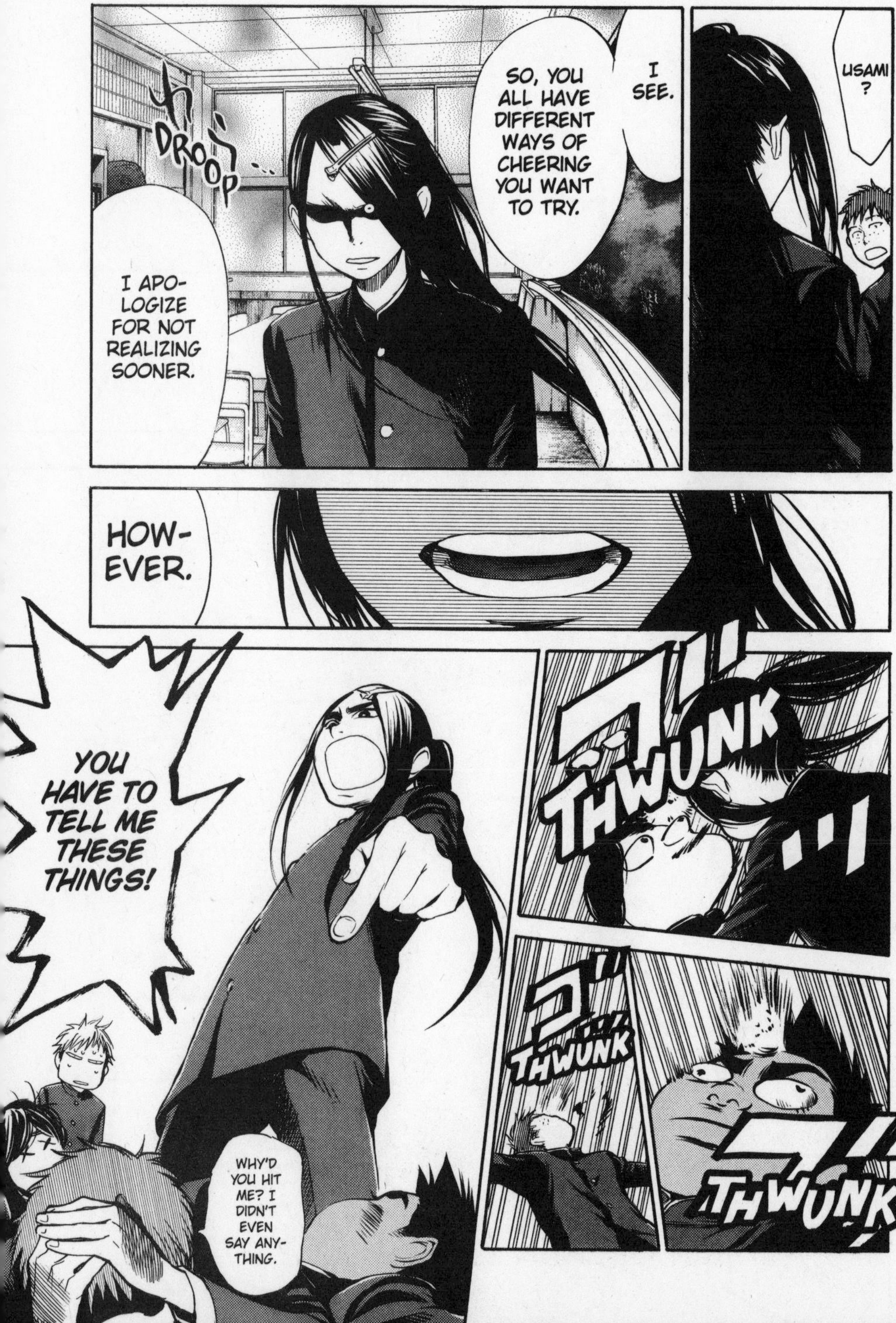
USAMI ?
I SEE.
SO, YOU ALL HAVE DIFFERENT WAYS OF CHEERING YOU WANT TO TRY.
DROOP ...
I APOLOGIZE FOR NOT REALIZING SOONER.
HOW-EVER.
THWUNK
...!
THWUNK
THWUNK
YOU HAVE TO TELL ME THESE THINGS!
WHY'D YOU HIT ME? I DIDN'T EVEN SAY ANYTHING.

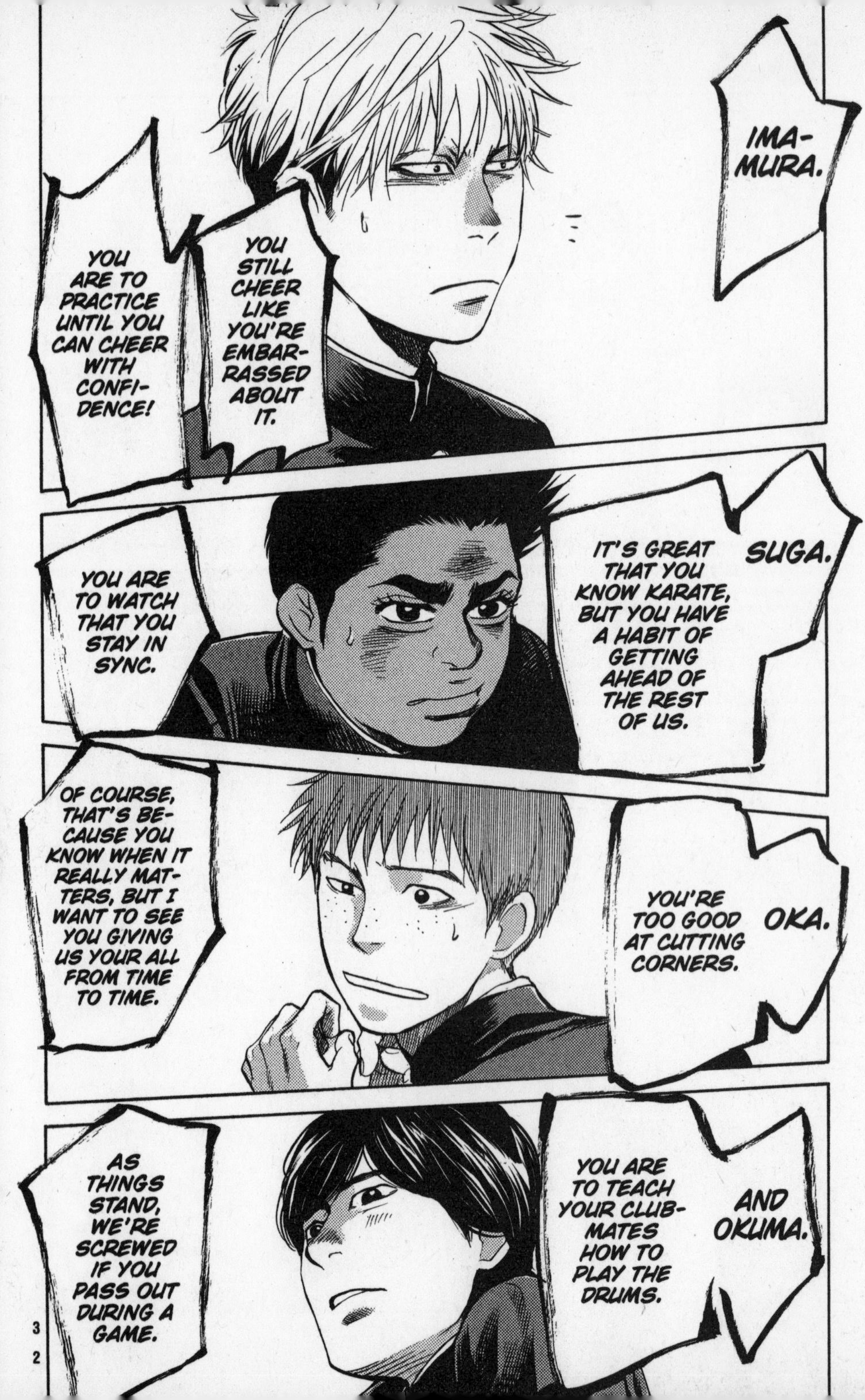
IMA-MURA.
YOU STILL CHEER LIKE YOU'RE EMBARRASSED ABOUT IT.
YOU ARE TO PRACTICE UNTIL YOU CAN CHEER WITH CONFIDENCE!
SUGA.
IT'S GREAT THAT YOU KNOW KARATE, BUT YOU HAVE A HABIT OF GETTING AHEAD OF THE REST OF US.
YOU ARE TO WATCH THAT YOU STAY IN SYNC.
OKA.
YOU'RE TOO GOOD AT CUTTING CORNERS.
OF COURSE, THAT'S BECAUSE YOU KNOW WHEN IT REALLY MATTERS, BUT I WANT TO SEE YOU GIVING US YOUR ALL FROM TIME TO TIME.
AND OKUMA.
YOU ARE TO TEACH YOUR CLUBMATES HOW TO PLAY THE DRUMS.
AS THINGS STAND, WE'RE SCREWED IF YOU PASS OUT DURING A GAME.

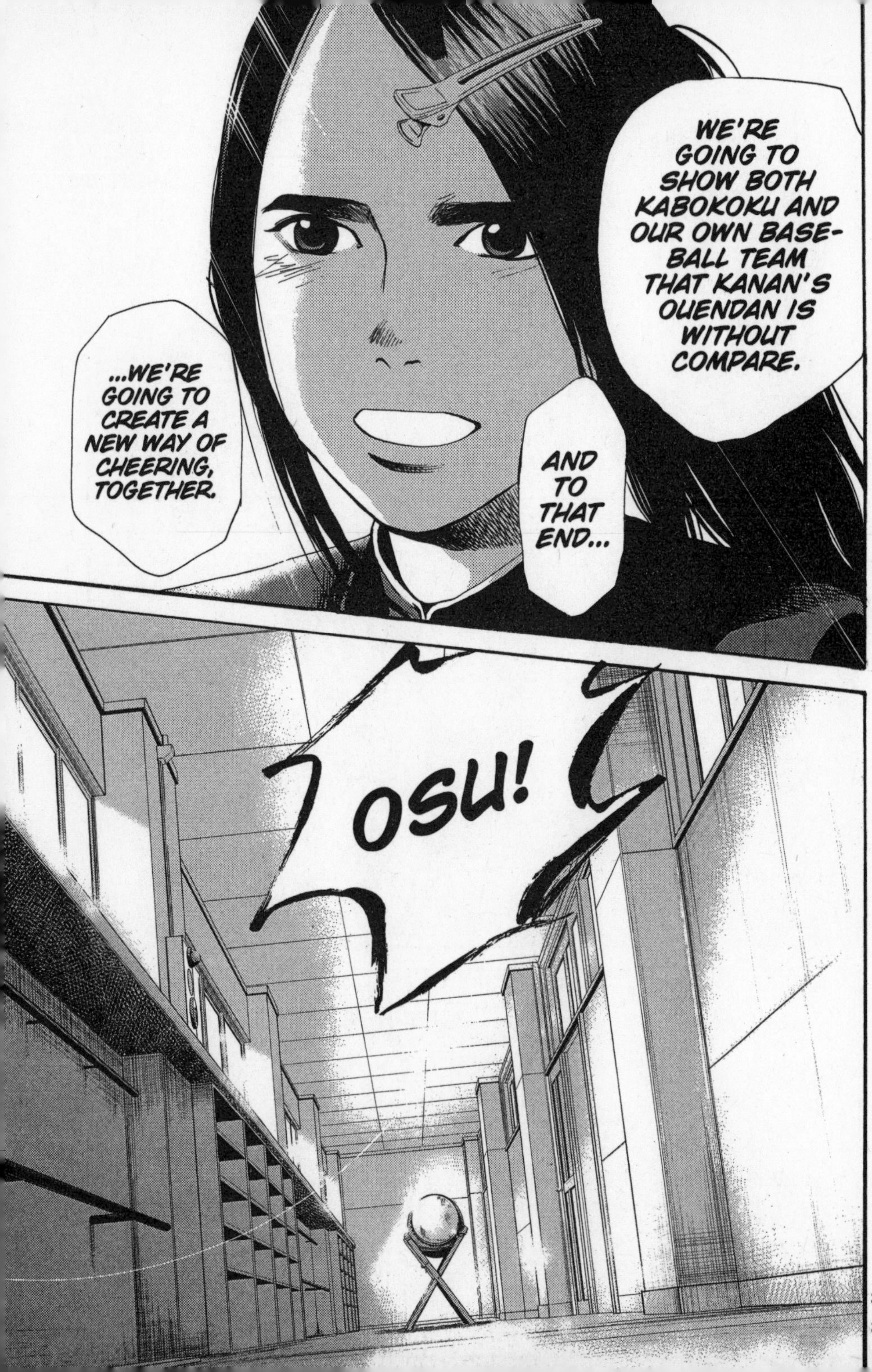
WE'RE GOING TO SHOW BOTH KABOKOKU AND OUR OWN BASE-BALL TEAM THAT KANAN'S OUENDAN IS WITHOUT COMPARE.
AND TO THAT END...
...WE'RE GOING TO CREATE A NEW WAY OF CHEERING, TOGETHER.
OSU!

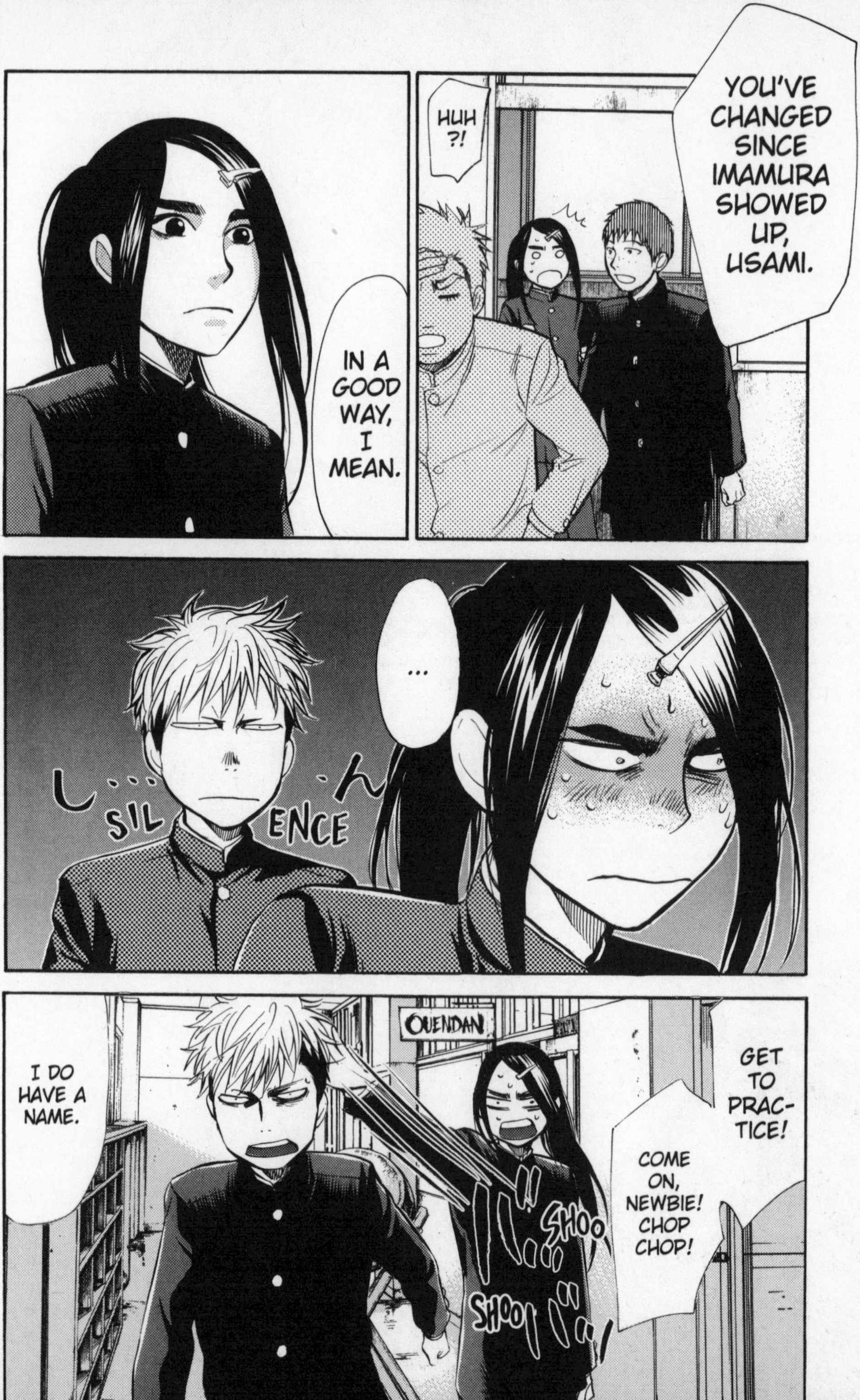
YOU'VE CHANGED SINCE IMAMURA SHOWED UP, USAMI.
HUH ?!
IN A GOOD WAY, I MEAN.
...
し…ん
SILENCE
OUENDAN
GET TO PRAC-TICE!
COME ON, NEWBIE! CHOP CHOP!
SHOO
SHOO
I DO HAVE A NAME.

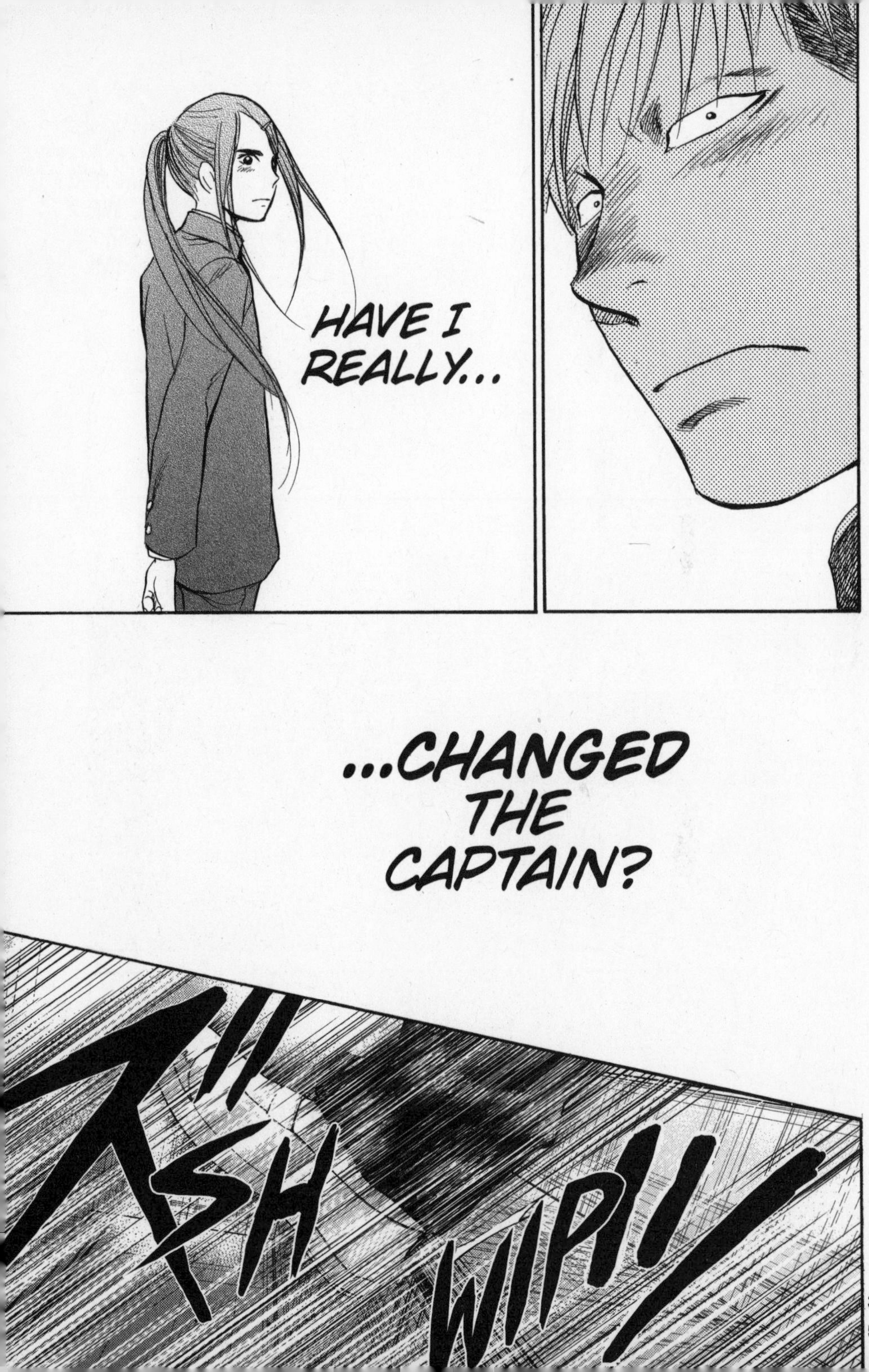
HAVE I REALLY...
...CHANGED THE CAPTAIN?
SH
WIP!!

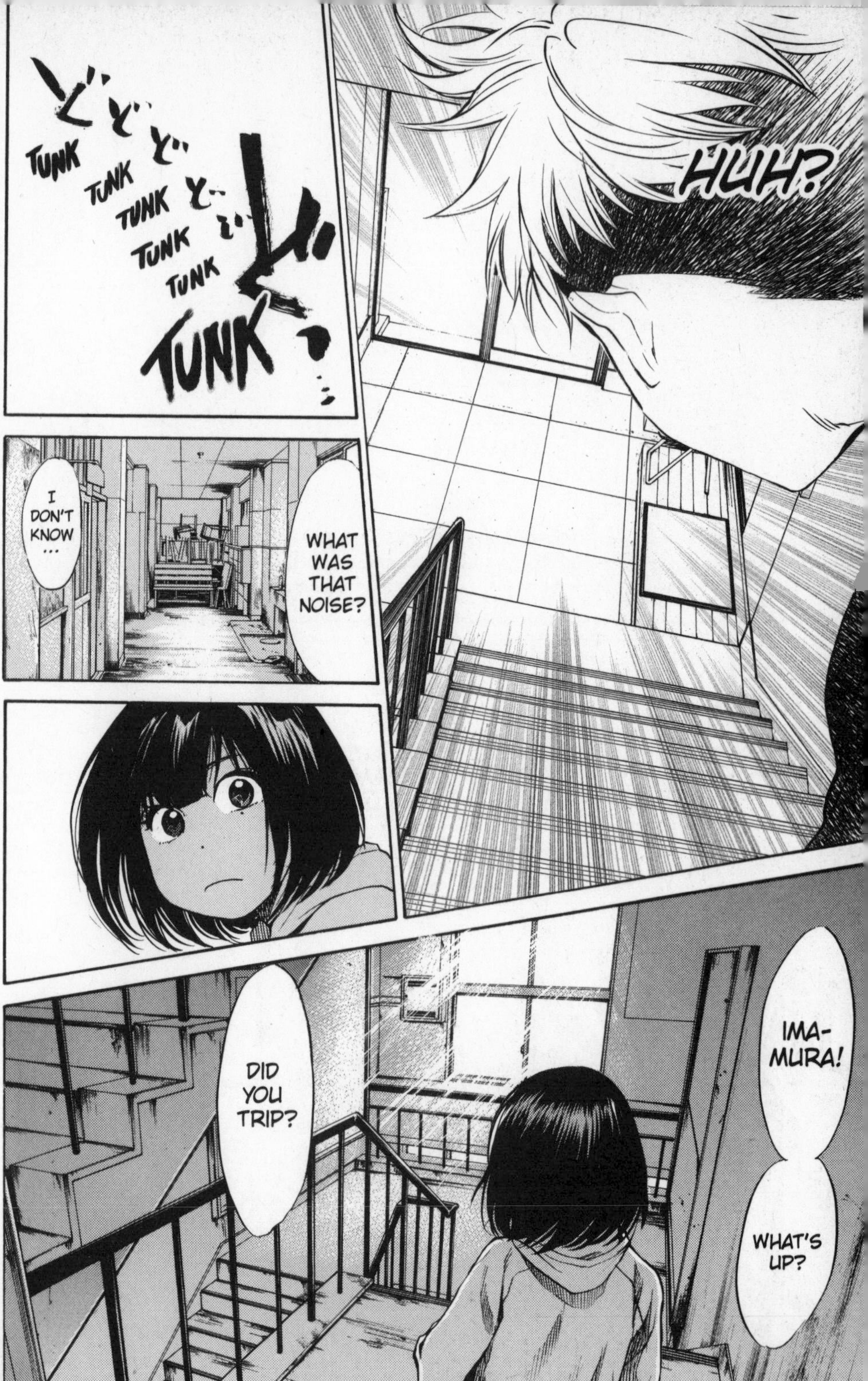
HUH?
TUNK
TUNK
TUNK
TUNK
TUNK
TUNK
WHAT WAS THAT NOISE?
I DON'T KNOW...
IMA-MURA!
WHAT'S UP?
DID YOU TRIP?

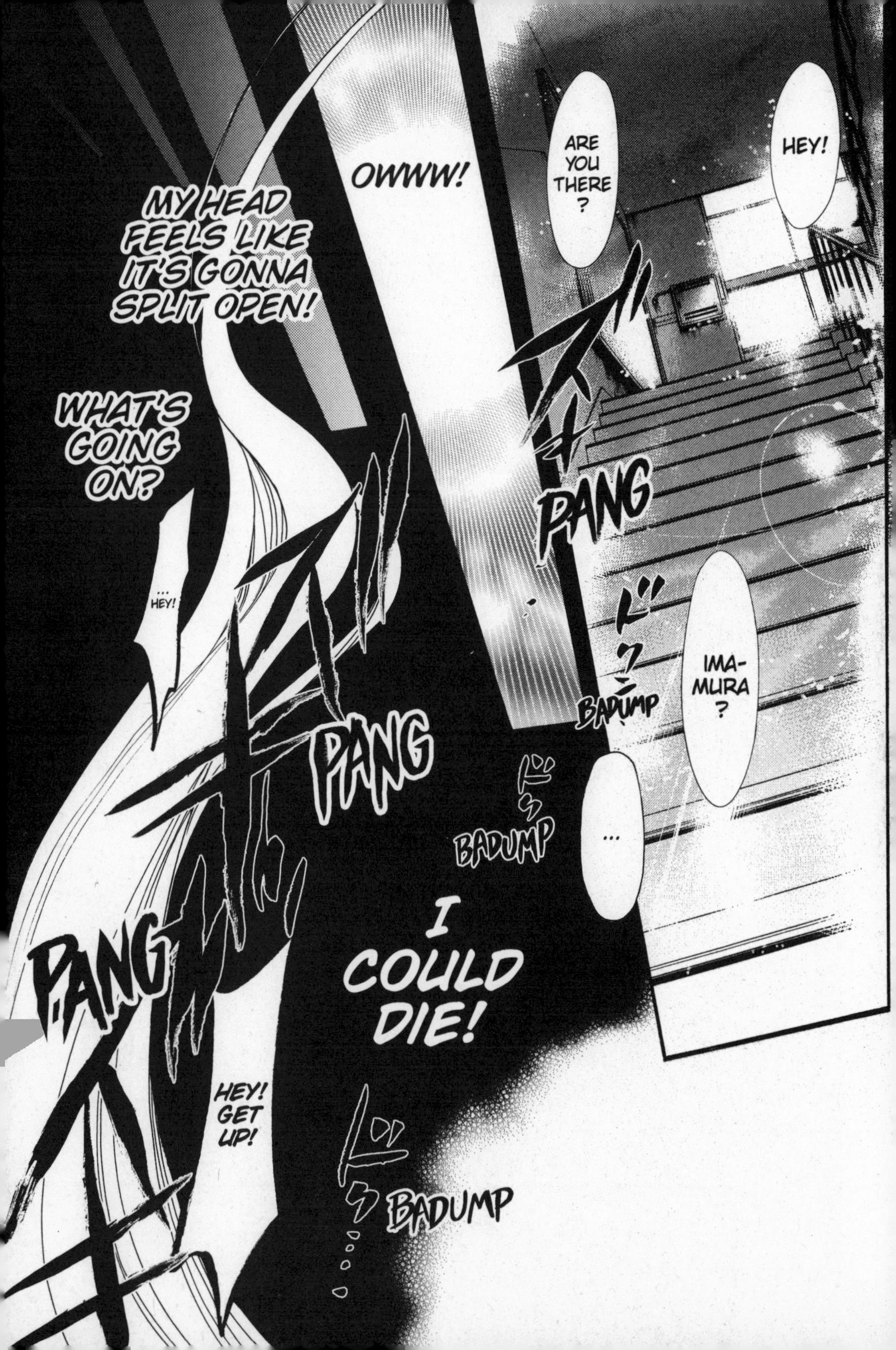
HEY!
ARE YOU THERE?
PANG
BADUMP
IMA-MURA?
...
OWWW!
MY HEAD FEELS LIKE IT'S GONNA SPLIT OPEN!
WHAT'S GOING ON?
...HEY!
PANG
BADUMP
I COULD DIE!
PANG
HEY! GET UP!
BADUMP

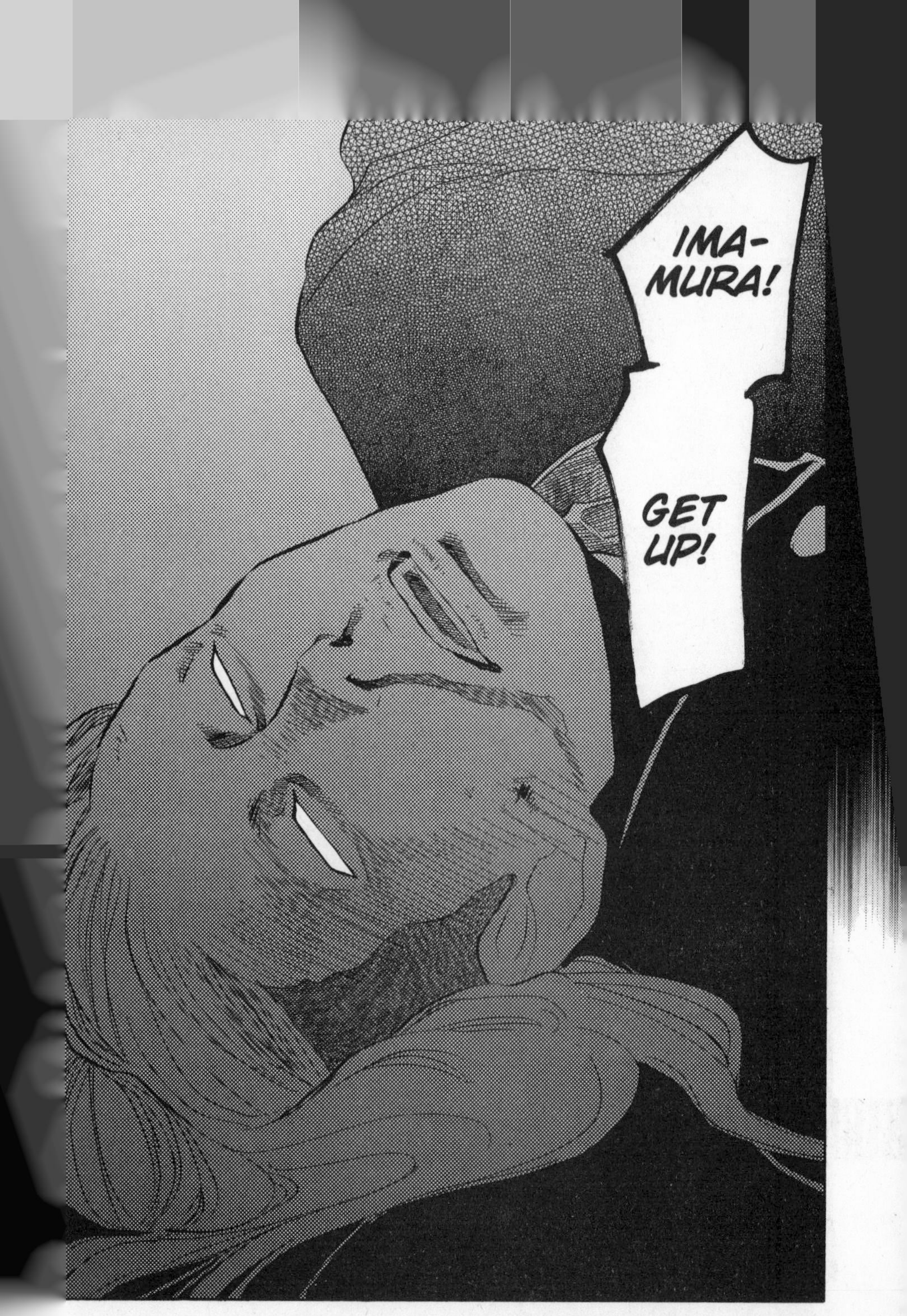
IMA-
MURA!
GET
UP!

33. LEFT BEHIND

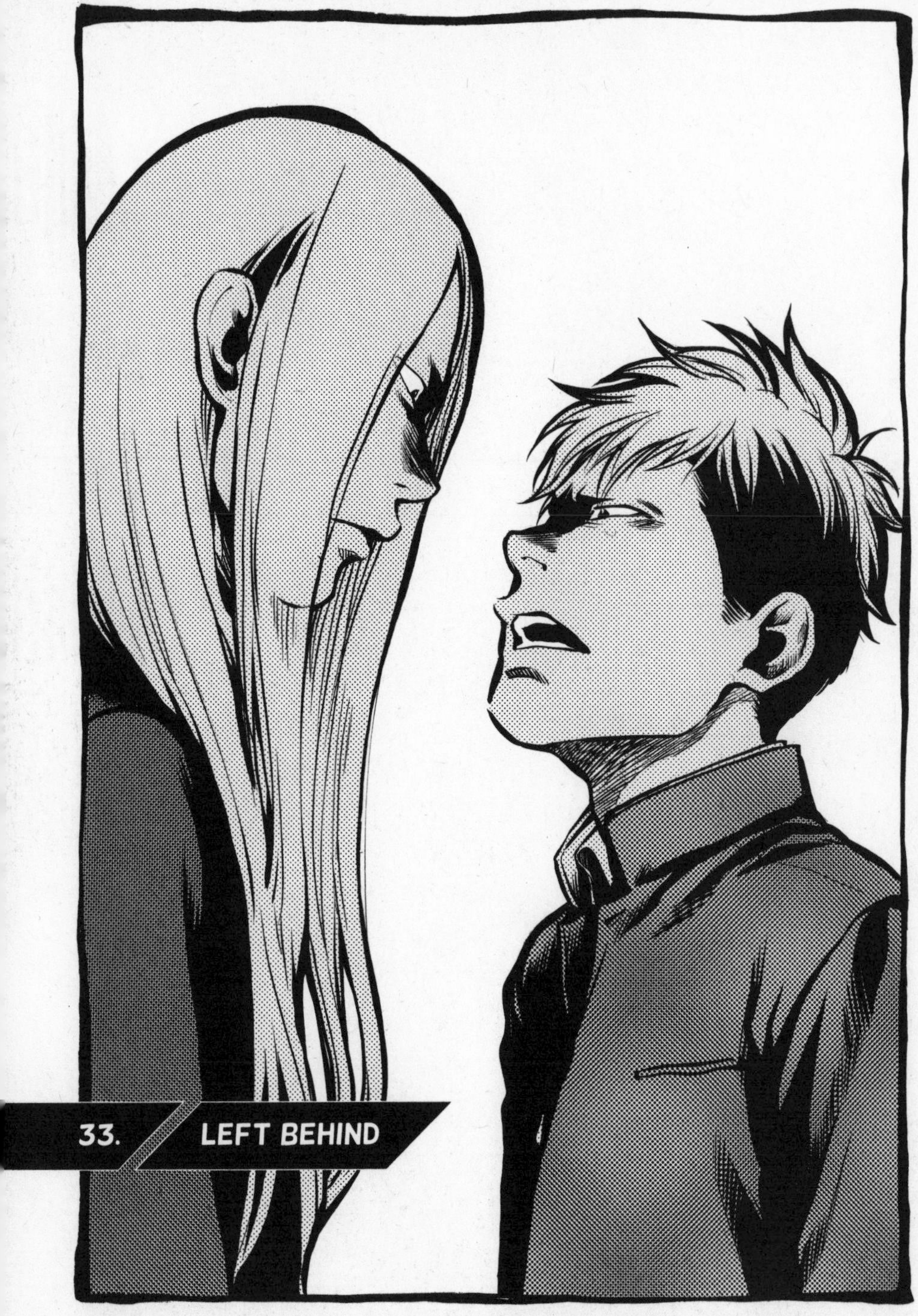

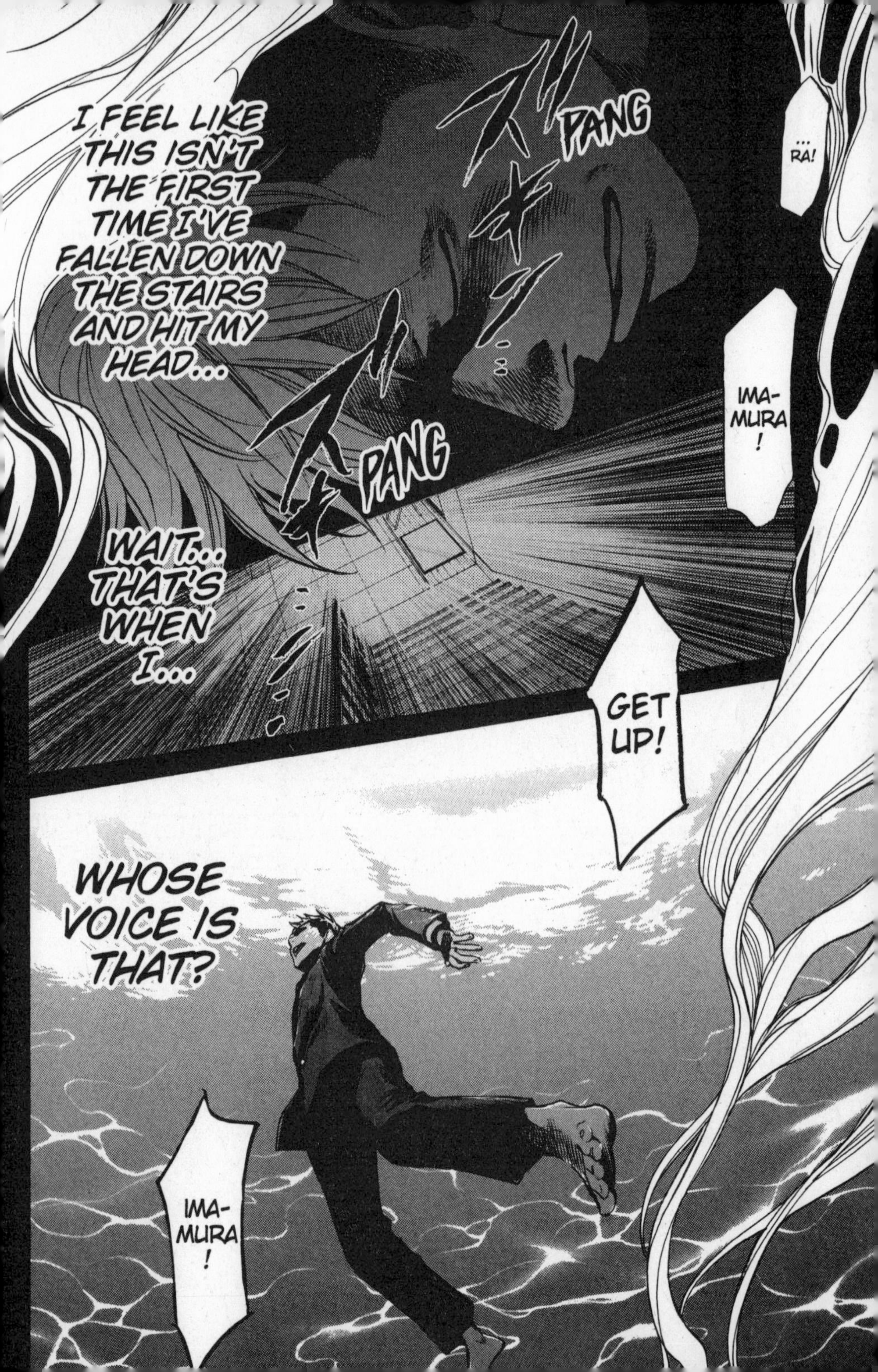

...RA!
PANG
I FEEL LIKE THIS ISN'T THE FIRST TIME I'VE FALLEN DOWN THE STAIRS AND HIT MY HEAD...
IMA-MURA!
PANG
WAIT... THAT'S WHEN I...
GET UP!
WHOSE VOICE IS THAT?
IMA-MURA!

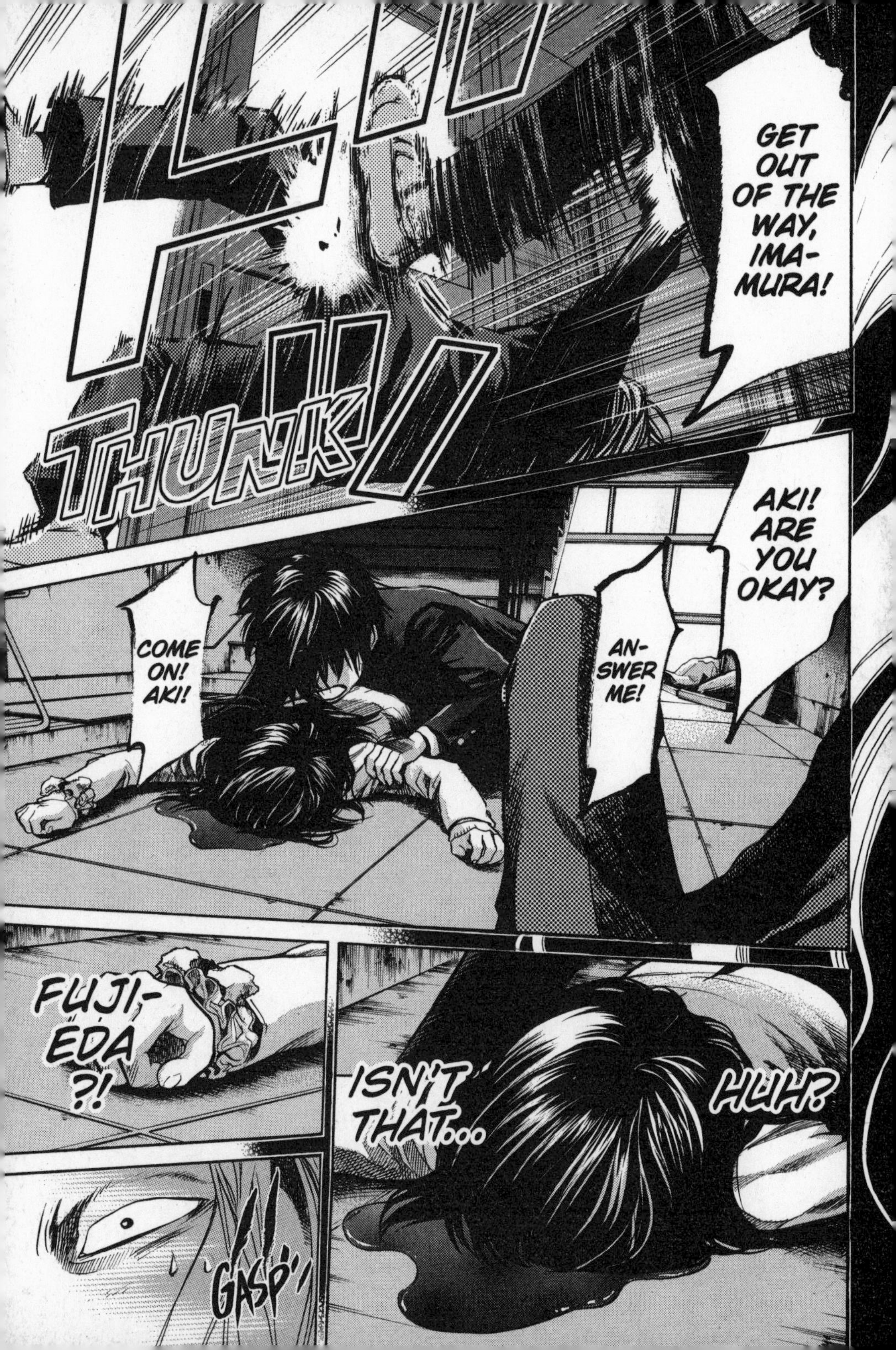
GET OUT OF THE WAY, IMAMURA!
THUNK
AKI! ARE YOU OKAY?
AN-SWER ME!
COME ON! AKI!
HUH?
ISN'T THAT...
FUJI-EDA ?!
GASP

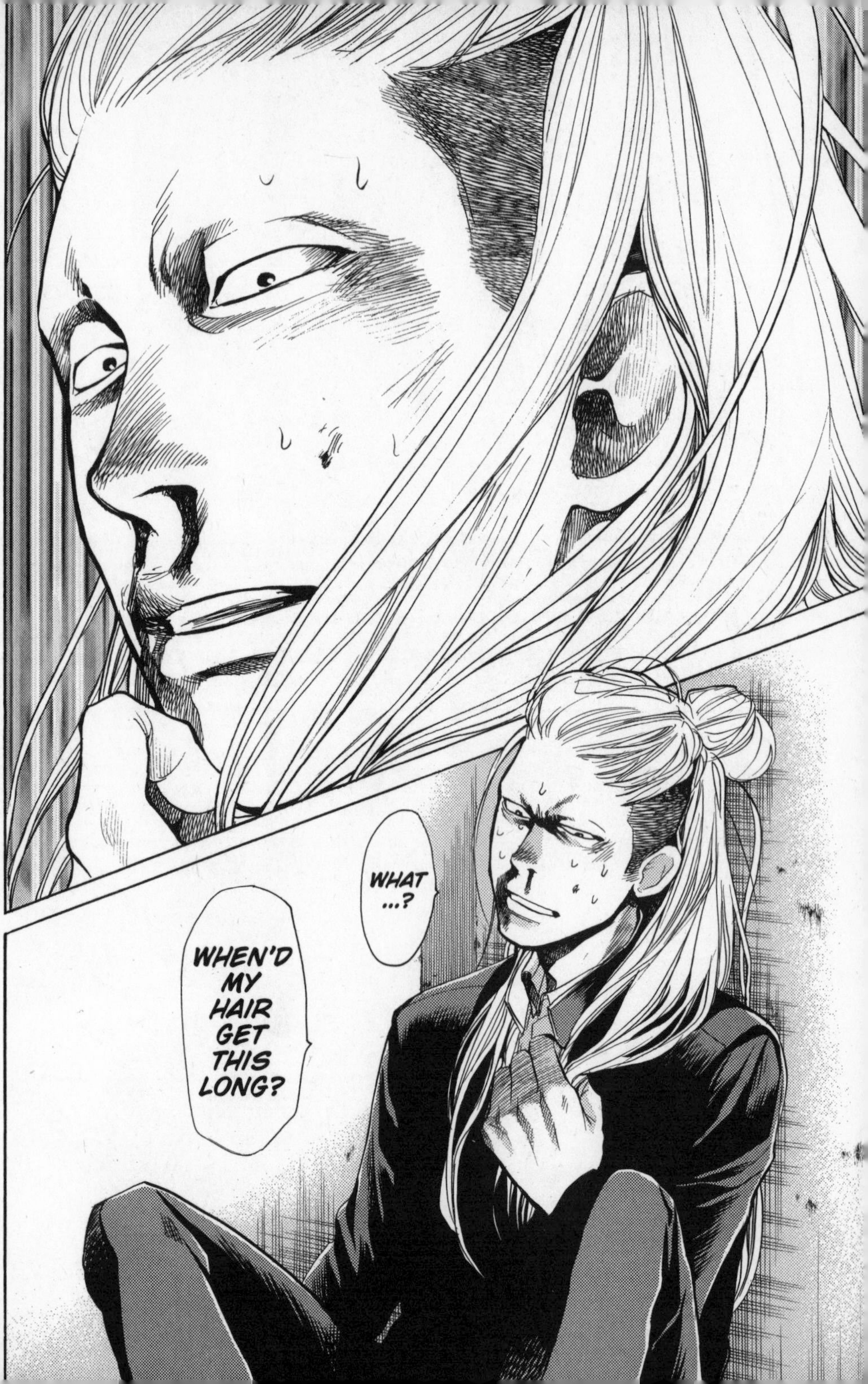
WHAT ...?
WHEN'D MY HAIR GET THIS LONG?

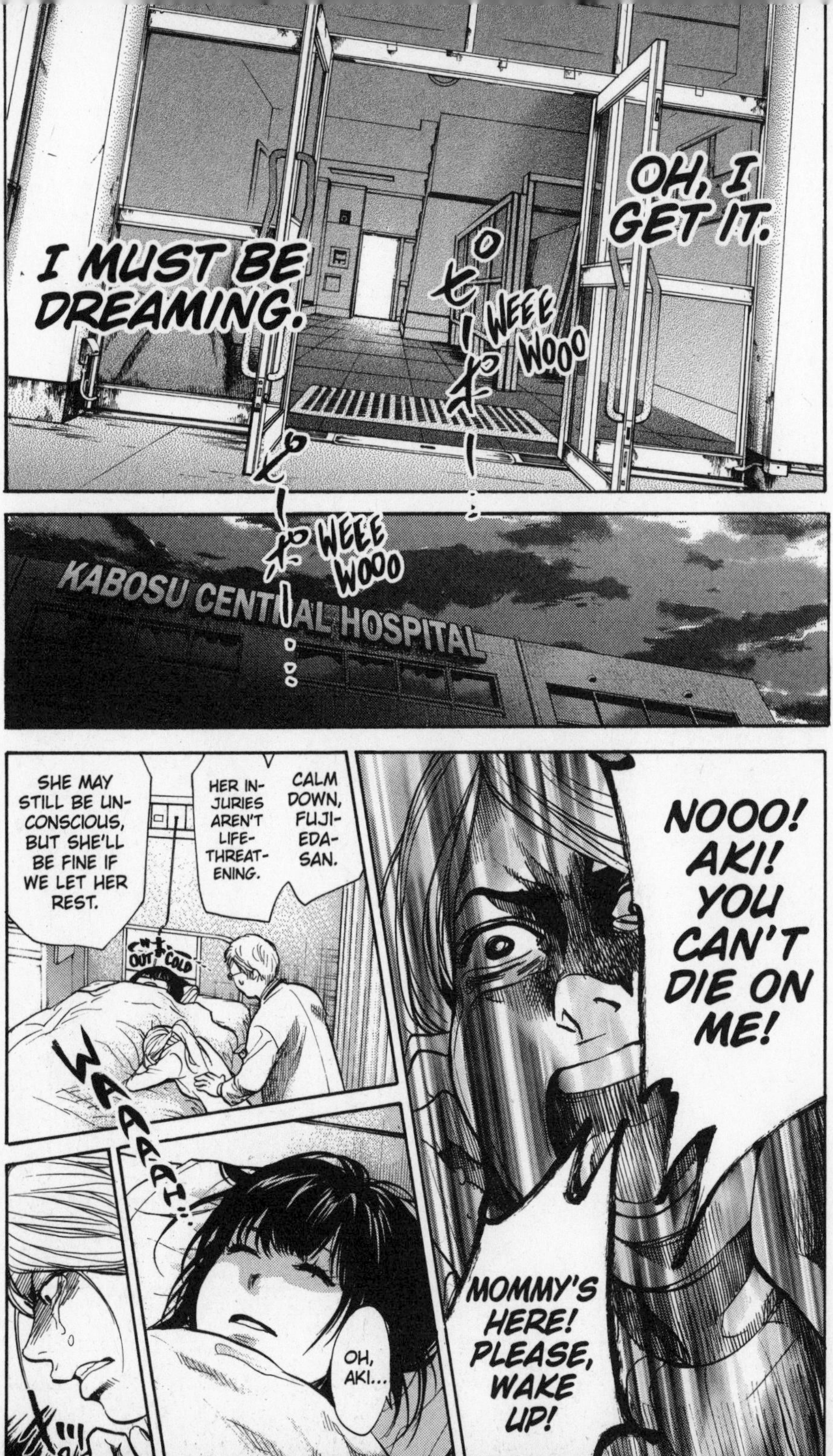
OH, I GET IT.
I MUST BE DREAMING.
WEEE WOOO
WEEE WOOO
KABOSU CENT AL HOSPITAL
NOOO! AKI! YOU CAN'T DIE ON ME!
CALM DOWN, FUJIEDA-SAN.
HER INJURIES AREN'T LIFE-THREATENING.
SHE MAY STILL BE UNCONSCIOUS, BUT SHE'LL BE FINE IF WE LET HER REST.
OUT COLD
WAAAAH!!
MOMMY'S HERE! PLEASE, WAKE UP!
OH, AKI...

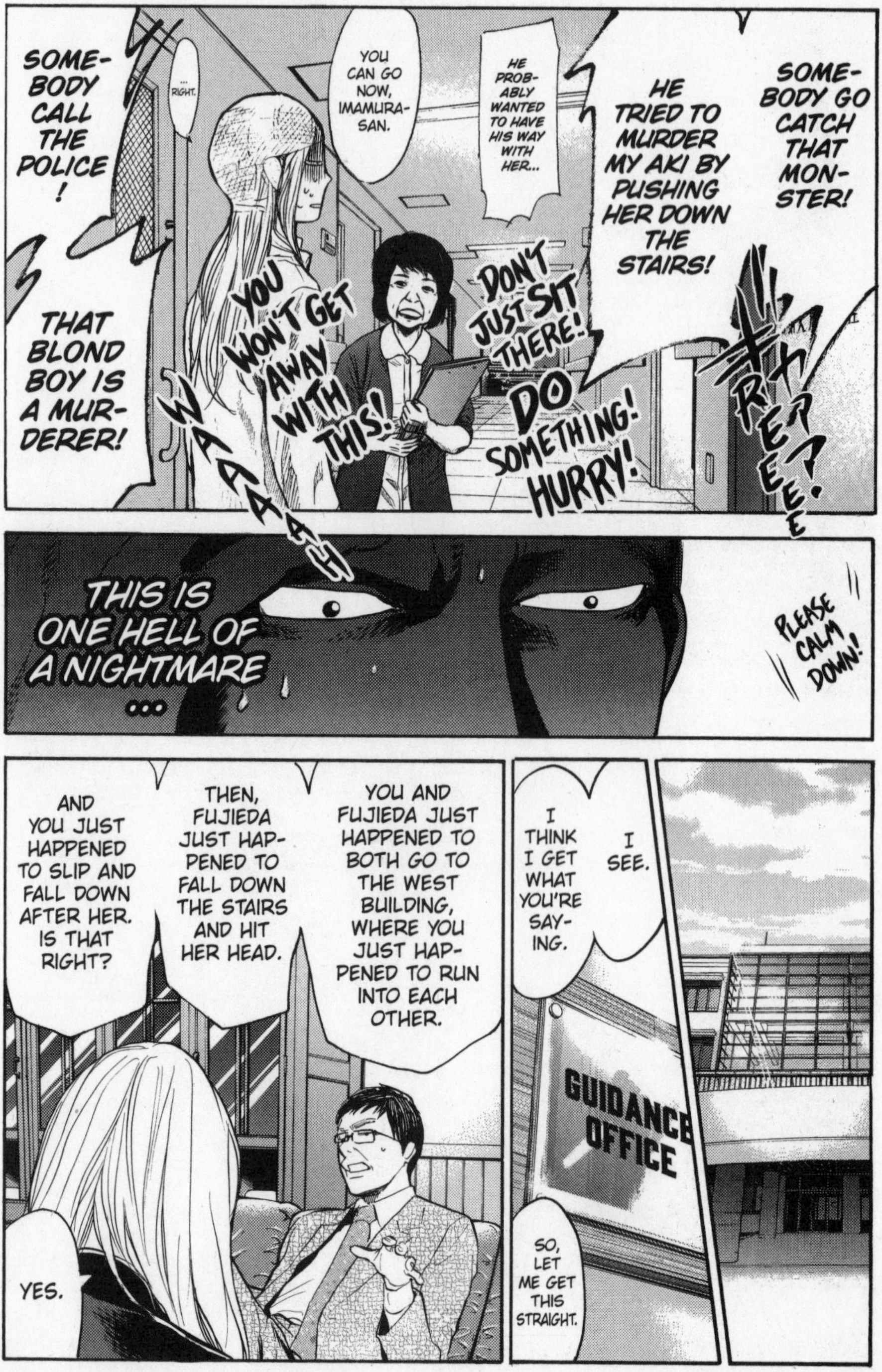
SOME-BODY GO CATCH THAT MON-STER!
HE TRIED TO MURDER MY AKI BY PUSHING HER DOWN THE STAIRS!
REEEE
HE PROB-ABLY WANTED TO HAVE HIS WAY WITH HER...
YOU CAN GO NOW, IMAMURA-SAN.
... RIGHT.
SOME-BODY CALL THE POLICE!
DON'T JUST SIT THERE! DO SOMETHING! HURRY!
YOU WON'T GET AWAY WITH THIS!
THAT BLOND BOY IS A MUR-DERER!
WAAAAH
PLEASE CALM DOWN!
THIS IS ONE HELL OF A NIGHTMARE ...
I SEE.
I THINK I GET WHAT YOU'RE SAY-ING.
GUIDANCE OFFICE
SO, LET ME GET THIS STRAIGHT.
YOU AND FUJIEDA JUST HAPPENED TO BOTH GO TO THE WEST BUILDING, WHERE YOU JUST HAP-PENED TO RUN INTO EACH OTHER.
THEN, FUJIEDA JUST HAP-PENED TO FALL DOWN THE STAIRS AND HIT HER HEAD.
AND YOU JUST HAPPENED TO SLIP AND FALL DOWN AFTER HER. IS THAT RIGHT?
YES.

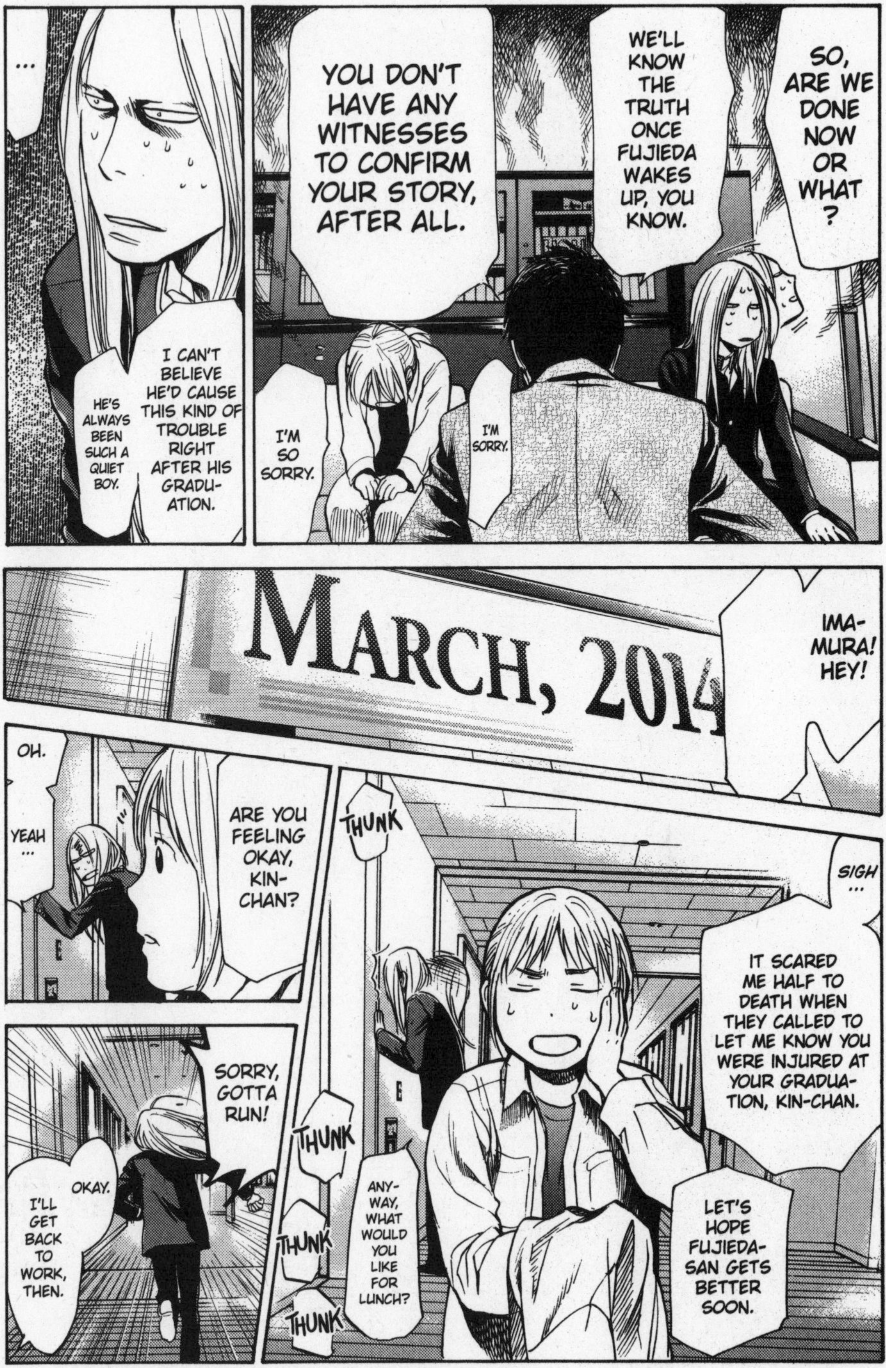
SO, ARE WE DONE NOW OR WHAT?
WE'LL KNOW THE TRUTH ONCE FUJIEDA WAKES UP, YOU KNOW.
YOU DON'T HAVE ANY WITNESSES TO CONFIRM YOUR STORY, AFTER ALL.
I'M SORRY.
I'M SO SORRY.
...
I CAN'T BELIEVE HE'D CAUSE THIS KIND OF TROUBLE RIGHT AFTER HIS GRADUATION.
HE'S ALWAYS BEEN SUCH A QUIET BOY.
IMAMURA! HEY!
MARCH, 2014
SIGH...
IT SCARED ME HALF TO DEATH WHEN THEY CALLED TO LET ME KNOW YOU WERE INJURED AT YOUR GRADUATION, KIN-CHAN.
LET'S HOPE FUJIEDA-SAN GETS BETTER SOON.
THUNK
ANYWAY, WHAT WOULD YOU LIKE FOR LUNCH?
THUNK
THUNK
THUNK
ARE YOU FEELING OKAY, KIN-CHAN?
OH.
YEAH...
SORRY, GOTTA RUN!
OKAY.
I'LL GET BACK TO WORK, THEN.

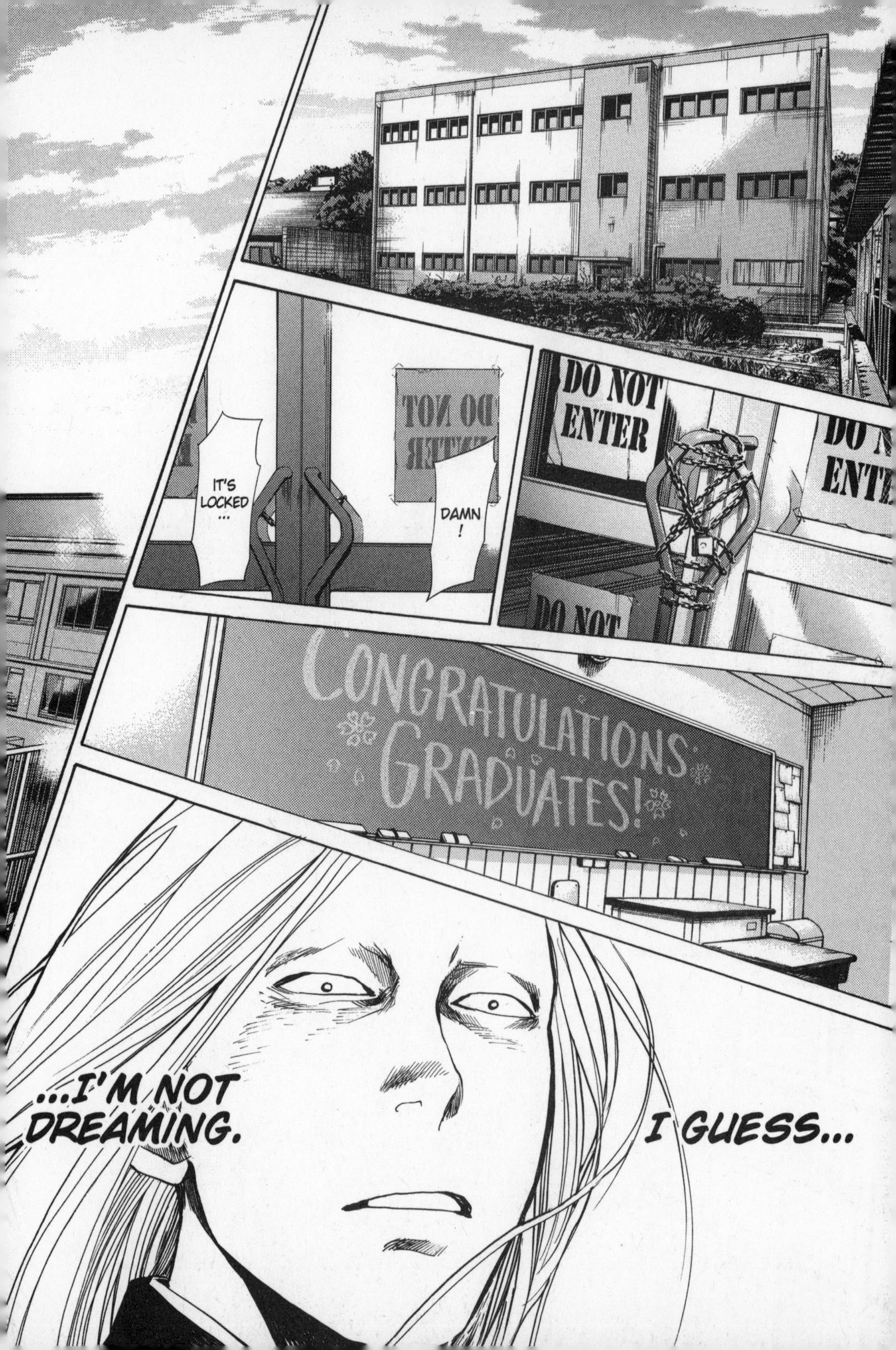
DO NOT ENTER
DO NOT
DAMN!
IT'S LOCKED...
CONGRATULATIONS GRADUATES!
I GUESS...
...I'M NOT DREAMING.

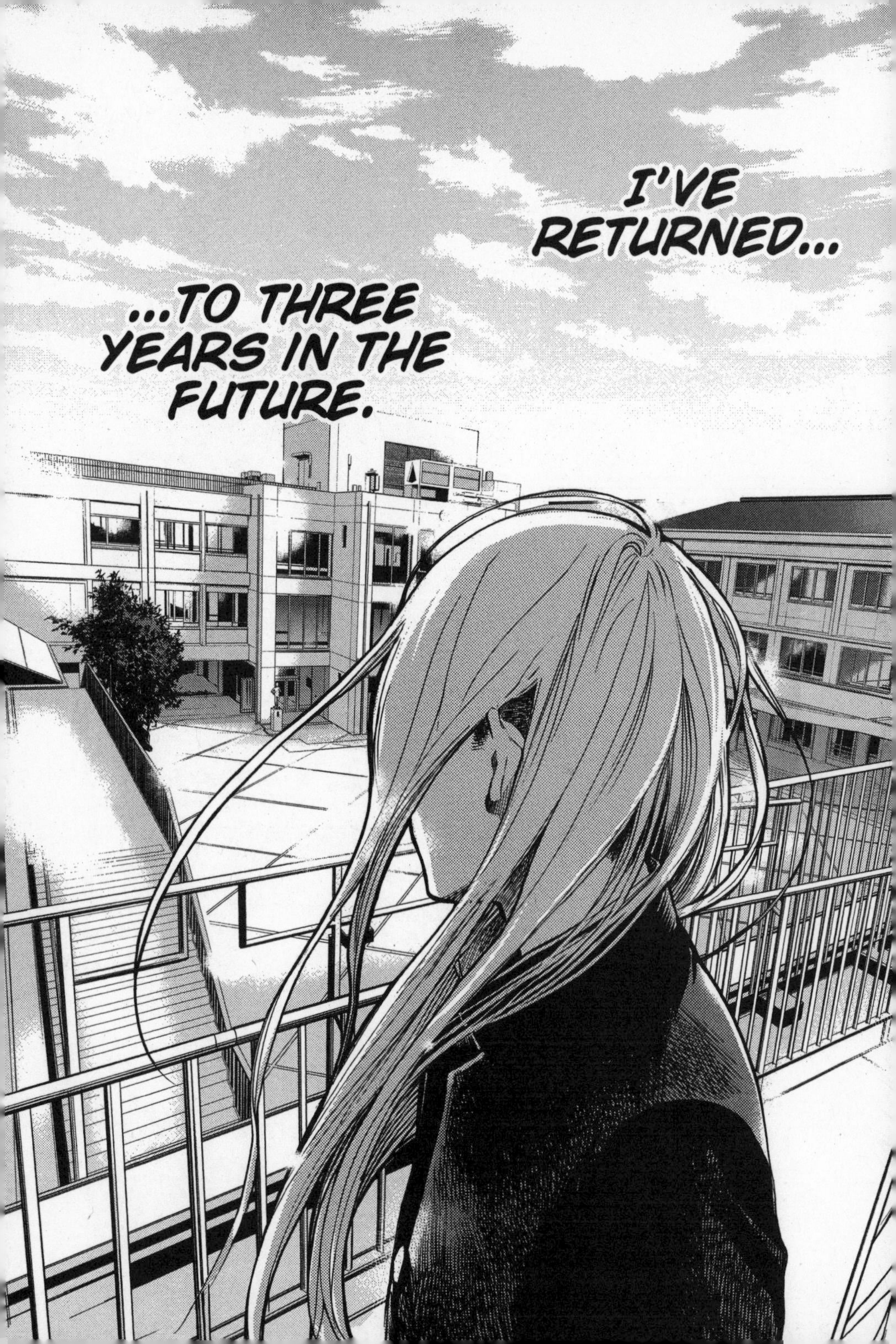
I'VE RETURNED...
...TO THREE YEARS IN THE FUTURE.

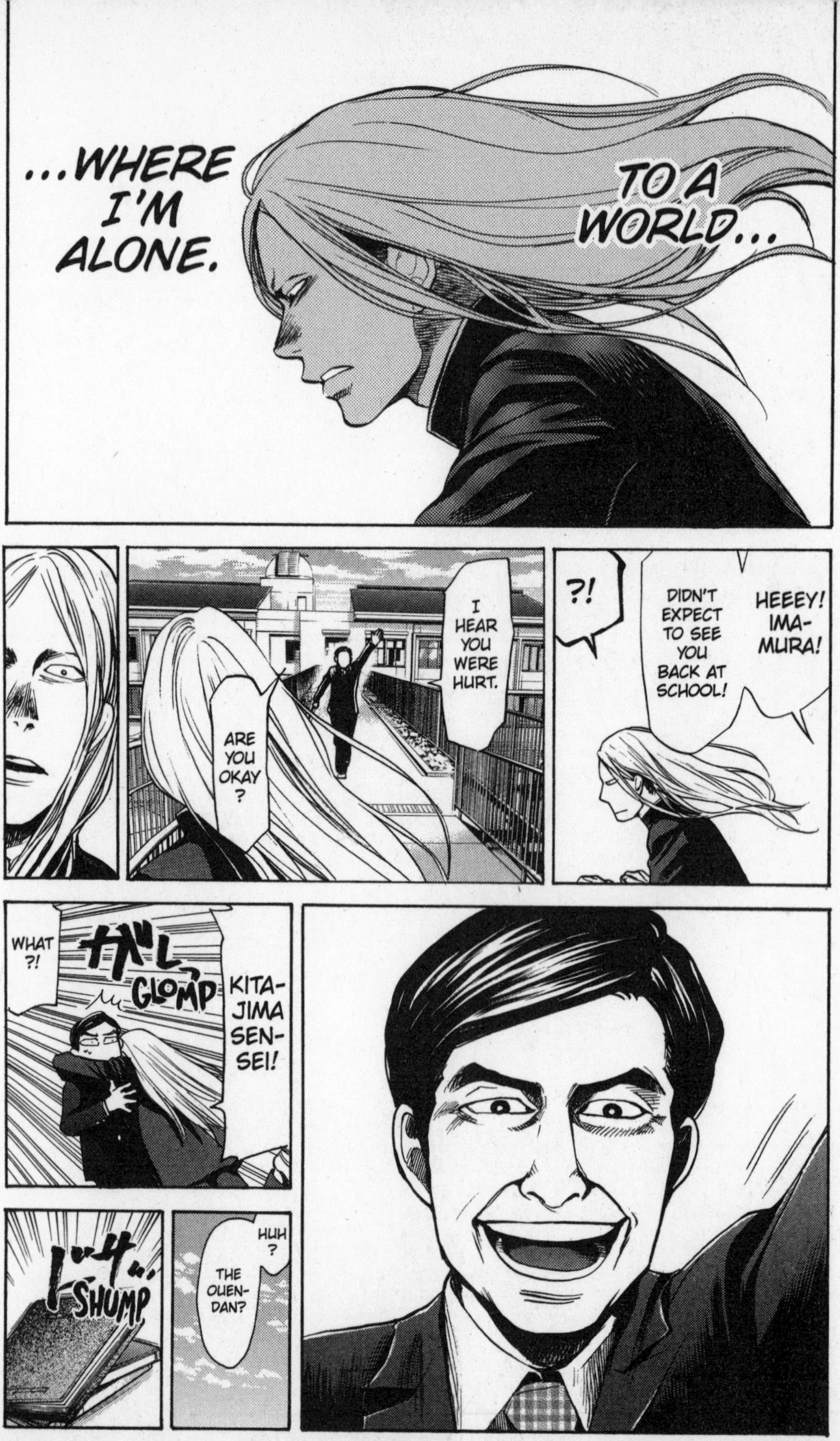
TO A WORLD...
...WHERE I'M ALONE.
HEEEY! IMA-MURA!
DIDN'T EXPECT TO SEE YOU BACK AT SCHOOL!
?!
I HEAR YOU WERE HURT.
ARE YOU OKAY?
KITA-JIMA SEN-SEI!
GLOMP
WHAT?!
HUH?
THE OUEN-DAN?
SHUMP

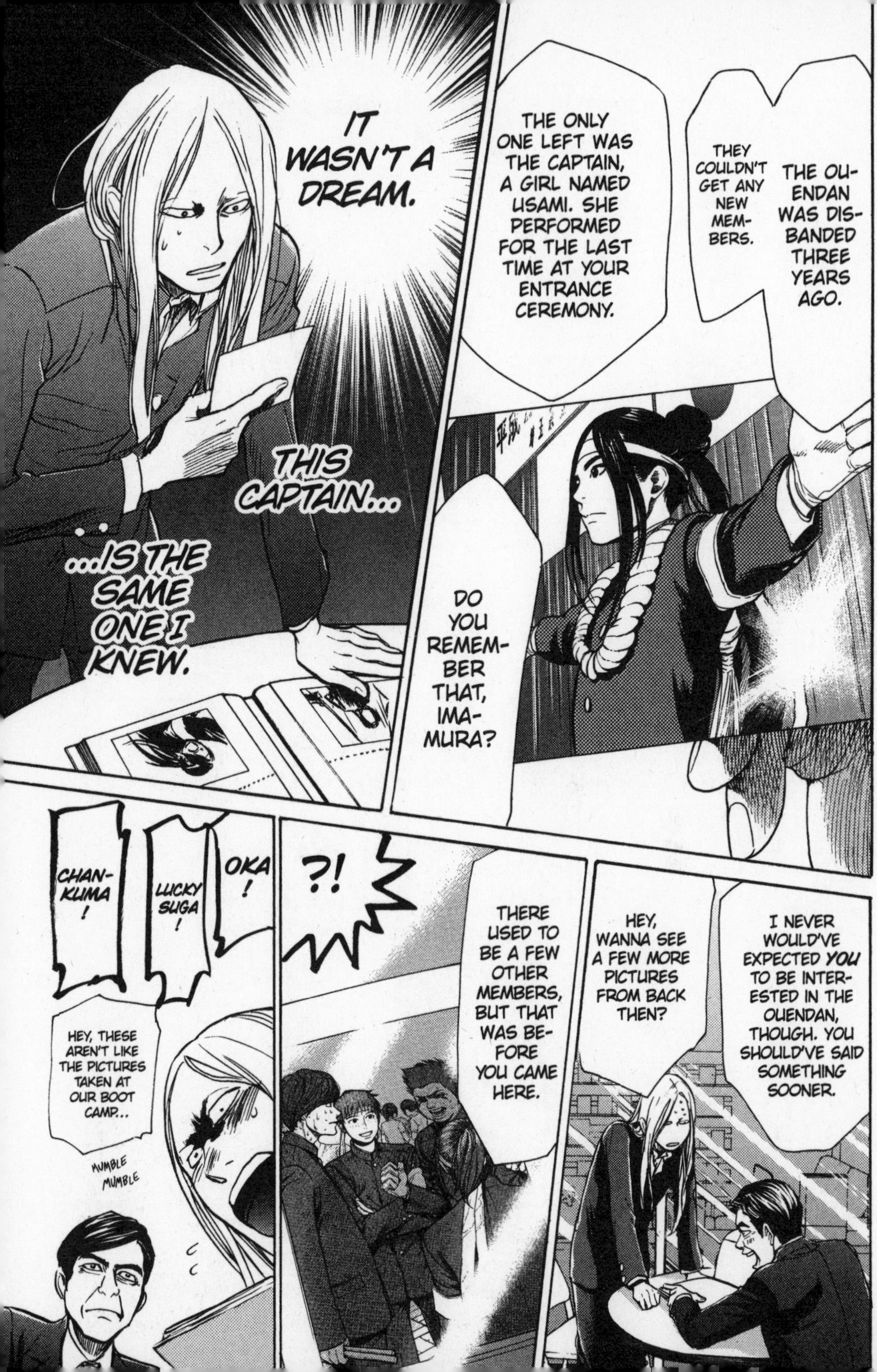
THE OU-ENDAN WAS DISBANDED THREE YEARS AGO.
THEY COULDN'T GET ANY NEW MEMBERS.
THE ONLY ONE LEFT WAS THE CAPTAIN, A GIRL NAMED USAMI. SHE PERFORMED FOR THE LAST TIME AT YOUR ENTRANCE CEREMONY.
DO YOU REMEMBER THAT, IMAMURA?
IT WASN'T A DREAM.
THIS CAPTAIN...
...IS THE SAME ONE I KNEW.
I NEVER WOULD'VE EXPECTED *YOU* TO BE INTERESTED IN THE OUENDAN, THOUGH. YOU SHOULD'VE SAID SOMETHING SOONER.
HEY, WANNA SEE A FEW MORE PICTURES FROM BACK THEN?
THERE USED TO BE A FEW OTHER MEMBERS, BUT THAT WAS BEFORE YOU CAME HERE.
?!
OKA!
LUCKY SUGA!
CHAN-KUMA!
HEY, THESE AREN'T LIKE THE PICTURES TAKEN AT OUR BOOT CAMP...
MUMBLE MUMBLE

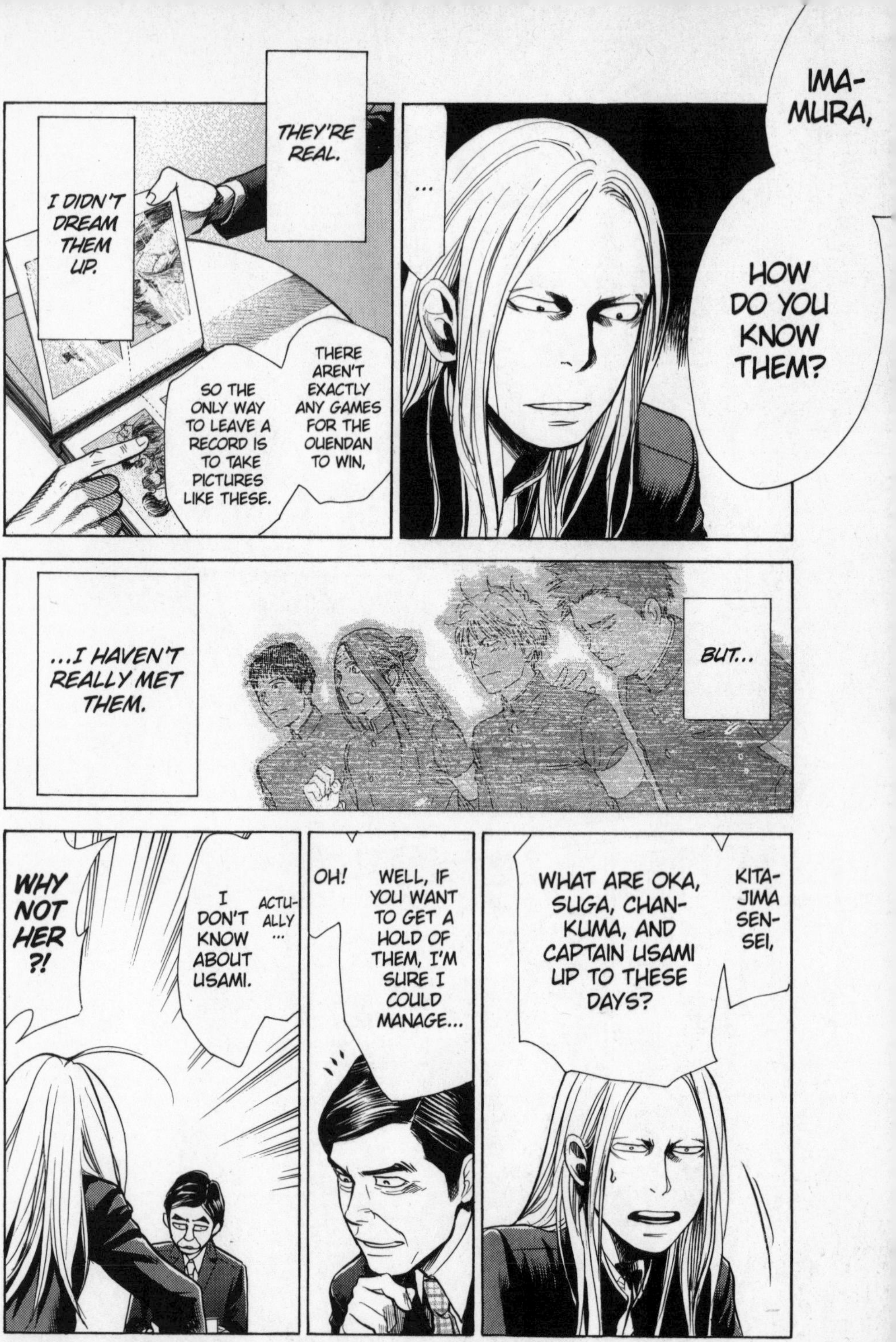
IMA-MURA,
HOW DO YOU KNOW THEM?
...
THEY'RE REAL.
I DIDN'T DREAM THEM UP.
THERE AREN'T EXACTLY ANY GAMES FOR THE OUENDAN TO WIN,
SO THE ONLY WAY TO LEAVE A RECORD IS TO TAKE PICTURES LIKE THESE.
BUT...
...I HAVEN'T REALLY MET THEM.
KITA-JIMA SEN-SEI,
WHAT ARE OKA, SUGA, CHAN-KUMA, AND CAPTAIN USAMI UP TO THESE DAYS?
OH!
WELL, IF YOU WANT TO GET A HOLD OF THEM, I'M SURE I COULD MANAGE...
ACTU-ALLY...
I DON'T KNOW ABOUT USAMI.
WHY NOT HER?!

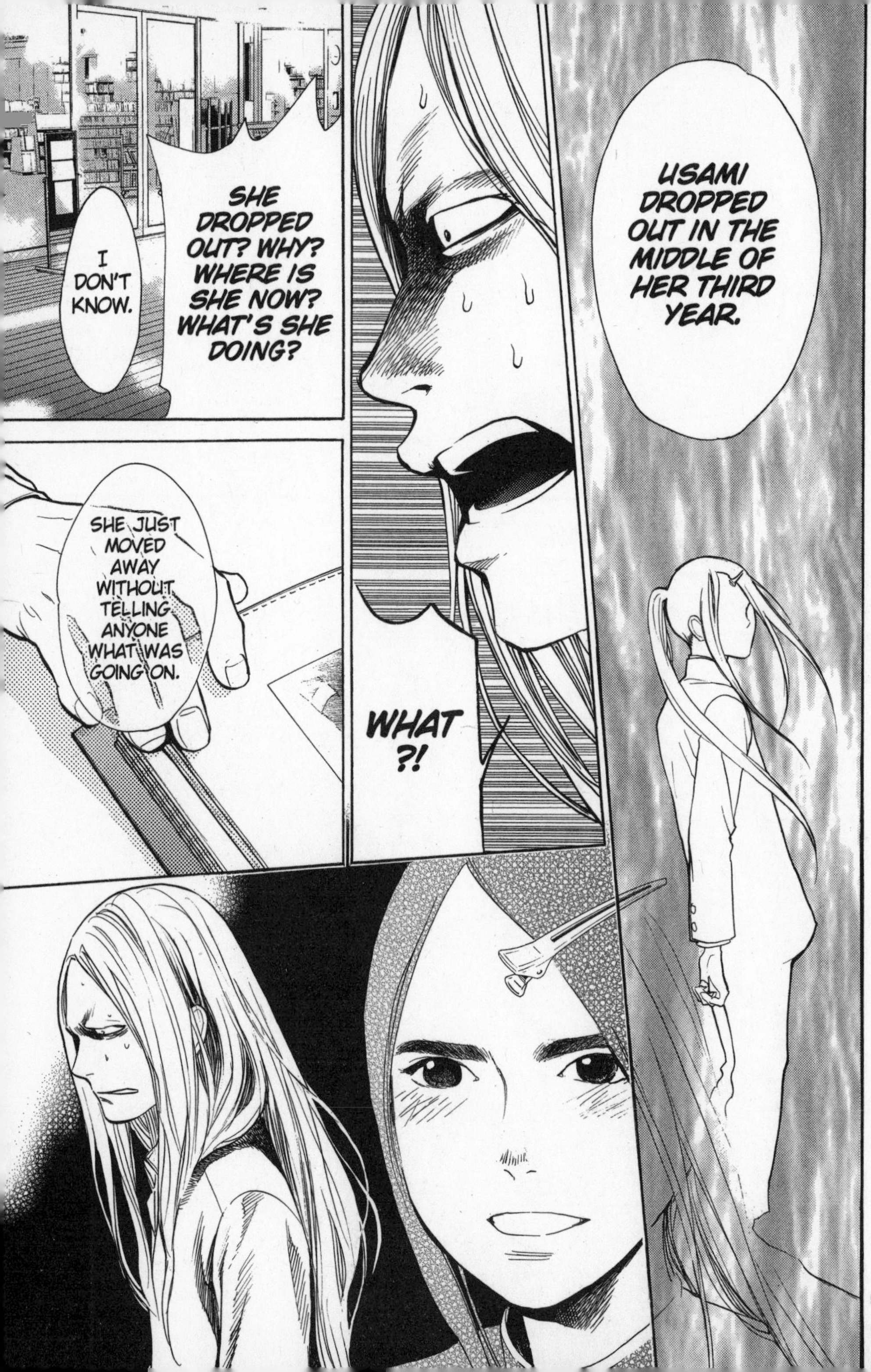
USAMI DROPPED OUT IN THE MIDDLE OF HER THIRD YEAR.
WHAT ?!
SHE DROPPED OUT? WHY? WHERE IS SHE NOW? WHAT'S SHE DOING?
I DON'T KNOW.
SHE JUST MOVED AWAY WITHOUT TELLING ANYONE WHAT WAS GOING ON.

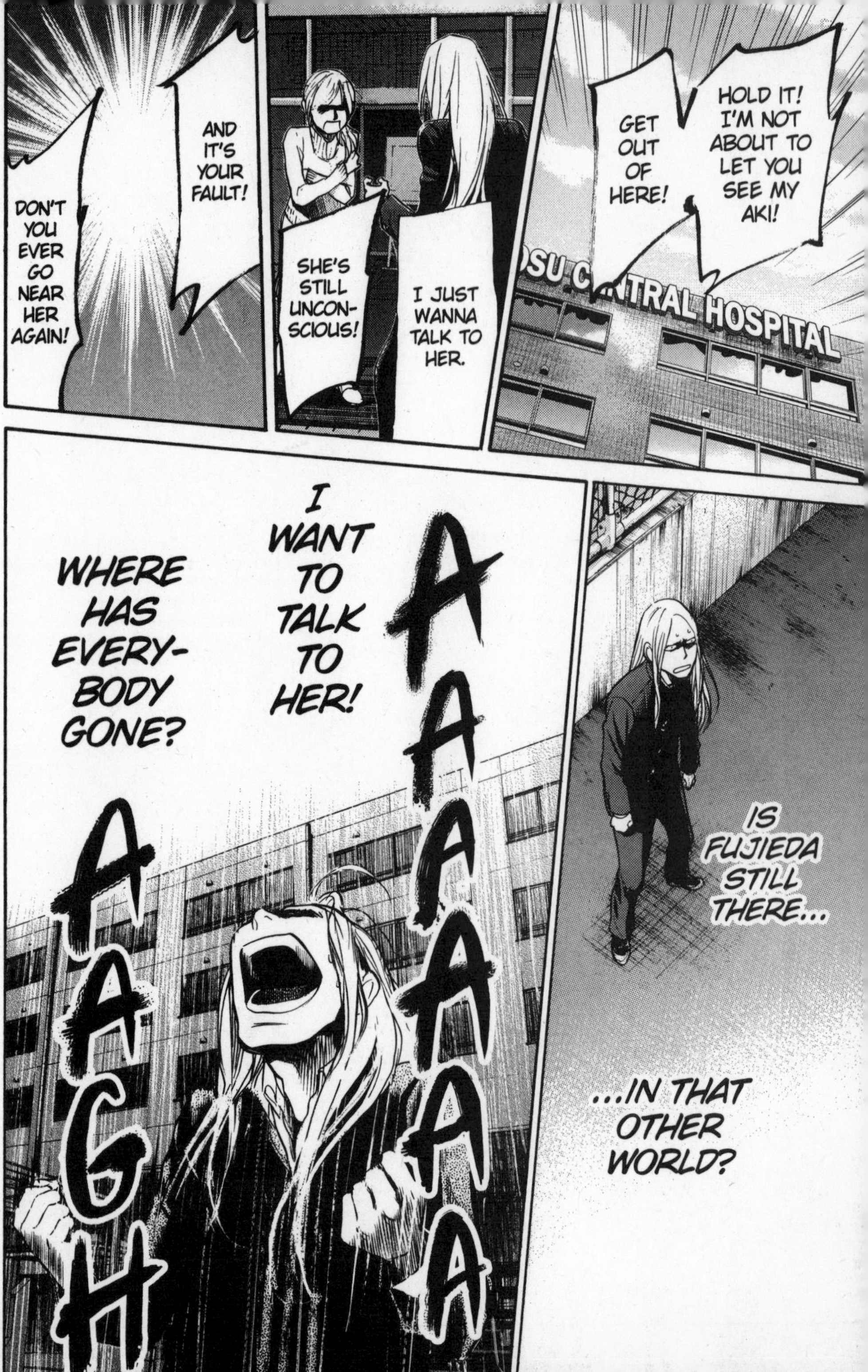
HOLD IT! I'M NOT ABOUT TO LET YOU SEE MY AKI!
GET OUT OF HERE!
I JUST WANNA TALK TO HER.
SHE'S STILL UNCONSCIOUS!
AND IT'S YOUR FAULT!
DON'T YOU EVER GO NEAR HER AGAIN!
IS FUJIEDA STILL THERE...
...IN THAT OTHER WORLD?
AAAAAAA
I WANT TO TALK TO HER!
WHERE HAS EVERYBODY GONE?
AAAAGH

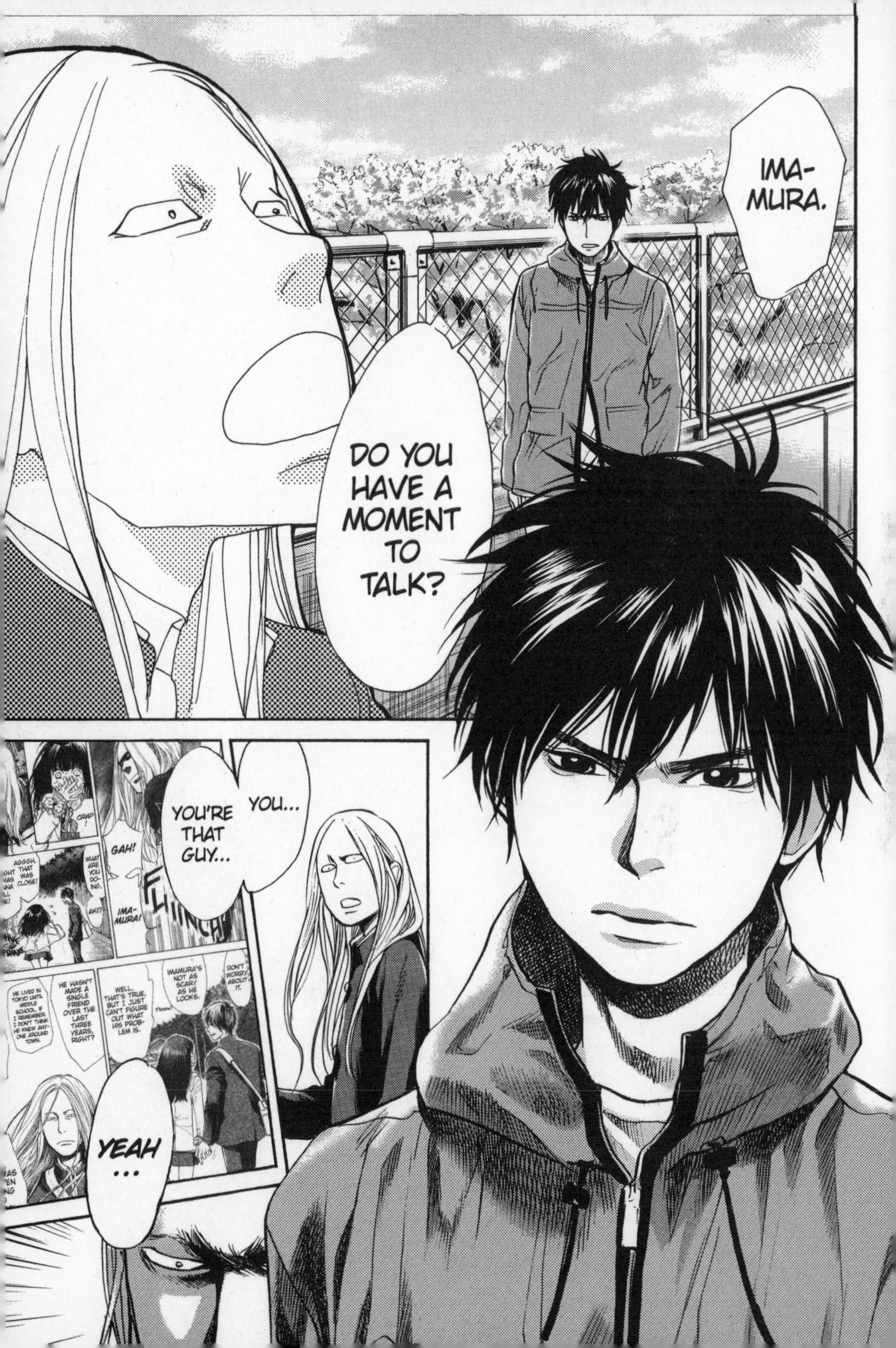
IMA-MURA.
DO YOU HAVE A MOMENT TO TALK?
YOU...
YOU'RE THAT GUY...
GAH!
IMA-MURA!
CRAP!
WHAT ARE YOU DO-ING,
AKI?
AGGGH, THAT WAS CLOSE!
DON'T WORRY ABOUT IT.
IMAMURA'S NOT AS SCARY AS HE LOOKS.
Y'know?
WELL, THAT'S TRUE, BUT I JUST CAN'T FIGURE OUT WHAT HIS PROB-LEM IS.
HE HASN'T MADE A SINGLE FRIEND OVER THE LAST THREE YEARS, RIGHT?
HE LIVED IN TOKYO UNTIL MIDDLE SCHOOL, IF I REMEMBER. I DON'T THINK HE KNEW ANY-ONE AROUND TOWN.
YEAH...

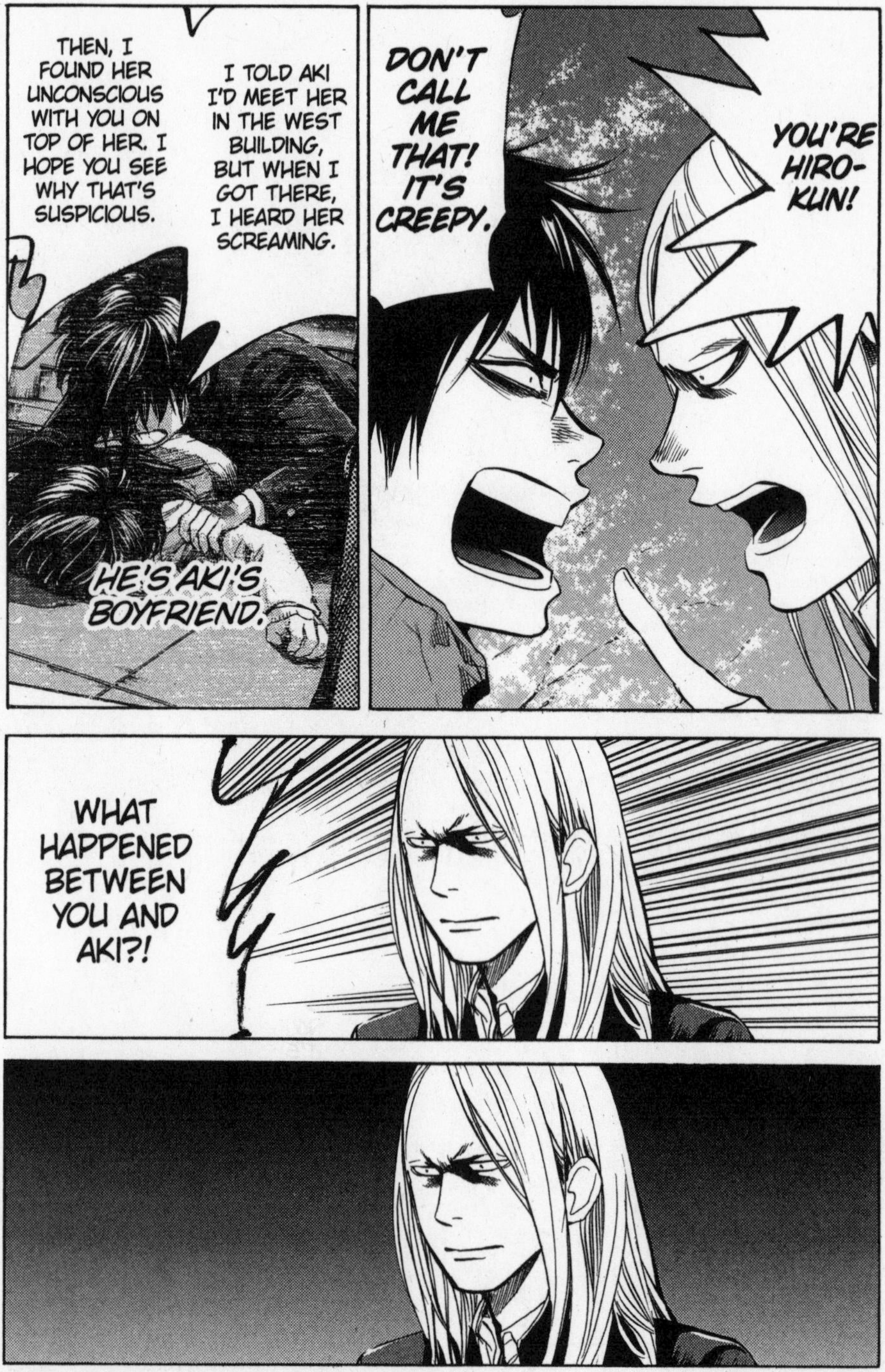
YOU'RE HIRO-KUN!
DON'T CALL ME THAT! IT'S CREEPY.
I TOLD AKI I'D MEET HER IN THE WEST BUILDING, BUT WHEN I GOT THERE, I HEARD HER SCREAMING.
THEN, I FOUND HER UNCONSCIOUS WITH YOU ON TOP OF HER. I HOPE YOU SEE WHY THAT'S SUSPICIOUS.
HE'S AKI'S BOYFRIEND.
WHAT HAPPENED BETWEEN YOU AND AKI?!

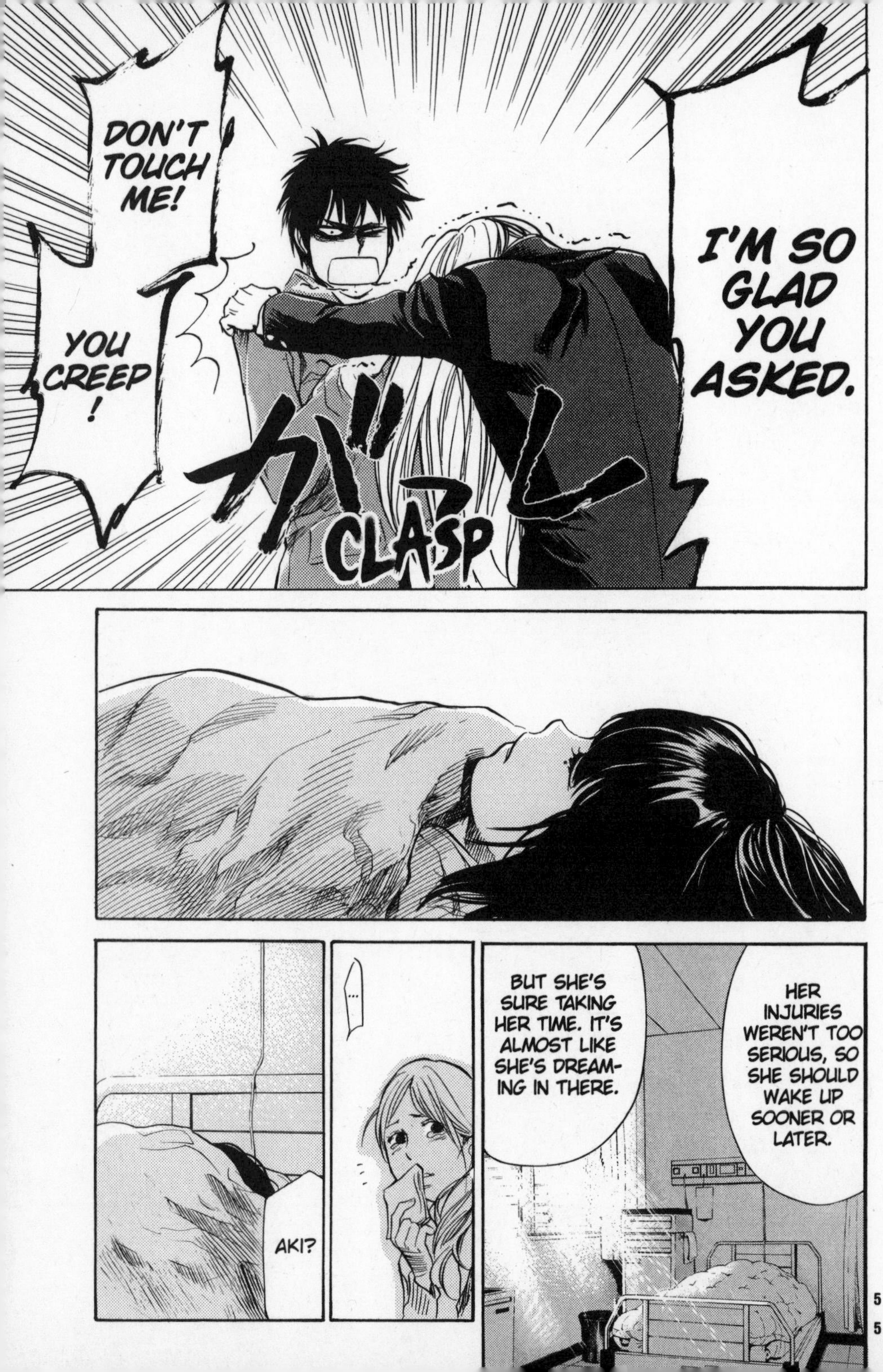
I'M SO GLAD YOU ASKED.
DON'T TOUCH ME!
YOU CREEP!
CLASP
HER INJURIES WEREN'T TOO SERIOUS, SO SHE SHOULD WAKE UP SOONER OR LATER.
BUT SHE'S SURE TAKING HER TIME. IT'S ALMOST LIKE SHE'S DREAMING IN THERE.
...
AKI?

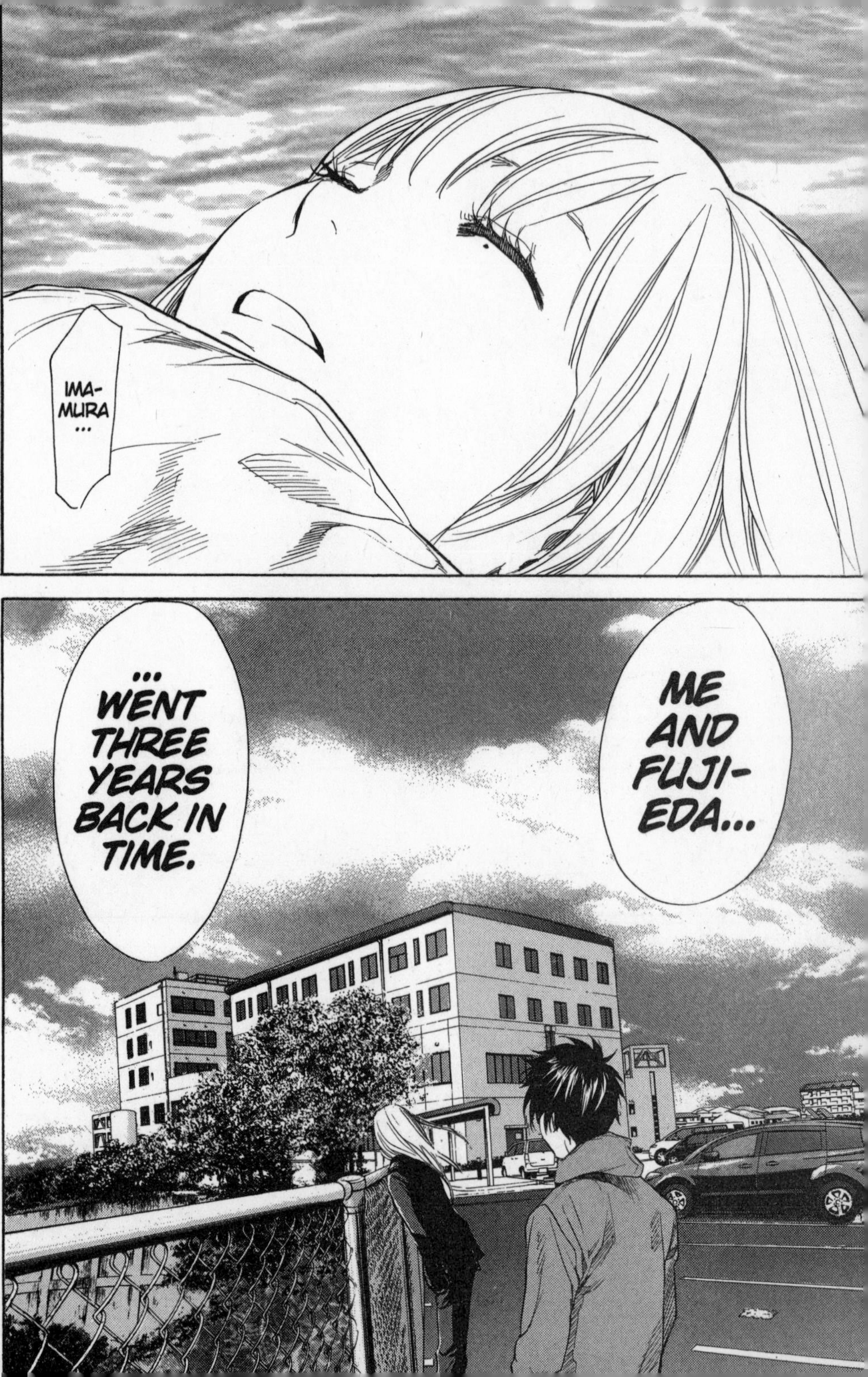
IMA-MURA ...
ME AND FUJI-EDA...
...WENT THREE YEARS BACK IN TIME.

34. CHANGE THE WORLD

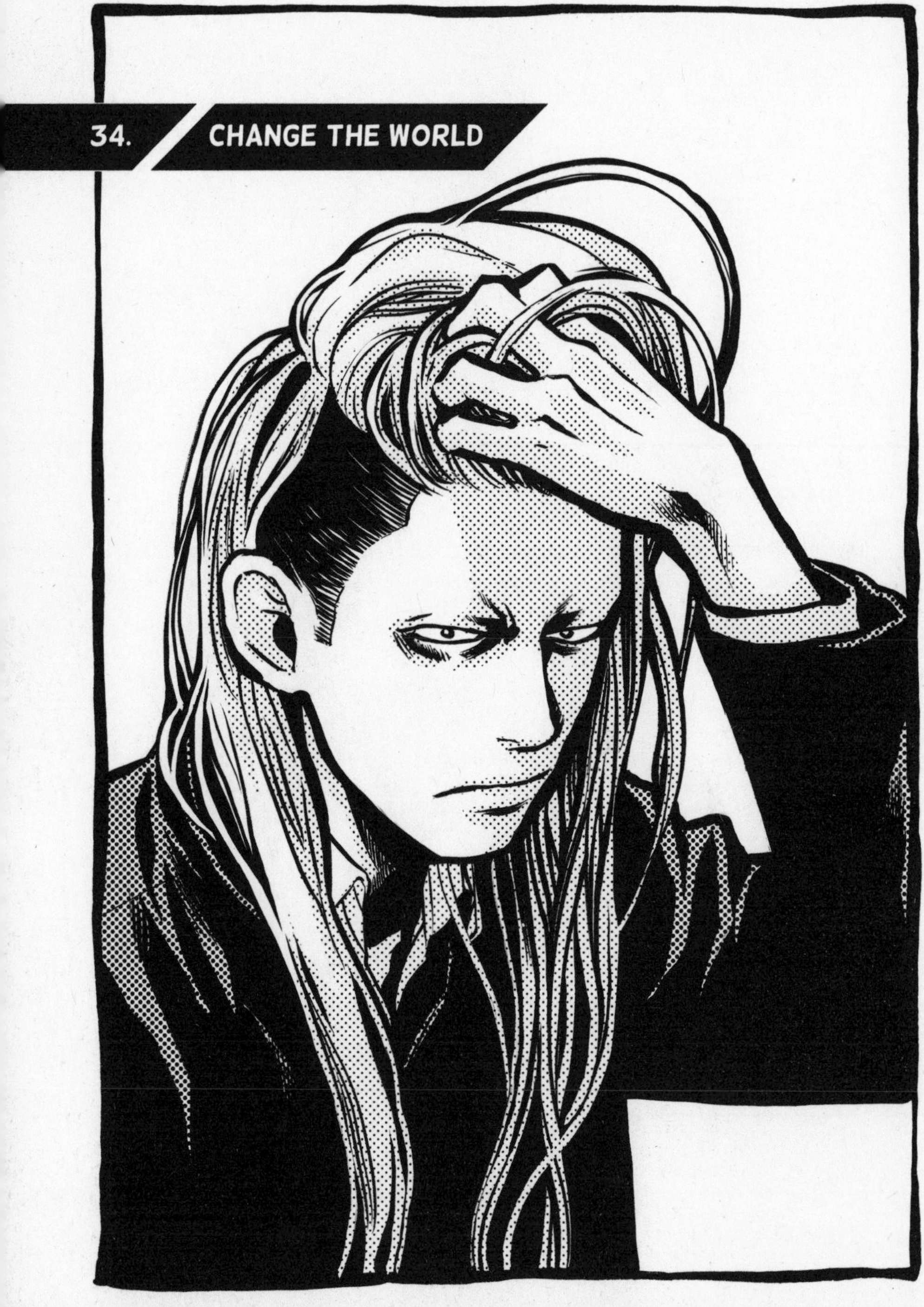

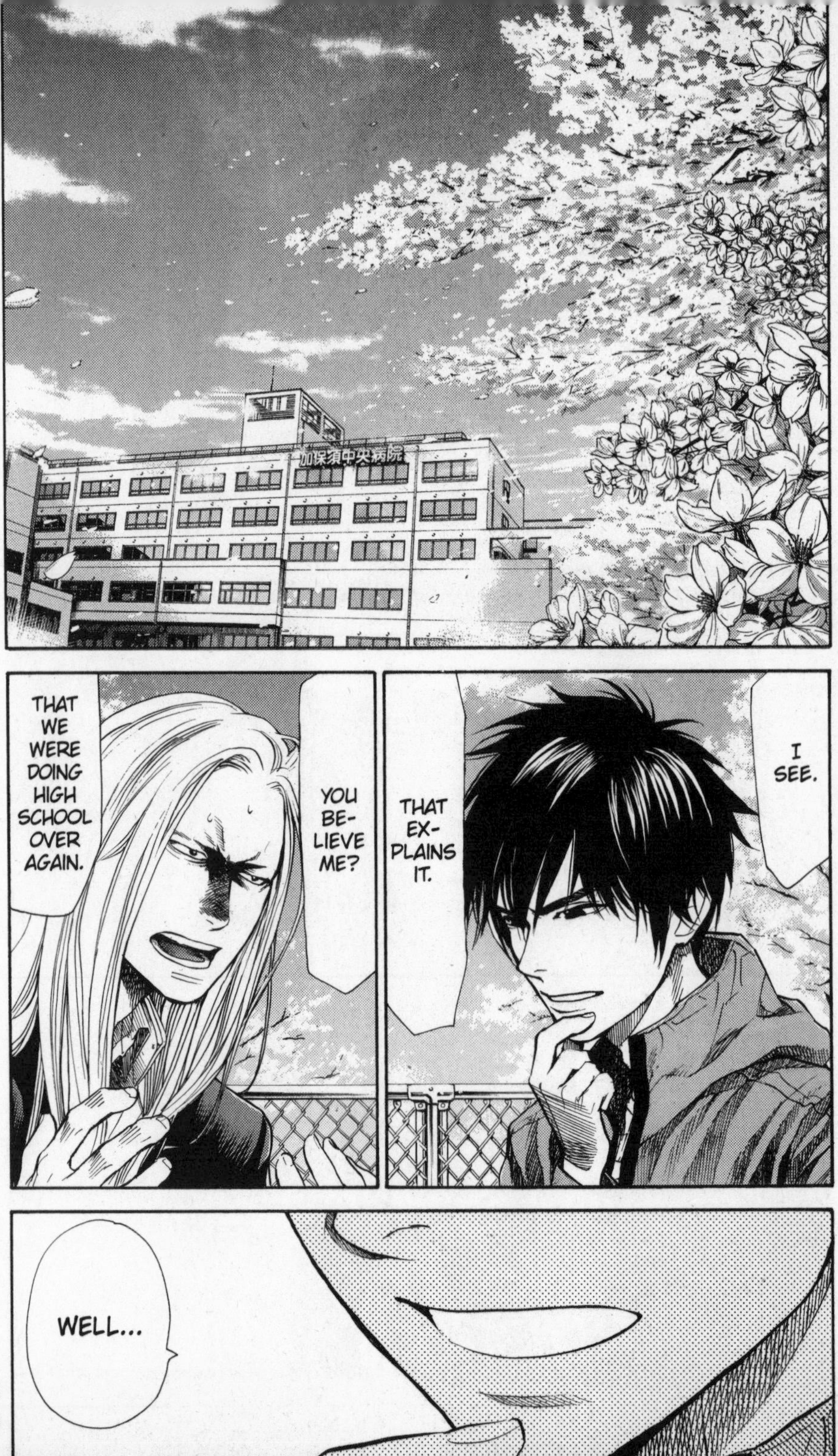
加保須中央病院
I SEE.
THAT EXPLAINS IT.
YOU BELIEVE ME?
THAT WE WERE DOING HIGH SCHOOL OVER AGAIN.
WELL...

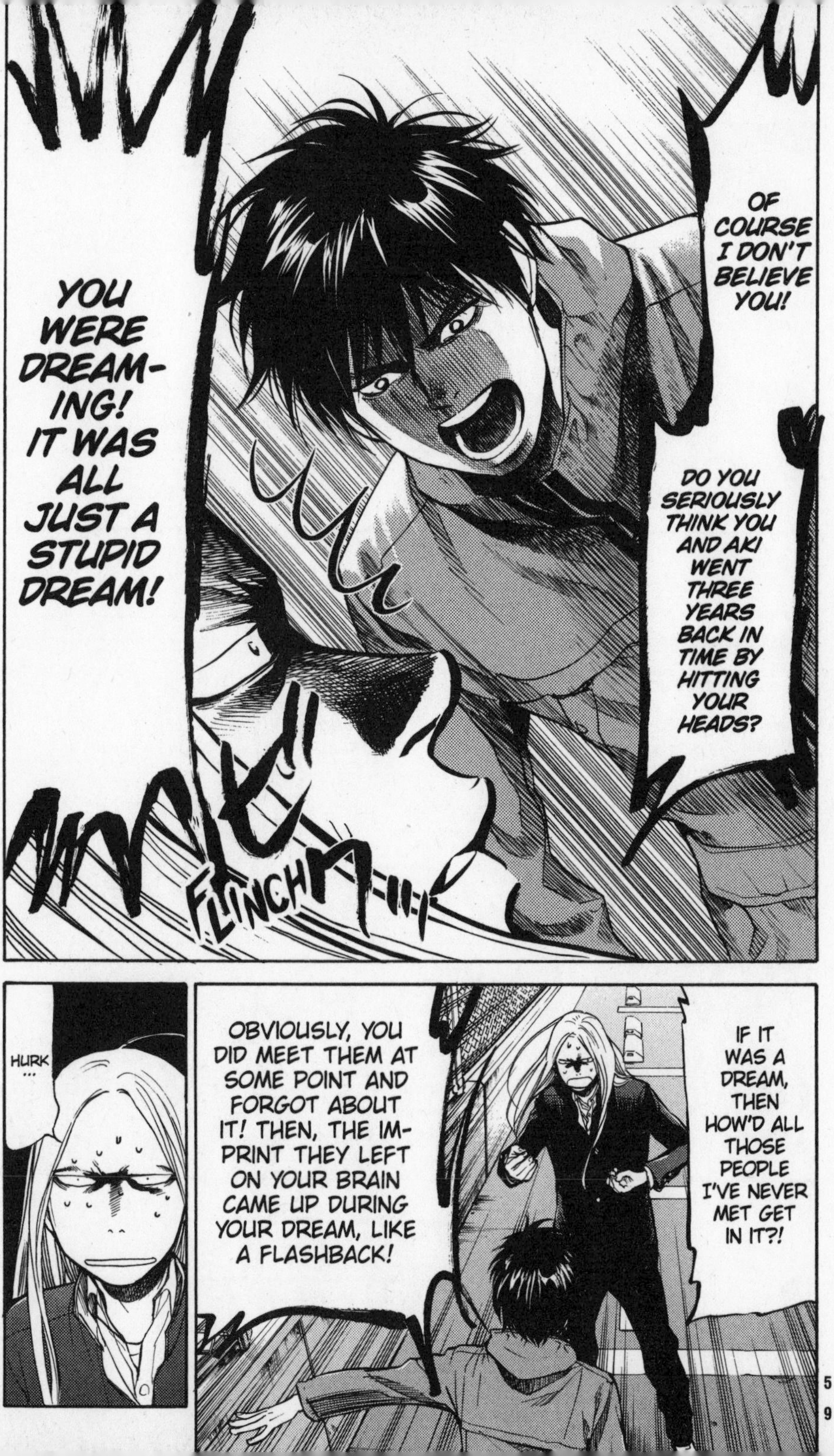
OF COURSE I DON'T BELIEVE YOU!
YOU WERE DREAMING! IT WAS ALL JUST A STUPID DREAM!
DO YOU SERIOUSLY THINK YOU AND AKI WENT THREE YEARS BACK IN TIME BY HITTING YOUR HEADS?
FLINCH!!!
IF IT WAS A DREAM, THEN HOW'D ALL THOSE PEOPLE I'VE NEVER MET GET IN IT?!
OBVIOUSLY, YOU DID MEET THEM AT SOME POINT AND FORGOT ABOUT IT! THEN, THE IMPRINT THEY LEFT ON YOUR BRAIN CAME UP DURING YOUR DREAM, LIKE A FLASHBACK!
HURK ...

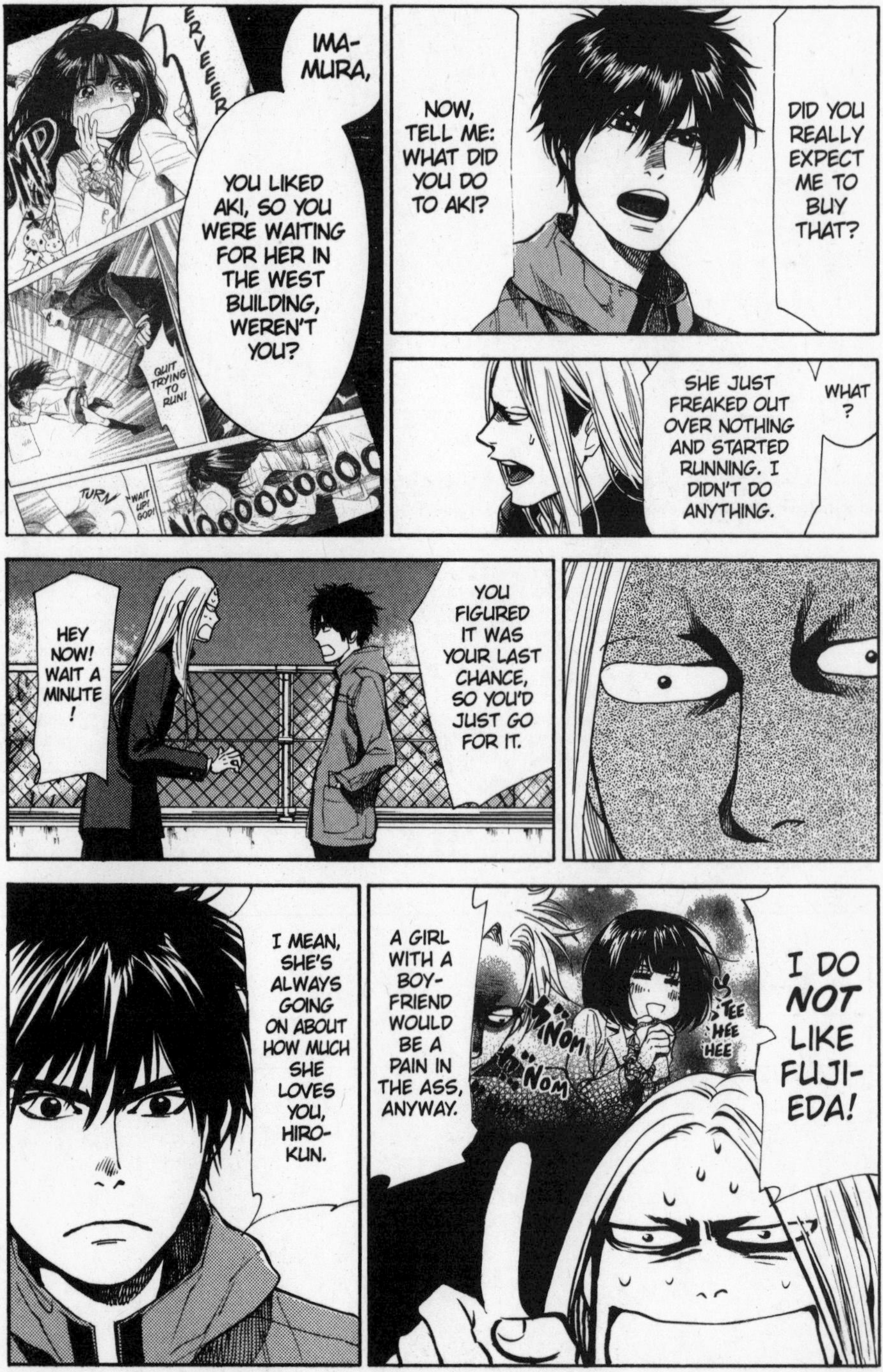
DID YOU REALLY EXPECT ME TO BUY THAT?
NOW, TELL ME: WHAT DID YOU DO TO AKI?
WHAT?
SHE JUST FREAKED OUT OVER NOTHING AND STARTED RUNNING. I DIDN'T DO ANYTHING.
IMA-MURA,
YOU LIKED AKI, SO YOU WERE WAITING FOR HER IN THE WEST BUILDING, WEREN'T YOU?
ERVEEEER
QUIT TRYING TO RUN!
WAIT UP! GOD!
TURN
NOOOOOOOOOOOO
YOU FIGURED IT WAS YOUR LAST CHANCE, SO YOU'D JUST GO FOR IT.
HEY NOW! WAIT A MINUTE!
I DO *NOT* LIKE FUJI-EDA!
TEE HEE HEE
NOM
NOM
A GIRL WITH A BOY-FRIEND WOULD BE A PAIN IN THE ASS, ANYWAY.
I MEAN, SHE'S ALWAYS GOING ON ABOUT HOW MUCH SHE LOVES YOU, HIRO-KUN.

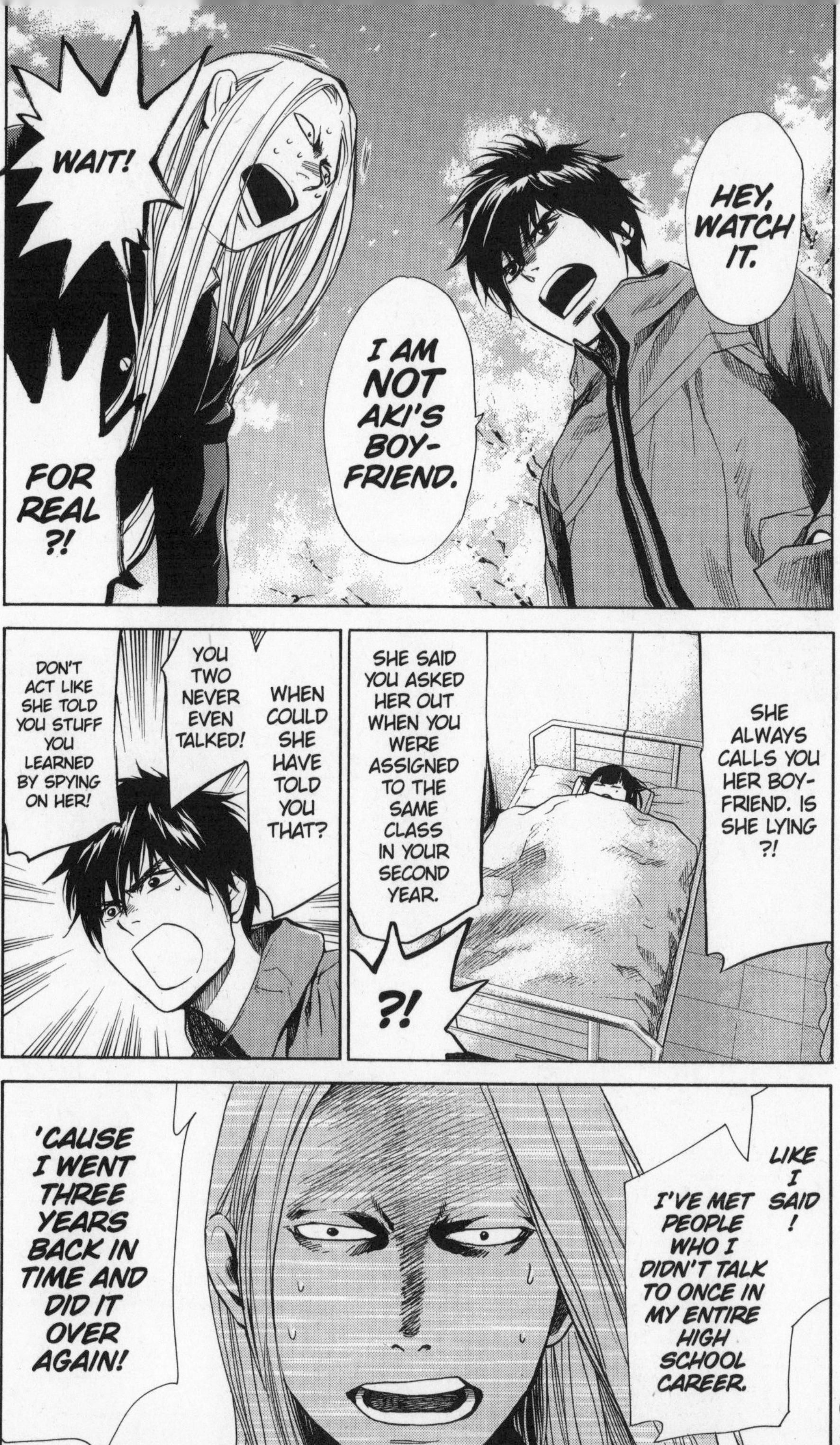
HEY, WATCH IT.
I AM NOT AKI'S BOY-FRIEND.
WAIT!
FOR REAL ?!
SHE ALWAYS CALLS YOU HER BOY-FRIEND. IS SHE LYING ?!
SHE SAID YOU ASKED HER OUT WHEN YOU WERE ASSIGNED TO THE SAME CLASS IN YOUR SECOND YEAR.
?!
WHEN COULD SHE HAVE TOLD YOU THAT?
YOU TWO NEVER EVEN TALKED!
DON'T ACT LIKE SHE TOLD YOU STUFF YOU LEARNED BY SPYING ON HER!
LIKE I SAID!
I'VE MET PEOPLE WHO I DIDN'T TALK TO ONCE IN MY ENTIRE HIGH SCHOOL CAREER.
'CAUSE I WENT THREE YEARS BACK IN TIME AND DID IT OVER AGAIN!

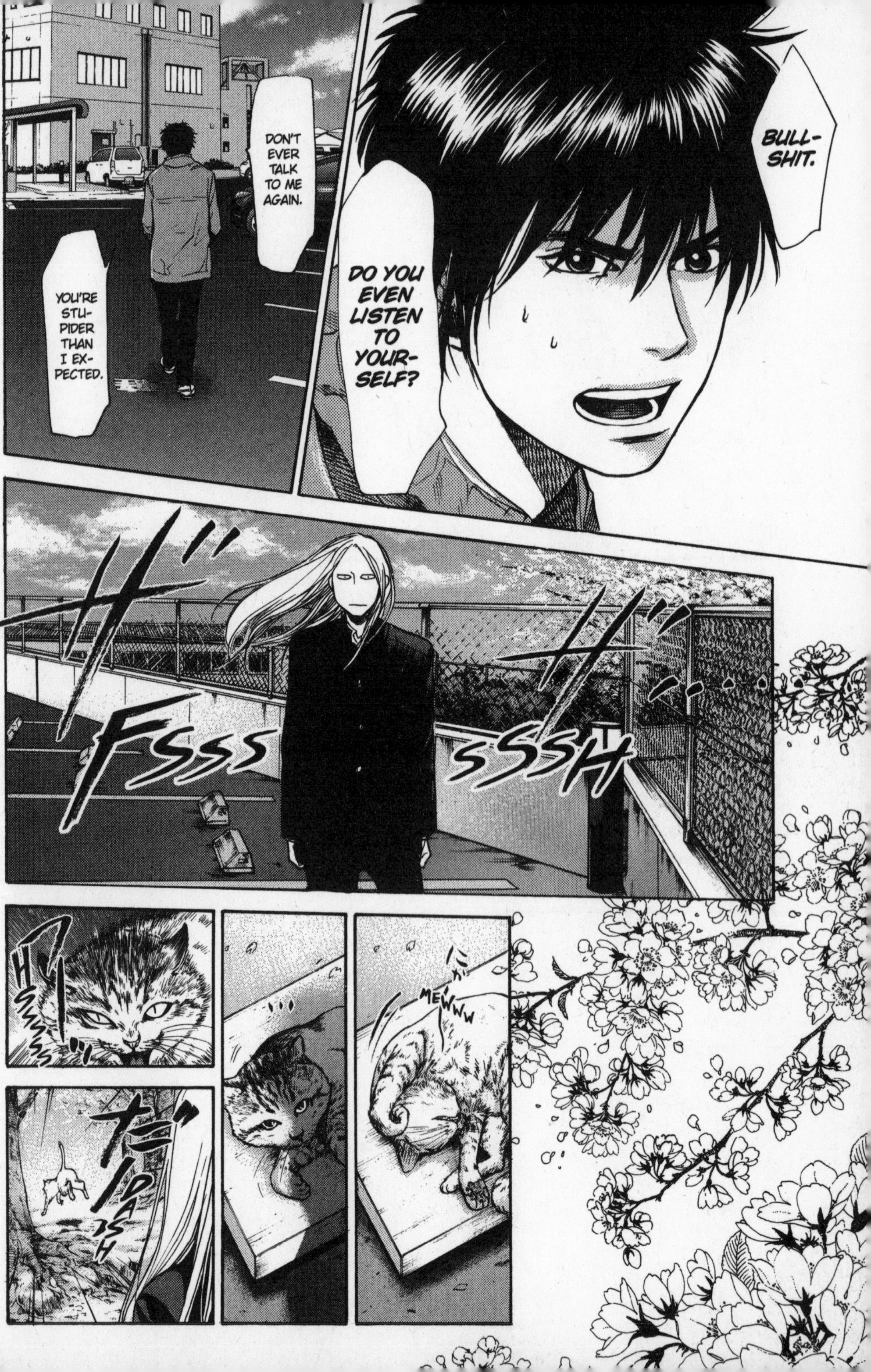
BULL-SHIT.
DO YOU EVEN LISTEN TO YOURSELF?
DON'T EVER TALK TO ME AGAIN.
YOU'RE STU-PIDER THAN I EX-PECTED.
FSSS
SSSH
MEWWW
...
HSSSSS
DASH

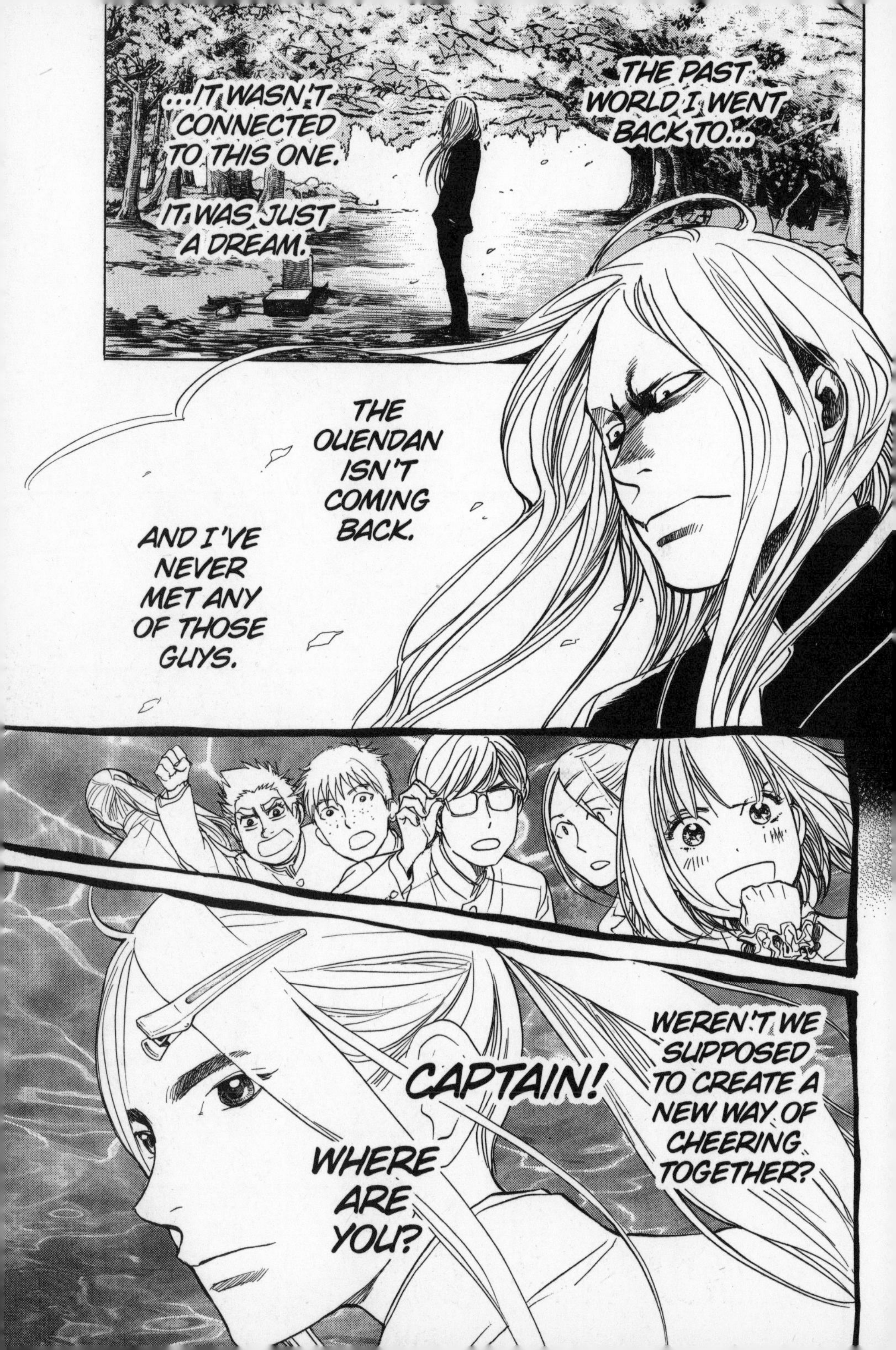
THE PAST WORLD I WENT BACK TO...
...IT WASN'T CONNECTED TO THIS ONE.
IT WAS JUST A DREAM.
THE OUENDAN ISN'T COMING BACK.
AND I'VE NEVER MET ANY OF THOSE GUYS.
WEREN'T WE SUPPOSED TO CREATE A NEW WAY OF CHEERING TOGETHER?
CAPTAIN!
WHERE ARE YOU?

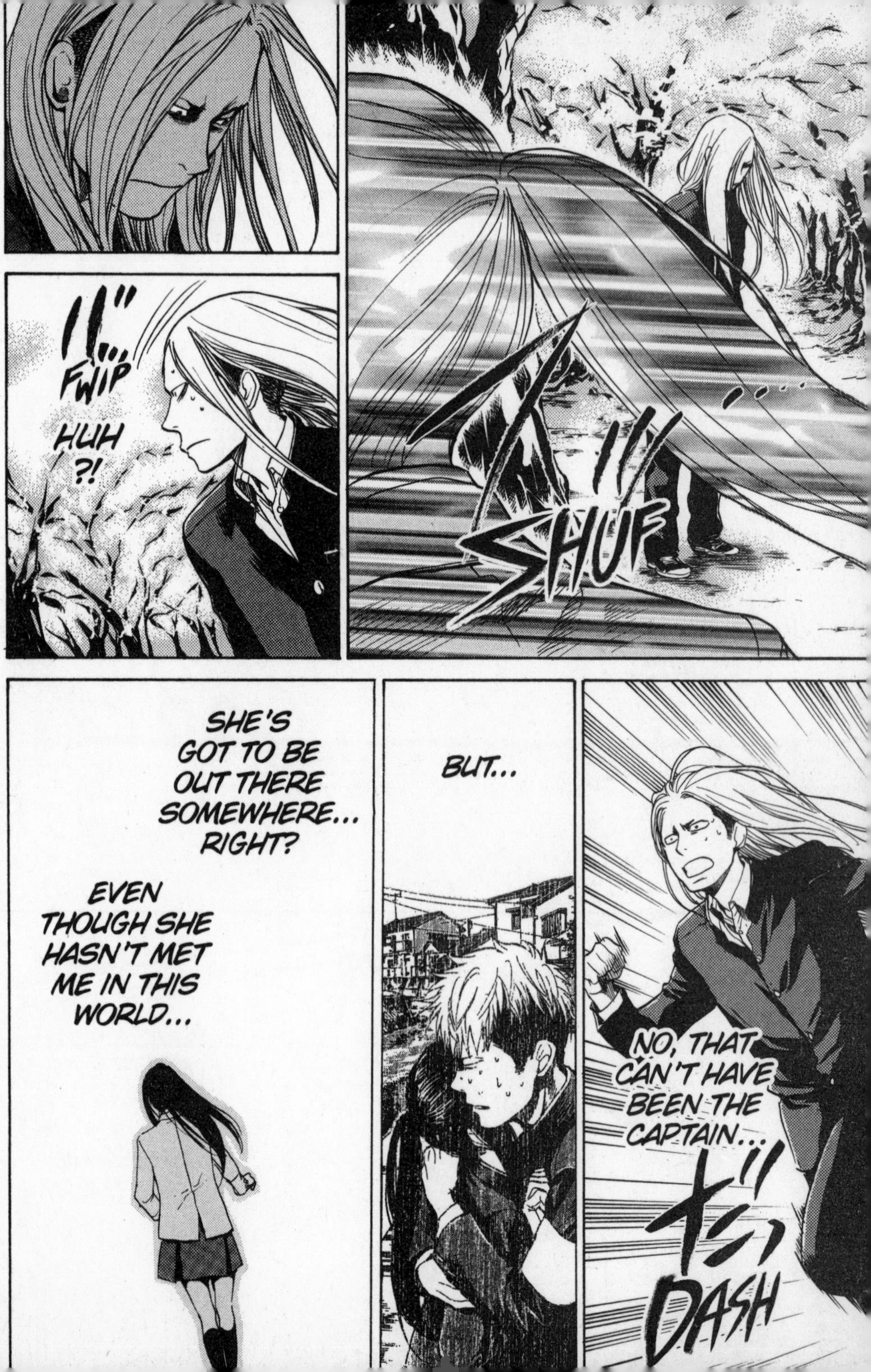
...
SHUF
!!...
FWIP
HUH ?!
NO, THAT CAN'T HAVE BEEN THE CAPTAIN...
DASH
BUT...
SHE'S GOT TO BE OUT THERE SOMEWHERE... RIGHT?
EVEN THOUGH SHE HASN'T MET ME IN THIS WORLD...

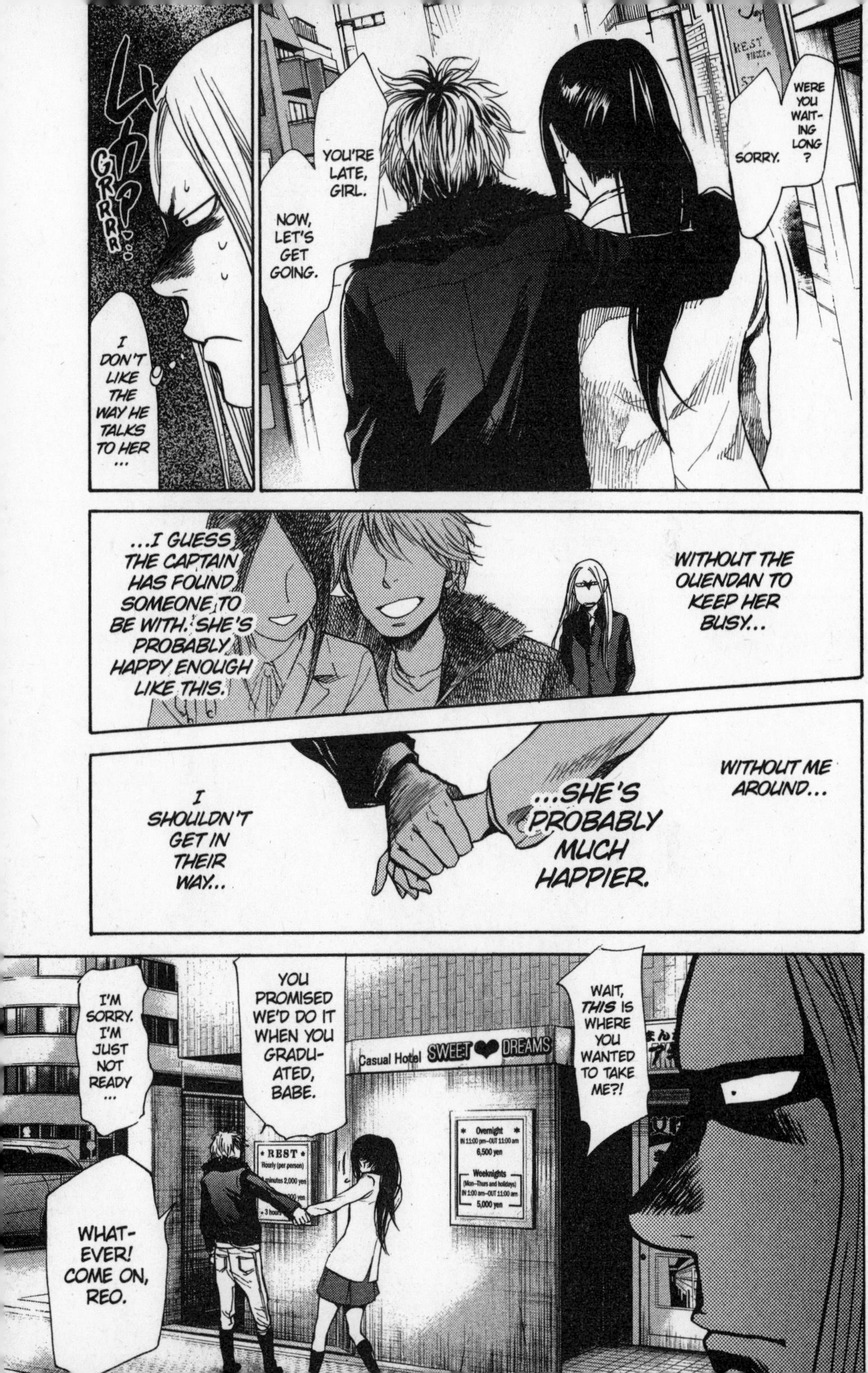
WERE YOU WAITING LONG?
SORRY.
YOU'RE LATE, GIRL.
NOW, LET'S GET GOING.
GRRRR
I DON'T LIKE THE WAY HE TALKS TO HER...
WITHOUT THE OUENDAN TO KEEP HER BUSY...
...I GUESS THE CAPTAIN HAS FOUND SOMEONE TO BE WITH. SHE'S PROBABLY HAPPY ENOUGH LIKE THIS.
WITHOUT ME AROUND...
...SHE'S PROBABLY MUCH HAPPIER.
I SHOULDN'T GET IN THEIR WAY...
WAIT, THIS IS WHERE YOU WANTED TO TAKE ME?!
Casual Hotel SWEET DREAMS
Overnight
IN 11:00 pm–OUT 11:00 am
6,500 yen
Weeknights
(Mon–Thurs and holidays)
IN 1:00 am–OUT 11:00 am
5,000 yen
REST
Hourly (per person)
YOU PROMISED WE'D DO IT WHEN YOU GRADUATED, BABE.
I'M SORRY. I'M JUST NOT READY...
WHATEVER! COME ON, REO.

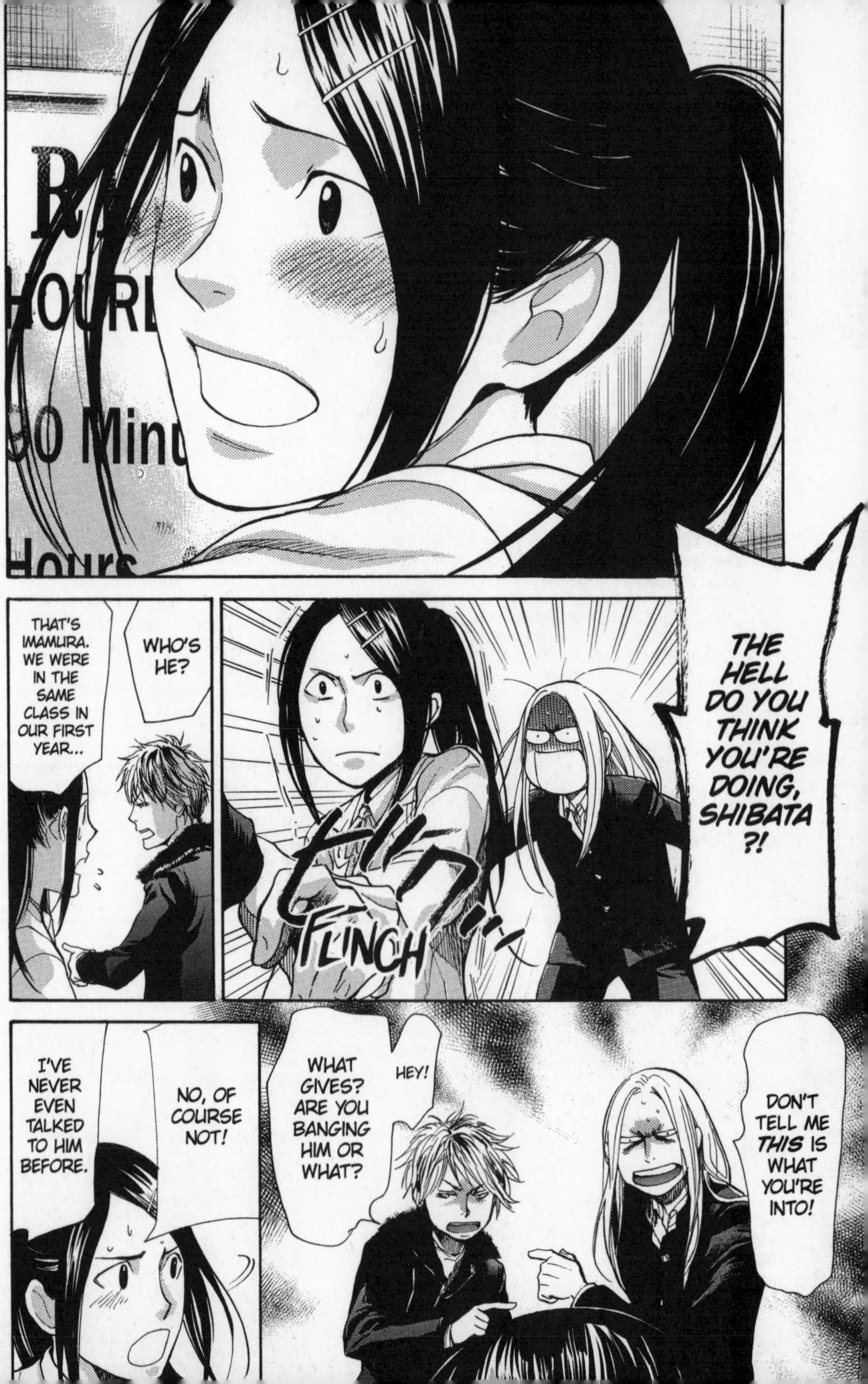
THE HELL DO YOU THINK YOU'RE DOING, SHIBATA?!
FLINCH
WHO'S HE?
THAT'S IMAMURA. WE WERE IN THE SAME CLASS IN OUR FIRST YEAR...
DON'T TELL ME *THIS* IS WHAT YOU'RE INTO!
HEY!
WHAT GIVES? ARE YOU BANGING HIM OR WHAT?
NO, OF COURSE NOT!
I'VE NEVER EVEN TALKED TO HIM BEFORE.

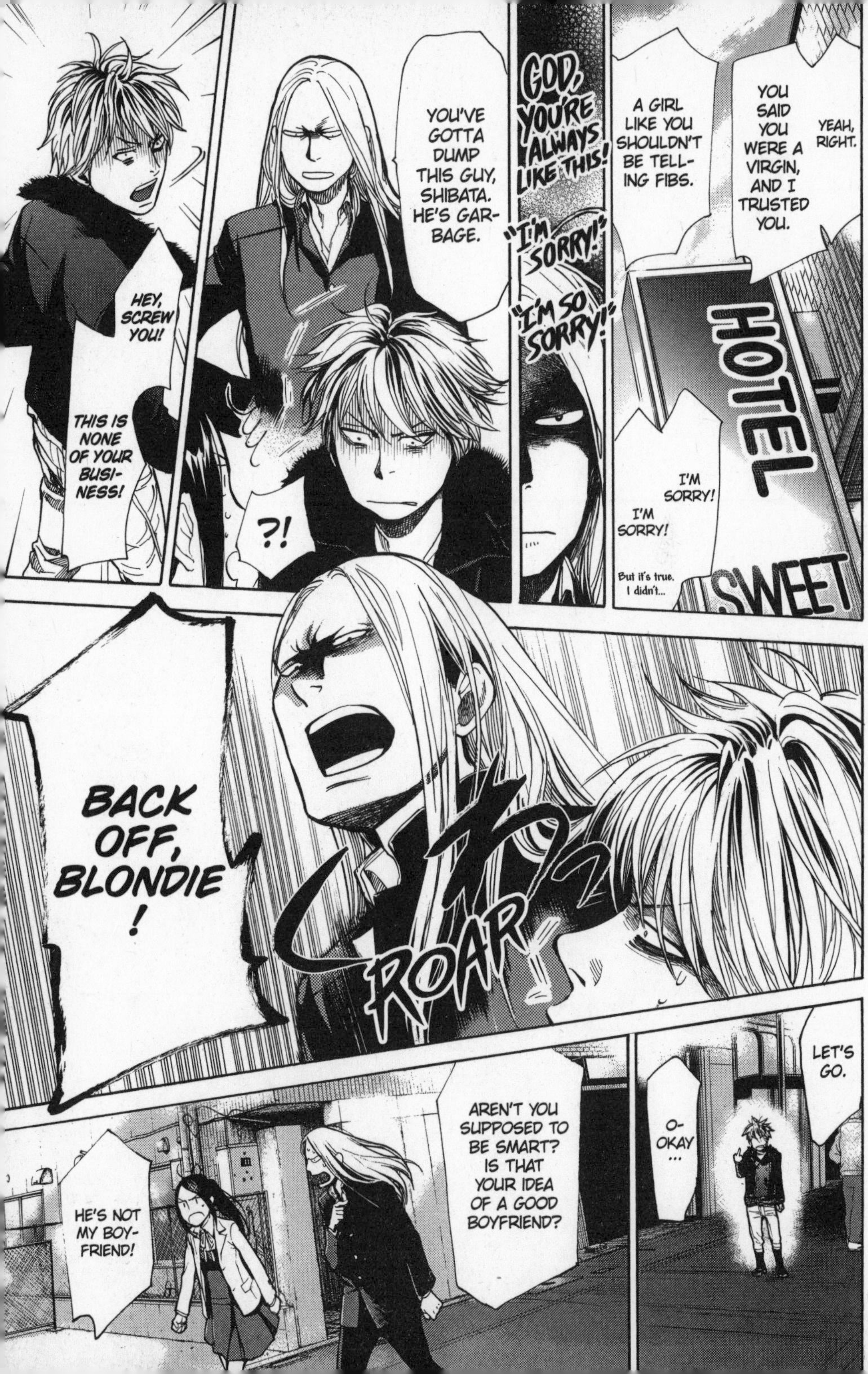
YEAH, RIGHT.
YOU SAID YOU WERE A VIRGIN, AND I TRUSTED YOU.
A GIRL LIKE YOU SHOULDN'T BE TELLING FIBS.
HOTEL
I'M SORRY!
I'M SORRY!
But it's true. I didn't...
SWEET
GOD, YOU'RE ALWAYS LIKE THIS!
"I'M SORRY!"
"I'M SO SORRY!"
YOU'VE GOTTA DUMP THIS GUY, SHIBATA. HE'S GARBAGE.
?!
HEY, SCREW YOU!
THIS IS NONE OF YOUR BUSINESS!
BACK OFF, BLONDIE!
ROAR
LET'S GO.
O-OKAY...
AREN'T YOU SUPPOSED TO BE SMART? IS THAT YOUR IDEA OF A GOOD BOYFRIEND?
HE'S NOT MY BOYFRIEND!

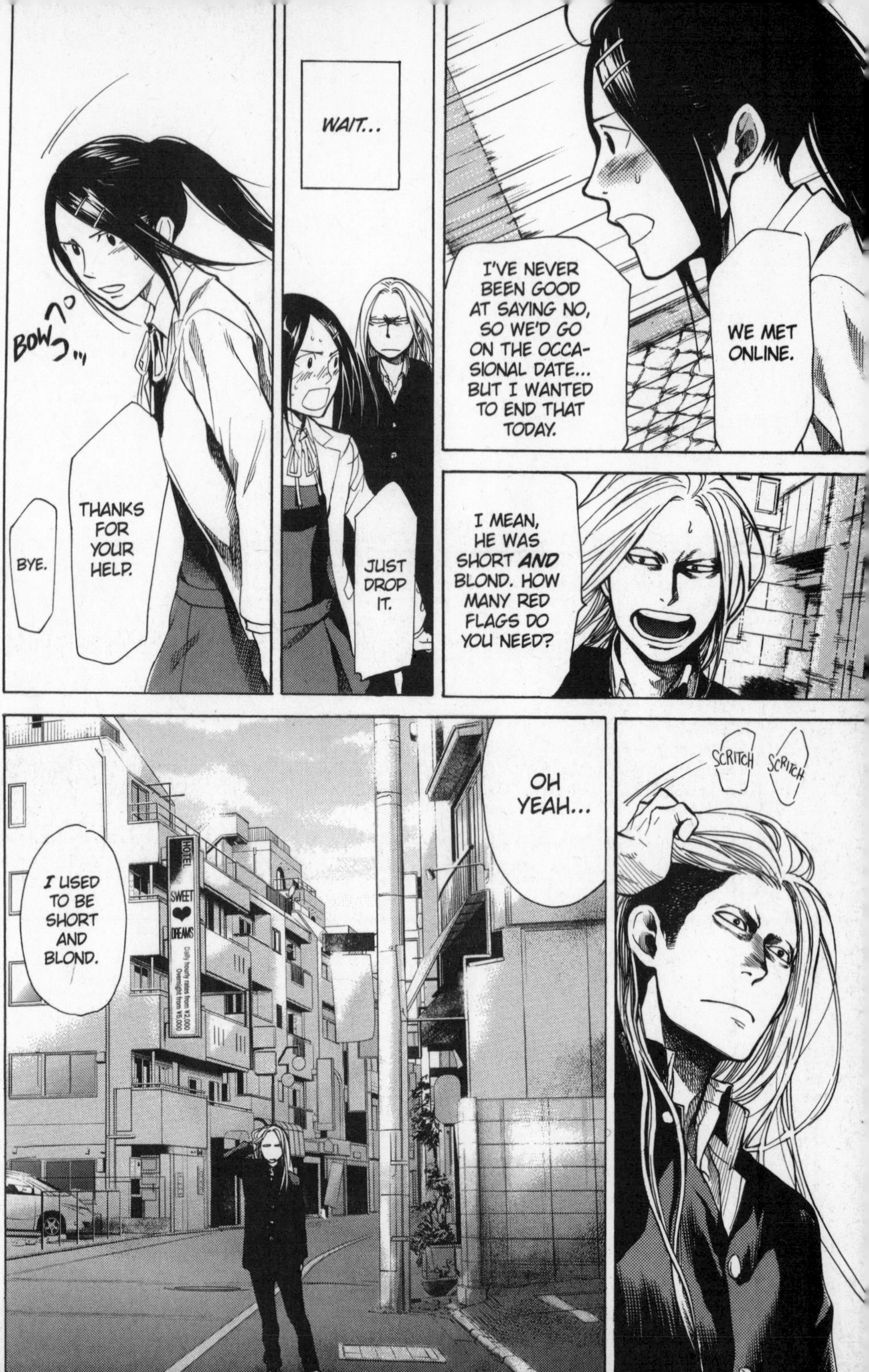
WE MET ONLINE.
I'VE NEVER BEEN GOOD AT SAYING NO, SO WE'D GO ON THE OCCA-SIONAL DATE... BUT I WANTED TO END THAT TODAY.
I MEAN, HE WAS SHORT AND BLOND. HOW MANY RED FLAGS DO YOU NEED?
WAIT...
JUST DROP IT.
BOW
THANKS FOR YOUR HELP.
BYE.
SCRITCH
SCRITCH
OH YEAH...
HOTEL
SWEET DREAMS
Daily hourly rates from ¥2,000
Overnight from ¥5,000
I USED TO BE SHORT AND BLOND.

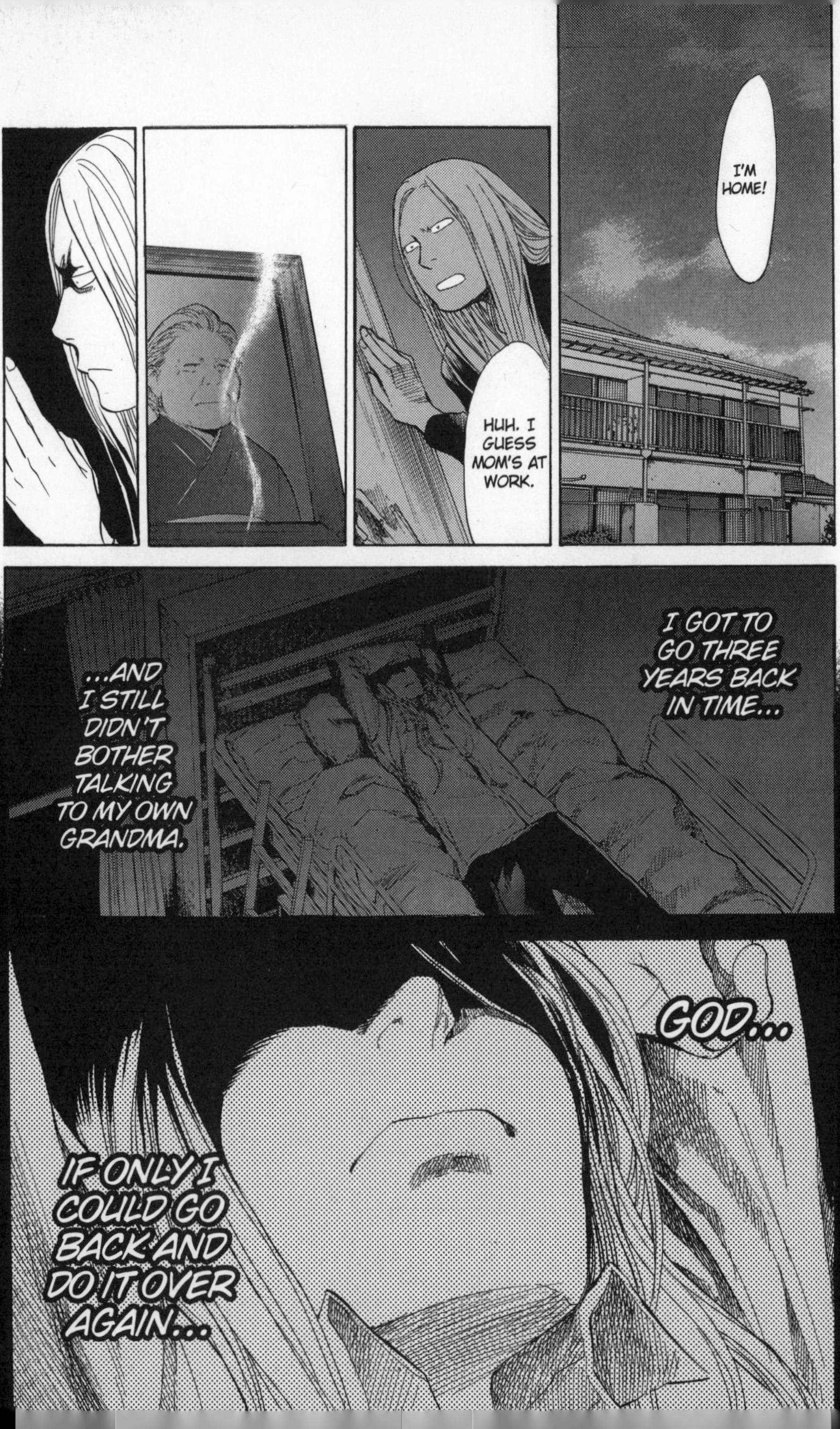
I'M HOME!
HUH. I GUESS MOM'S AT WORK.
I GOT TO GO THREE YEARS BACK IN TIME...
...AND I STILL DIDN'T BOTHER TALKING TO MY OWN GRANDMA.
GOD...
IF ONLY I COULD GO BACK AND DO IT OVER AGAIN...

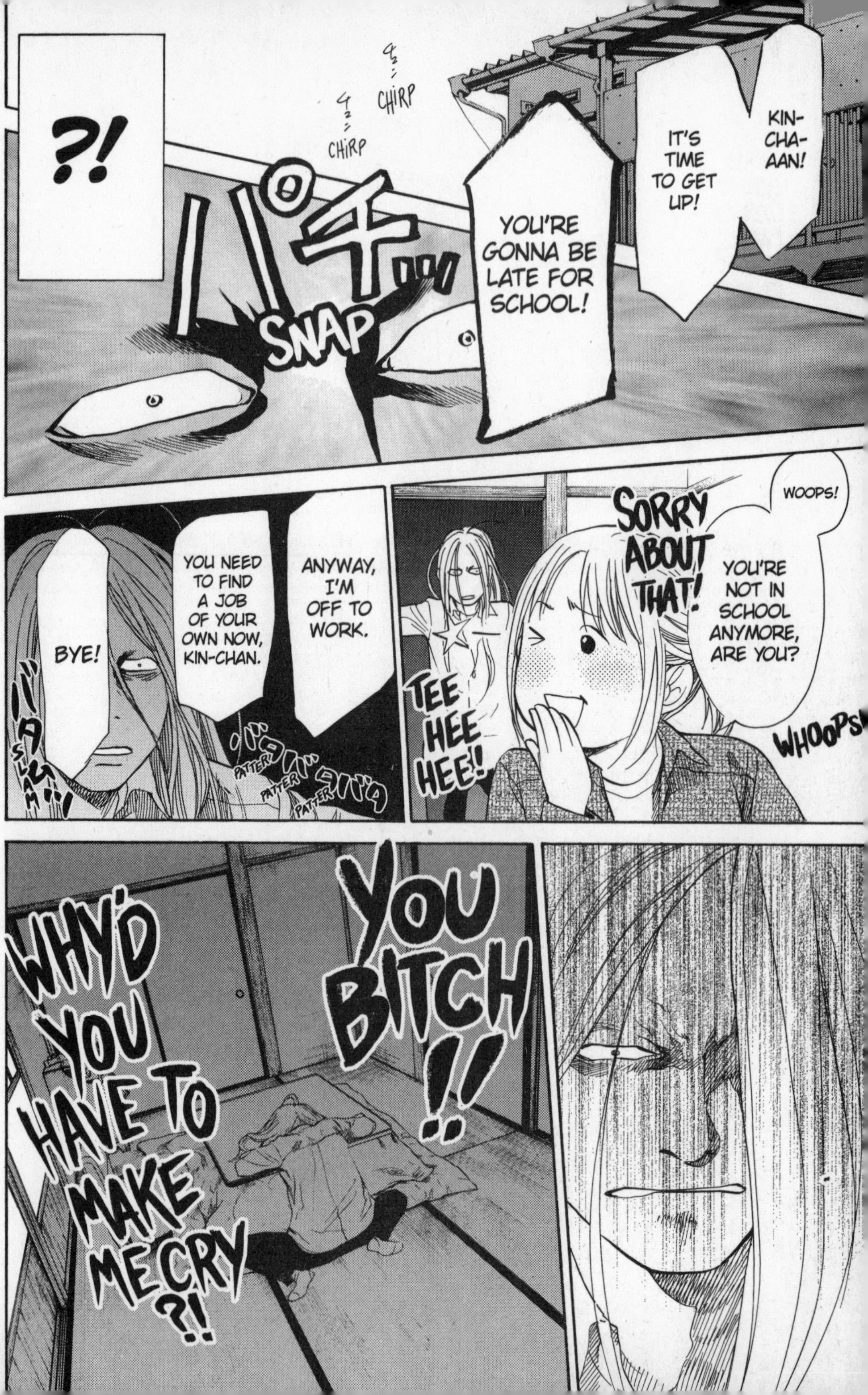
KIN-CHAAAN!
IT'S TIME TO GET UP!
YOU'RE GONNA BE LATE FOR SCHOOL!
CHIRP
CHIRP
SNAP
?!
WOOPS!
SORRY ABOUT THAT!
YOU'RE NOT IN SCHOOL ANYMORE, ARE YOU?
WHOOPS
TEE HEE HEE!
ANYWAY, I'M OFF TO WORK.
YOU NEED TO FIND A JOB OF YOUR OWN NOW, KIN-CHAN.
BYE!
PATTER
PATTER
PATTER
SLAM
YOU BITCH!!
WHY'D YOU HAVE TO MAKE ME CRY?!

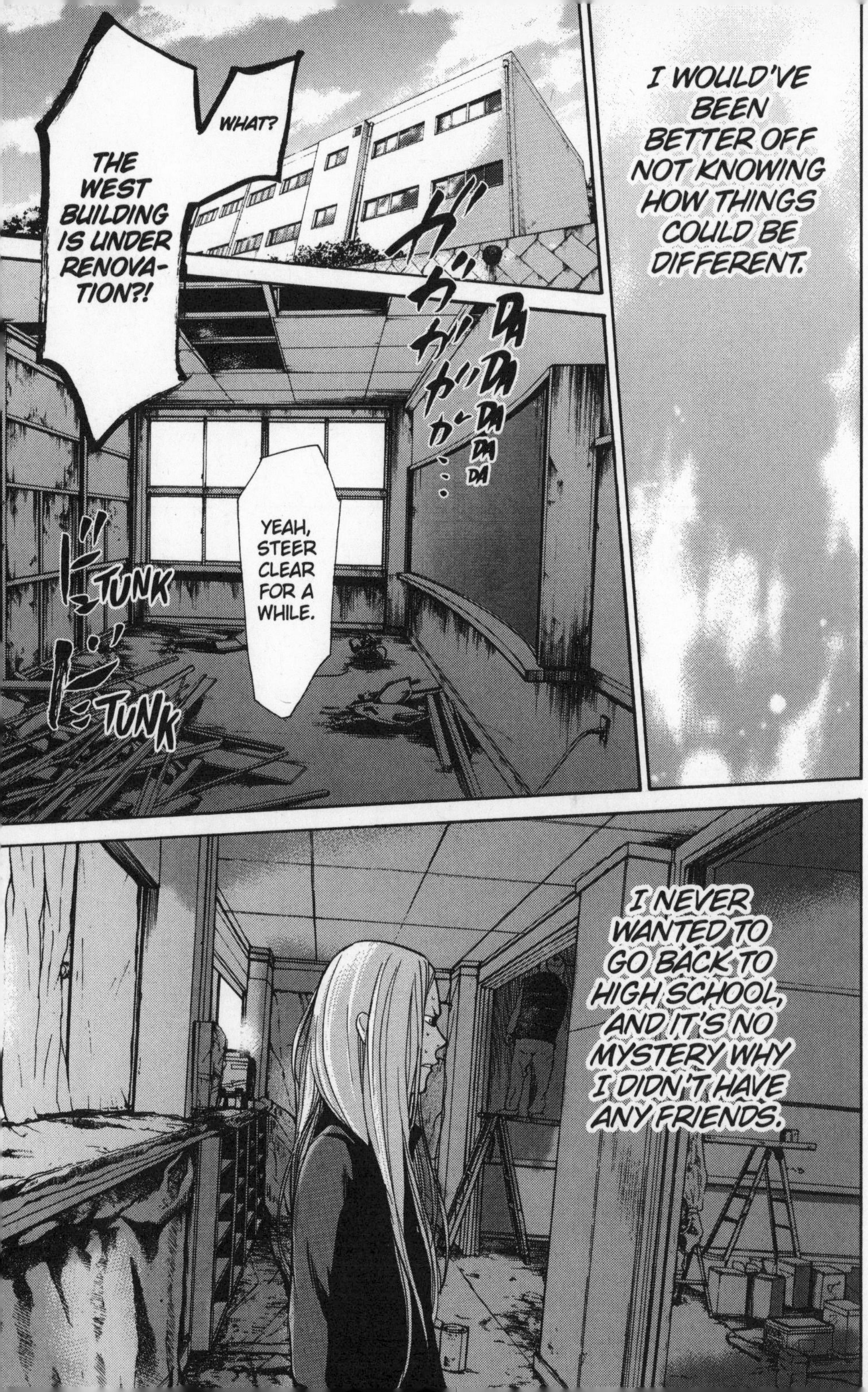
I WOULD'VE BEEN BETTER OFF NOT KNOWING HOW THINGS COULD BE DIFFERENT.
WHAT?
THE WEST BUILDING IS UNDER RENOVA-TION?!
DA DA DA DA DA
YEAH, STEER CLEAR FOR A WHILE.
TUNK
TUNK
I NEVER WANTED TO GO BACK TO HIGH SCHOOL, AND IT'S NO MYSTERY WHY I DIDN'T HAVE ANY FRIENDS.

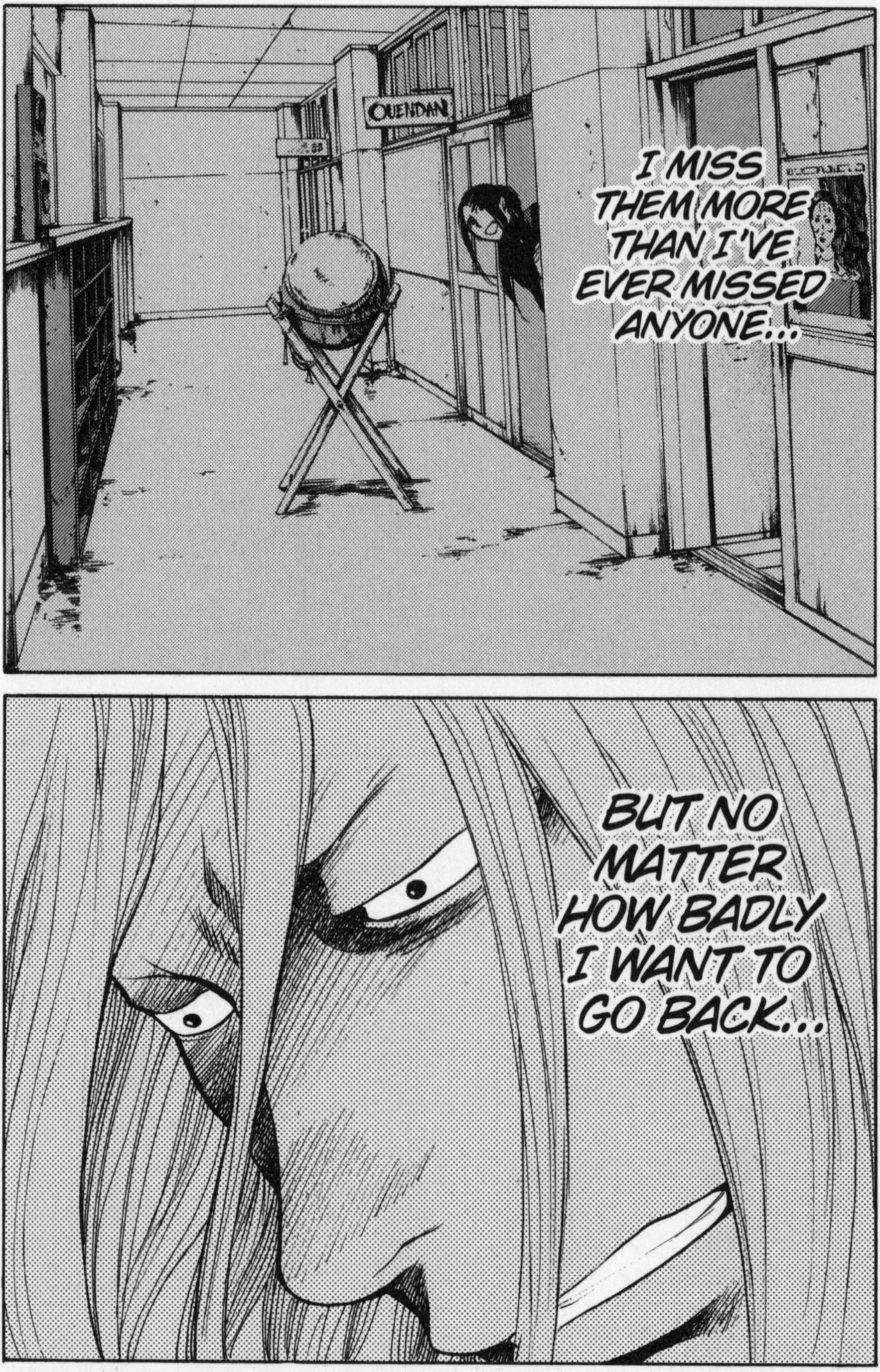
I MISS THEM MORE THAN I'VE EVER MISSED ANYONE...
OUENDAN
BUT NO MATTER HOW BADLY I WANT TO GO BACK...

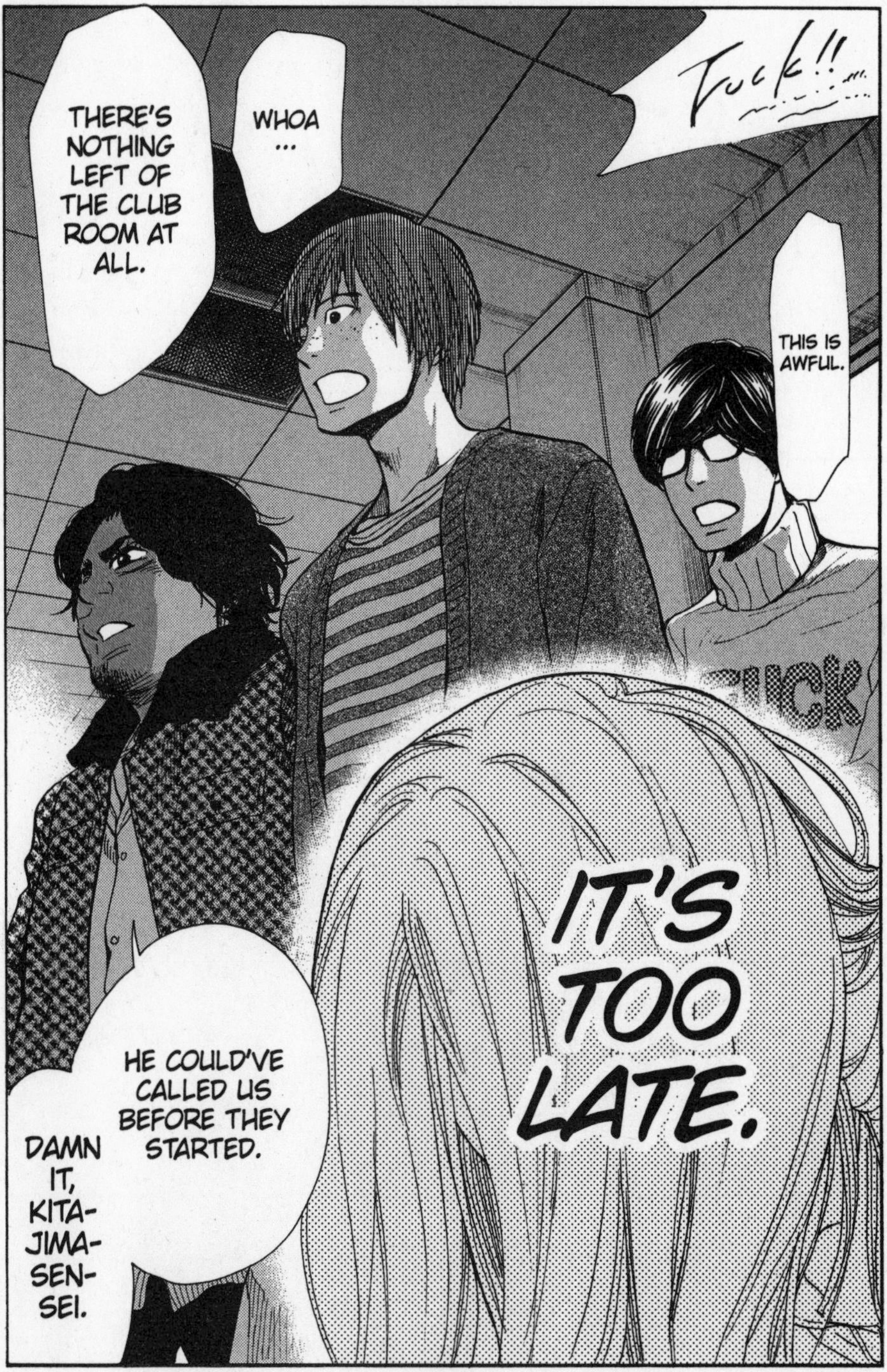
Fuck!!...
THIS IS AWFUL.
WHOA ...
THERE'S NOTHING LEFT OF THE CLUB ROOM AT ALL.
IT'S TOO LATE.
HE COULD'VE CALLED US BEFORE THEY STARTED.
DAMN IT, KITA-JIMA-SEN-SEI.

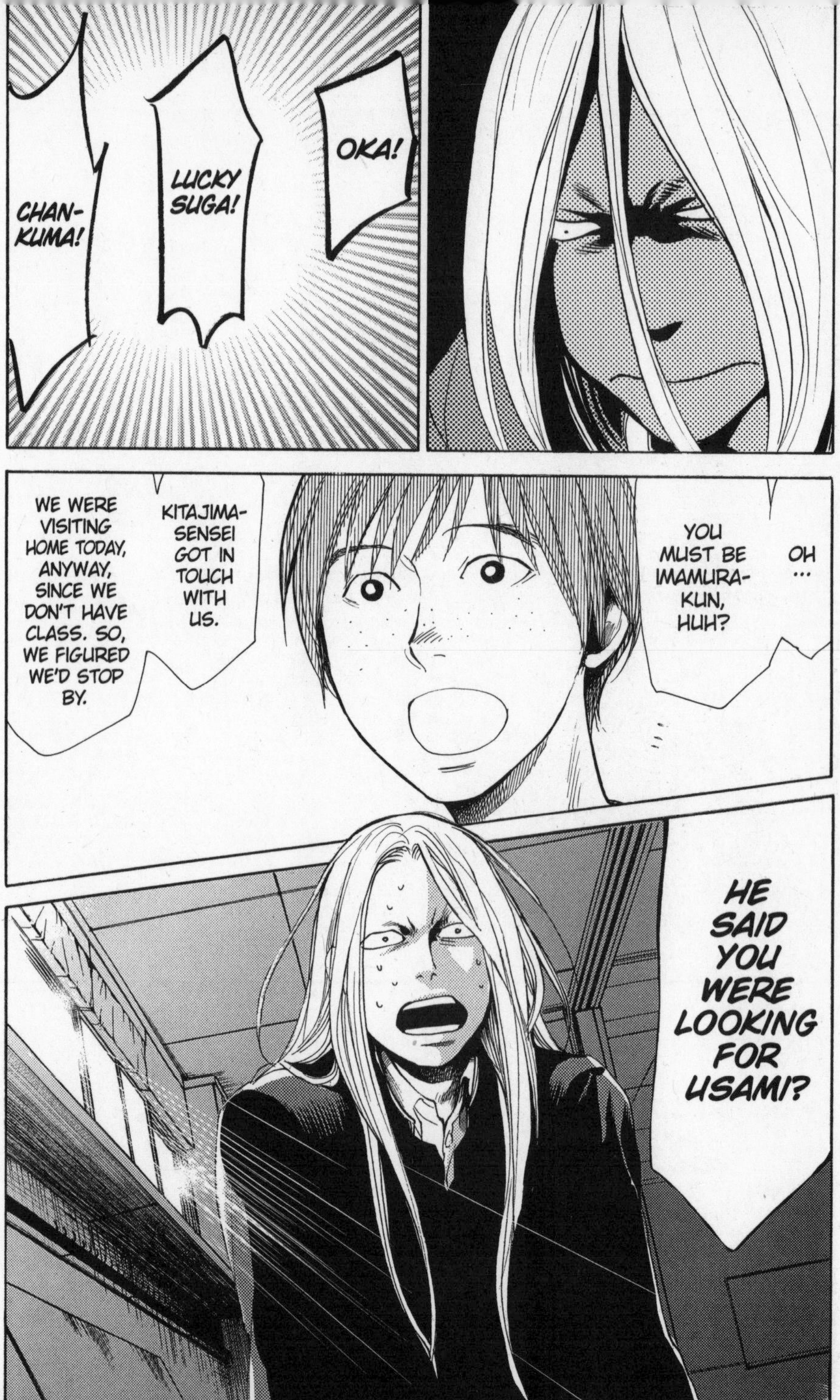
OKA!
LUCKY SUGA!
CHAN-KUMA!
OH ...
YOU MUST BE IMAMURA-KUN, HUH?
KITAJIMA-SENSEI GOT IN TOUCH WITH US.
WE WERE VISITING HOME TODAY, ANYWAY, SINCE WE DON'T HAVE CLASS. SO, WE FIGURED WE'D STOP BY.
HE SAID YOU WERE LOOKING FOR USAMI?

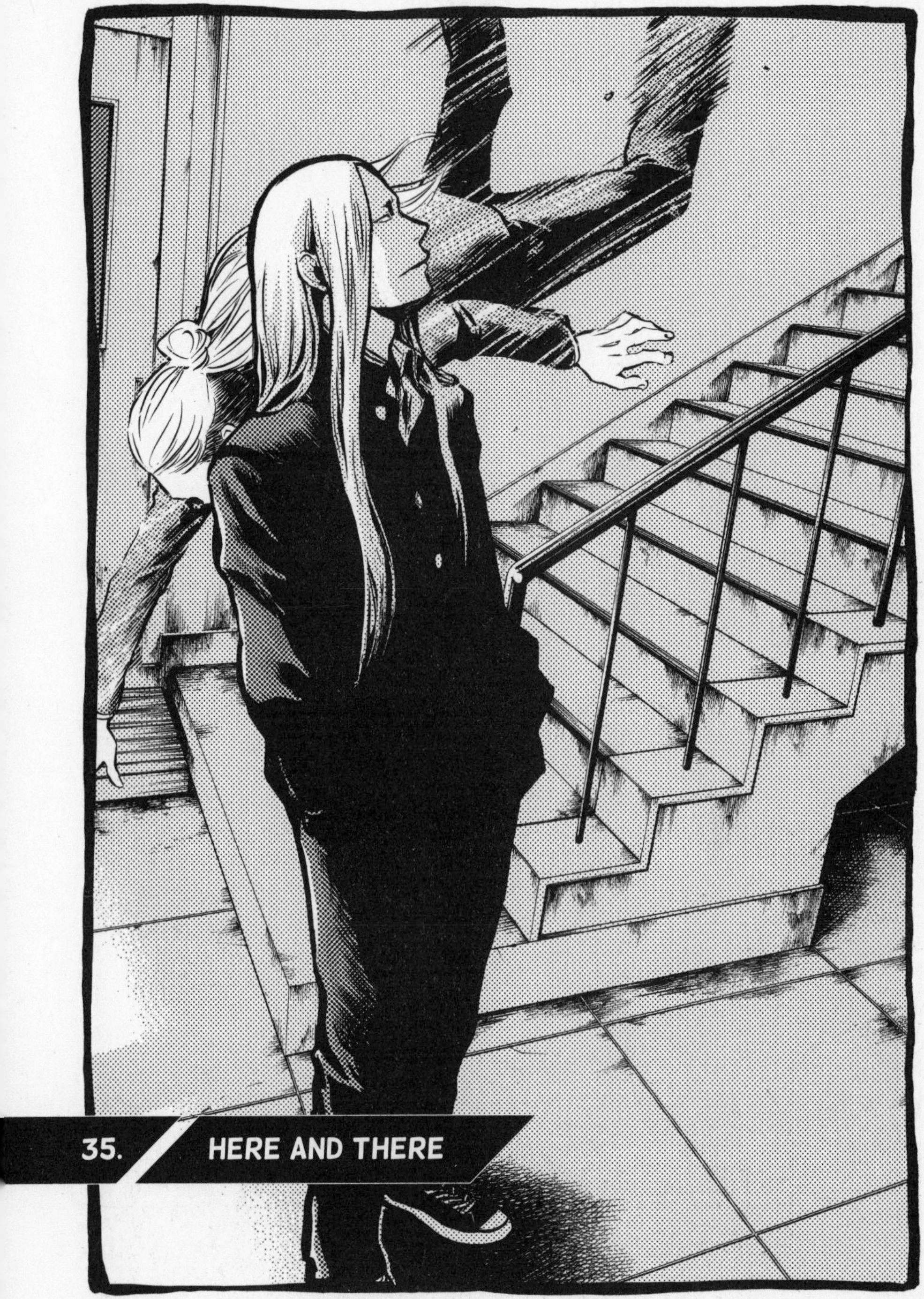
35.
HERE AND THERE

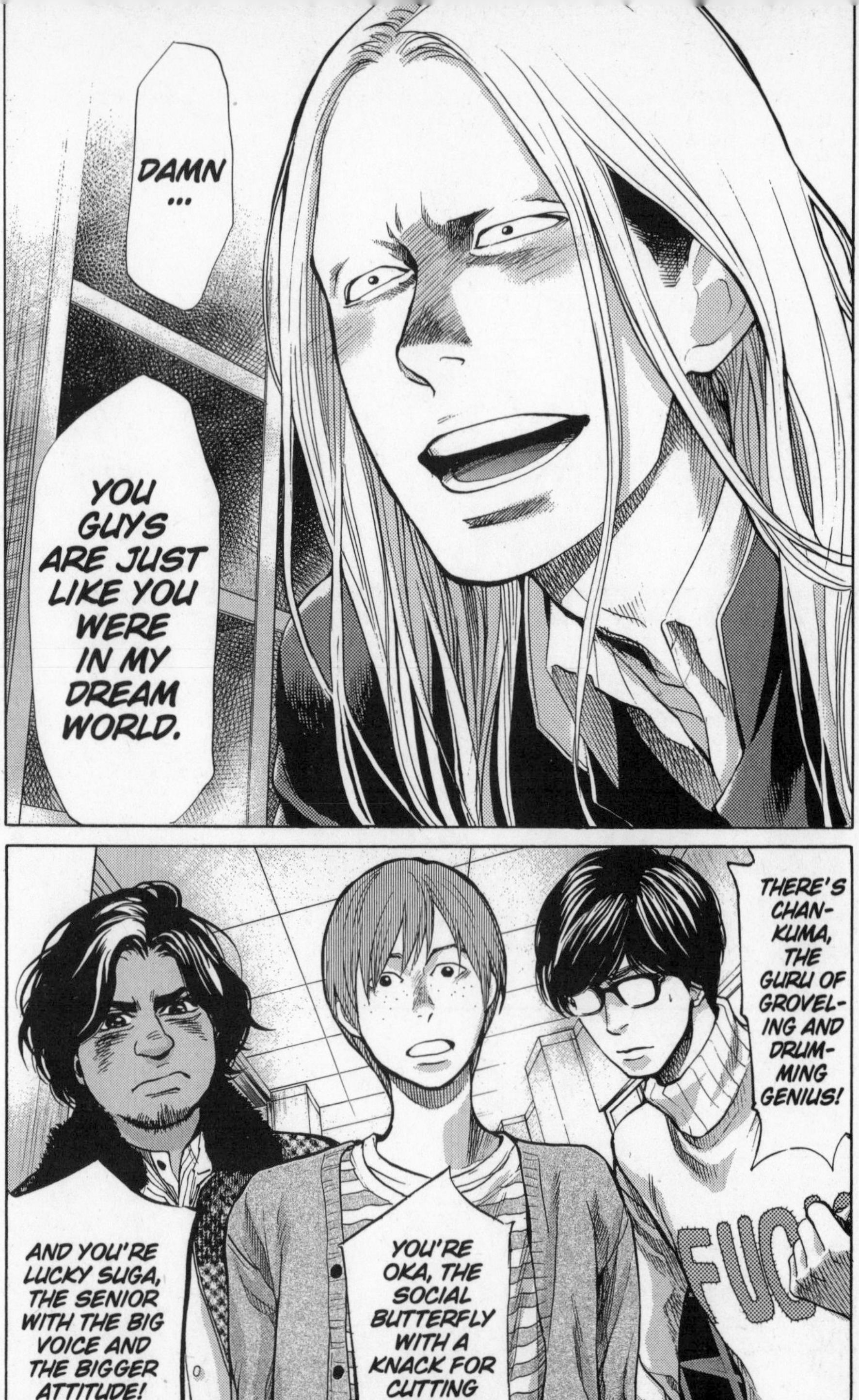
DAMN ...
YOU GUYS ARE JUST LIKE YOU WERE IN MY DREAM WORLD.
THERE'S CHAN-KUMA, THE GURU OF GROVEL-ING AND DRUM-MING GENIUS!
FUC
YOU'RE OKA, THE SOCIAL BUTTERFLY WITH A KNACK FOR CUTTING CORNERS!
AND YOU'RE LUCKY SUGA, THE SENIOR WITH THE BIG VOICE AND THE BIGGER ATTITUDE!

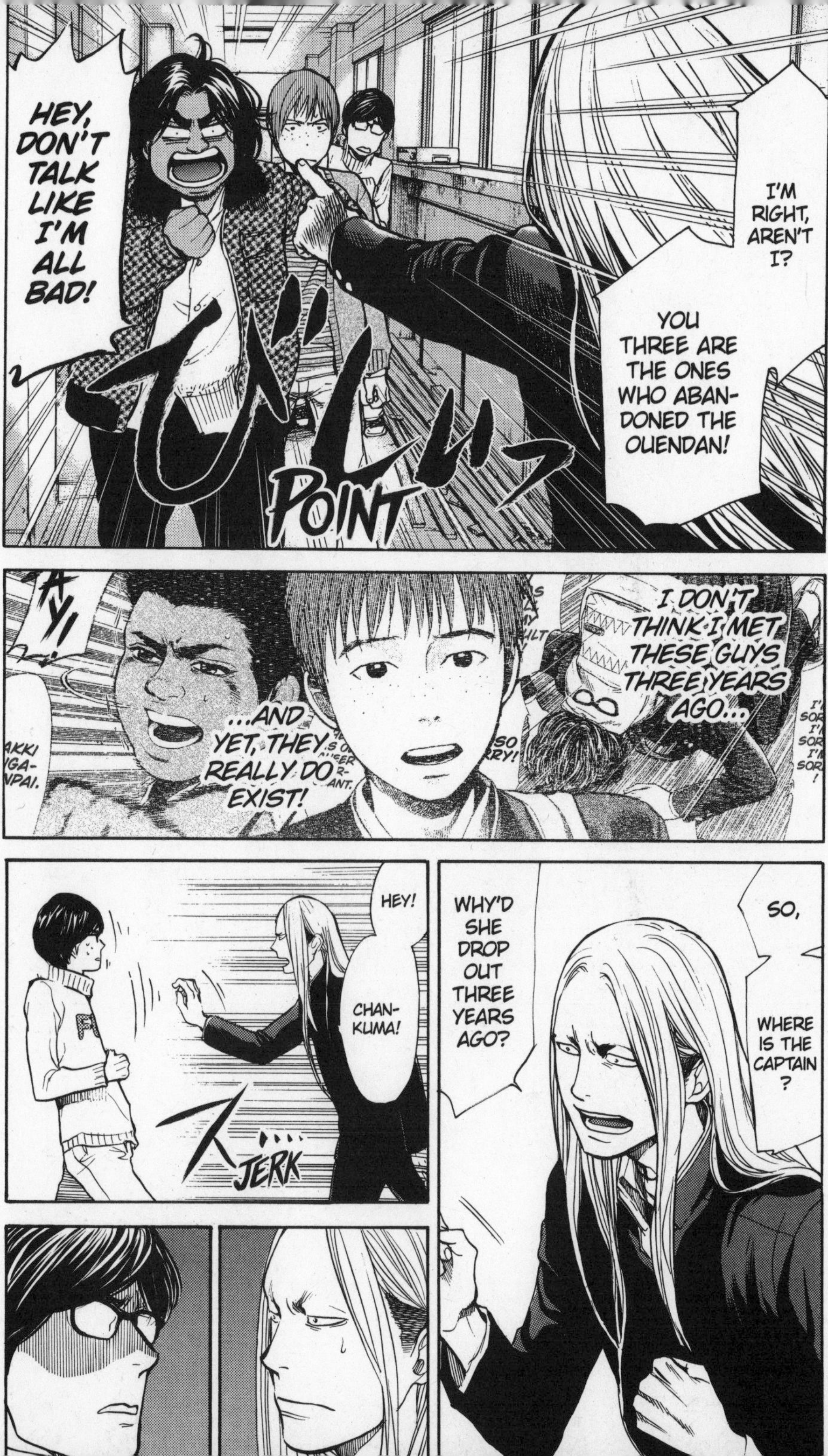
I'M RIGHT, AREN'T I?
YOU THREE ARE THE ONES WHO ABAN-DONED THE OUENDAN!
HEY, DON'T TALK LIKE I'M ALL BAD!
POINT
I DON'T THINK I MET THESE GUYS THREE YEARS AGO...
...AND YET, THEY REALLY DO EXIST!
SO,
WHERE IS THE CAPTAIN?
WHY'D SHE DROP OUT THREE YEARS AGO?
HEY!
CHAN-KUMA!
JERK

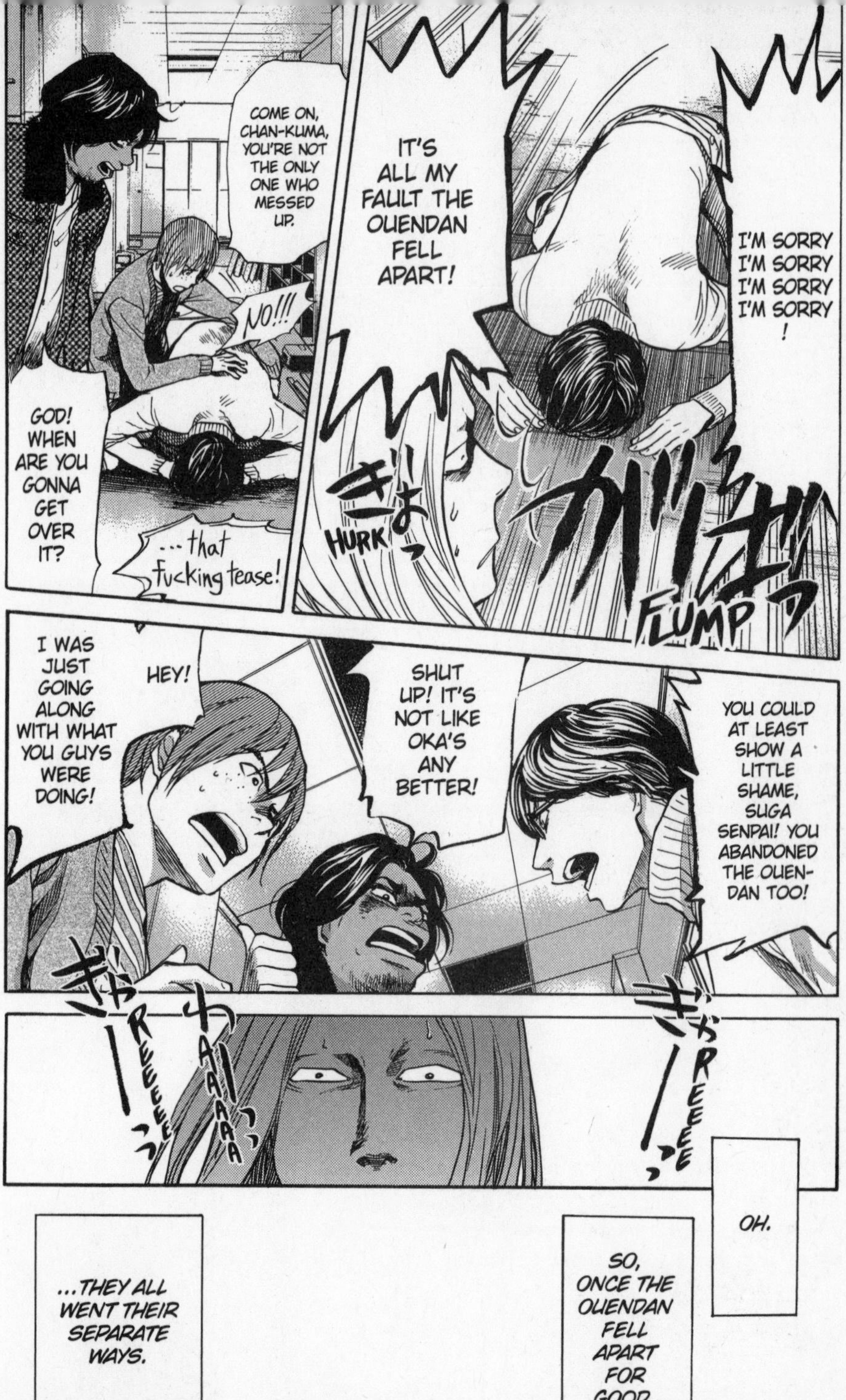
I'M SORRY I'M SORRY I'M SORRY I'M SORRY!
IT'S ALL MY FAULT THE OUENDAN FELL APART!
FLUMP
HURK
COME ON, CHAN-KUMA, YOU'RE NOT THE ONLY ONE WHO MESSED UP.
NO!!!
GOD! WHEN ARE YOU GONNA GET OVER IT?
...that fucking tease!
YOU COULD AT LEAST SHOW A LITTLE SHAME, SUGA SENPAI! YOU ABANDONED THE OUEN-DAN TOO!
SHUT UP! IT'S NOT LIKE OKA'S ANY BETTER!
HEY!
I WAS JUST GOING ALONG WITH WHAT YOU GUYS WERE DOING!
REEEE
AAAAAA
REEEEE
OH.
SO, ONCE THE OUENDAN FELL APART FOR GOOD...
...THEY ALL WENT THEIR SEPARATE WAYS.

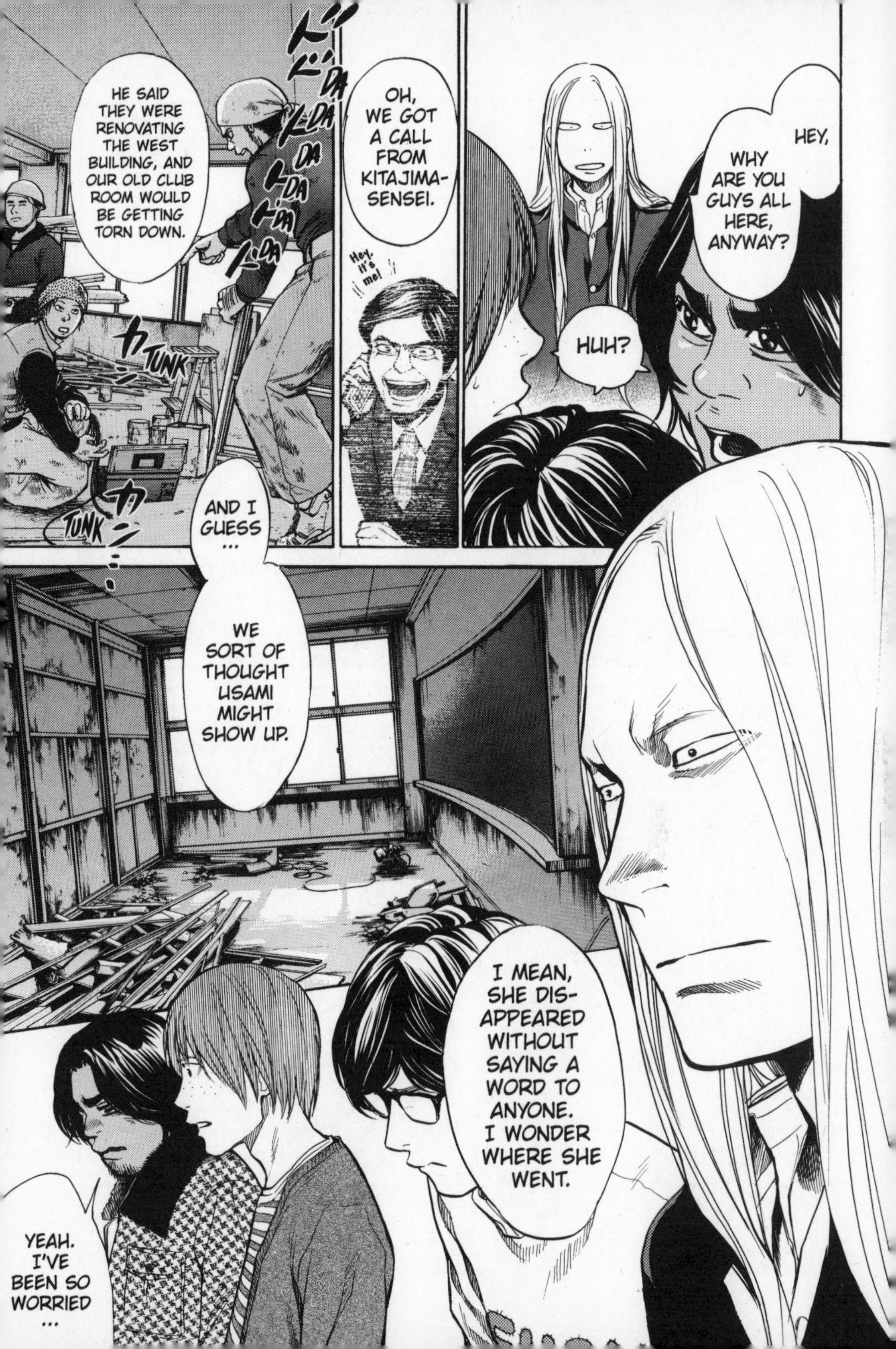

HEY, WHY ARE YOU GUYS ALL HERE, ANYWAY?
HUH?
OH, WE GOT A CALL FROM KITAJIMA-SENSEI.
Hey, it's me!
DA DA DA DA DA DA
HE SAID THEY WERE RENOVATING THE WEST BUILDING, AND OUR OLD CLUB ROOM WOULD BE GETTING TORN DOWN.
TUNK
TUNK
AND I GUESS ...
WE SORT OF THOUGHT USAMI MIGHT SHOW UP.
I MEAN, SHE DIS-APPEARED WITHOUT SAYING A WORD TO ANYONE. I WONDER WHERE SHE WENT.
YEAH. I'VE BEEN SO WORRIED ...

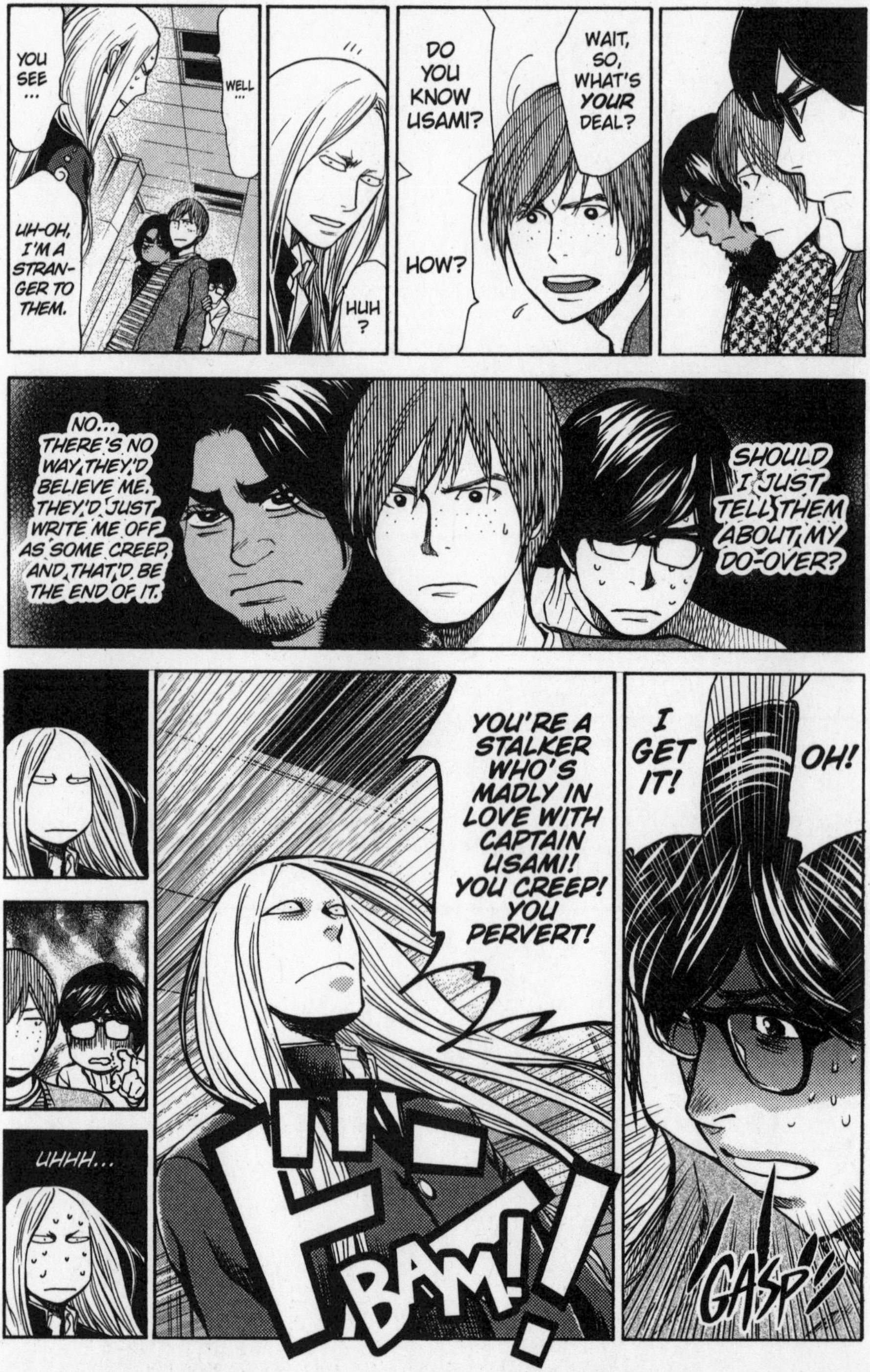
WAIT, SO, WHAT'S YOUR DEAL?
DO YOU KNOW USAMI?
HOW?
HUH?
WELL...
YOU SEE...
UH-OH, I'M A STRANGER TO THEM.
SHOULD I JUST TELL THEM ABOUT MY DO-OVER?
NO... THERE'S NO WAY THEY'D BELIEVE ME. THEY'D JUST WRITE ME OFF AS SOME CREEP, AND THAT'D BE THE END OF IT.
OH!
I GET IT!
GASP!!
YOU'RE A STALKER WHO'S MADLY IN LOVE WITH CAPTAIN USAMI! YOU CREEP! YOU PERVERT!
BAM!!
UHHH...

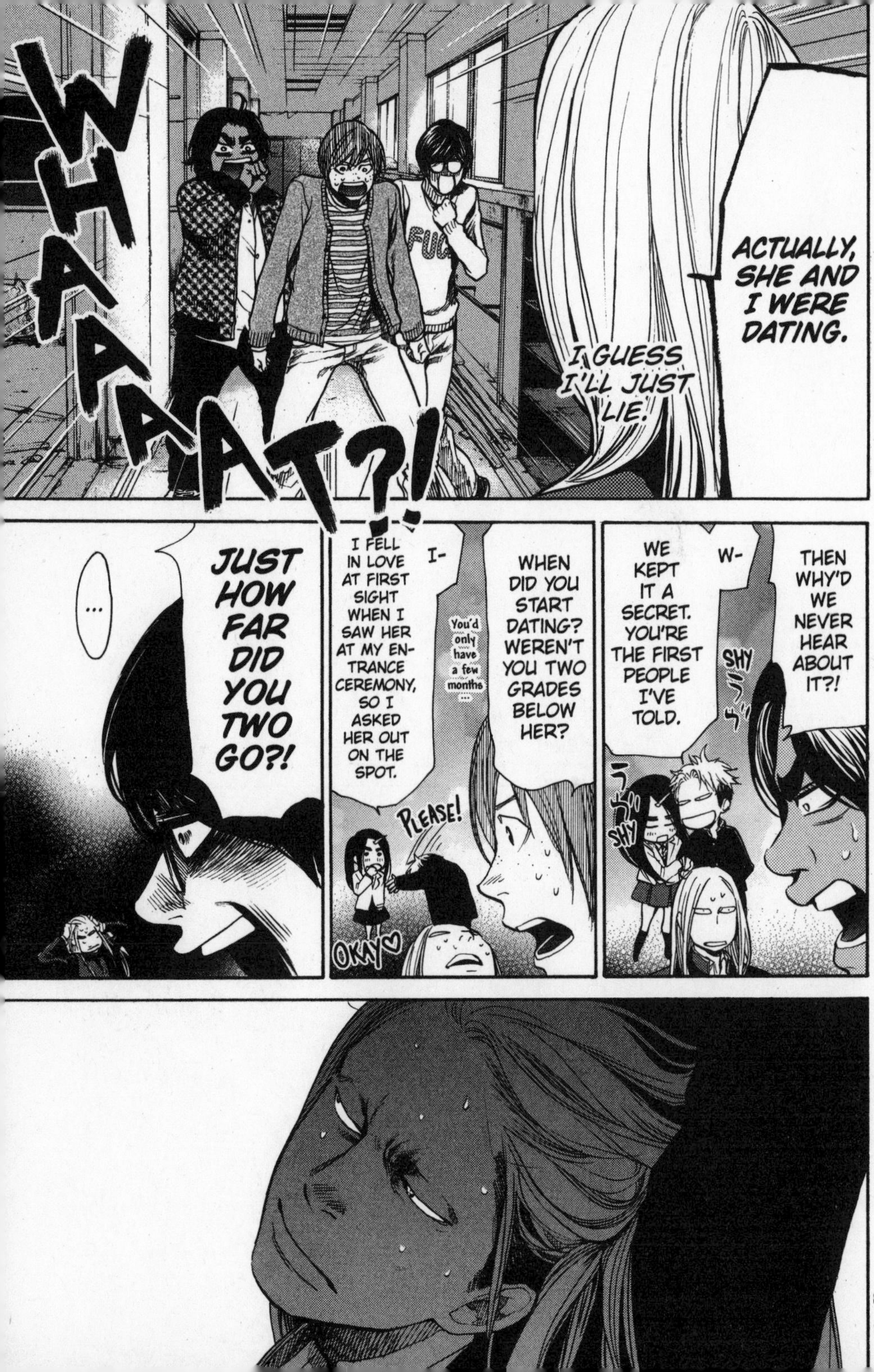
ACTUALLY, SHE AND I WERE DATING.
I GUESS I'LL JUST LIE.
WHAAAAT?!!
THEN WHY'D WE NEVER HEAR ABOUT IT?!
W-
WE KEPT IT A SECRET. YOU'RE THE FIRST PEOPLE I'VE TOLD.
SHY
SHY
WHEN DID YOU START DATING? WEREN'T YOU TWO GRADES BELOW HER?
I-
You'd only have a few months...
I FELL IN LOVE AT FIRST SIGHT WHEN I SAW HER AT MY ENTRANCE CEREMONY, SO I ASKED HER OUT ON THE SPOT.
PLEASE!
OKAY♡
JUST HOW FAR DID YOU TWO GO?!
...

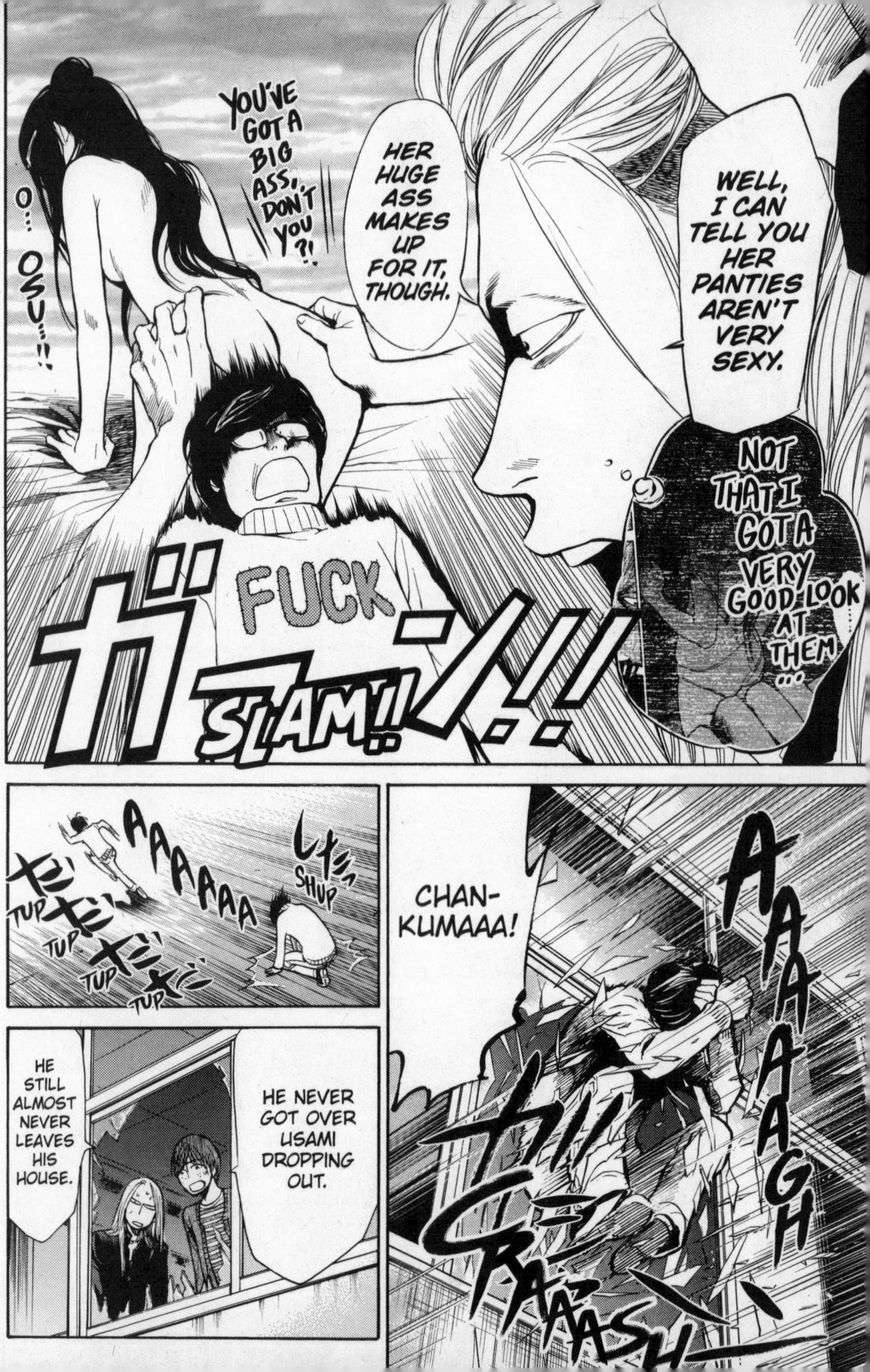
WELL, I CAN TELL YOU HER PANTIES AREN'T VERY SEXY.
NOT THAT I GOT A VERY GOOD LOOK AT THEM...
HER HUGE ASS MAKES UP FOR IT, THOUGH.
YOU'VE GOT A BIG ASS, DON'T YOU?!
O... OSU...!!
FUCK
SLAM!!
CHAN-KUMAAA!
AAAAAAGH
CRAAASH
AAAAAAA
SHUP
TUP TUP TUP TUP
HE NEVER GOT OVER USAMI DROPPING OUT.
HE STILL ALMOST NEVER LEAVES HIS HOUSE.

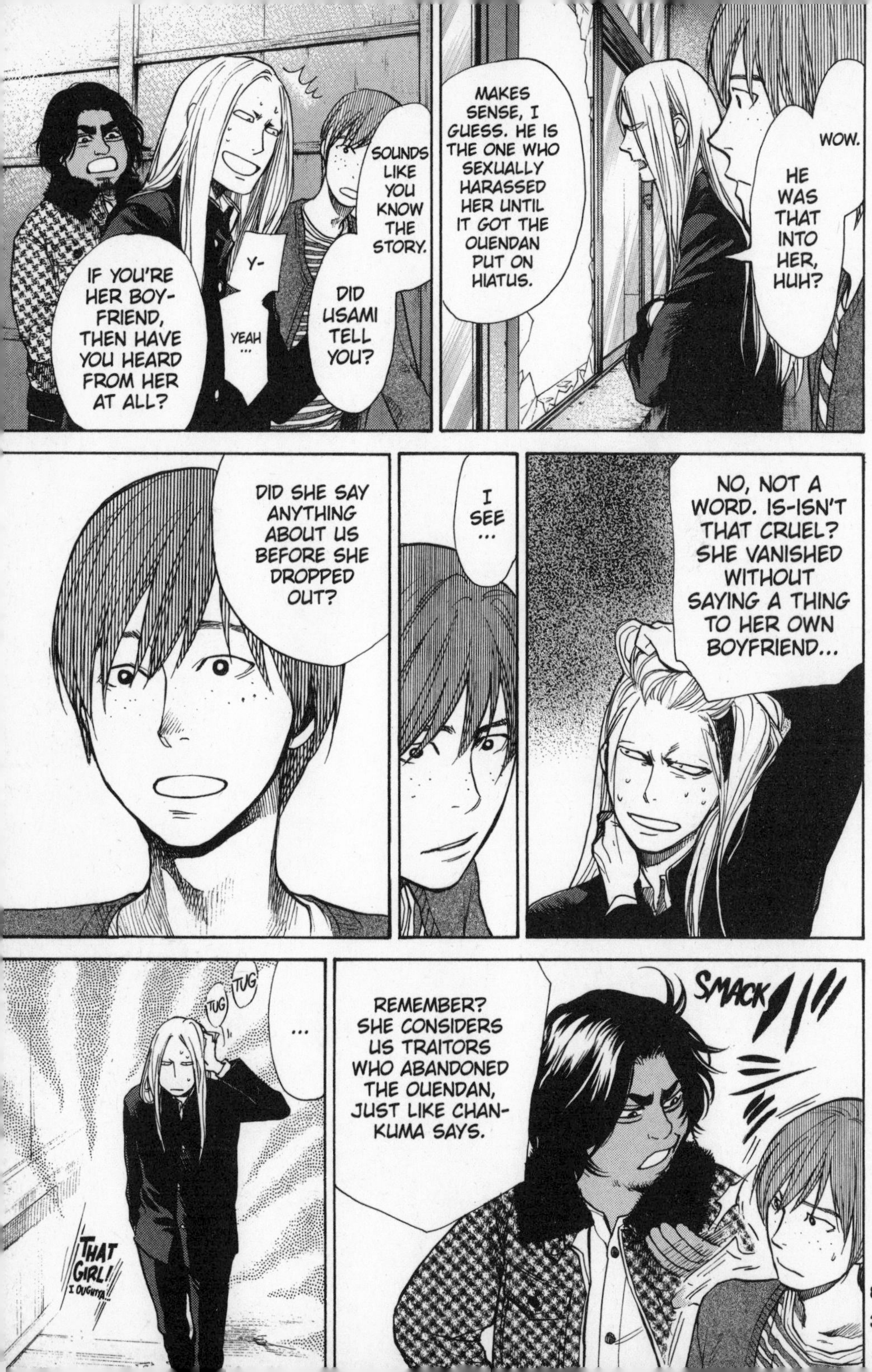
WOW.
HE WAS THAT INTO HER, HUH?
MAKES SENSE, I GUESS. HE IS THE ONE WHO SEXUALLY HARASSED HER UNTIL IT GOT THE OUENDAN PUT ON HIATUS.
SOUNDS LIKE YOU KNOW THE STORY.
DID USAMI TELL YOU?
Y-
YEAH...
IF YOU'RE HER BOY-FRIEND, THEN HAVE YOU HEARD FROM HER AT ALL?
NO, NOT A WORD. IS-ISN'T THAT CRUEL? SHE VANISHED WITHOUT SAYING A THING TO HER OWN BOYFRIEND...
I SEE...
DID SHE SAY ANYTHING ABOUT US BEFORE SHE DROPPED OUT?
SMACK
REMEMBER? SHE CONSIDERS US TRAITORS WHO ABANDONED THE OUENDAN, JUST LIKE CHAN-KUMA SAYS.
...
TUG
TUG
THAT GIRL!

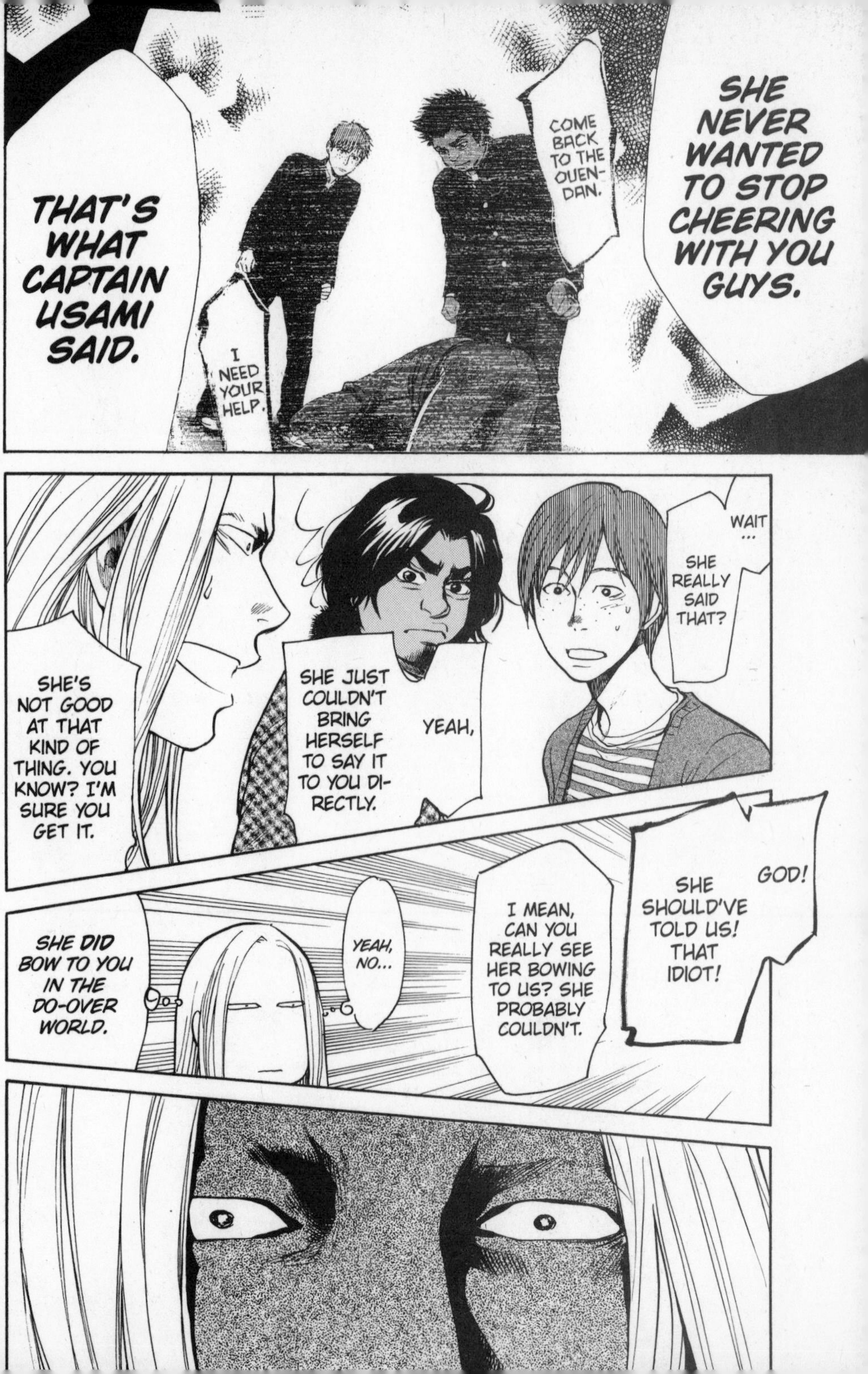

SHE NEVER WANTED TO STOP CHEERING WITH YOU GUYS.
COME BACK TO THE OUEN-DAN.
I NEED YOUR HELP.
THAT'S WHAT CAPTAIN USAMI SAID.
WAIT...
SHE REALLY SAID THAT?
YEAH,
SHE JUST COULDN'T BRING HERSELF TO SAY IT TO YOU DI-RECTLY.
SHE'S NOT GOOD AT THAT KIND OF THING. YOU KNOW? I'M SURE YOU GET IT.
GOD!
SHE SHOULD'VE TOLD US! THAT IDIOT!
I MEAN, CAN YOU REALLY SEE HER BOWING TO US? SHE PROBABLY COULDN'T.
YEAH, NO...
SHE DID BOW TO YOU IN THE DO-OVER WORLD.

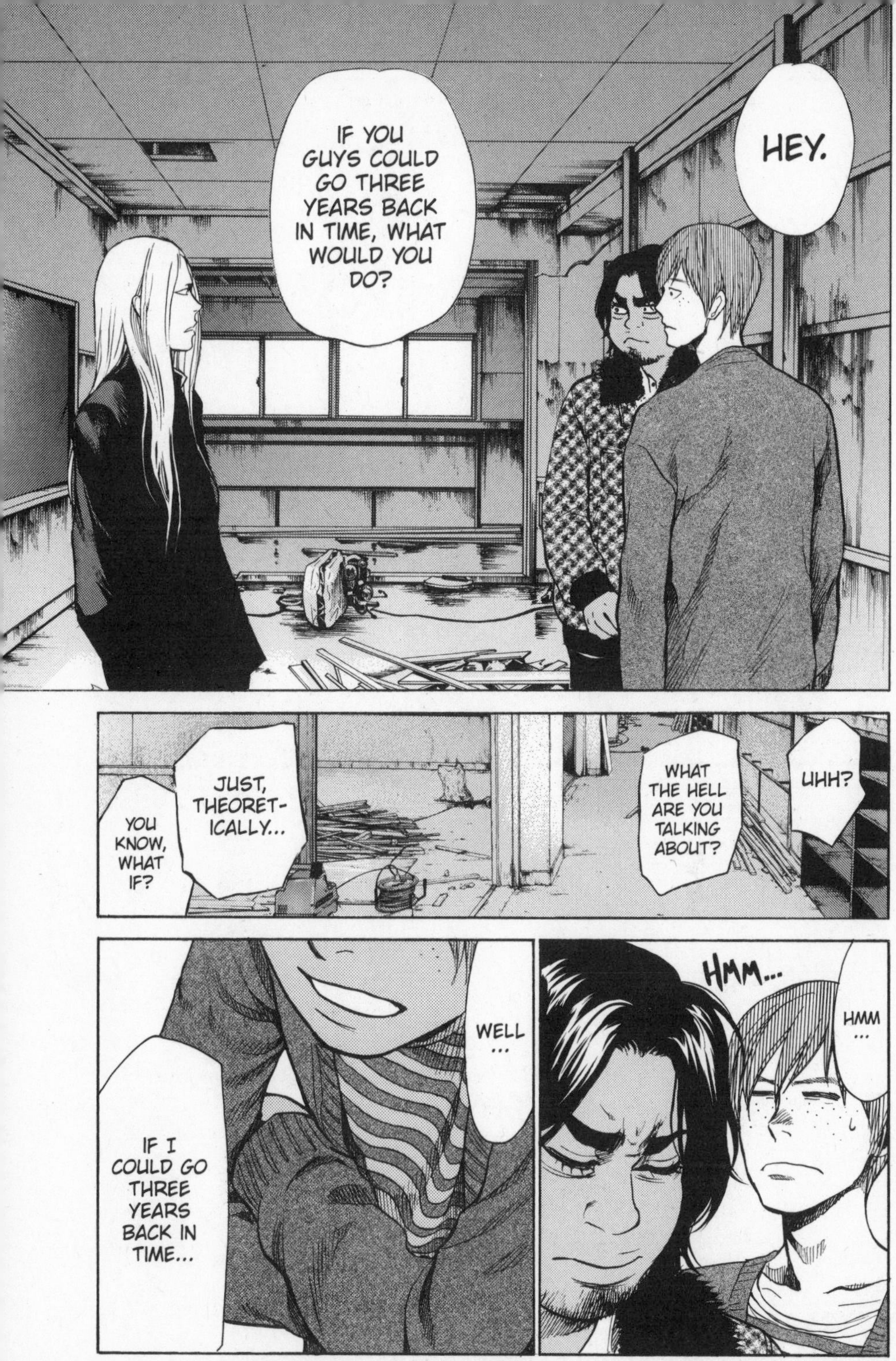
HEY.
IF YOU GUYS COULD GO THREE YEARS BACK IN TIME, WHAT WOULD YOU DO?
UHH?
WHAT THE HELL ARE YOU TALKING ABOUT?
JUST, THEORET-ICALLY...
YOU KNOW, WHAT IF?
HMM...
HMM ...
WELL ...
IF I COULD GO THREE YEARS BACK IN TIME...

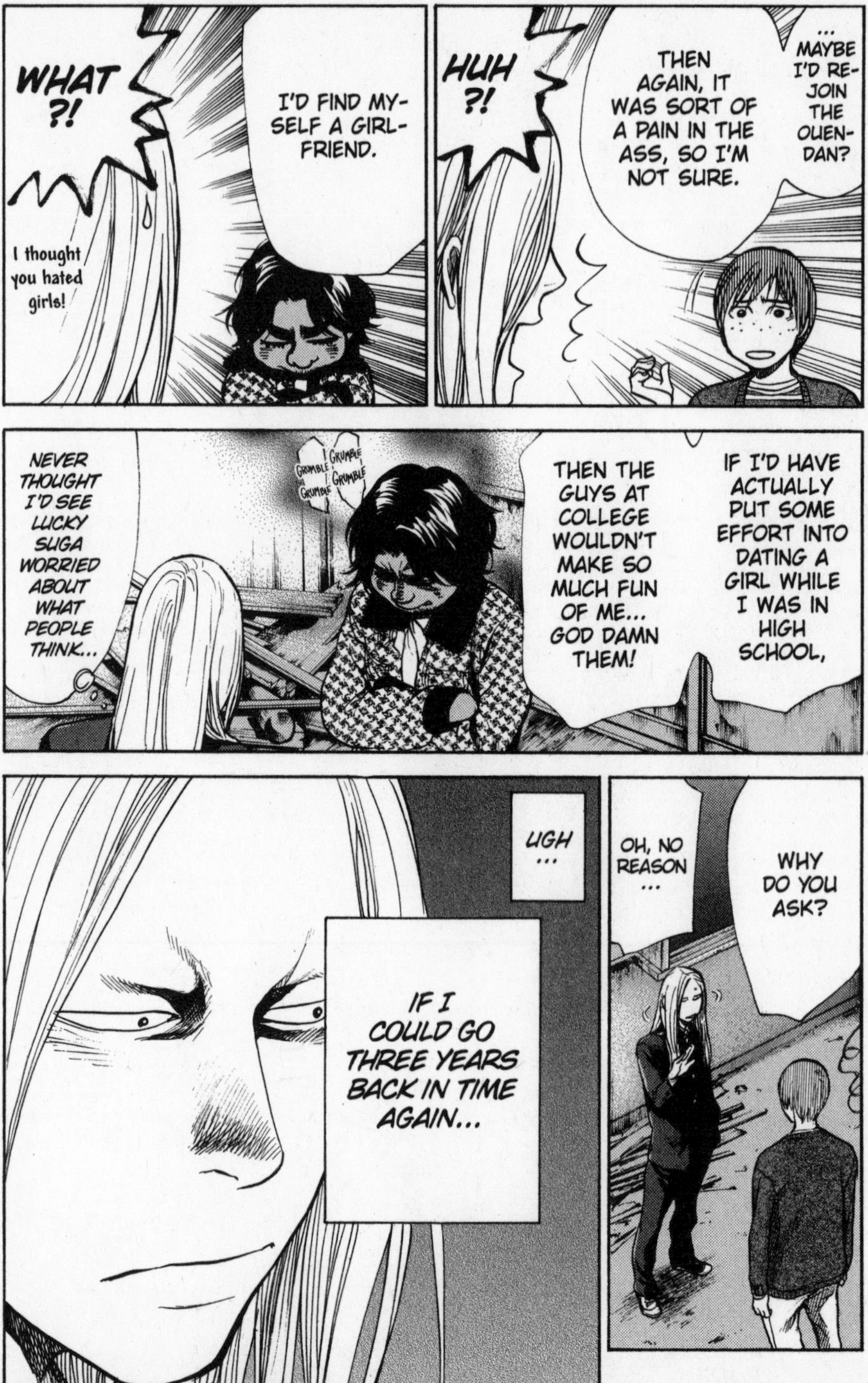

... MAYBE I'D RE-JOIN THE OUEN-DAN?
THEN AGAIN, IT WAS SORT OF A PAIN IN THE ASS, SO I'M NOT SURE.
HUH ?!
I'D FIND MY-SELF A GIRL-FRIEND.
WHAT ?!
I thought you hated girls!
IF I'D HAVE ACTUALLY PUT SOME EFFORT INTO DATING A GIRL WHILE I WAS IN HIGH SCHOOL,
THEN THE GUYS AT COLLEGE WOULDN'T MAKE SO MUCH FUN OF ME... GOD DAMN THEM!
GRUMBLE GRUMBLE GRUMBLE GRUMBLE
NEVER THOUGHT I'D SEE LUCKY SUGA WORRIED ABOUT WHAT PEOPLE THINK...
WHY DO YOU ASK?
OH, NO REASON ...
UGH ...
IF I COULD GO THREE YEARS BACK IN TIME AGAIN...

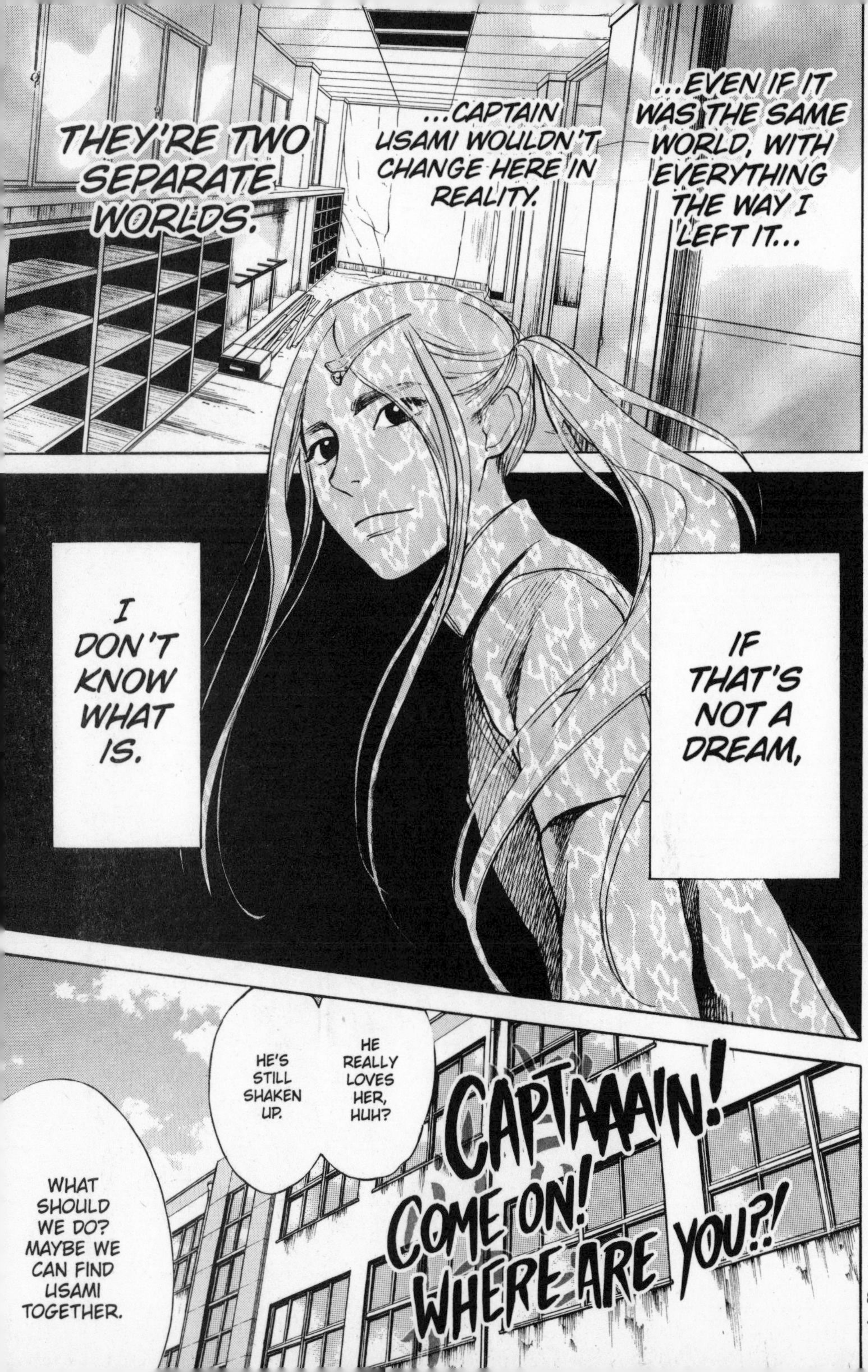
...EVEN IF IT WAS THE SAME WORLD, WITH EVERYTHING THE WAY I LEFT IT...
...CAPTAIN USAMI WOULDN'T CHANGE HERE IN REALITY.
THEY'RE TWO SEPARATE WORLDS.
IF THAT'S NOT A DREAM,
I DON'T KNOW WHAT IS.
CAPTAAAIN! COME ON! WHERE ARE YOU?!
HE REALLY LOVES HER, HUH?
HE'S STILL SHAKEN UP.
WHAT SHOULD WE DO? MAYBE WE CAN FIND USAMI TOGETHER.

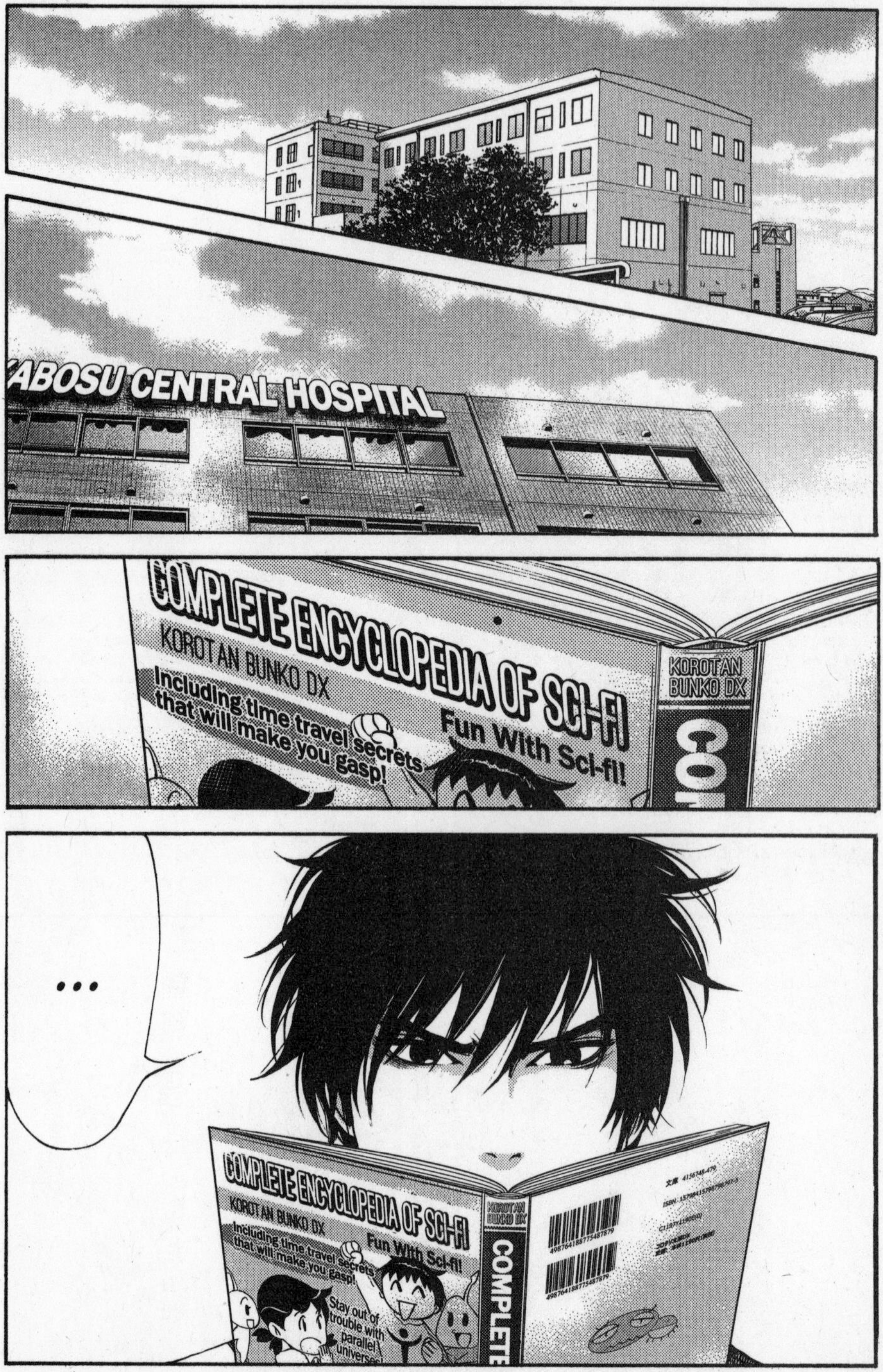
KABOSU CENTRAL HOSPITAL
COMPLETE ENCYCLOPEDIA OF SCI-FI
KOROTAN BUNKO DX
Including time travel secrets that will make you gasp!
Fun With Sci-fi!
KOROTAN BUNKO DX
...
COMPLETE ENCYCLOPEDIA OF SCI-FI
KOROTAN BUNKO DX
Including time travel secrets that will make you gasp!
Fun With Sci-fi!
Stay out of trouble with parallel universes
KOROTAN BUNKO DX
COMPLETE

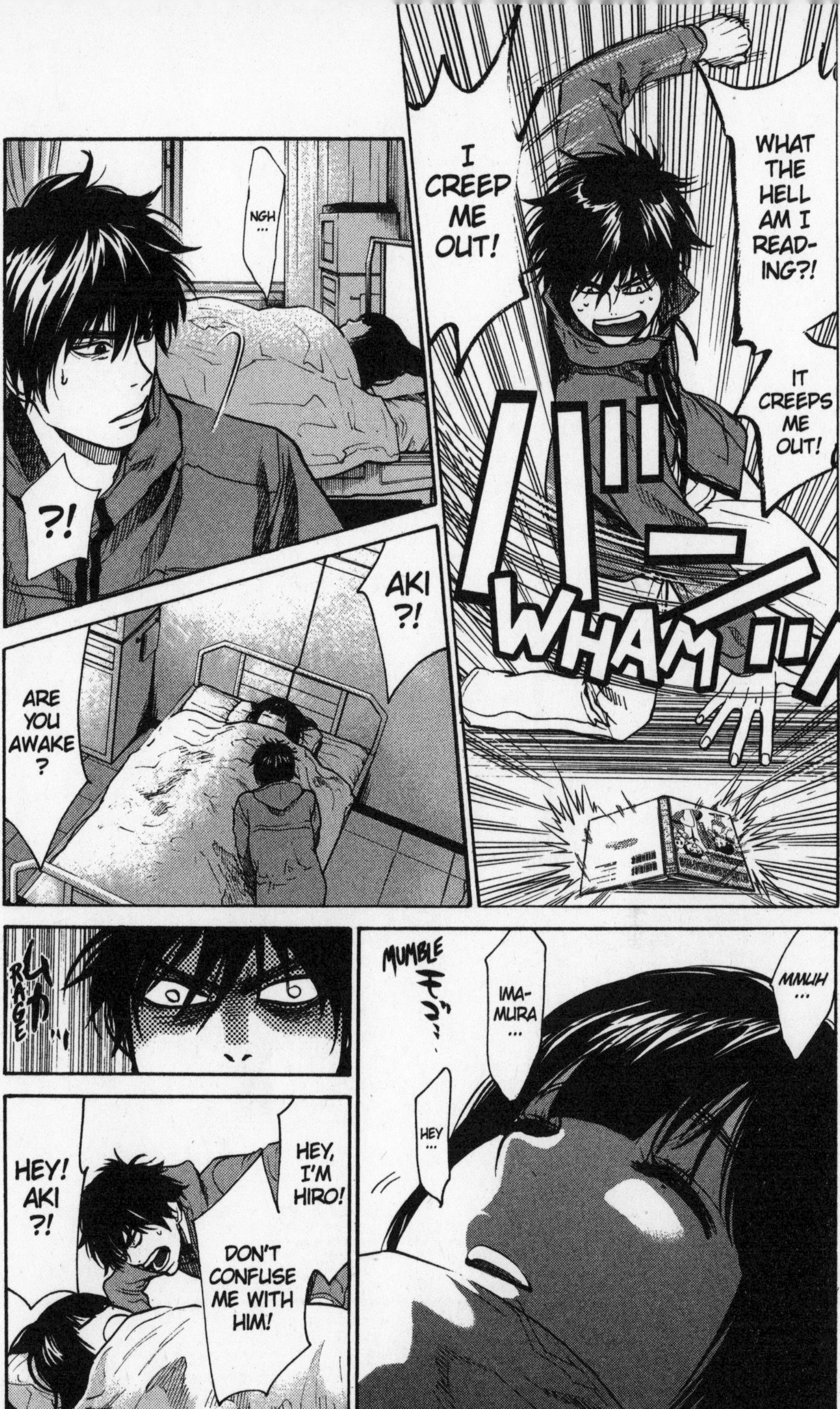
WHAT THE HELL AM I READING?!
I CREEP ME OUT!
IT CREEPS ME OUT!
WHAM
NGH...
?!
AKI?!
ARE YOU AWAKE?
MMUH...
IMA-MURA...
MUMBLE
HEY...
RAGE
HEY, I'M HIRO!
HEY! AKI?!
DON'T CONFUSE ME WITH HIM!

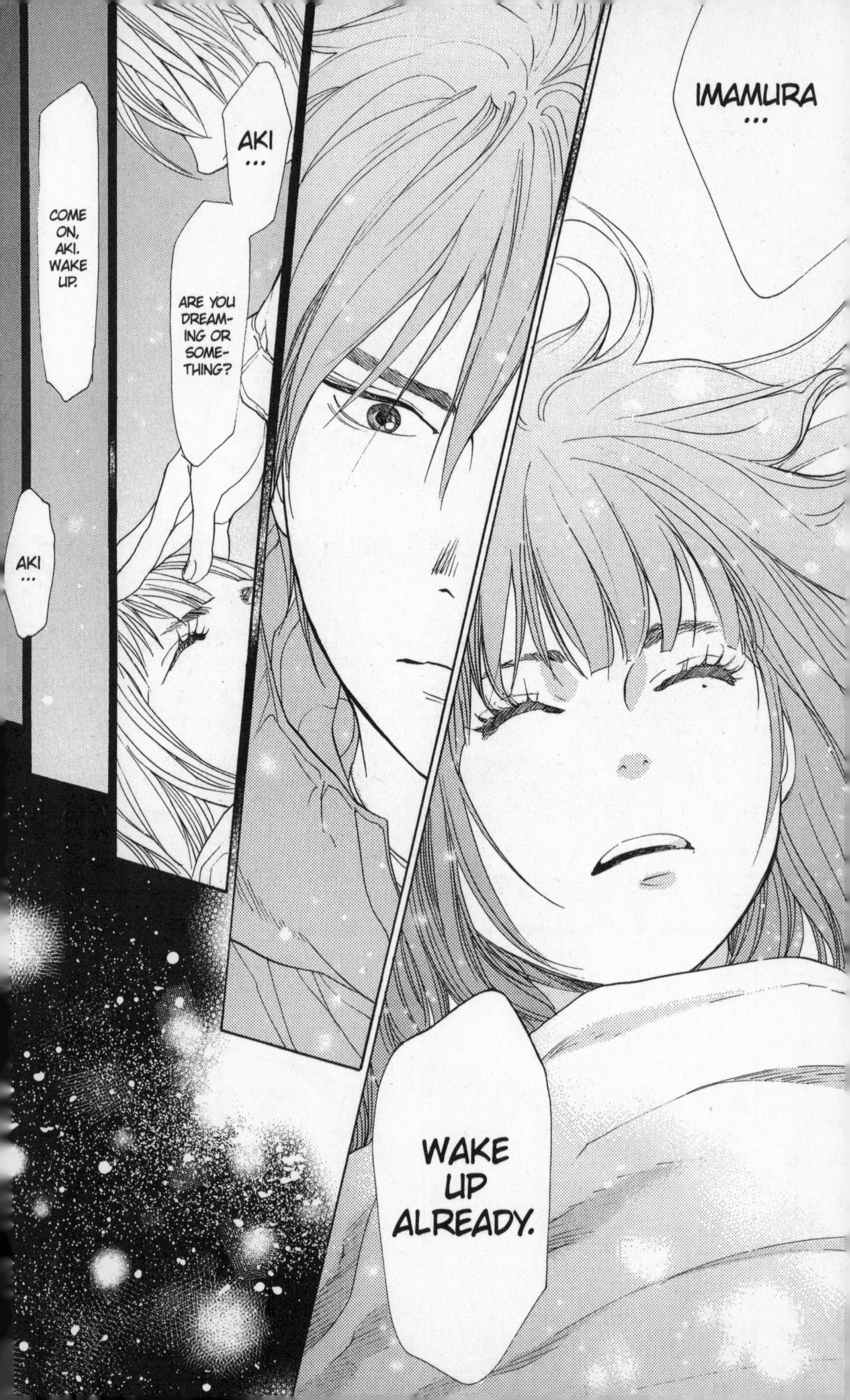
IMAMURA ...
WAKE UP ALREADY.
AKI ...
ARE YOU DREAMING OR SOMETHING?
COME ON, AKI. WAKE UP.
AKI ...

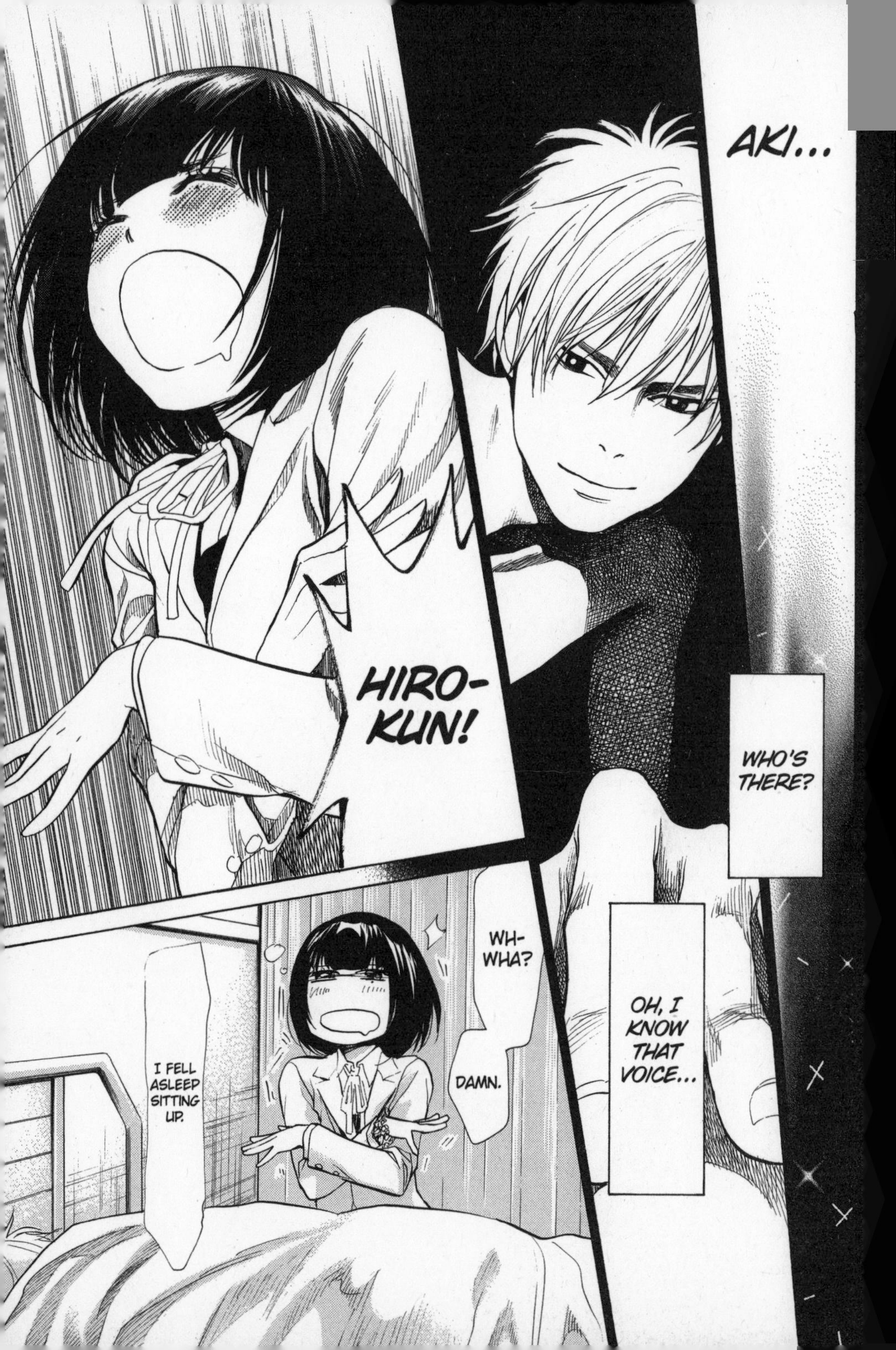
AKI...
WHO'S THERE?
OH, I KNOW THAT VOICE...
HIRO-KUN!
WH-WHA?
DAMN.
I FELL ASLEEP SITTING UP.

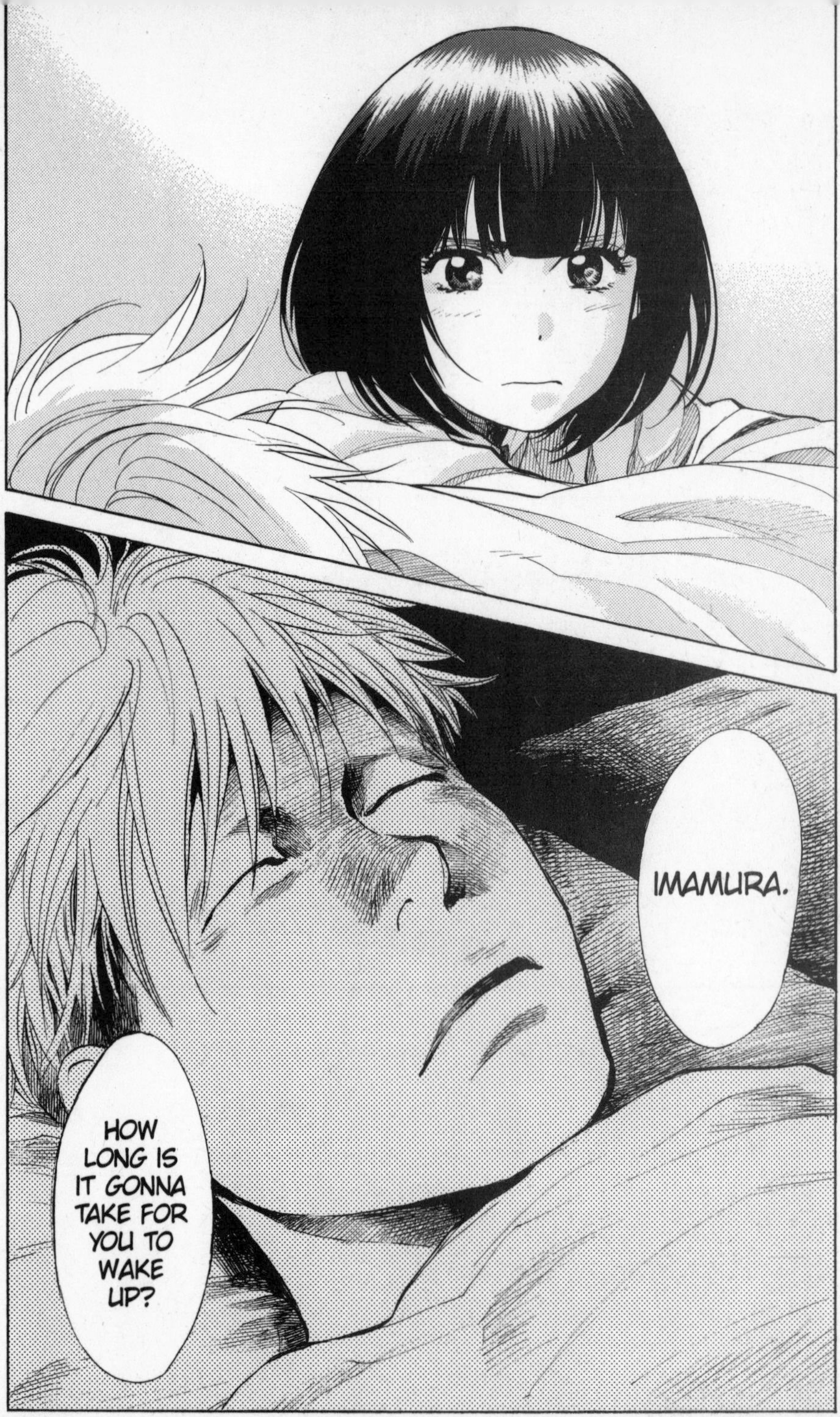
IMAMURA.
HOW LONG IS IT GONNA TAKE FOR YOU TO WAKE UP?

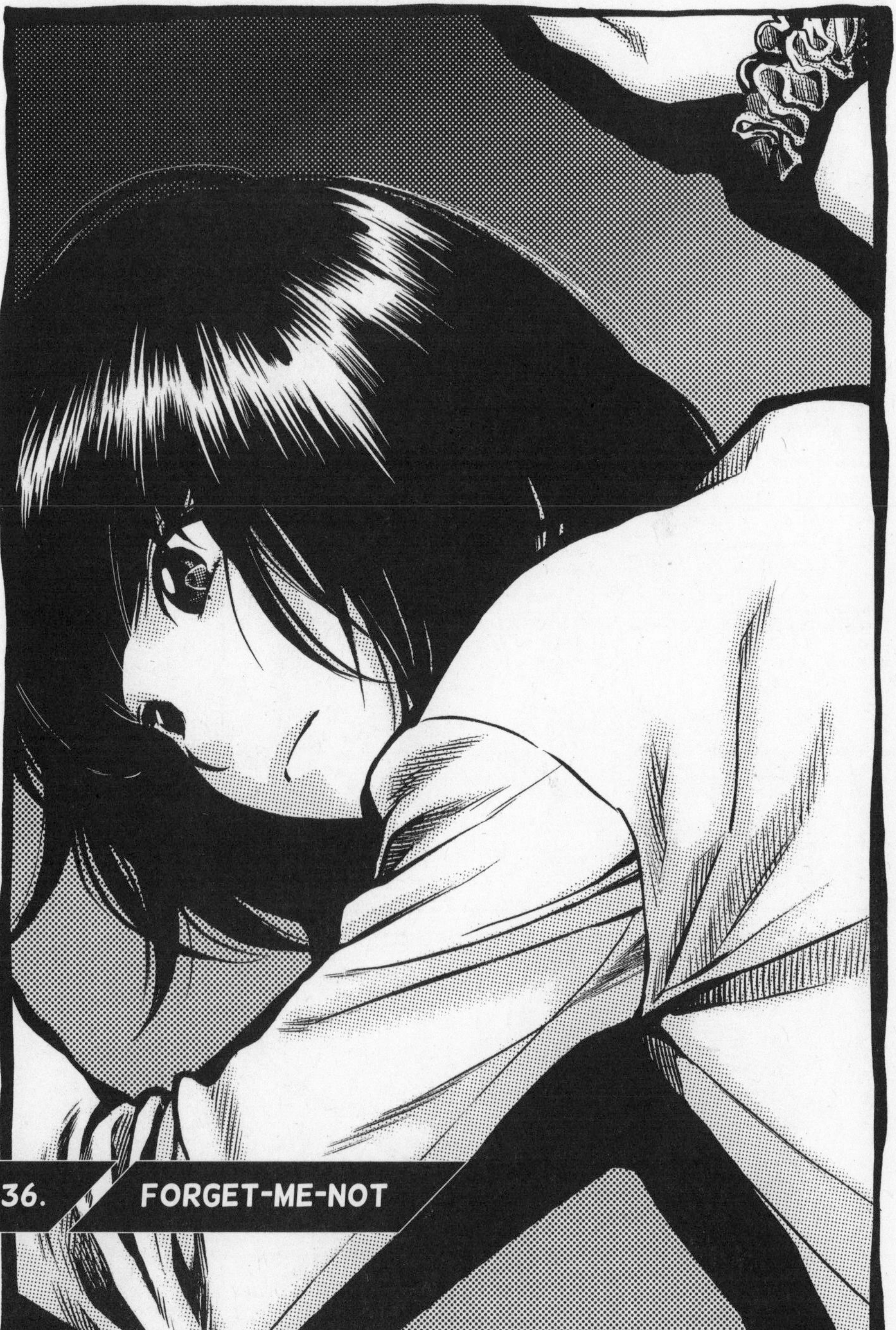

36. FORGET-ME-NOT

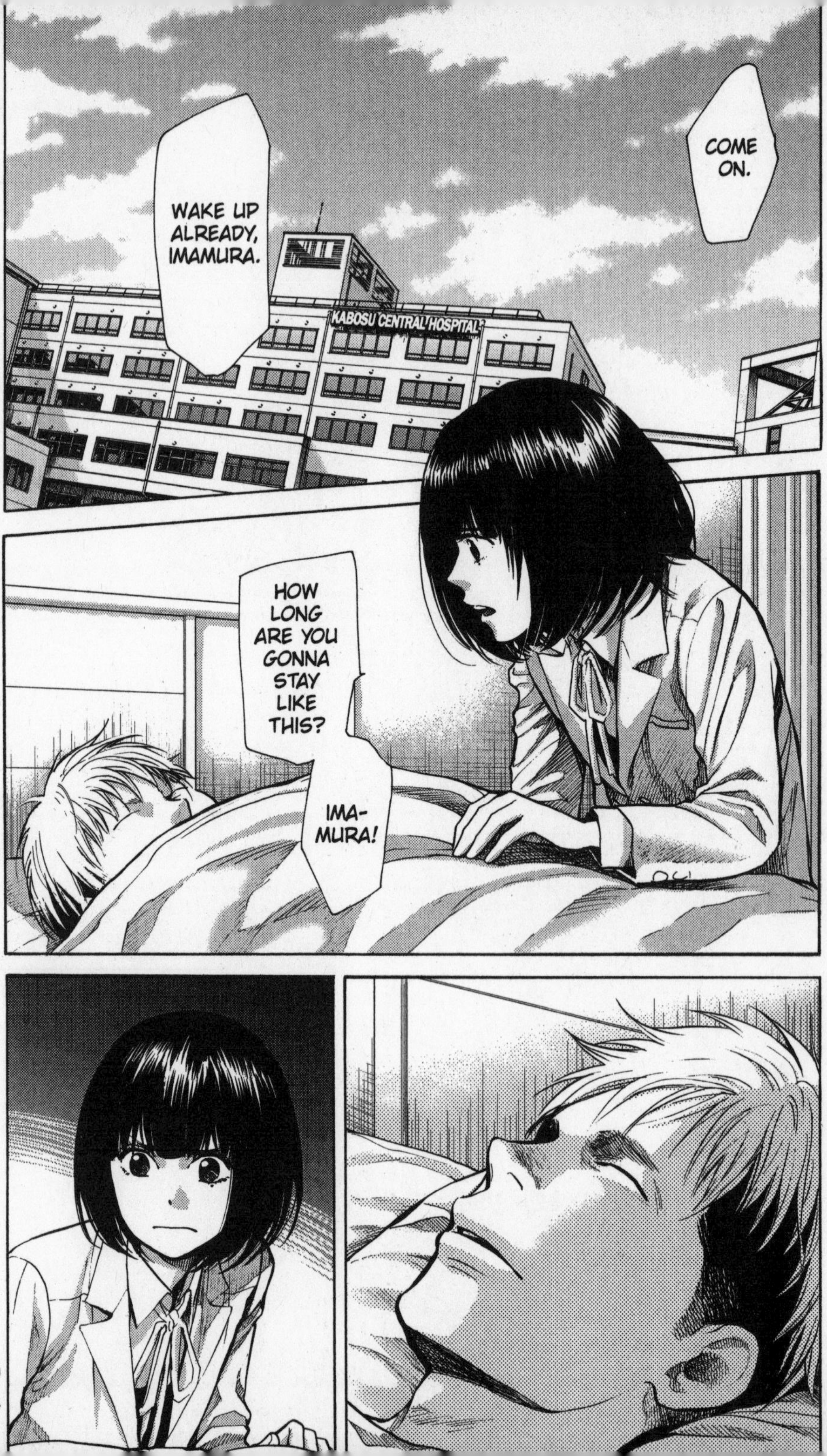
COME ON.
WAKE UP ALREADY, IMAMURA.
KABOSU CENTRAL HOSPITAL
HOW LONG ARE YOU GONNA STAY LIKE THIS?
IMA-MURA!

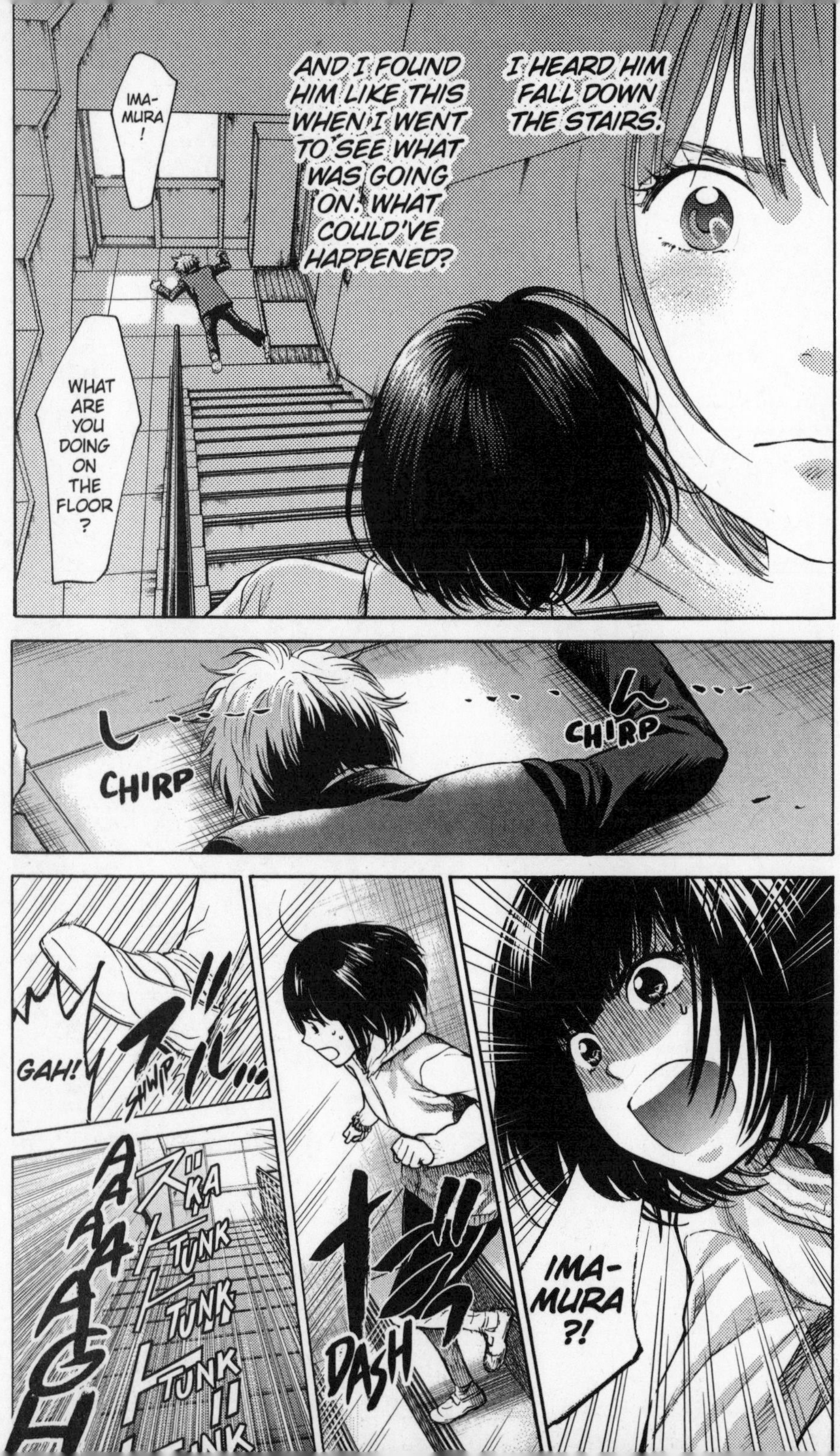
I HEARD HIM FALL DOWN THE STAIRS.
AND I FOUND HIM LIKE THIS WHEN I WENT TO SEE WHAT WAS GOING ON. WHAT COULD'VE HAPPENED?
IMA-MURA!
WHAT ARE YOU DOING ON THE FLOOR?
CHIRP
CHIRP
IMA-MURA?!
DASH
GAH!
SHWIP
KA
TUNK
TUNK
TUNK
TUNK
TUNK

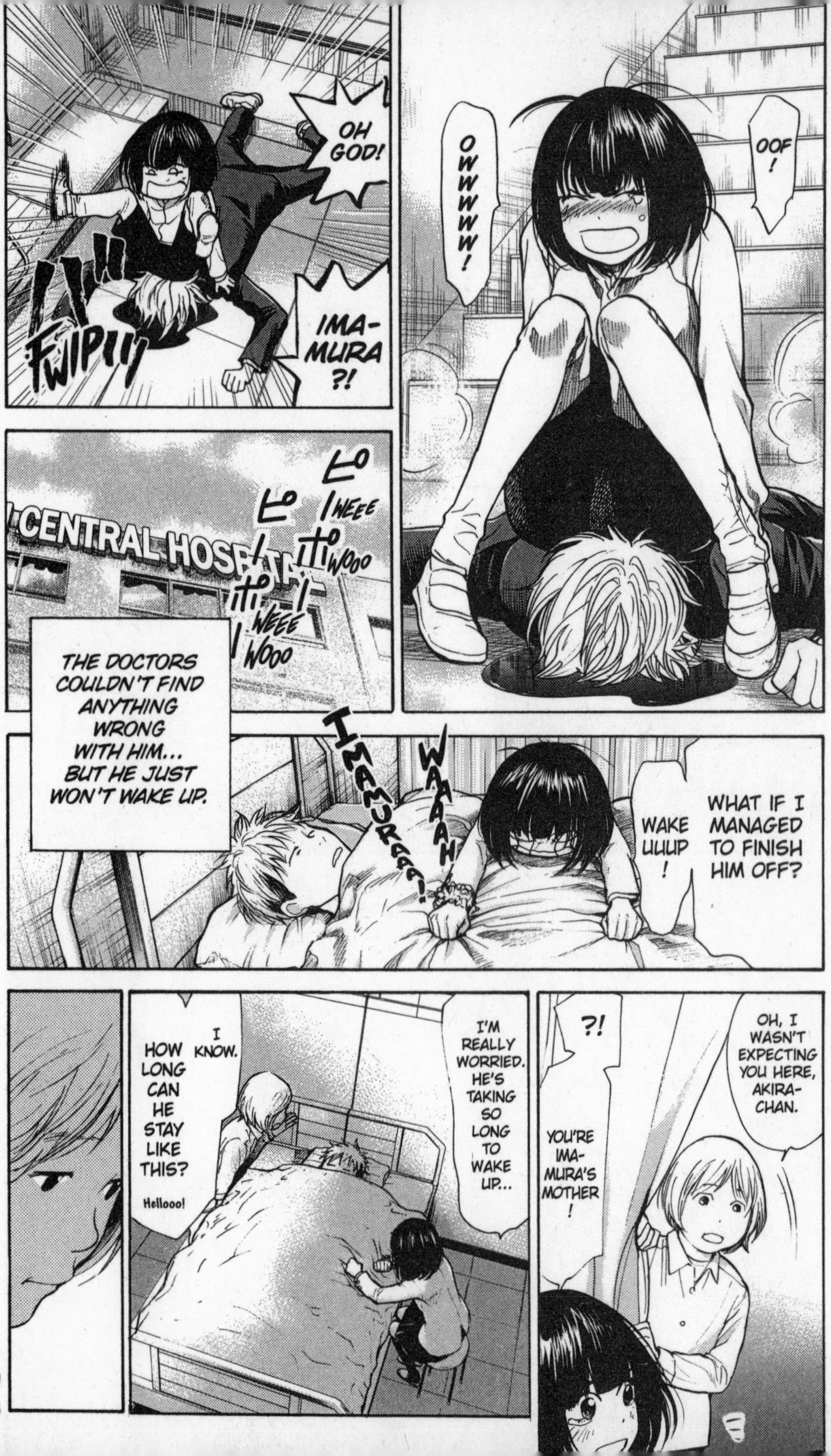
OOF!
OWWWWWW!
OH GOD!
IMA-MURA?!
FWIP!!
ピ WEEE
ポ WOOO
ピ WEEE
ポ WOOO
CENTRAL HOS
THE DOCTORS COULDN'T FIND ANYTHING WRONG WITH HIM... BUT HE JUST WON'T WAKE UP.
WHAT IF I MANAGED TO FINISH HIM OFF?
WAKE UUUP!
WAAAAH!
IMAMURAAA!
OH, I WASN'T EXPECTING YOU HERE, AKIRA-CHAN.
?!
YOU'RE IMA-MURA'S MOTHER!
I'M REALLY WORRIED. HE'S TAKING SO LONG TO WAKE UP...
I KNOW.
HOW LONG CAN HE STAY LIKE THIS?
Hellooo!

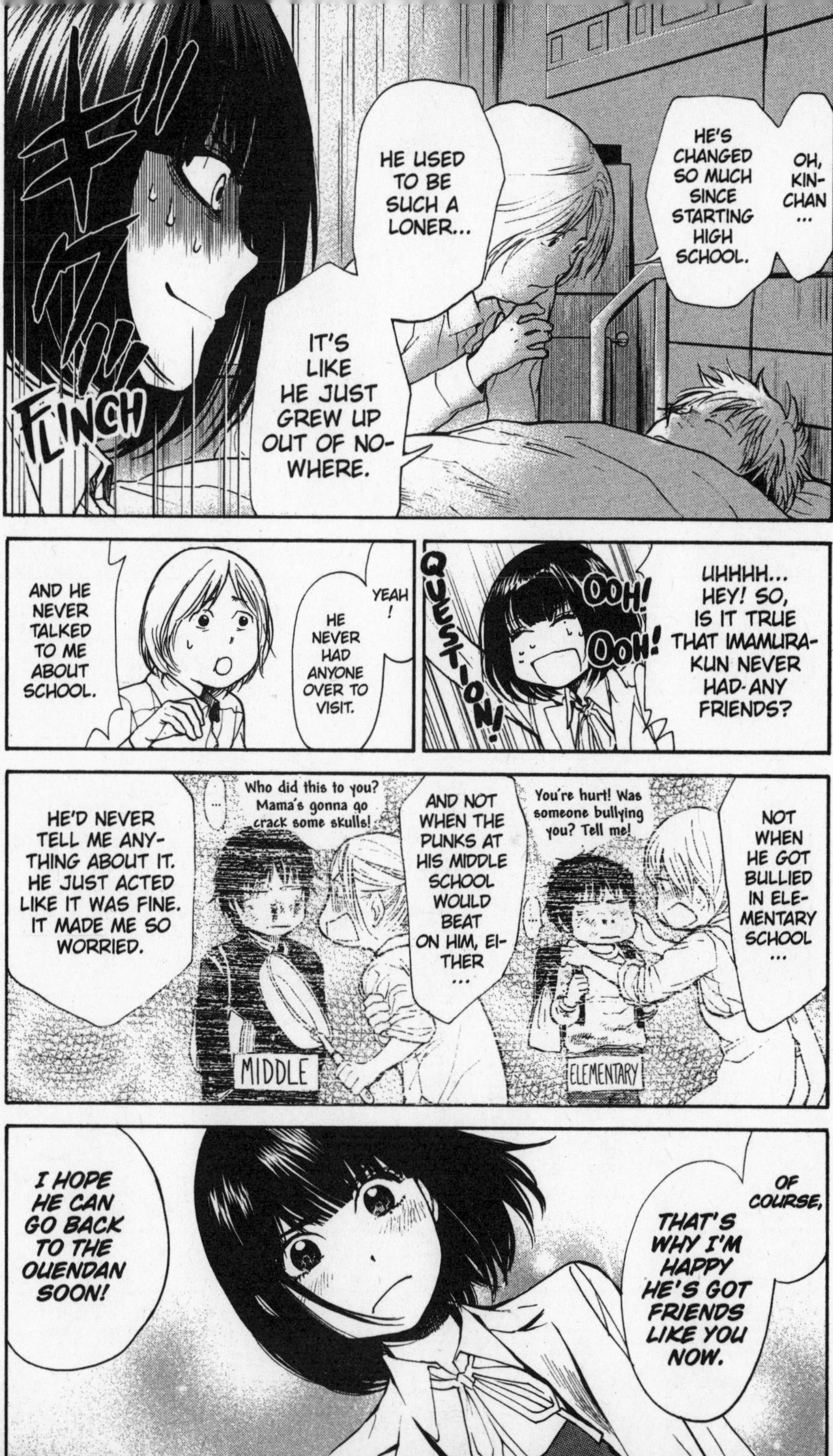
OH, KIN-CHAN...
HE'S CHANGED SO MUCH SINCE STARTING HIGH SCHOOL.
HE USED TO BE SUCH A LONER...
IT'S LIKE HE JUST GREW UP OUT OF NOWHERE.
FLINCH
UHHHH... HEY! SO, IS IT TRUE THAT IMAMURA-KUN NEVER HAD ANY FRIENDS?
OOH! OOH!
QUESTION!
YEAH!
HE NEVER HAD ANYONE OVER TO VISIT.
AND HE NEVER TALKED TO ME ABOUT SCHOOL.
NOT WHEN HE GOT BULLIED IN ELEMENTARY SCHOOL...
You're hurt! Was someone bullying you? Tell me!
...
ELEMENTARY
AND NOT WHEN THE PUNKS AT HIS MIDDLE SCHOOL WOULD BEAT ON HIM, EITHER...
Who did this to you? Mama's gonna go crack some skulls!
...
MIDDLE
HE'D NEVER TELL ME ANYTHING ABOUT IT. HE JUST ACTED LIKE IT WAS FINE. IT MADE ME SO WORRIED.
OF COURSE, THAT'S WHY I'M HAPPY HE'S GOT FRIENDS LIKE YOU NOW.
I HOPE HE CAN GO BACK TO THE OUENDAN SOON!

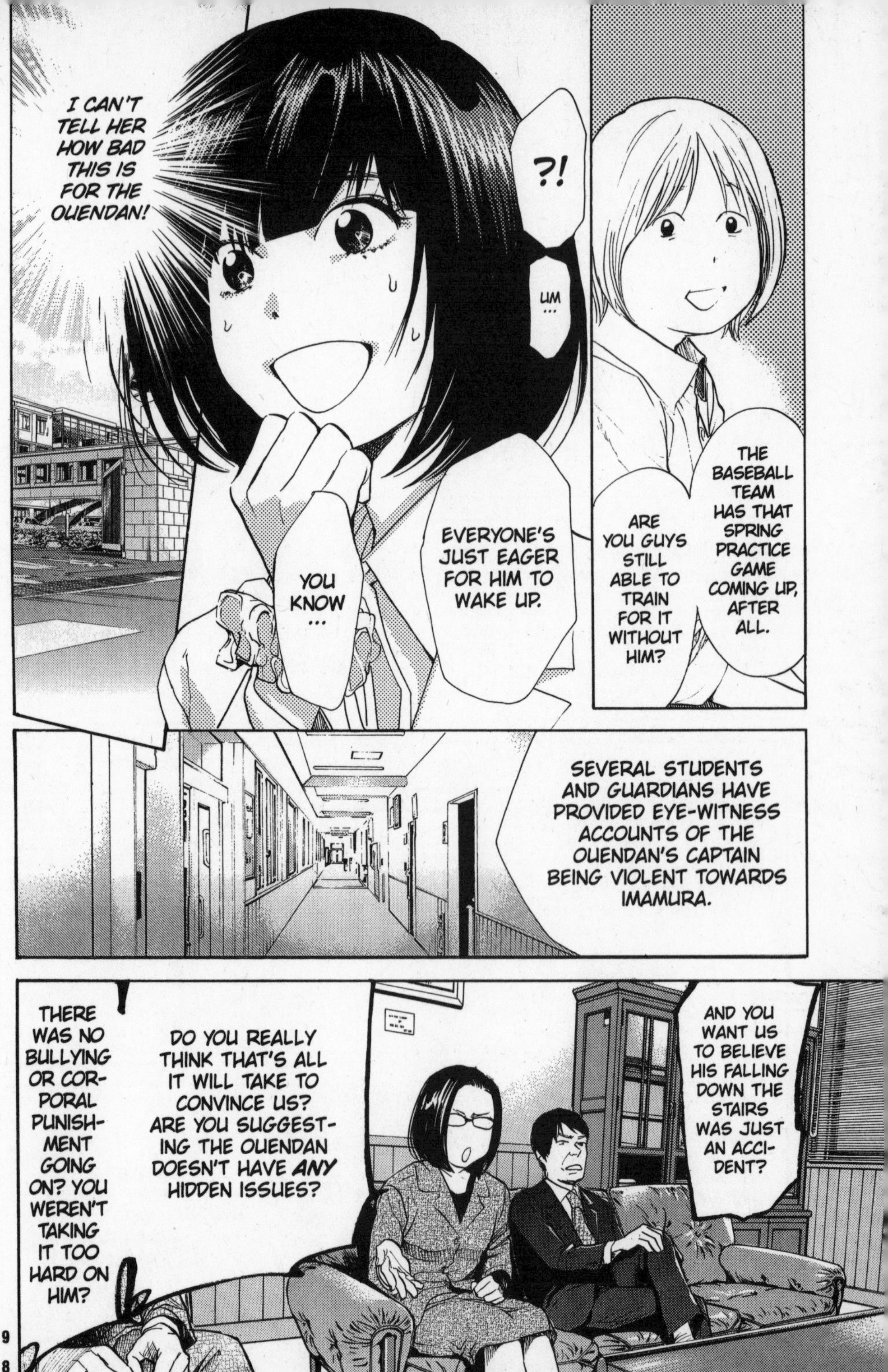
THE BASEBALL TEAM HAS THAT SPRING PRACTICE GAME COMING UP, AFTER ALL.
ARE YOU GUYS STILL ABLE TO TRAIN FOR IT WITHOUT HIM?
?!
UM ...
I CAN'T TELL HER HOW BAD THIS IS FOR THE OUENDAN!
EVERYONE'S JUST EAGER FOR HIM TO WAKE UP.
YOU KNOW ...
SEVERAL STUDENTS AND GUARDIANS HAVE PROVIDED EYE-WITNESS ACCOUNTS OF THE OUENDAN'S CAPTAIN BEING VIOLENT TOWARDS IMAMURA.
AND YOU WANT US TO BELIEVE HIS FALLING DOWN THE STAIRS WAS JUST AN ACCI-DENT?
DO YOU REALLY THINK THAT'S ALL IT WILL TAKE TO CONVINCE US? ARE YOU SUGGEST-ING THE OUENDAN DOESN'T HAVE *ANY* HIDDEN ISSUES?
THERE WAS NO BULLYING OR COR-PORAL PUNISH-MENT GOING ON? YOU WEREN'T TAKING IT TOO HARD ON HIM?

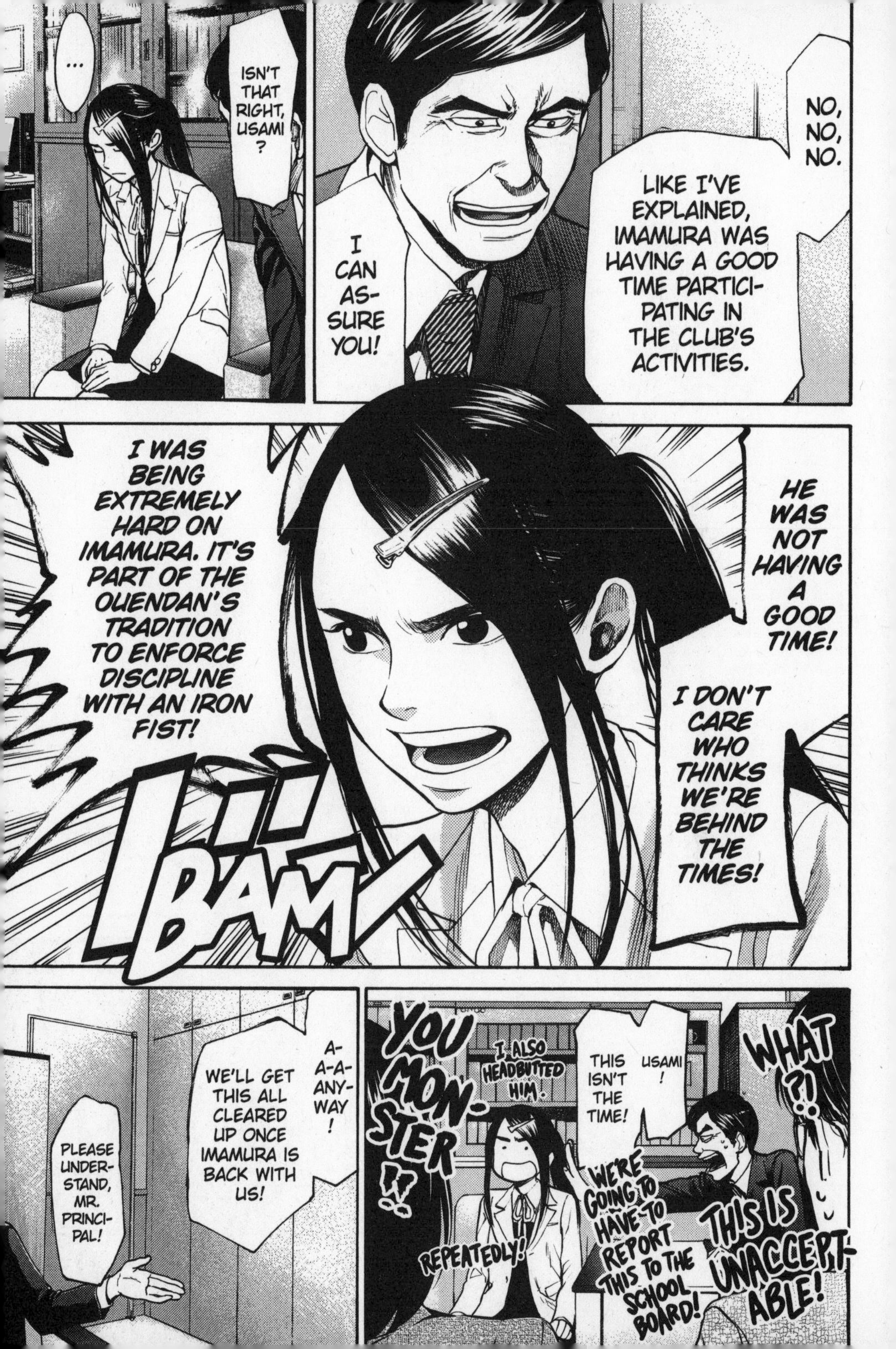
NO, NO, NO.
LIKE I'VE EXPLAINED, IMAMURA WAS HAVING A GOOD TIME PARTICIPATING IN THE CLUB'S ACTIVITIES.
I CAN ASSURE YOU!
ISN'T THAT RIGHT, USAMI?
...
HE WAS NOT HAVING A GOOD TIME!
I DON'T CARE WHO THINKS WE'RE BEHIND THE TIMES!
I WAS BEING EXTREMELY HARD ON IMAMURA. IT'S PART OF THE OUENDAN'S TRADITION TO ENFORCE DISCIPLINE WITH AN IRON FIST!
BAM!
WHAT?!
THIS IS UNACCEPTABLE!
WE'RE GOING TO HAVE TO REPORT THIS TO THE SCHOOL BOARD!
USAMI!
THIS ISN'T THE TIME!
I ALSO HEADBUTTED HIM.
REPEATEDLY!
YOU MONSTER!!
A-A-A-ANYWAY!
WE'LL GET THIS ALL CLEARED UP ONCE IMAMURA IS BACK WITH US!
PLEASE UNDERSTAND, MR. PRINCIPAL!

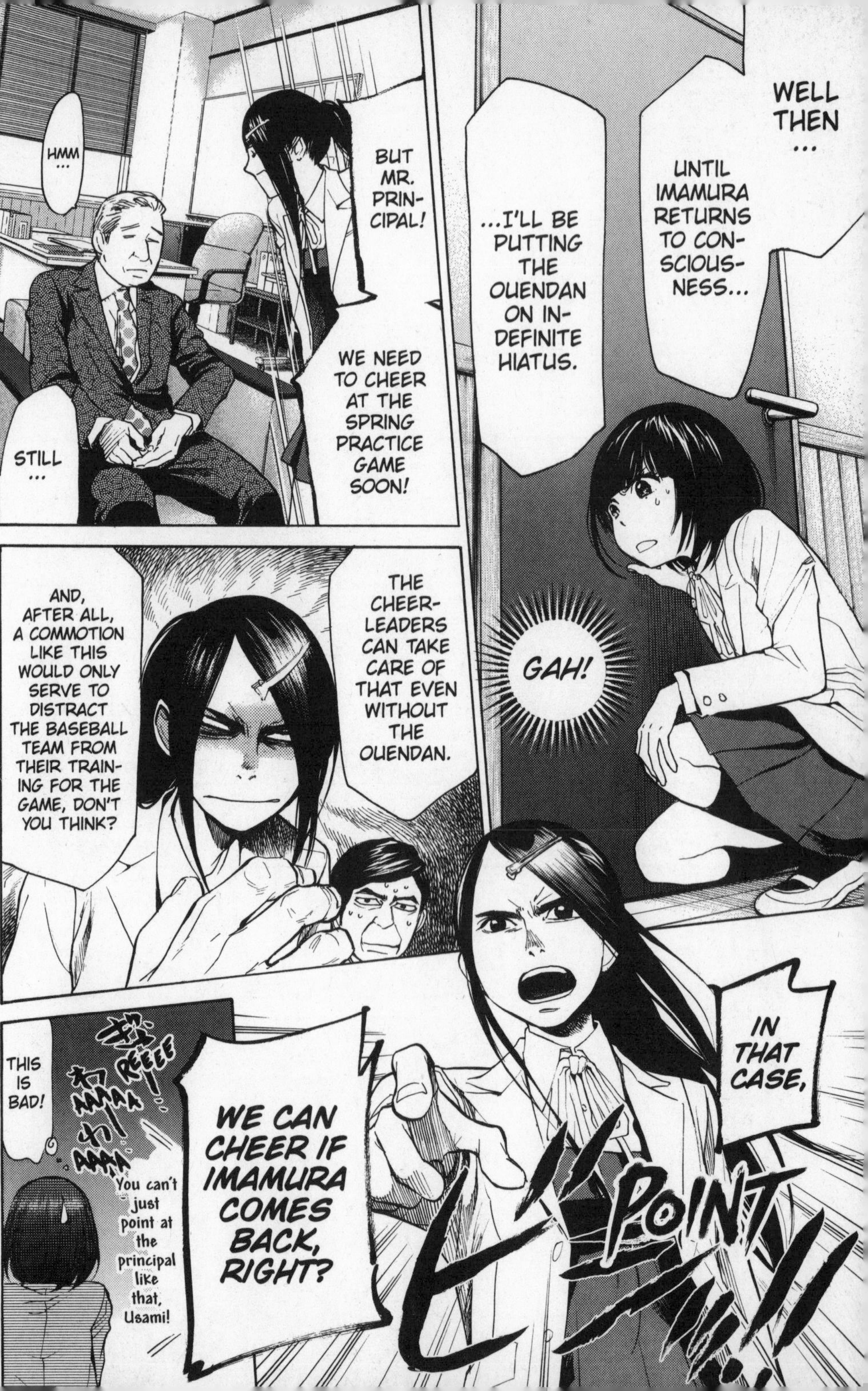
WELL THEN ...
UNTIL IMAMURA RETURNS TO CONSCIOUSNESS...
...I'LL BE PUTTING THE OUENDAN ON INDEFINITE HIATUS.
GAH!
BUT MR. PRINCIPAL!
WE NEED TO CHEER AT THE SPRING PRACTICE GAME SOON!
HMM ...
STILL ...
THE CHEERLEADERS CAN TAKE CARE OF THAT EVEN WITHOUT THE OUENDAN.
AND, AFTER ALL, A COMMOTION LIKE THIS WOULD ONLY SERVE TO DISTRACT THE BASEBALL TEAM FROM THEIR TRAINING FOR THE GAME, DON'T YOU THINK?
IN THAT CASE,
WE CAN CHEER IF IMAMURA COMES BACK, RIGHT?
POINT
THIS IS BAD!
REEEE
AAAAA
AAAA
You can't just point at the principal like that, Usami!

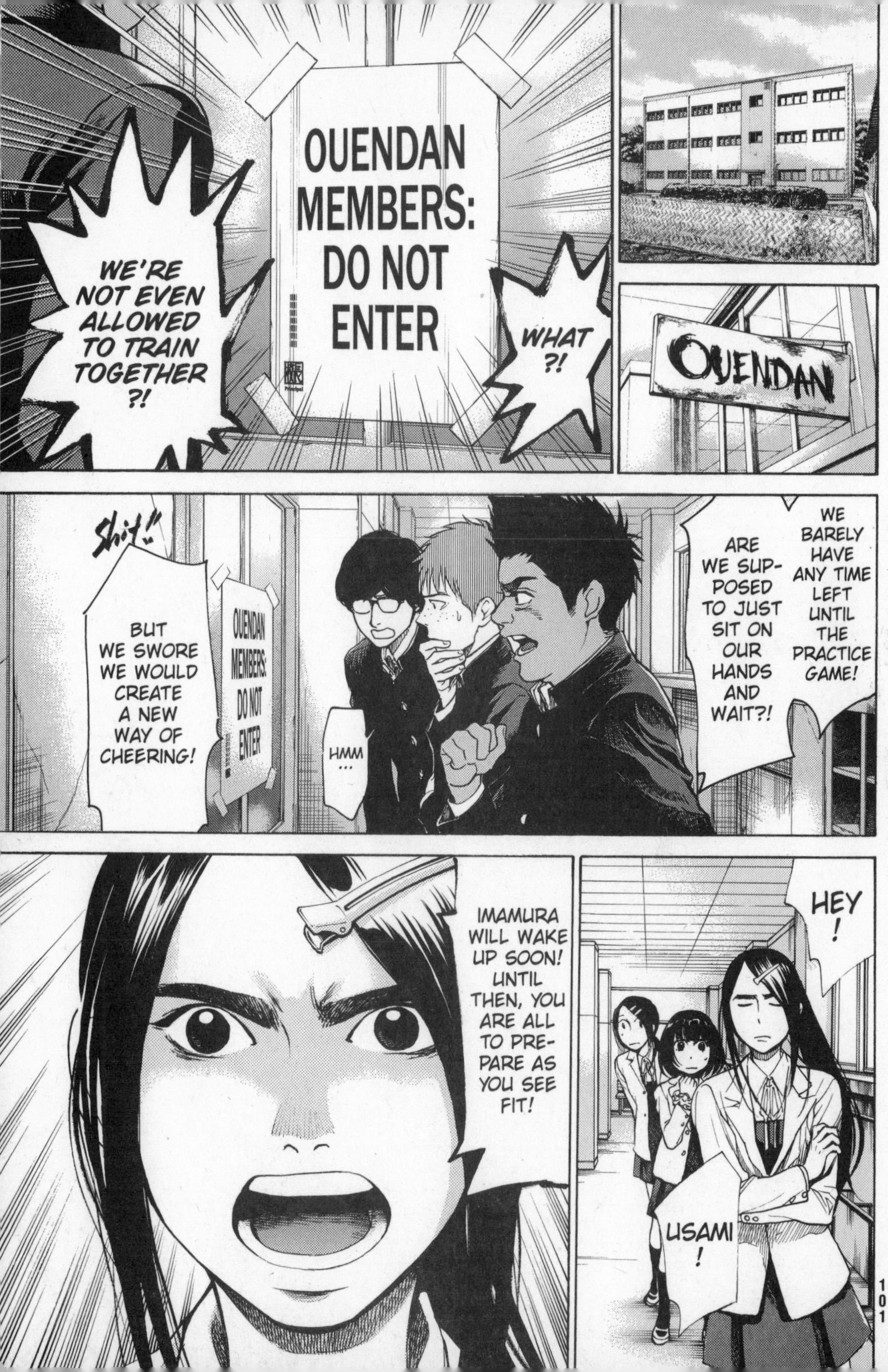
OUENDAN
OUENDAN MEMBERS: DO NOT ENTER
WHAT ?!
WE'RE NOT EVEN ALLOWED TO TRAIN TOGETHER ?!
WE BARELY HAVE ANY TIME LEFT UNTIL THE PRACTICE GAME!
ARE WE SUP-POSED TO JUST SIT ON OUR HANDS AND WAIT?!
HMM ...
OUENDAN MEMBERS: DO NOT ENTER
BUT WE SWORE WE WOULD CREATE A NEW WAY OF CHEERING!
Shit!!
HEY !
USAMI !
IMAMURA WILL WAKE UP SOON! UNTIL THEN, YOU ARE ALL TO PRE-PARE AS YOU SEE FIT!

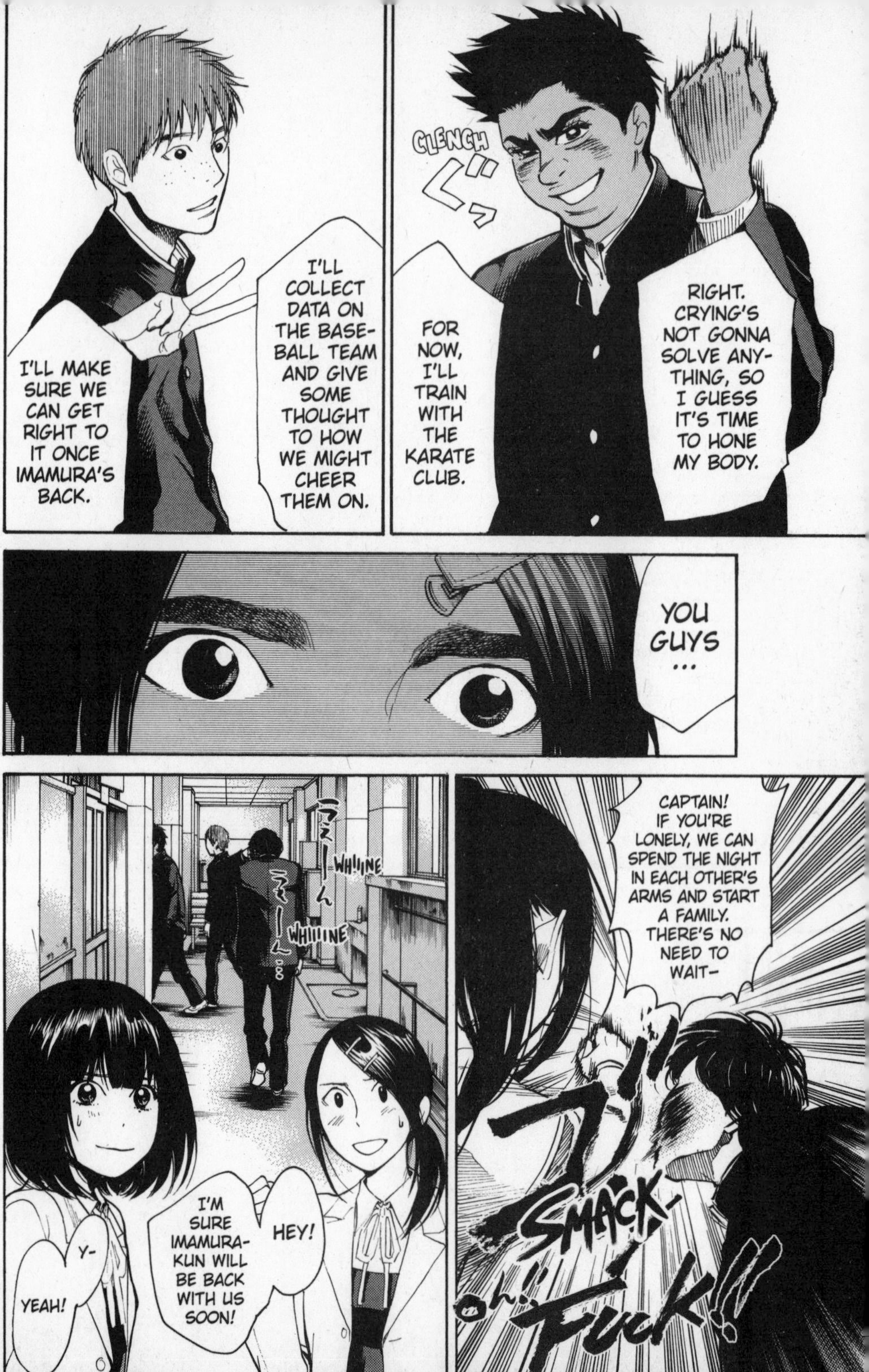
CLENCH
RIGHT. CRYING'S NOT GONNA SOLVE ANYTHING, SO I GUESS IT'S TIME TO HONE MY BODY.
FOR NOW, I'LL TRAIN WITH THE KARATE CLUB.
I'LL COLLECT DATA ON THE BASEBALL TEAM AND GIVE SOME THOUGHT TO HOW WE MIGHT CHEER THEM ON.
I'LL MAKE SURE WE CAN GET RIGHT TO IT ONCE IMAMURA'S BACK.
YOU GUYS...
CAPTAIN! IF YOU'RE LONELY, WE CAN SPEND THE NIGHT IN EACH OTHER'S ARMS AND START A FAMILY. THERE'S NO NEED TO WAIT–
SMACK–
oh!! Fuck!!
WHIIINE
WHIIINE
HEY!
I'M SURE IMAMURA-KUN WILL BE BACK WITH US SOON!
Y-
YEAH!

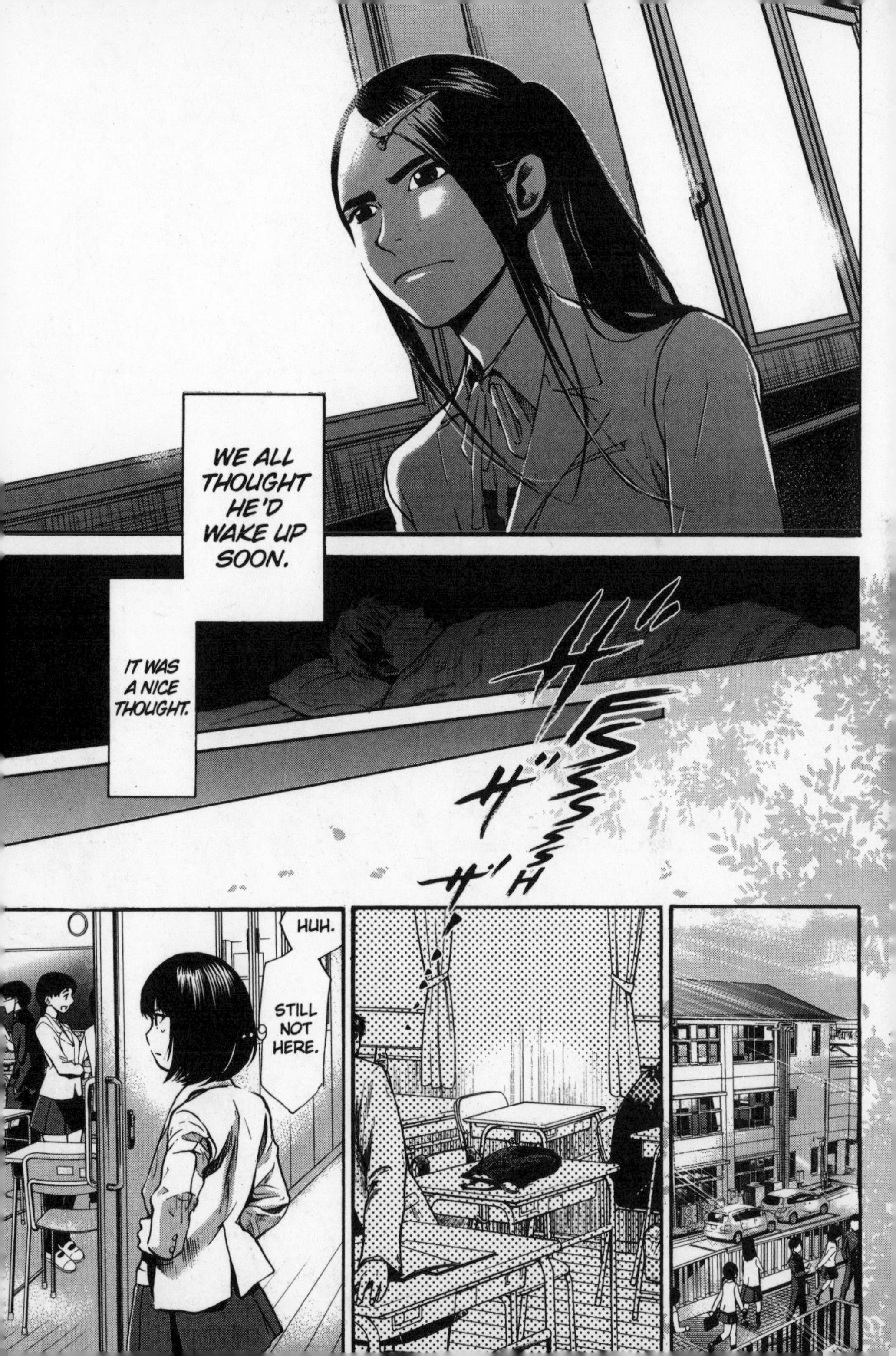
WE ALL THOUGHT HE'D WAKE UP SOON.
IT WAS A NICE THOUGHT.
FSSSSSSH
HUH.
STILL NOT HERE.

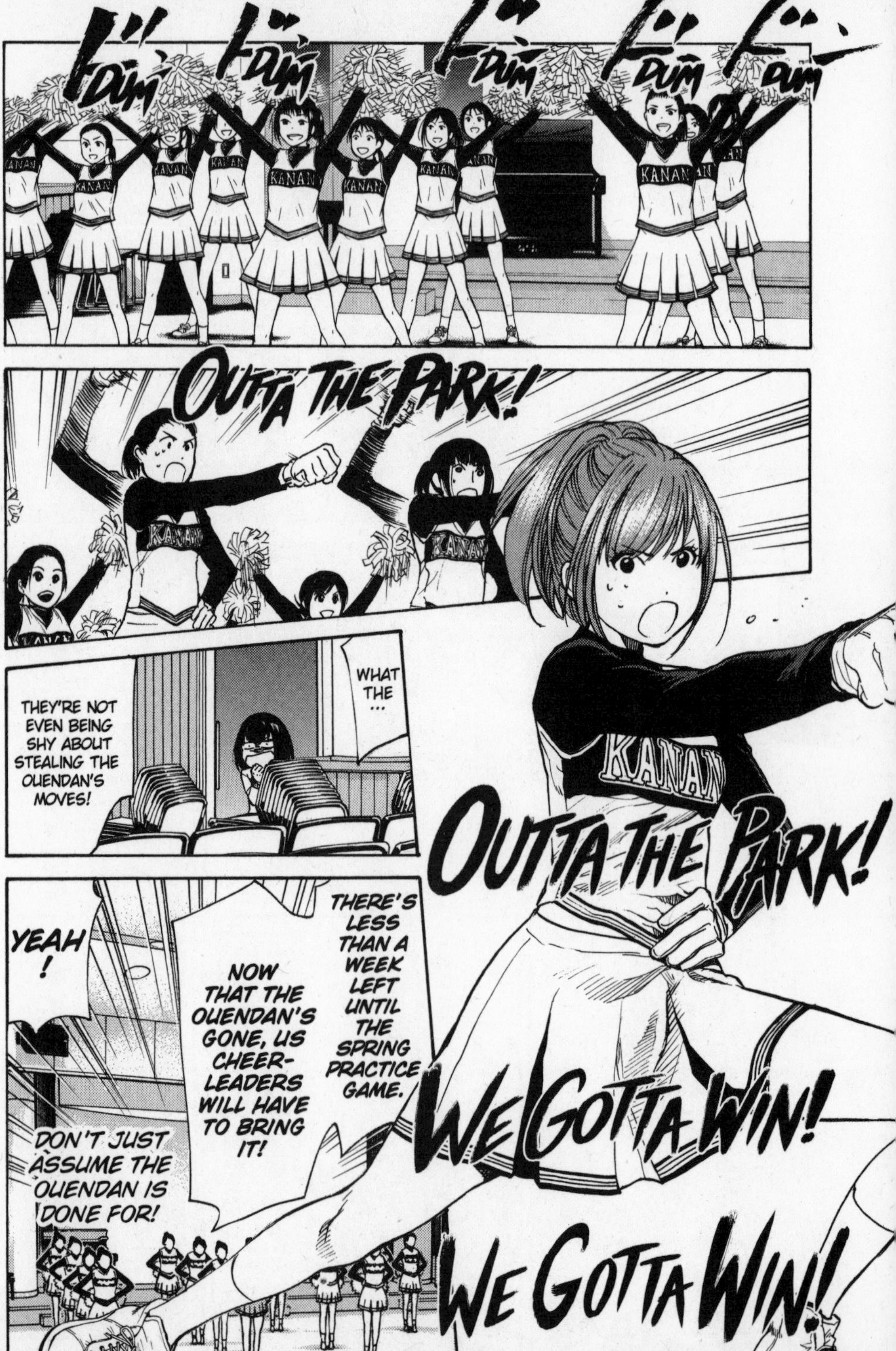
DUM
DUM
DUM
DUM
DUM
OUTTA THE PARK!
OUTTA THE PARK!
WE GOTTA WIN!
WE GOTTA WIN!
WHAT THE ...
THEY'RE NOT EVEN BEING SHY ABOUT STEALING THE OUENDAN'S MOVES!
THERE'S LESS THAN A WEEK LEFT UNTIL THE SPRING PRACTICE GAME.
NOW THAT THE OUENDAN'S GONE, US CHEER-LEADERS WILL HAVE TO BRING IT!
YEAH!
DON'T JUST ASSUME THE OUENDAN IS DONE FOR!

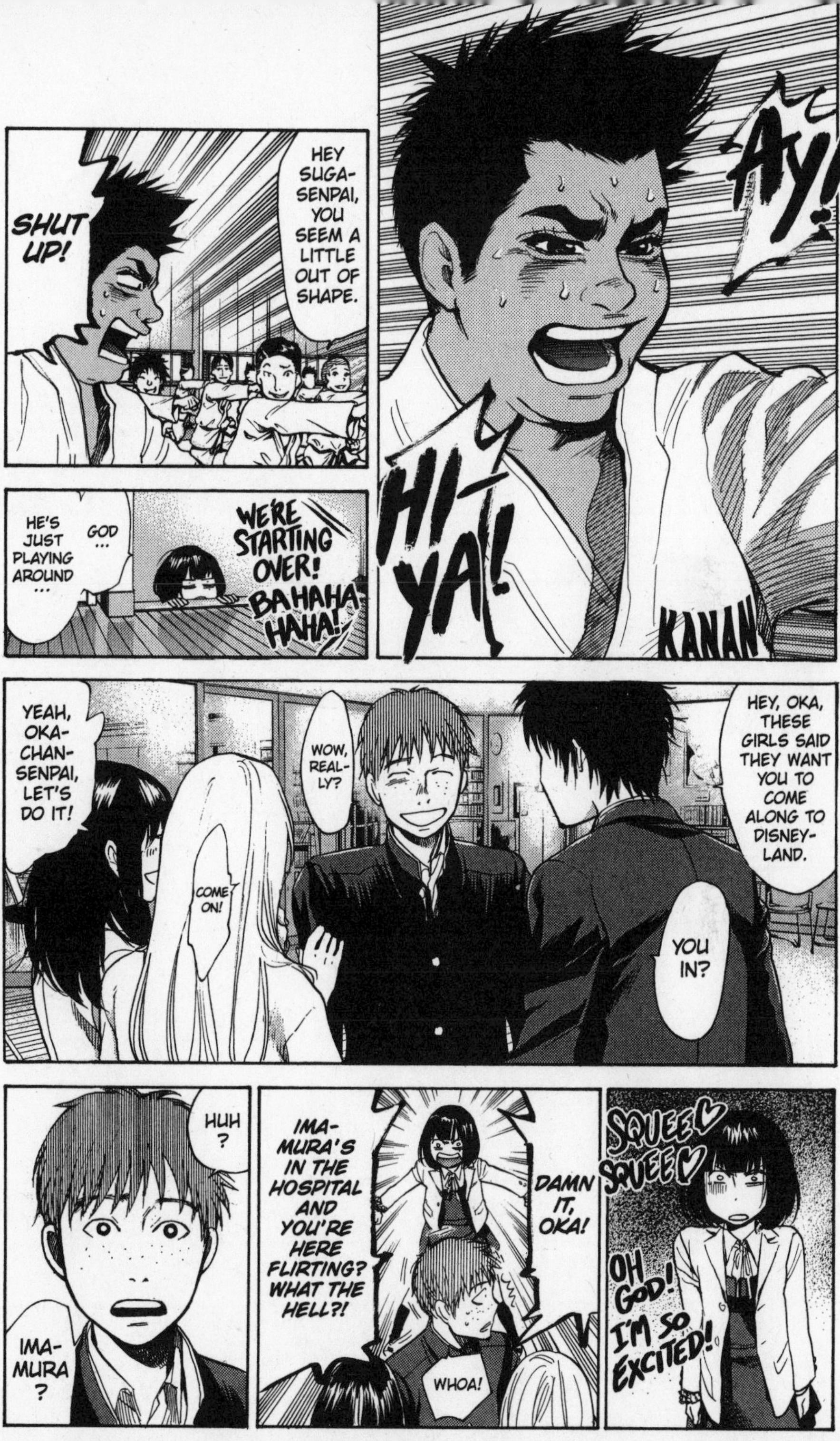
AY!
HI-YA!
KANAN
HEY SUGA-SENPAI, YOU SEEM A LITTLE OUT OF SHAPE.
SHUT UP!
WE'RE STARTING OVER! BAHAHA HAHA!
GOD ...
HE'S JUST PLAYING AROUND ...
HEY, OKA, THESE GIRLS SAID THEY WANT YOU TO COME ALONG TO DISNEY-LAND.
YOU IN?
WOW, REAL-LY?
COME ON!
YEAH, OKA-CHAN-SENPAI, LET'S DO IT!
SQUEE♡ SQUEE♡
OH GOD! I'M SO EXCITED!
DAMN IT, OKA!
IMA-MURA'S IN THE HOSPITAL AND YOU'RE HERE FLIRTING? WHAT THE HELL?!
WHOA!
HUH?
IMA-MURA?

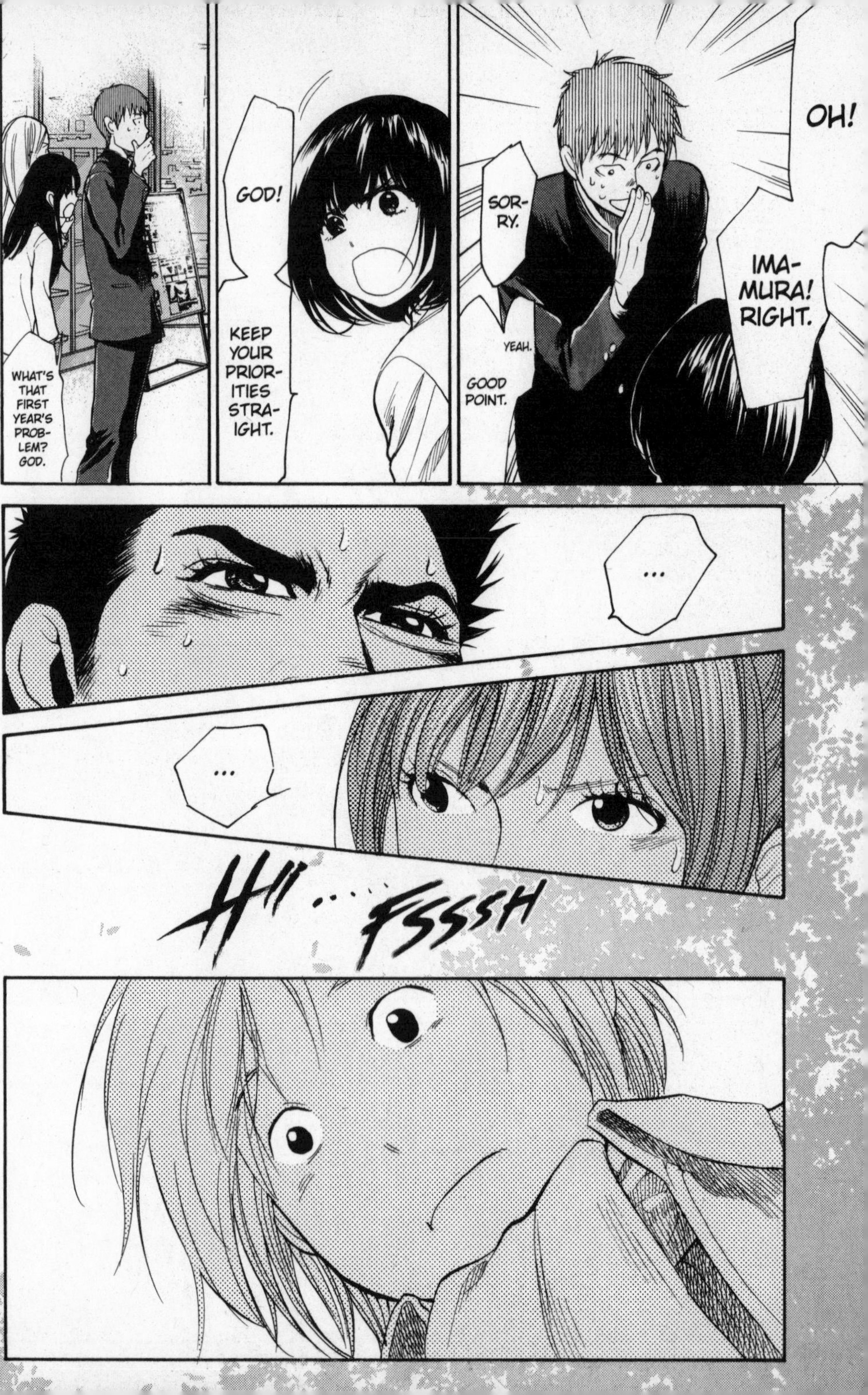
OH!
IMA-MURA! RIGHT.
SOR-RY.
YEAH.
GOOD POINT.
GOD!
KEEP YOUR PRIORI-TIES STRA-IGHT.
WHAT'S THAT FIRST YEAR'S PROB-LEM? GOD.
...
...
HII..... FSSSH

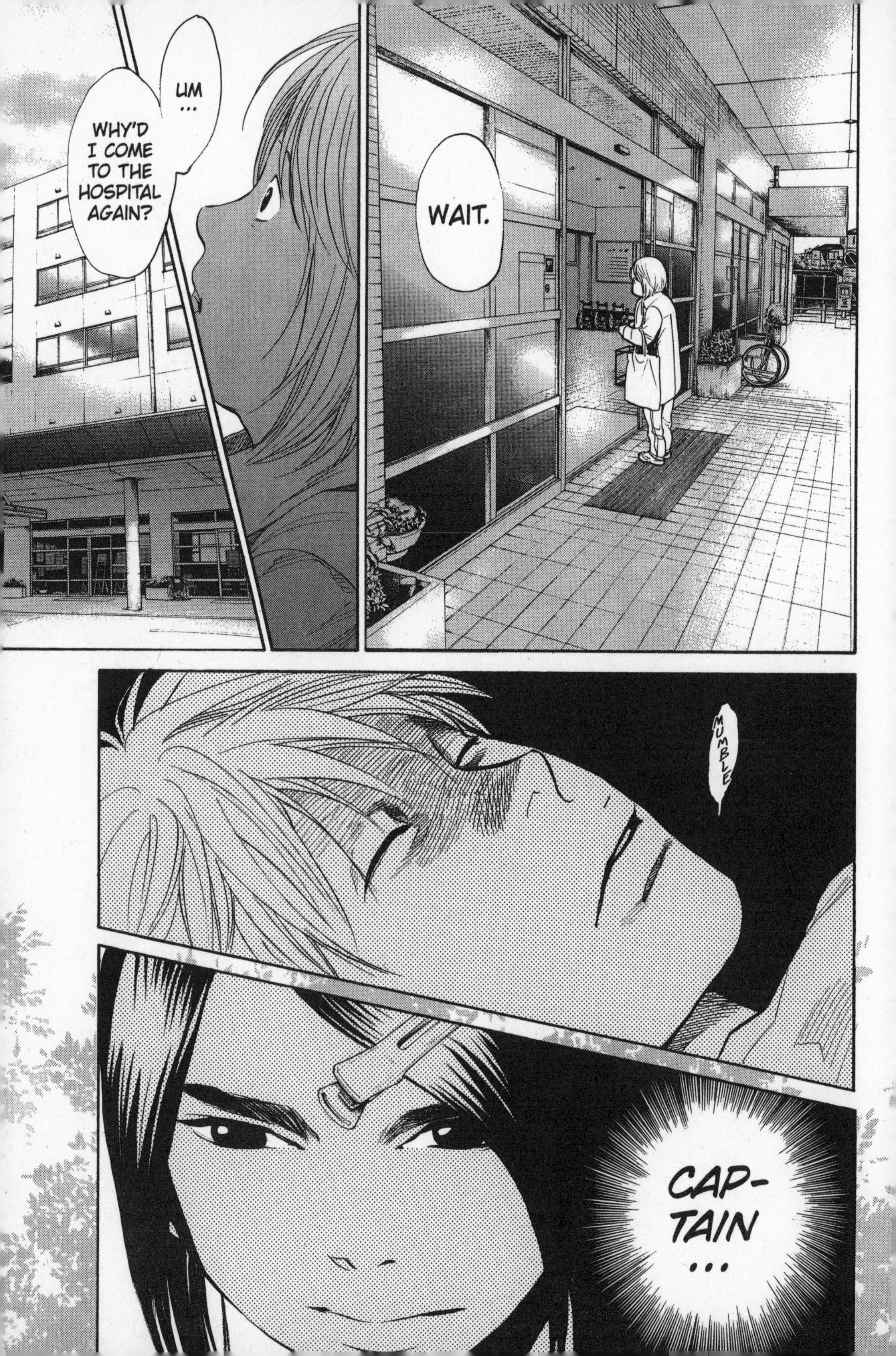
WAIT.
UM ...
WHY'D I COME TO THE HOSPITAL AGAIN?
MUMBLE
CAP-TAIN ...

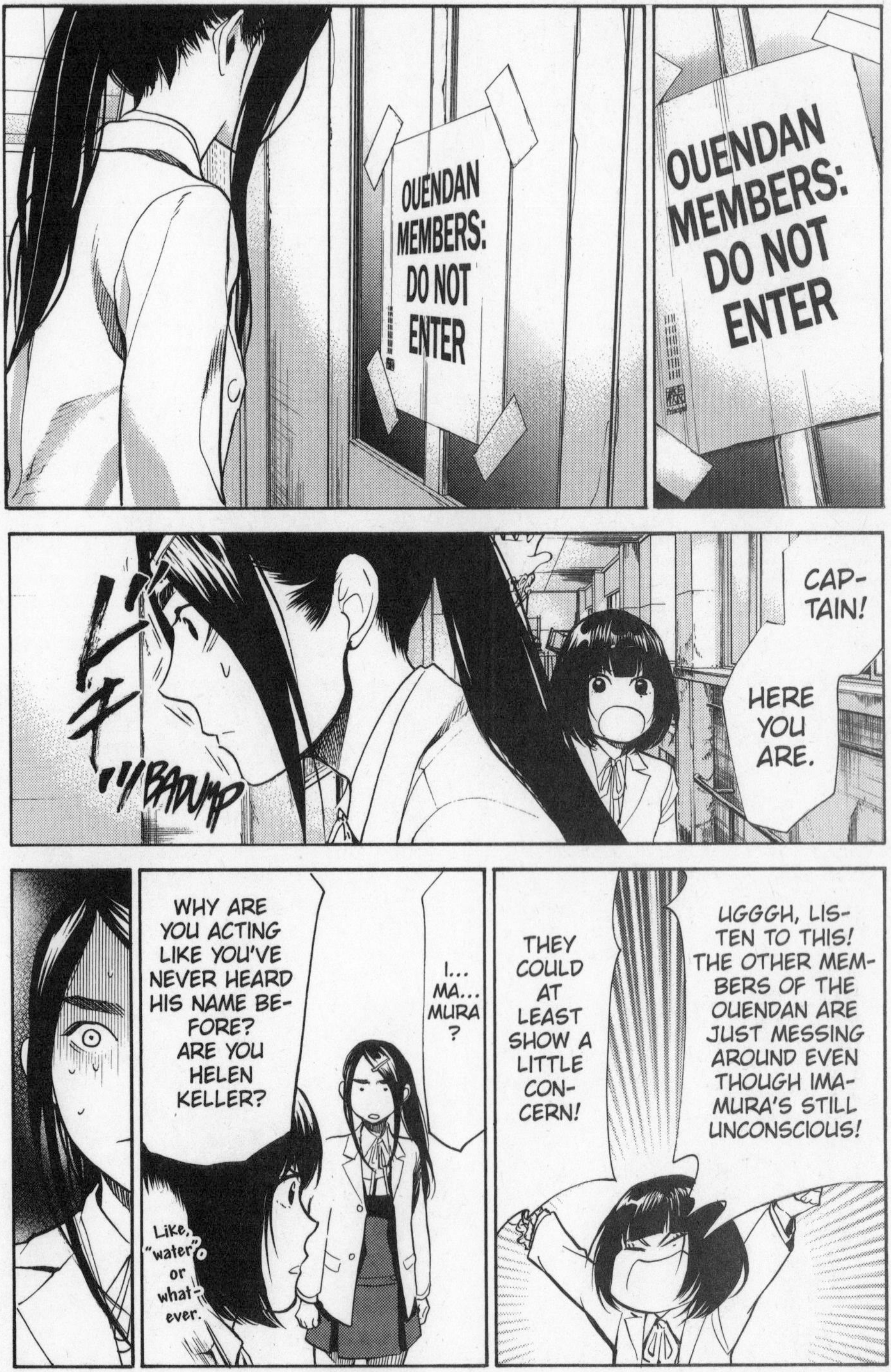
OUENDAN MEMBERS: DO NOT ENTER
OUENDAN MEMBERS: DO NOT ENTER
CAP-TAIN!
HERE YOU ARE.
BADUMP
UGGGH, LIS-TEN TO THIS! THE OTHER MEM-BERS OF THE OUENDAN ARE JUST MESSING AROUND EVEN THOUGH IMA-MURA'S STILL UNCONSCIOUS!
THEY COULD AT LEAST SHOW A LITTLE CON-CERN!
I... MA... MURA?
WHY ARE YOU ACTING LIKE YOU'VE NEVER HEARD HIS NAME BE-FORE? ARE YOU HELEN KELLER?
Like, "water" or what-ever.

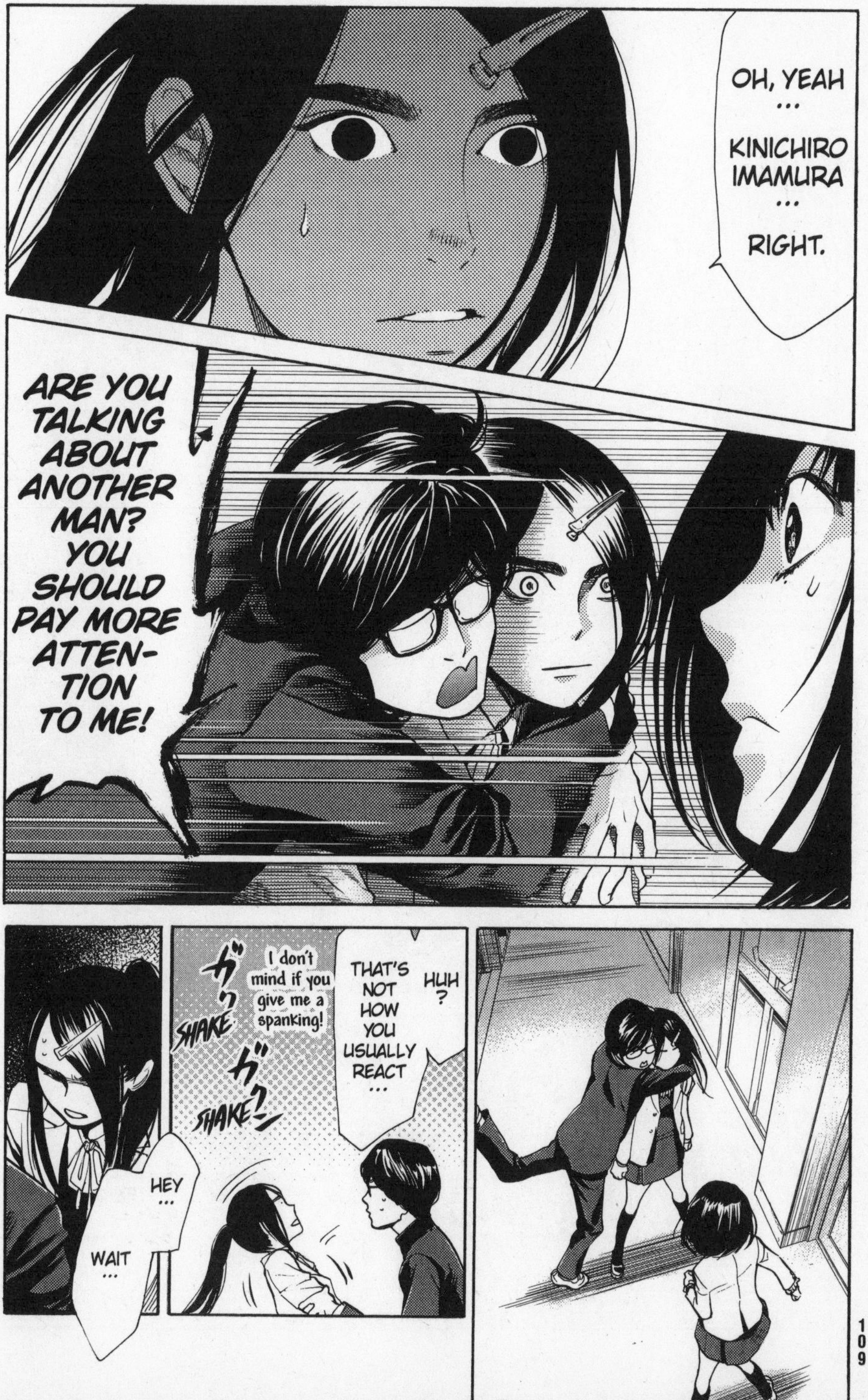
OH, YEAH ... KINICHIRO IMAMURA ... RIGHT.
ARE YOU TALKING ABOUT ANOTHER MAN? YOU SHOULD PAY MORE ATTEN-TION TO ME!
HUH?
THAT'S NOT HOW YOU USUALLY REACT ...
I don't mind if you give me a spanking!
SHAKE
SHAKE
HEY ...
WAIT ...

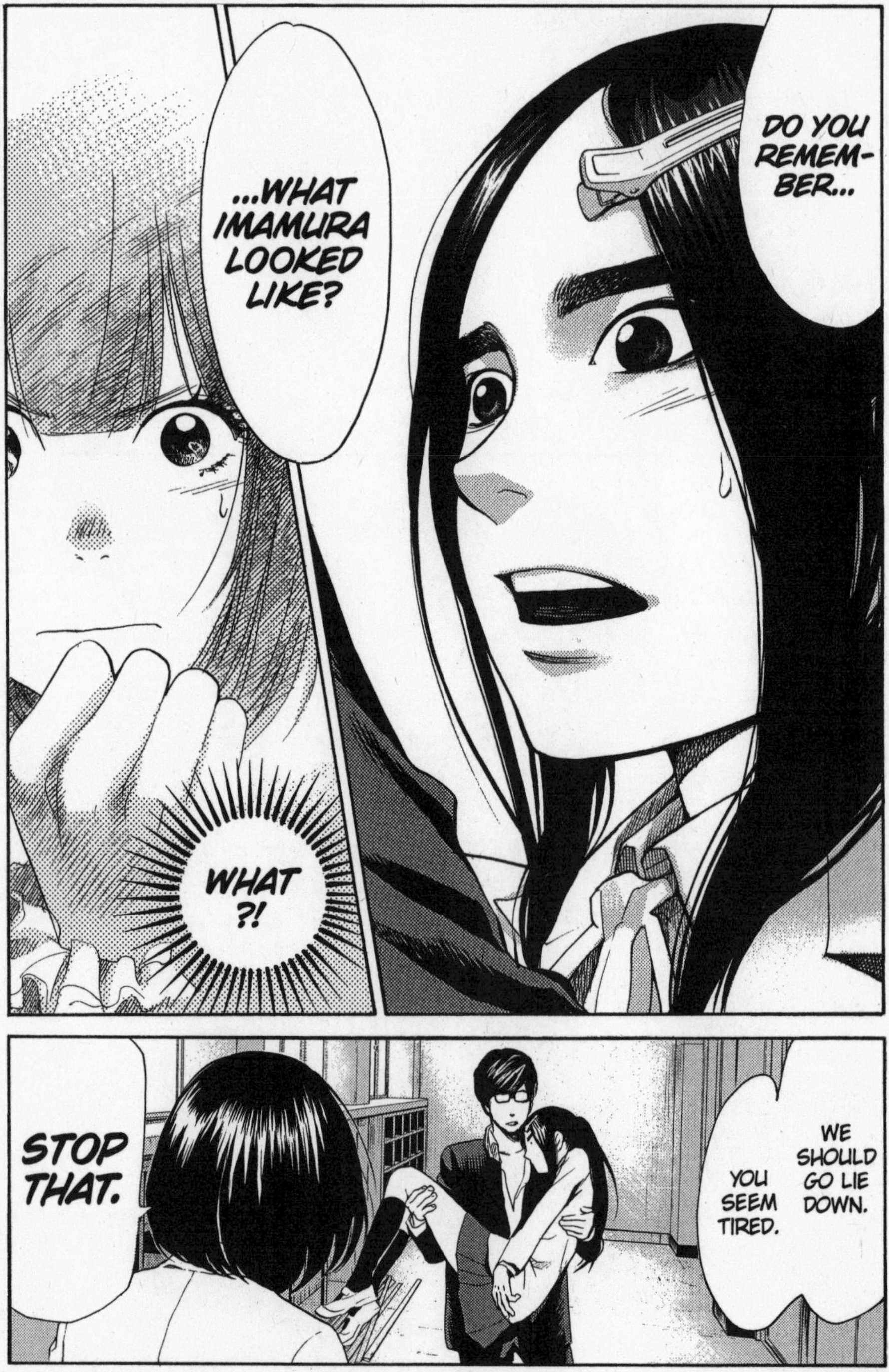
DO YOU REMEMBER...
...WHAT IMAMURA LOOKED LIKE?
WHAT?!
WE SHOULD GO LIE DOWN.
YOU SEEM TIRED.
STOP THAT.

37. I MISS YOU WHEN YOU'RE GONE

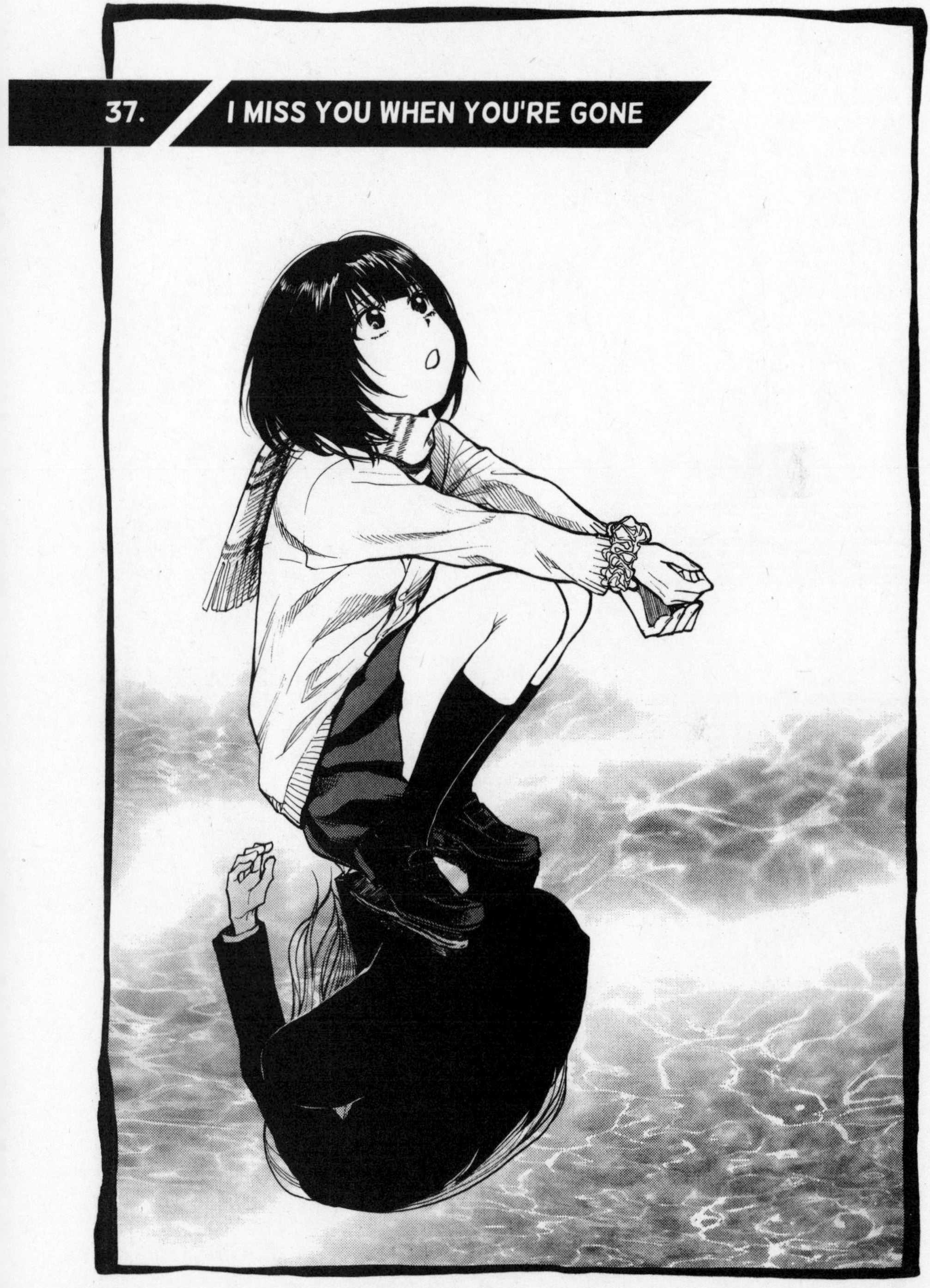

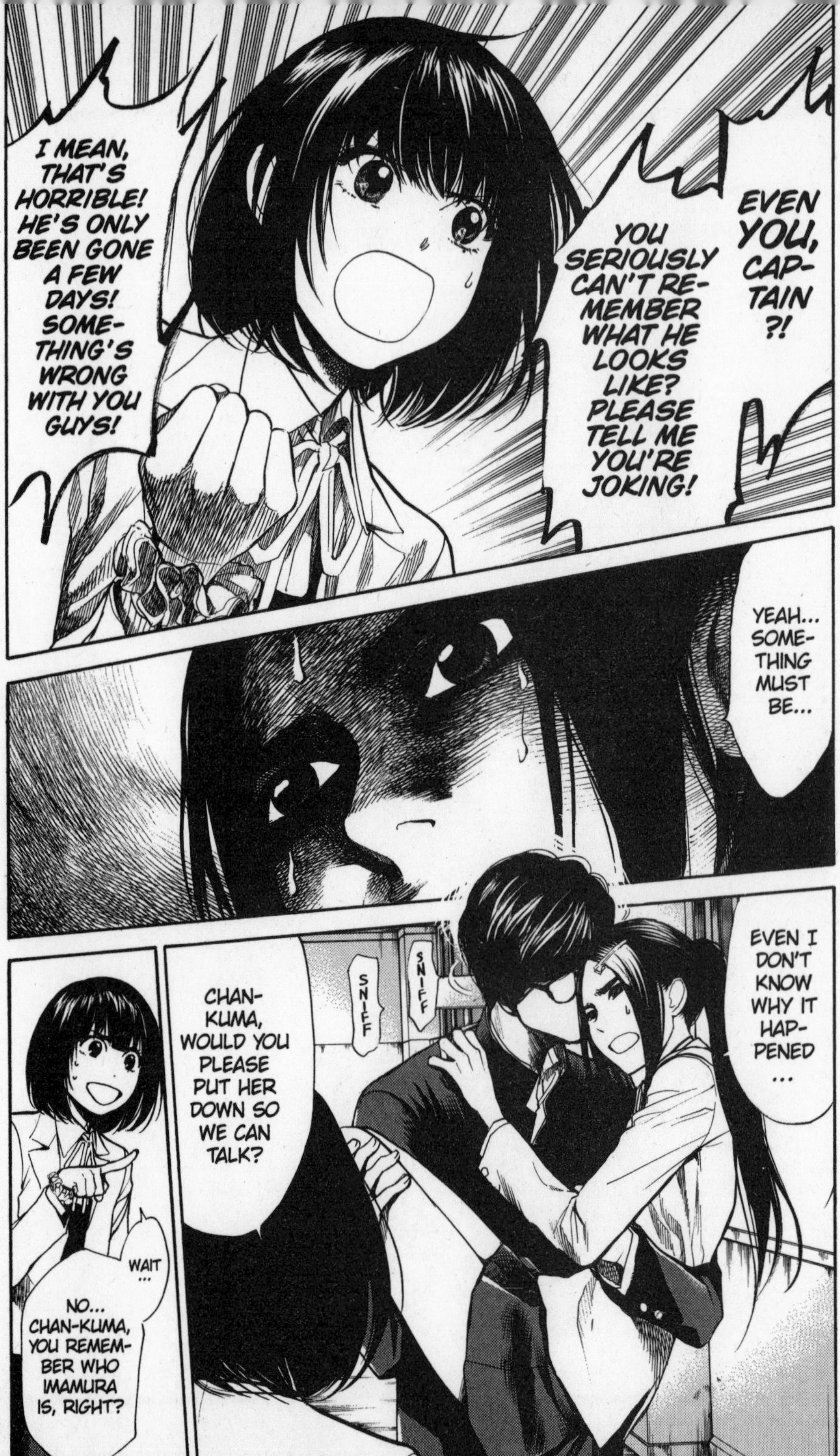
EVEN YOU, CAPTAIN?!
YOU SERIOUSLY CAN'T REMEMBER WHAT HE LOOKS LIKE? PLEASE TELL ME YOU'RE JOKING!
I MEAN, THAT'S HORRIBLE! HE'S ONLY BEEN GONE A FEW DAYS! SOMETHING'S WRONG WITH YOU GUYS!
YEAH... SOMETHING MUST BE...
EVEN I DON'T KNOW WHY IT HAPPENED...
SNIFF
SNIFF
CHAN-KUMA, WOULD YOU PLEASE PUT HER DOWN SO WE CAN TALK?
WAIT...
NO... CHAN-KUMA, YOU REMEMBER WHO IMAMURA IS, RIGHT?

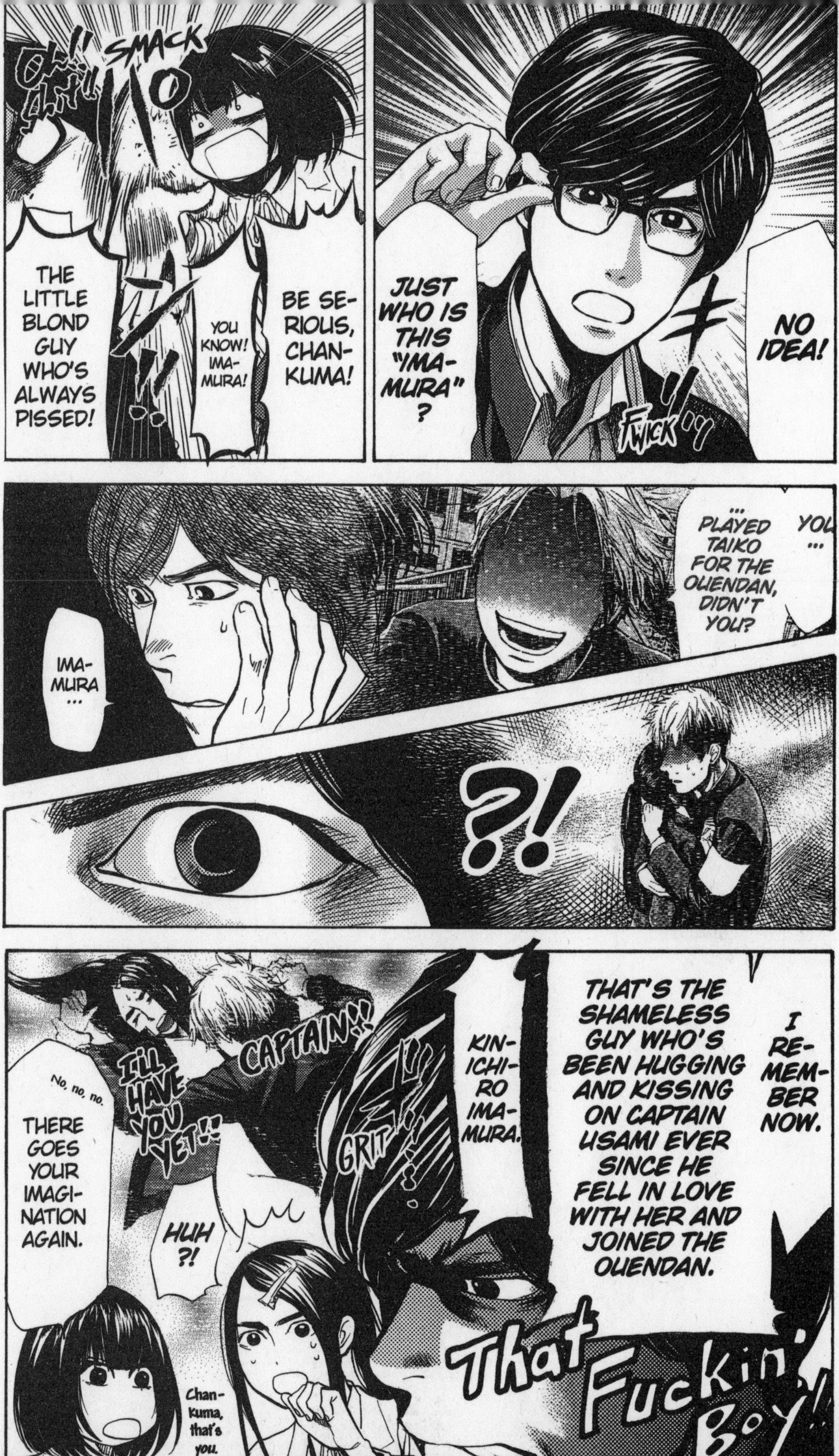
NO IDEA!
JUST WHO IS THIS "IMA-MURA"?
FWICK
SMACK
BE SE-RIOUS, CHAN-KUMA!
YOU KNOW! IMA-MURA!
THE LITTLE BLOND GUY WHO'S ALWAYS PISSED!
YOU...
...PLAYED TAIKO FOR THE OUENDAN, DIDN'T YOU?
IMA-MURA...
?!
I RE-MEM-BER NOW.
THAT'S THE SHAMELESS GUY WHO'S BEEN HUGGING AND KISSING ON CAPTAIN USAMI EVER SINCE HE FELL IN LOVE WITH HER AND JOINED THE OUENDAN.
KIN-ICHI-RO IMA-MURA.
GRIT
CAPTAIN!!
I'LL HAVE YOU YET!!
No, no, no.
THERE GOES YOUR IMAGI-NATION AGAIN.
HUH?!
That Fuckin' Boy!
Chan-kuma, that's you.

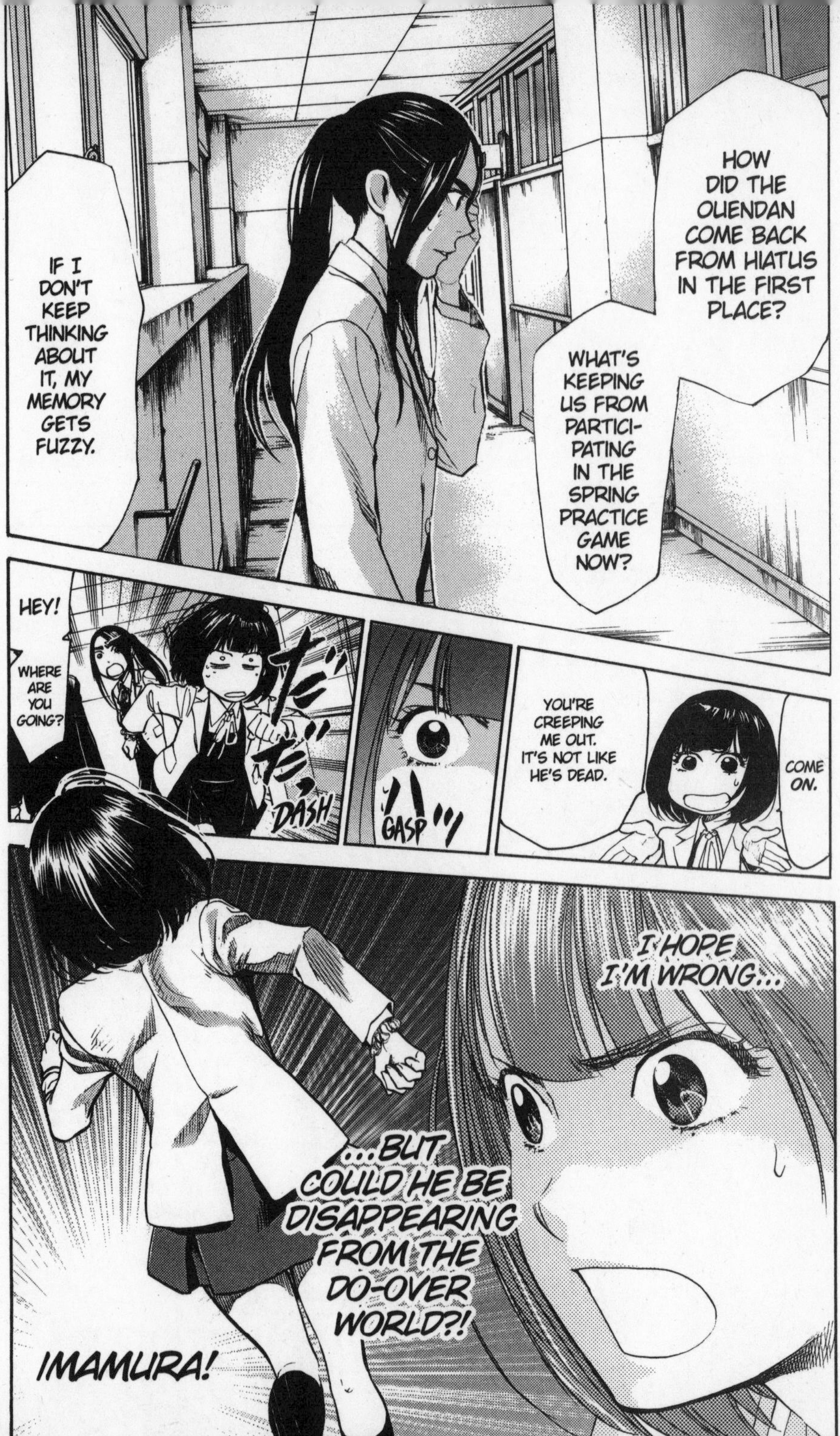
HOW DID THE OUENDAN COME BACK FROM HIATUS IN THE FIRST PLACE?
WHAT'S KEEPING US FROM PARTICI-PATING IN THE SPRING PRACTICE GAME NOW?
IF I DON'T KEEP THINKING ABOUT IT, MY MEMORY GETS FUZZY.
COME ON.
YOU'RE CREEPING ME OUT. IT'S NOT LIKE HE'S DEAD.
GASP
DASH
HEY!
WHERE ARE YOU GOING?
I HOPE I'M WRONG...
...BUT COULD HE BE DISAPPEARING FROM THE DO-OVER WORLD?!
IMAMURA!

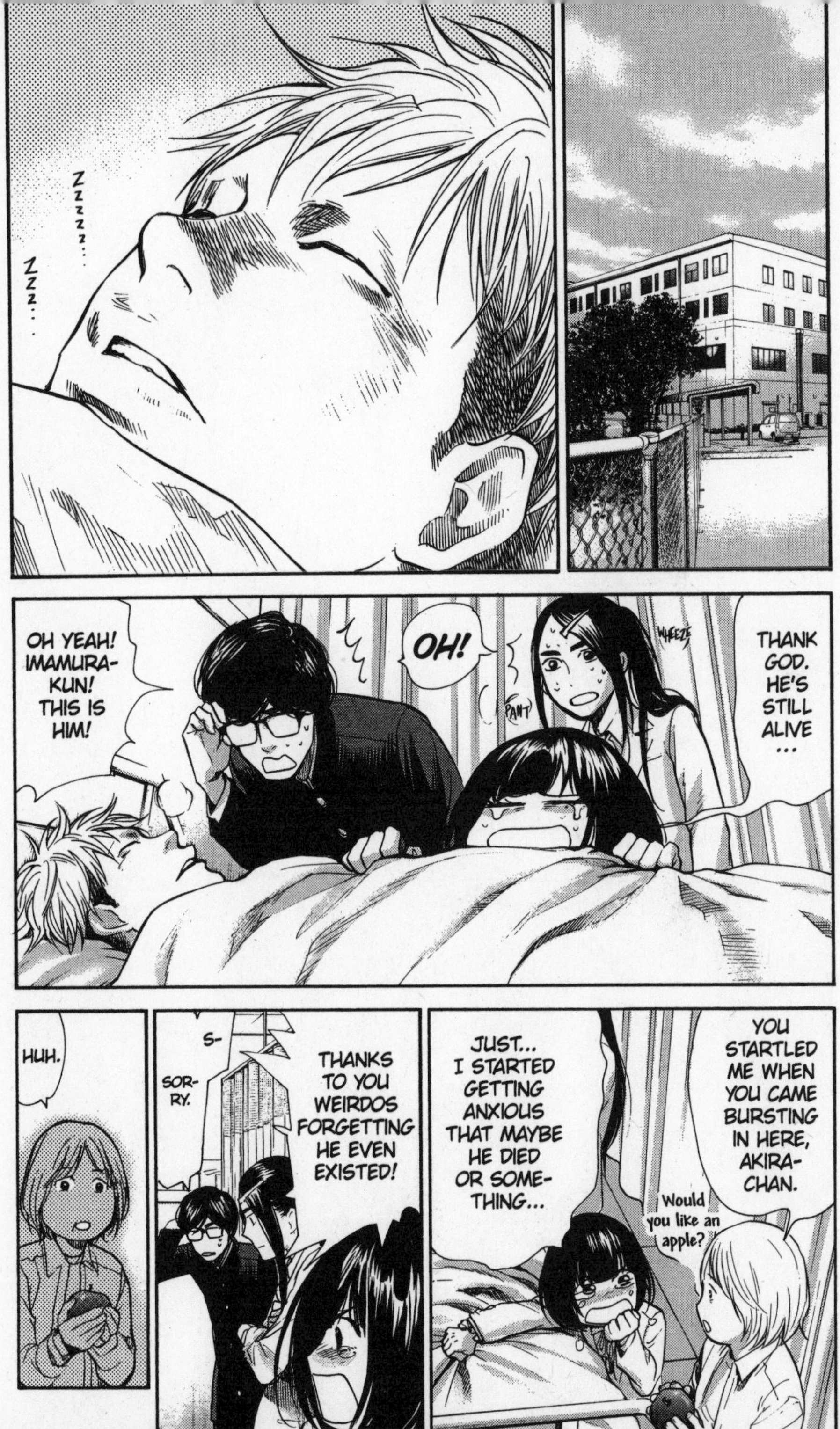

ZZZZZ...
ZZZ...
THANK GOD. HE'S STILL ALIVE...
WHEEZE
PANT
OH!
OH YEAH! IMAMURA-KUN! THIS IS HIM!
YOU STARTLED ME WHEN YOU CAME BURSTING IN HERE, AKIRA-CHAN.
Would you like an apple?
JUST... I STARTED GETTING ANXIOUS THAT MAYBE HE DIED OR SOME-THING...
THANKS TO YOU WEIRDOS FORGETTING HE EVEN EXISTED!
S- SOR-RY.
HUH.

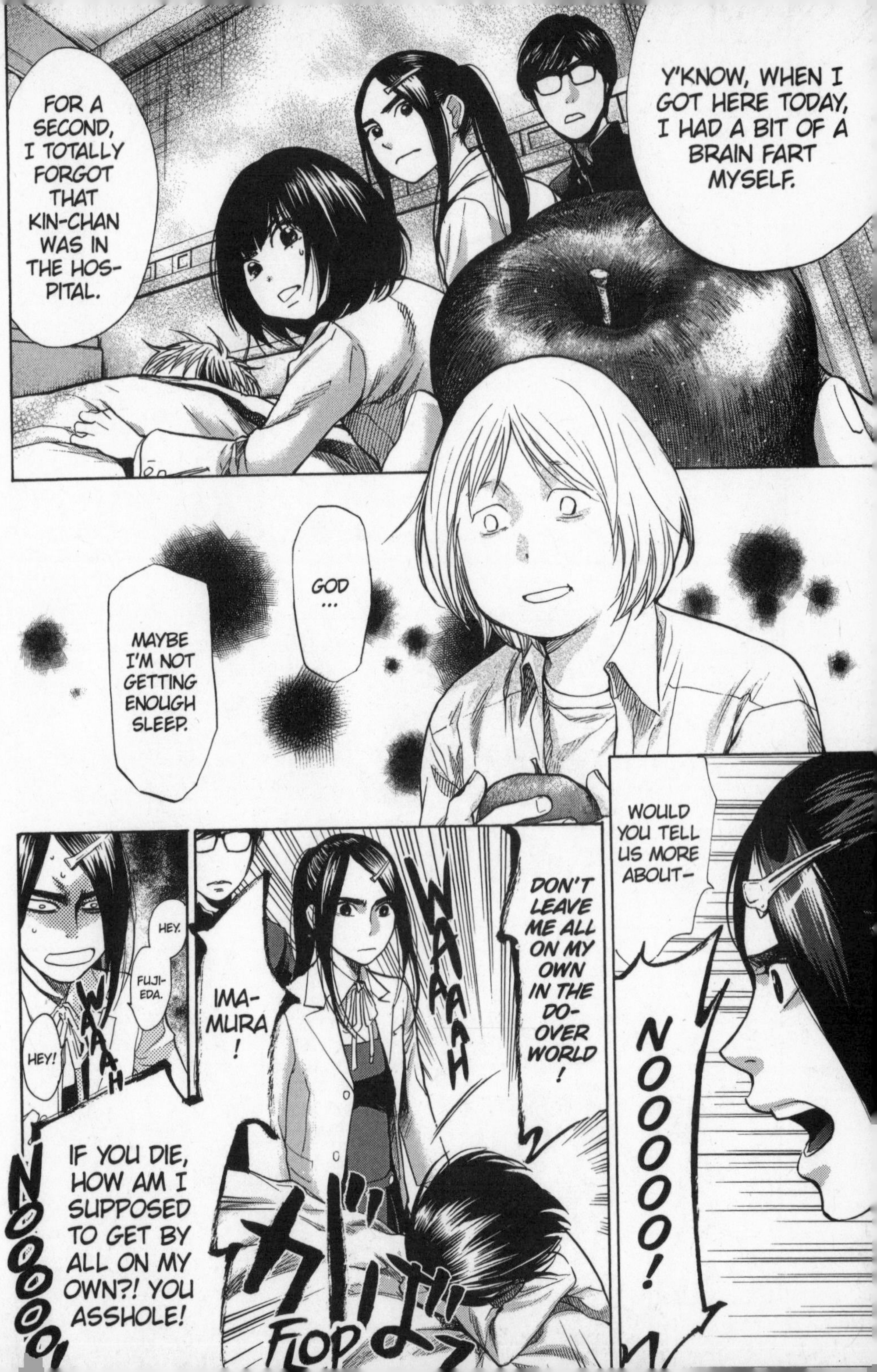

Y'KNOW, WHEN I GOT HERE TODAY, I HAD A BIT OF A BRAIN FART MYSELF.
FOR A SECOND, I TOTALLY FORGOT THAT KIN-CHAN WAS IN THE HOS-PITAL.
GOD ...
MAYBE I'M NOT GETTING ENOUGH SLEEP.
WOULD YOU TELL US MORE ABOUT–
NOOOOOO!
DON'T LEAVE ME ALL ON MY OWN IN THE DO-OVER WORLD!
WAAAAH
IMA-MURA!
HEY.
FUJI-EDA.
HEY!
WAAAAH
NOOOOOO
IF YOU DIE, HOW AM I SUPPOSED TO GET BY ALL ON MY OWN?! YOU ASSHOLE!
FLOP

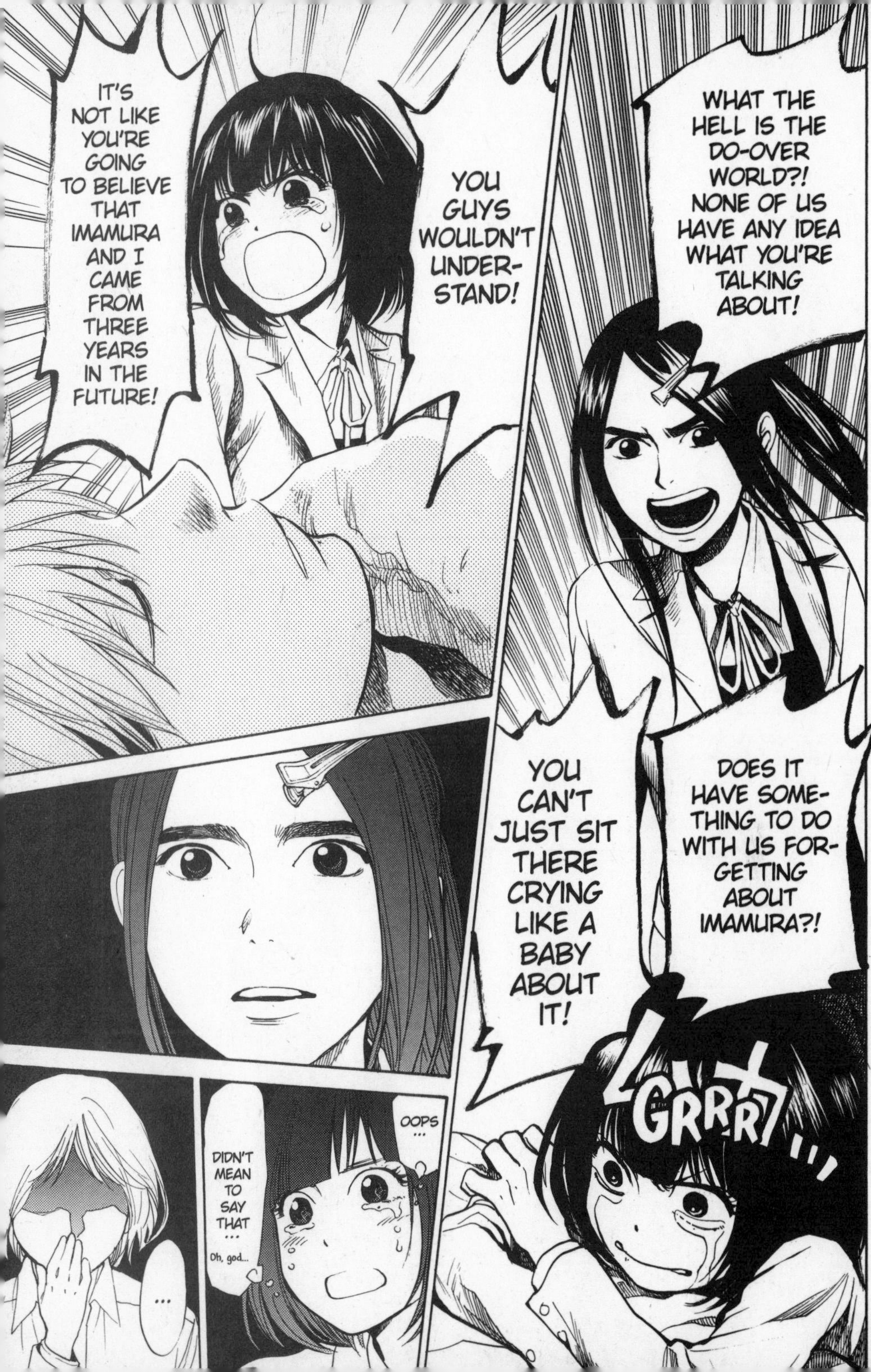

WHAT THE HELL IS THE DO-OVER WORLD?! NONE OF US HAVE ANY IDEA WHAT YOU'RE TALKING ABOUT!
DOES IT HAVE SOME-THING TO DO WITH US FOR-GETTING ABOUT IMAMURA?!
YOU CAN'T JUST SIT THERE CRYING LIKE A BABY ABOUT IT!
GRRR...!
YOU GUYS WOULDN'T UNDER-STAND!
IT'S NOT LIKE YOU'RE GOING TO BELIEVE THAT IMAMURA AND I CAME FROM THREE YEARS IN THE FUTURE!
OOPS...
DIDN'T MEAN TO SAY THAT...
Oh, god...
...

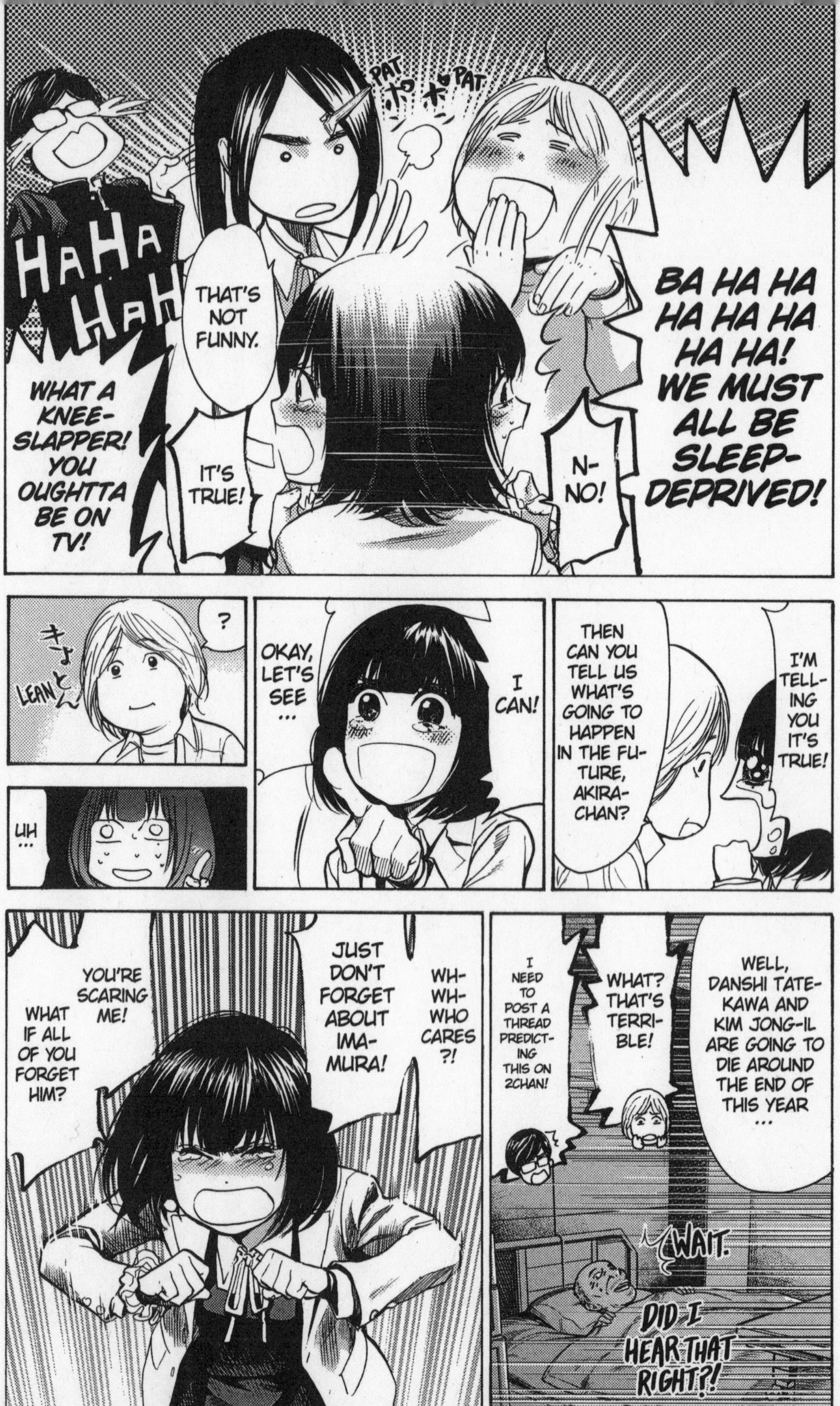

PAT PAT
BA HA HA HA HA HA HA HA! WE MUST ALL BE SLEEP-DEPRIVED!
N-NO!
THAT'S NOT FUNNY.
IT'S TRUE!
HAHAHAH
WHAT A KNEE-SLAPPER! YOU OUGHTTA BE ON TV!
I'M TELLING YOU IT'S TRUE!
THEN CAN YOU TELL US WHAT'S GOING TO HAPPEN IN THE FUTURE, AKIRA-CHAN?
I CAN!
OKAY, LET'S SEE ...
?
LEAN
UH ...
WELL, DANSHI TATEKAWA AND KIM JONG-IL ARE GOING TO DIE AROUND THE END OF THIS YEAR ...
WHAT? THAT'S TERRIBLE!
I NEED TO POST A THREAD PREDICTING THIS ON 2CHAN!
WAIT.
DID I HEAR THAT RIGHT?!
WH-WH-WHO CARES?!
JUST DON'T FORGET ABOUT IMAMURA!
YOU'RE SCARING ME!
WHAT IF ALL OF YOU FORGET HIM?

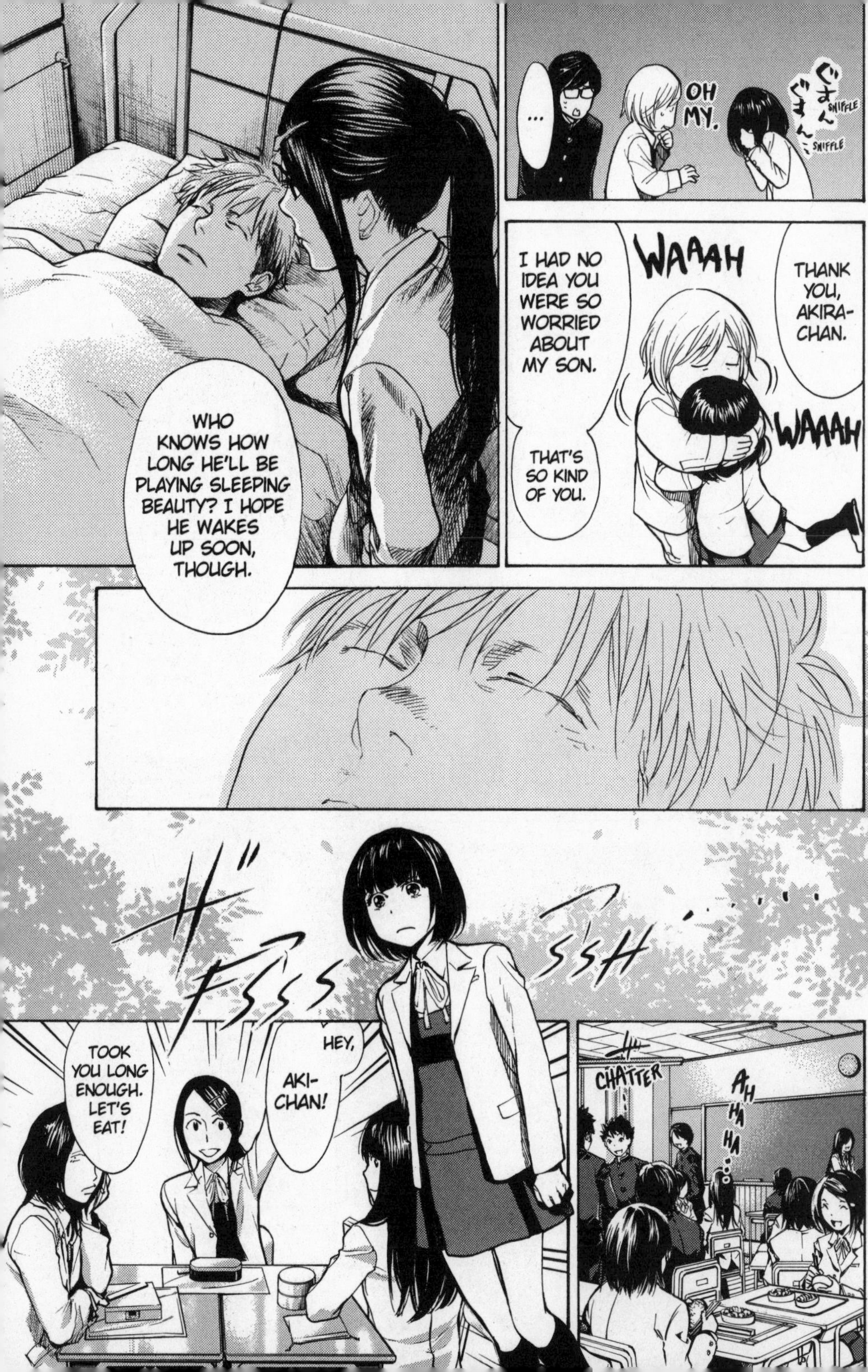

ぐすん ぐすん
SNIFFLE
SNIFFLE
OH MY.
...
THANK YOU, AKIRA-CHAN.
WAAAH
I HAD NO IDEA YOU WERE SO WORRIED ABOUT MY SON.
WAAAH
THAT'S SO KIND OF YOU.
WHO KNOWS HOW LONG HE'LL BE PLAYING SLEEPING BEAUTY? I HOPE HE WAKES UP SOON, THOUGH.
ザッ
FSSS
SSH
...
CHATTER
AHAHAHA...
HEY,
AKI-CHAN!
TOOK YOU LONG ENOUGH. LET'S EAT!

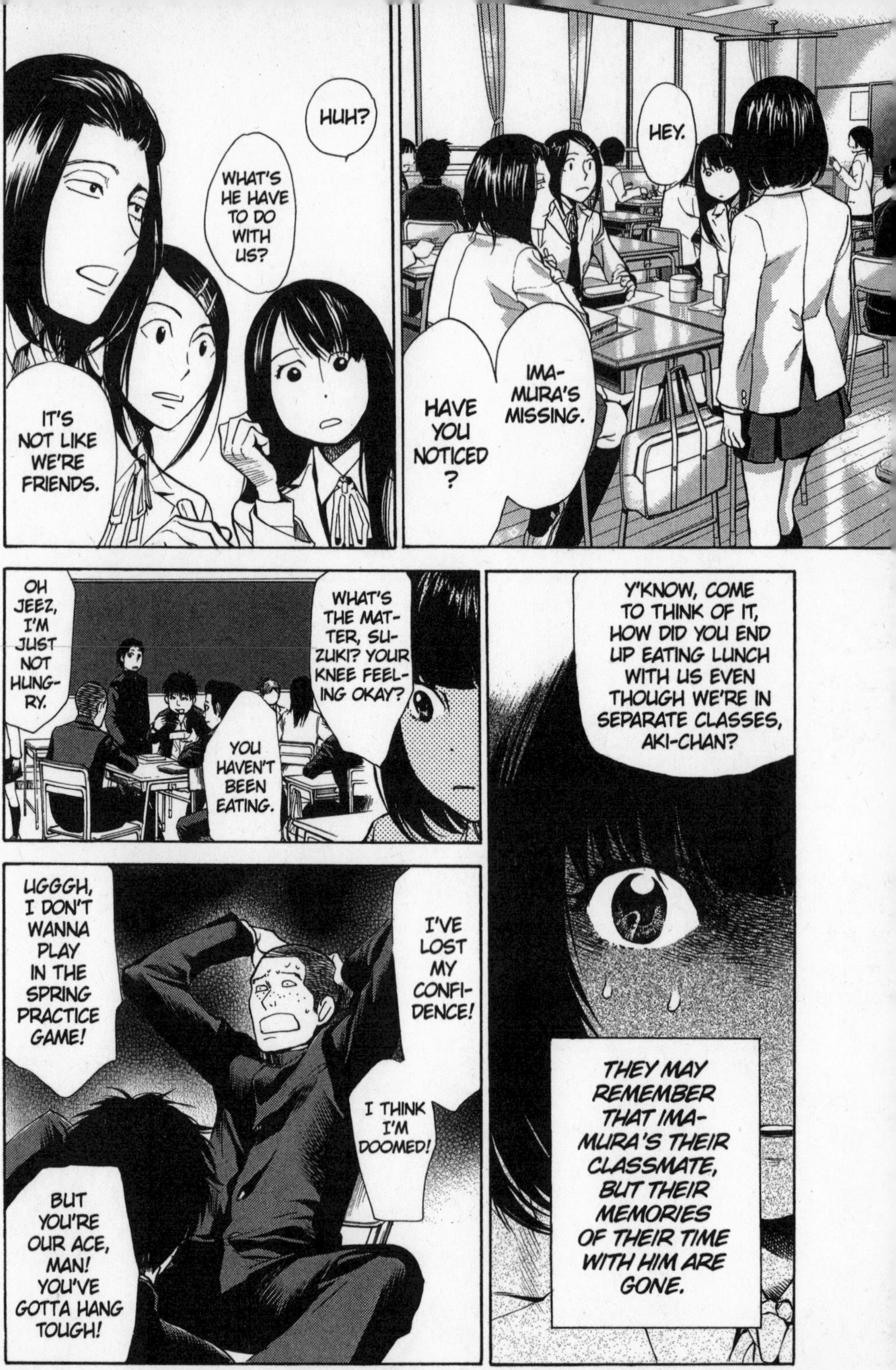
HEY.
IMA-MURA'S MISSING.
HAVE YOU NOTICED?
HUH?
WHAT'S HE HAVE TO DO WITH US?
IT'S NOT LIKE WE'RE FRIENDS.
Y'KNOW, COME TO THINK OF IT, HOW DID YOU END UP EATING LUNCH WITH US EVEN THOUGH WE'RE IN SEPARATE CLASSES, AKI-CHAN?
THEY MAY REMEMBER THAT IMA-MURA'S THEIR CLASSMATE, BUT THEIR MEMORIES OF THEIR TIME WITH HIM ARE GONE.
WHAT'S THE MAT-TER, SU-ZUKI? YOUR KNEE FEEL-ING OKAY?
YOU HAVEN'T BEEN EATING.
OH JEEZ, I'M JUST NOT HUNG-RY.
I'VE LOST MY CONFI-DENCE!
UGGGH, I DON'T WANNA PLAY IN THE SPRING PRACTICE GAME!
I THINK I'M DOOMED!
BUT YOU'RE OUR ACE, MAN! YOU'VE GOTTA HANG TOUGH!

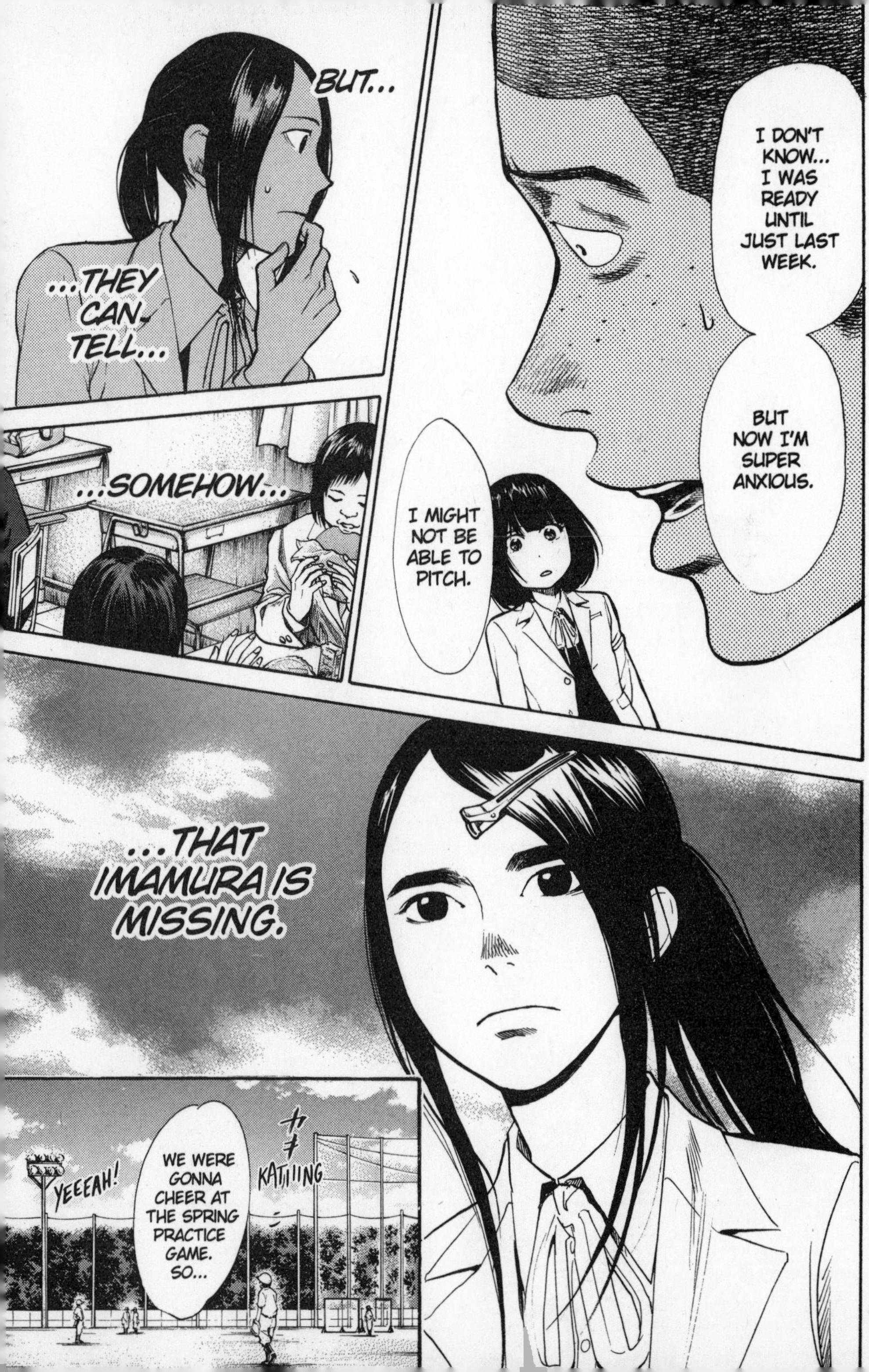
I DON'T KNOW... I WAS READY UNTIL JUST LAST WEEK.
BUT NOW I'M SUPER ANXIOUS.
I MIGHT NOT BE ABLE TO PITCH.
BUT...
...THEY CAN TELL...
...SOMEHOW...
...THAT IMAMURA IS MISSING.
カキ
KATIIING
WE WERE GONNA CHEER AT THE SPRING PRACTICE GAME. SO...
YEEEAH!

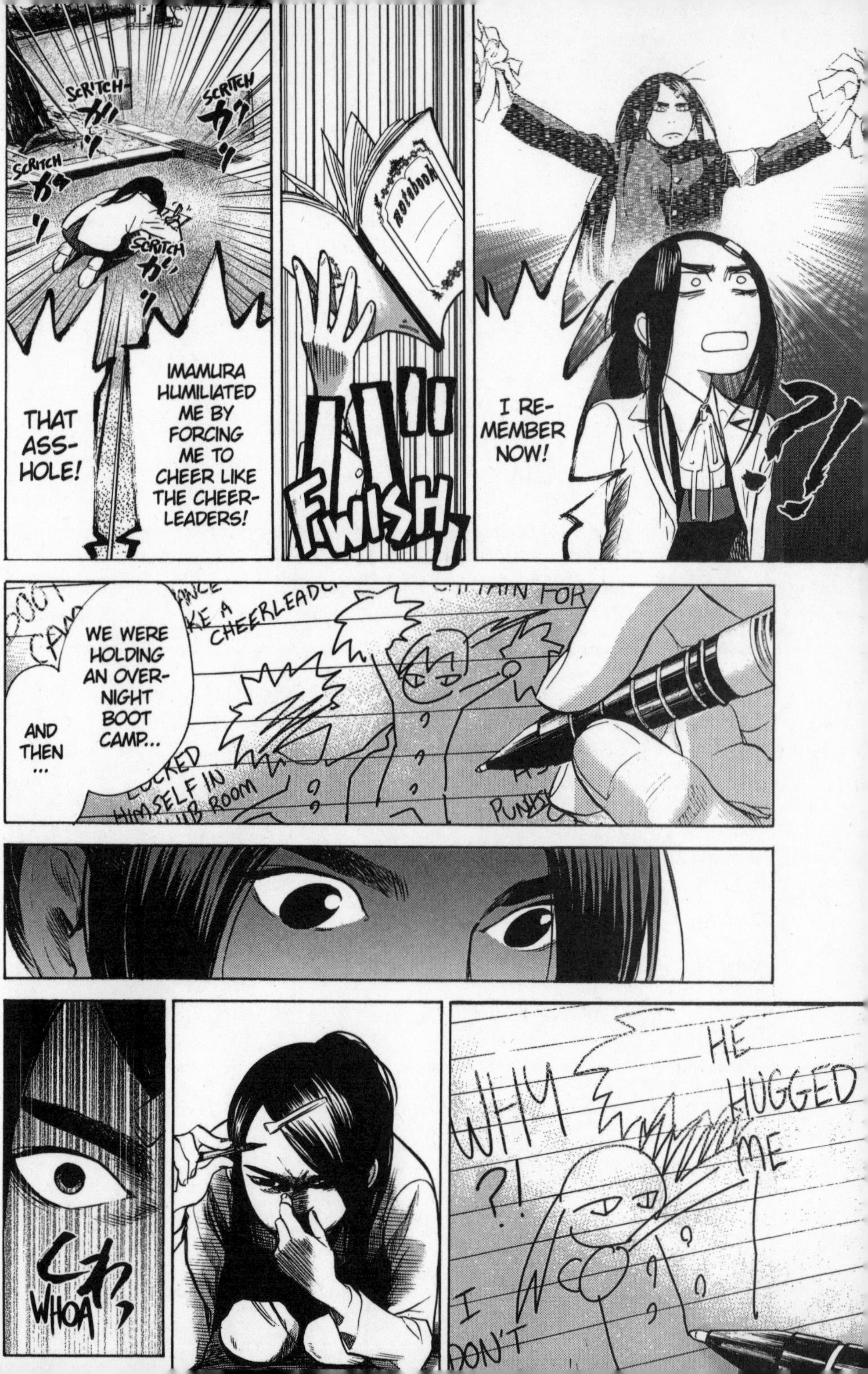
I RE-MEMBER NOW!
?!
FWISH
IMAMURA HUMILIATED ME BY FORCING ME TO CHEER LIKE THE CHEER-LEADERS!
THAT ASS-HOLE!
SCRITCH
SCRITCH
SCRITCH
SCRITCH
notebook
WE WERE HOLDING AN OVER-NIGHT BOOT CAMP...
AND THEN ...
LOCKED HIMSELF IN
HE HUGGED ME
WHY ?!
I DON'T
WHOA

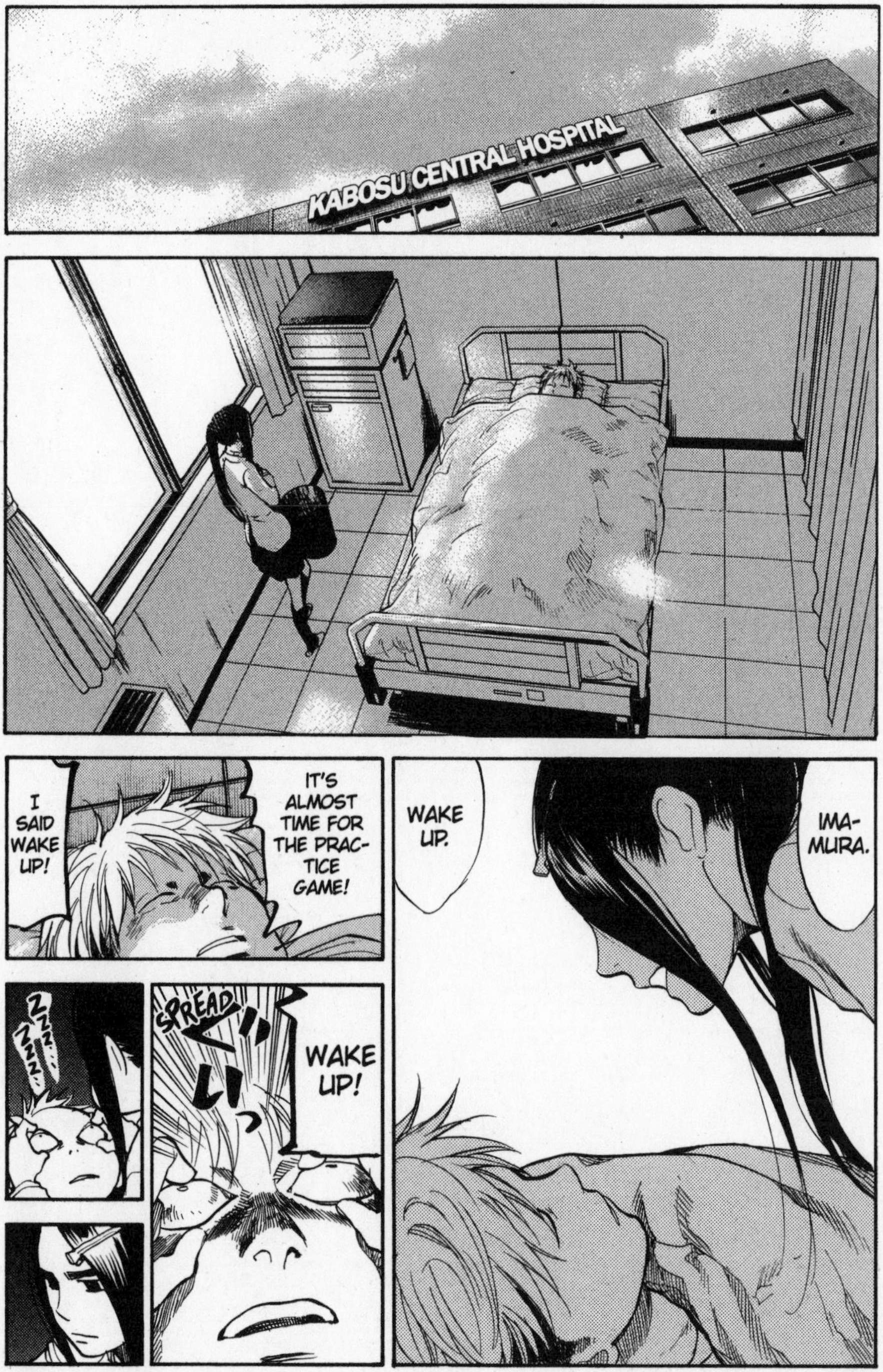
KABOSU CENTRAL HOSPITAL
IMA-MURA.
WAKE UP.
IT'S ALMOST TIME FOR THE PRAC-TICE GAME!
I SAID WAKE UP!
WAKE UP!
SPREAD
ZZZ...
ZZZ...

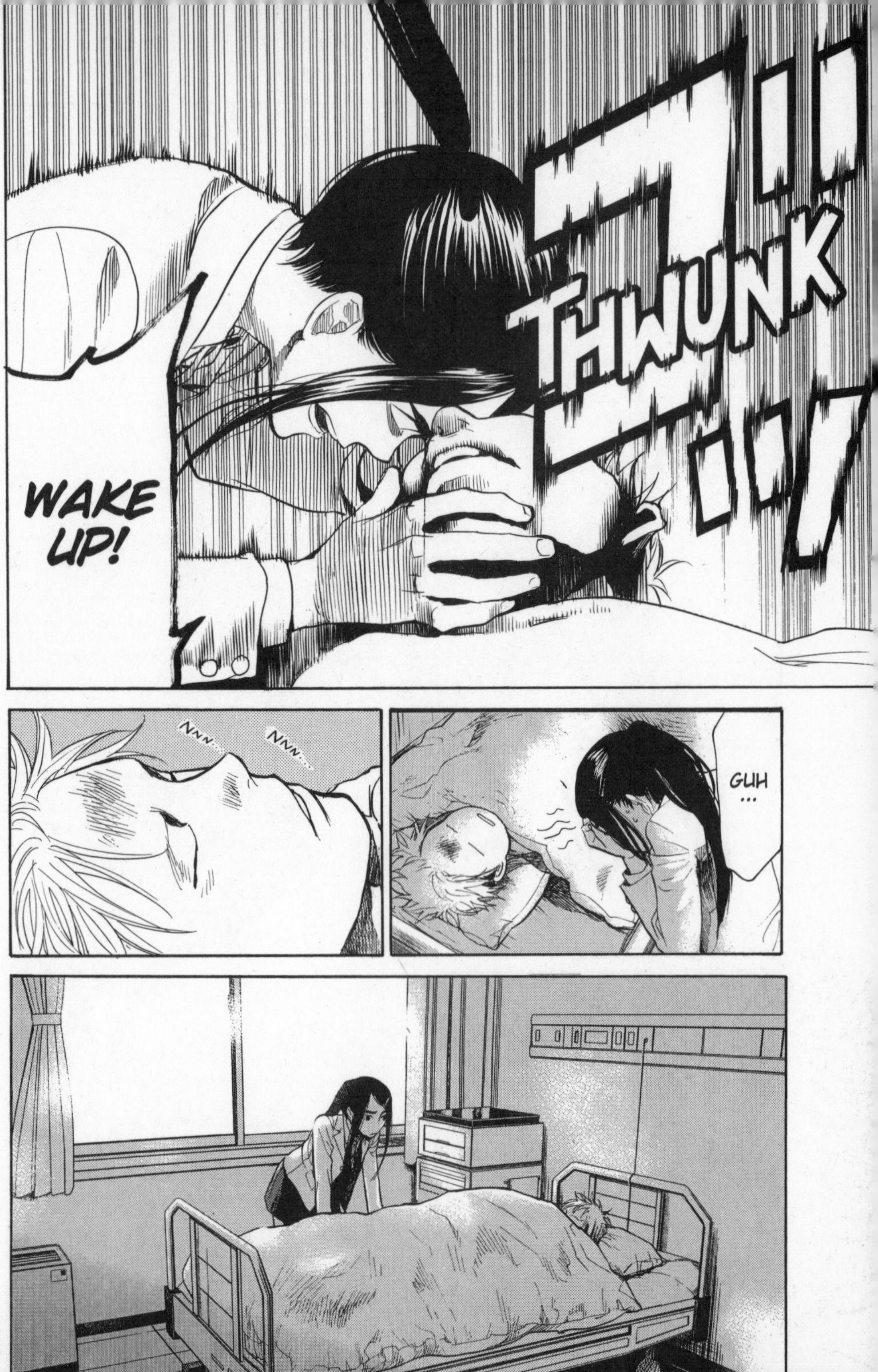
THWUNK
WAKE UP!
GUH ...
Nnn...
Nnn...

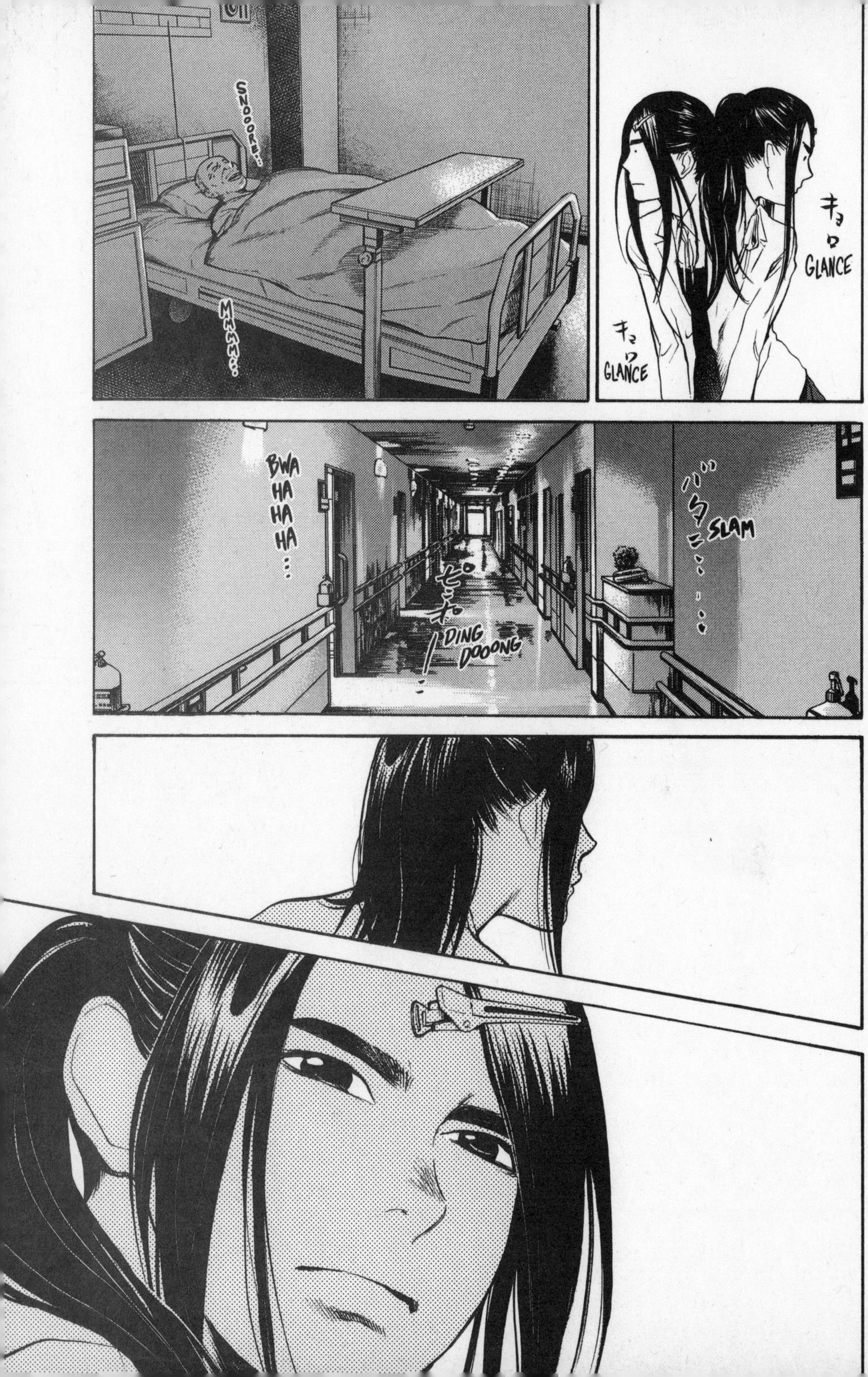
キョロ
GLANCE
キョロ
GLANCE
SNOOORE...
MMMM...
バタン...
SLAM
ピンポーン
DING DOOONG
BWA HA HA HA...

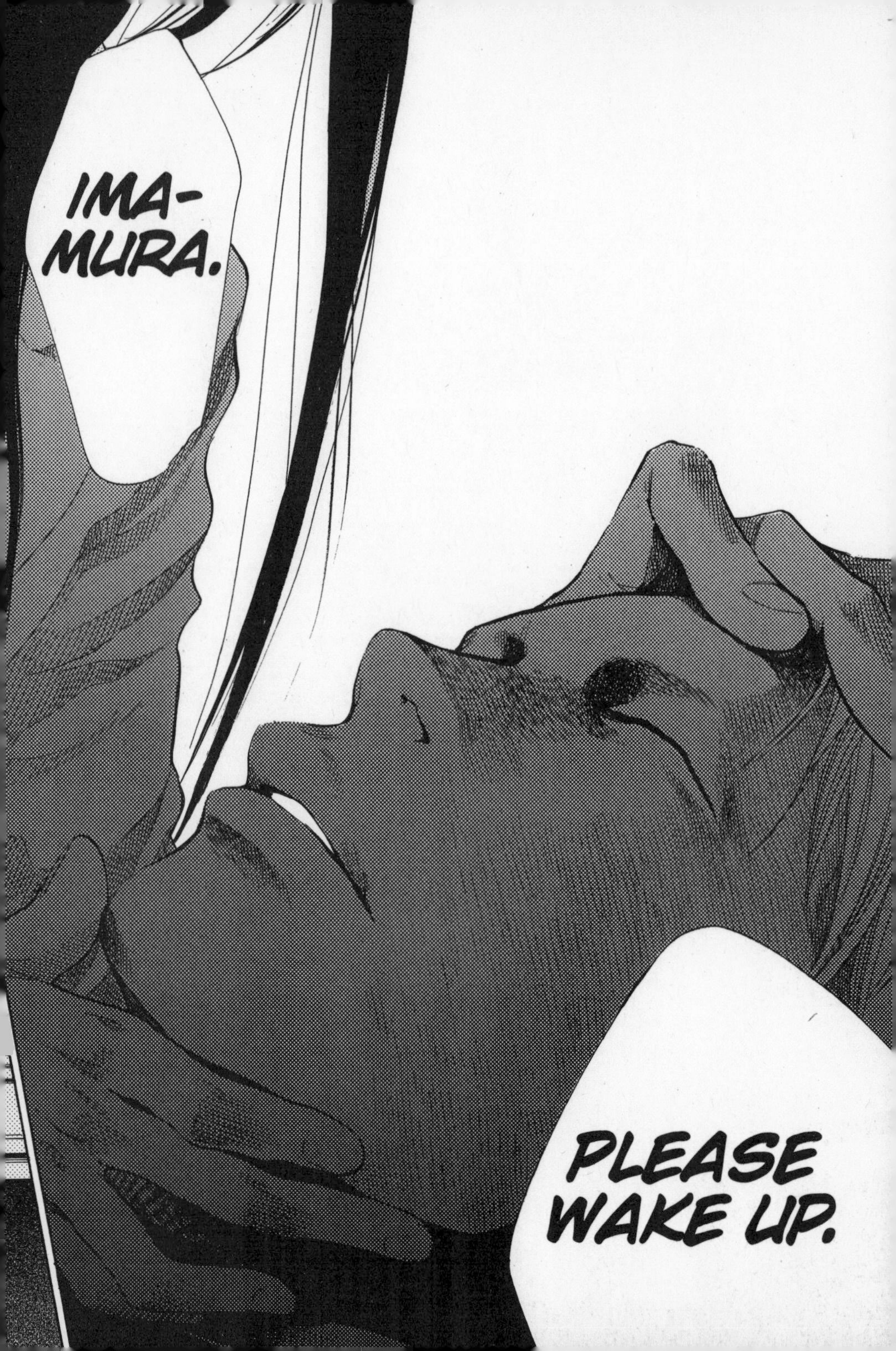
IMA-MURA.
PLEASE WAKE UP.

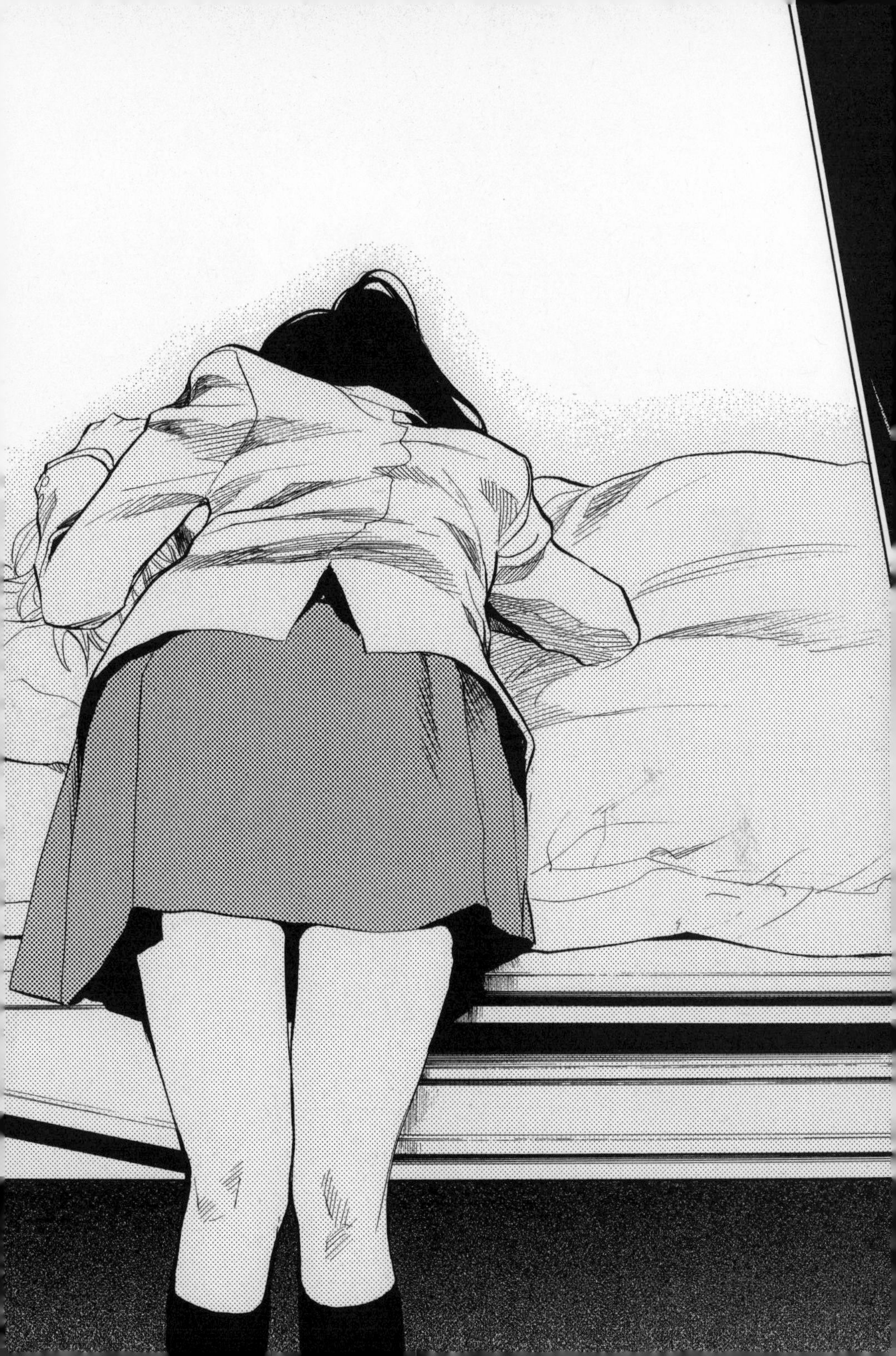

38. ONE HELL OF A KISS

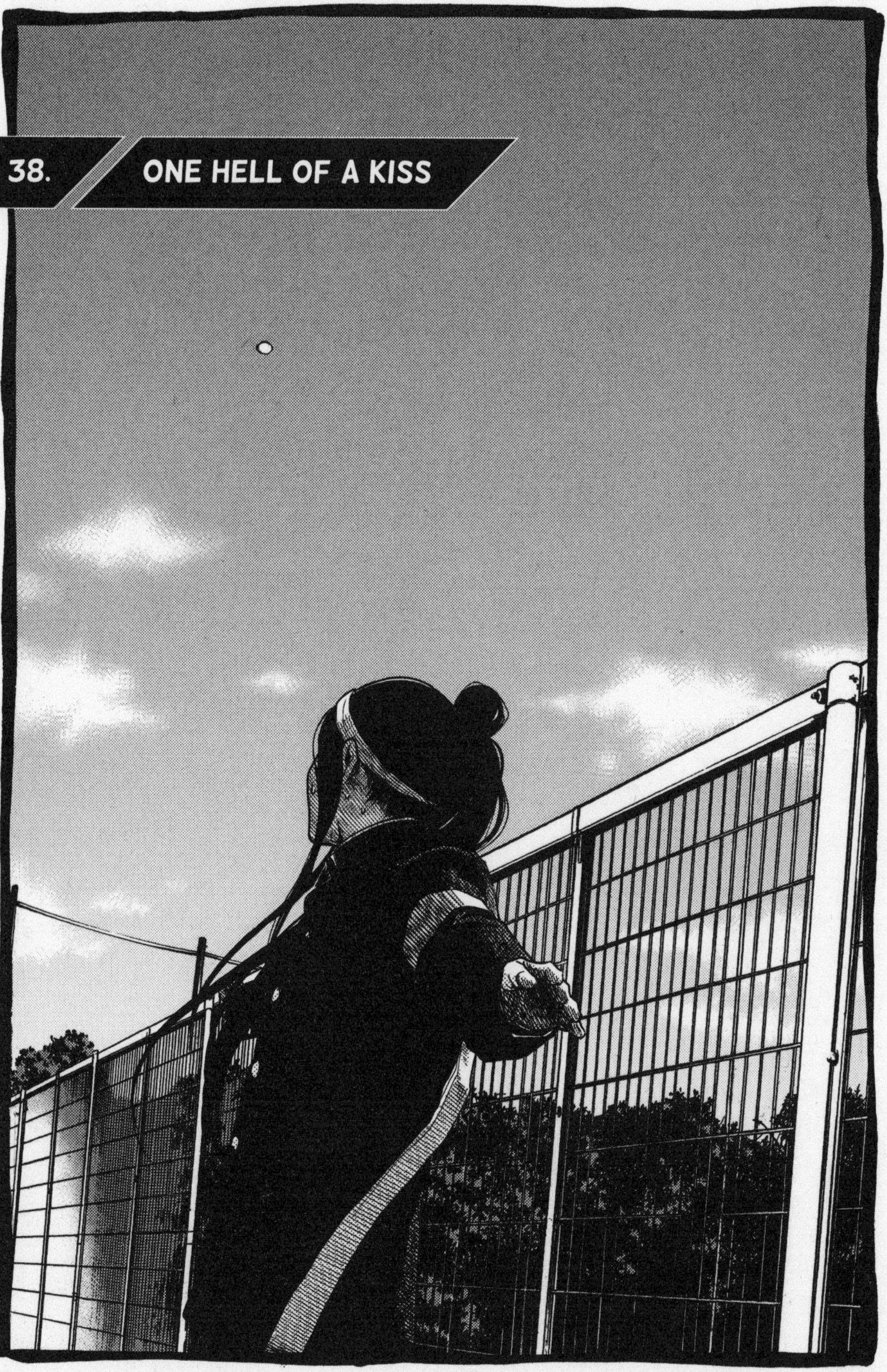

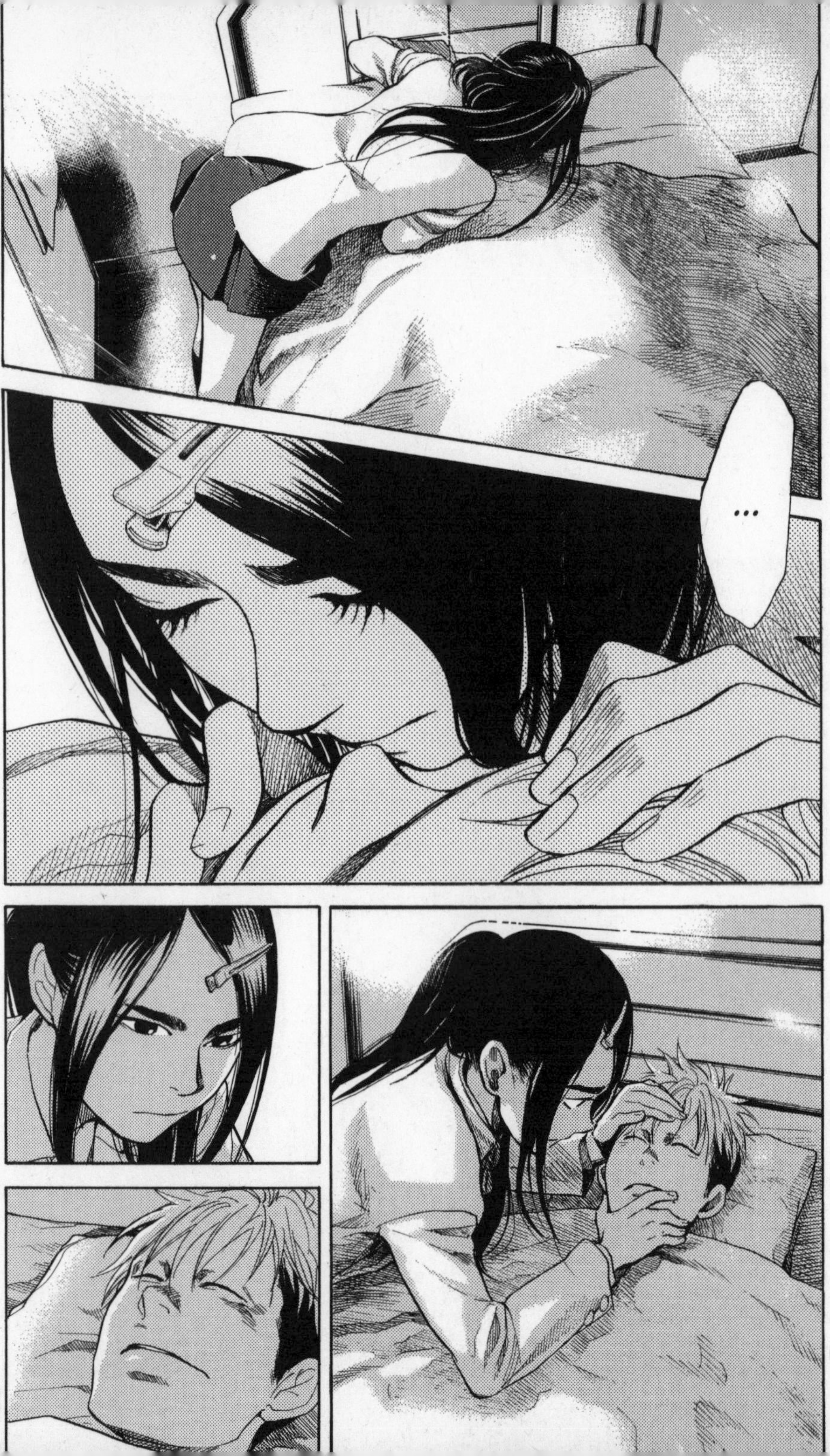
...

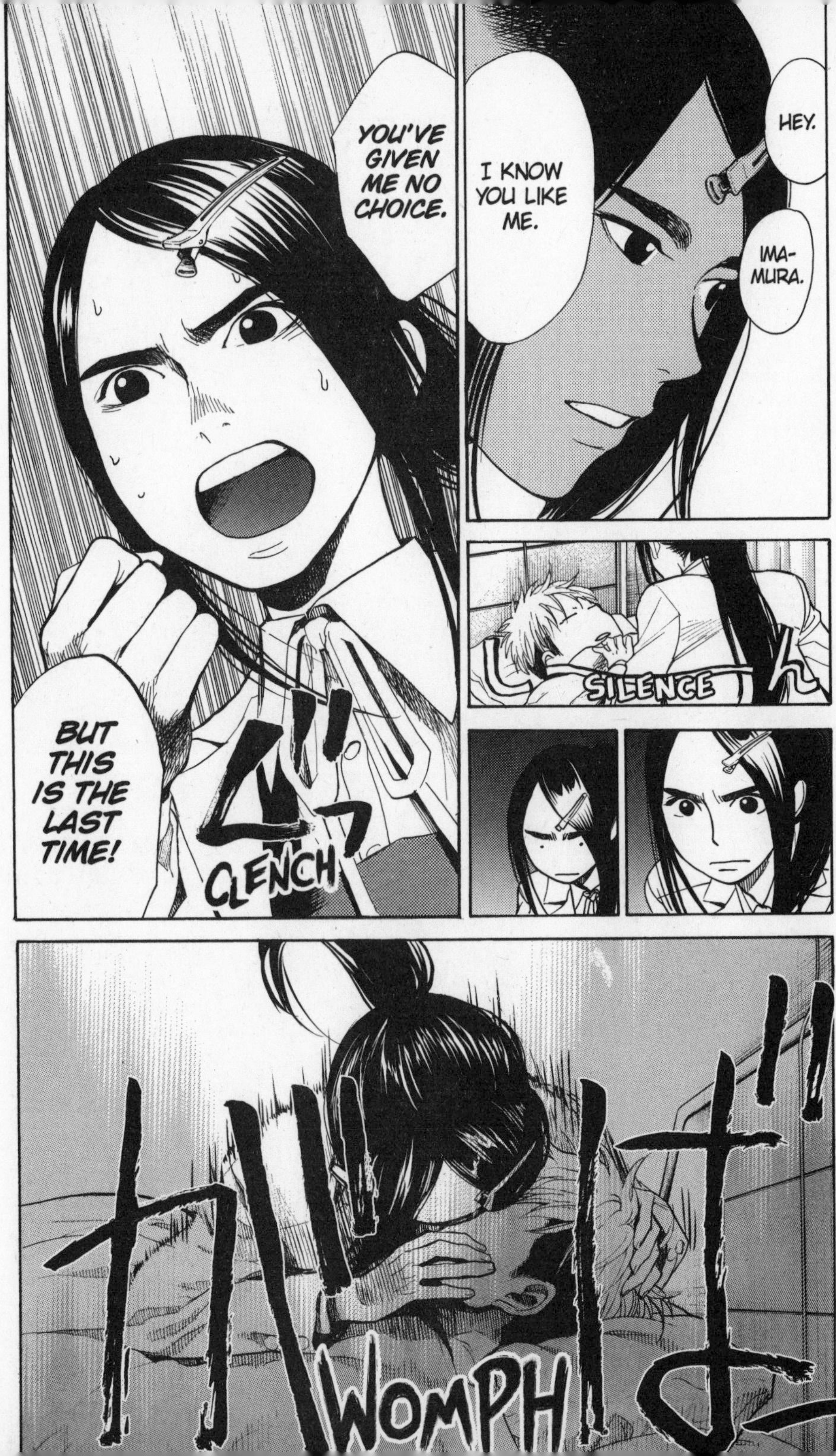
HEY.
IMA-MURA.
I KNOW YOU LIKE ME.
SILENCE
YOU'VE GIVEN ME NO CHOICE.
BUT THIS IS THE LAST TIME!
CLENCH
WOMPH

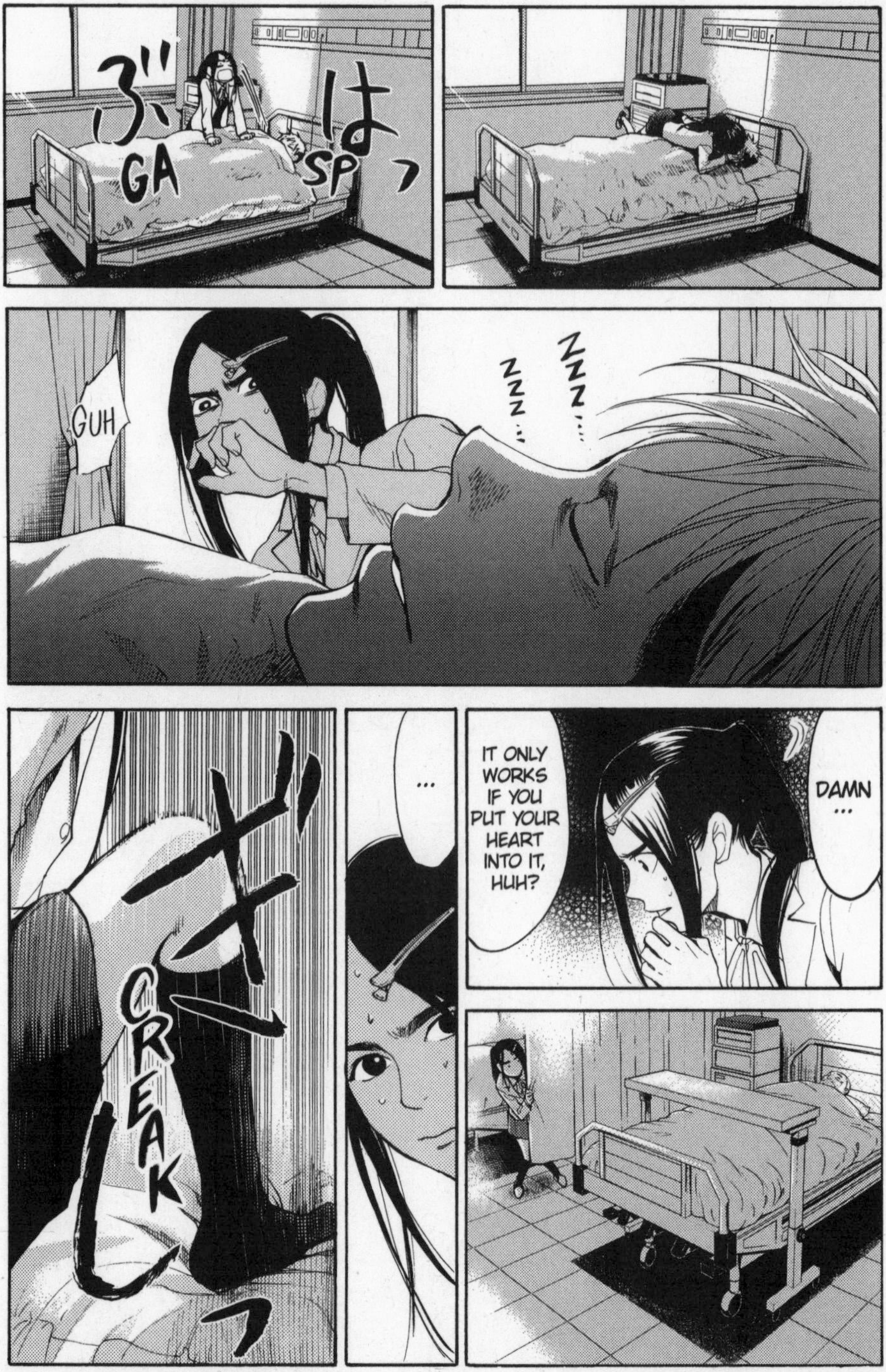
ぶはっ
GA
SP
ZZZ...
ZZZ...
GUH
DAMN ...
IT ONLY WORKS IF YOU PUT YOUR HEART INTO IT, HUH?
...
ギしっ
CREAK

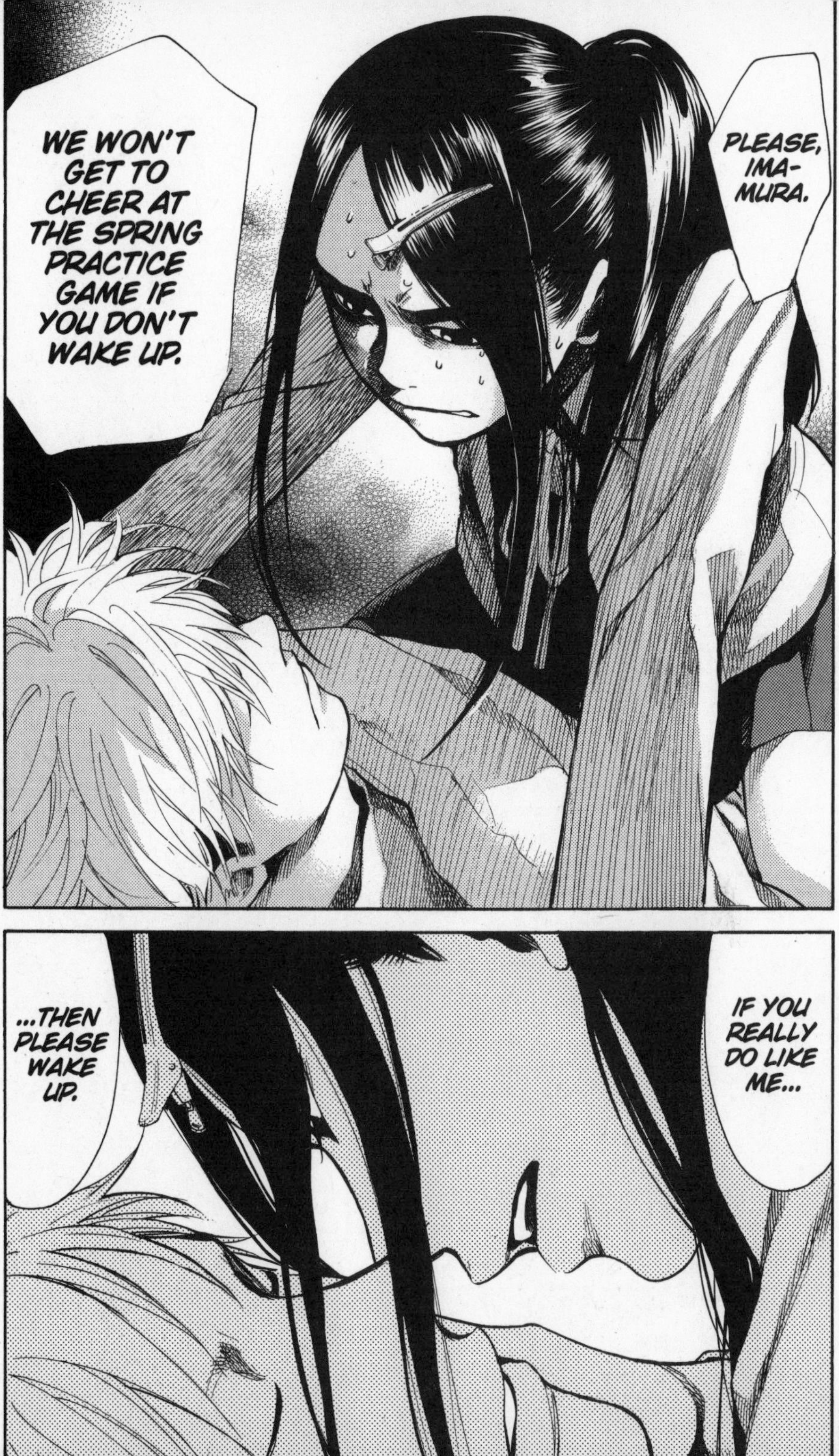
PLEASE, IMA-MURA.
WE WON'T GET TO CHEER AT THE SPRING PRACTICE GAME IF YOU DON'T WAKE UP.
IF YOU REALLY DO LIKE ME...
...THEN PLEASE WAKE UP.

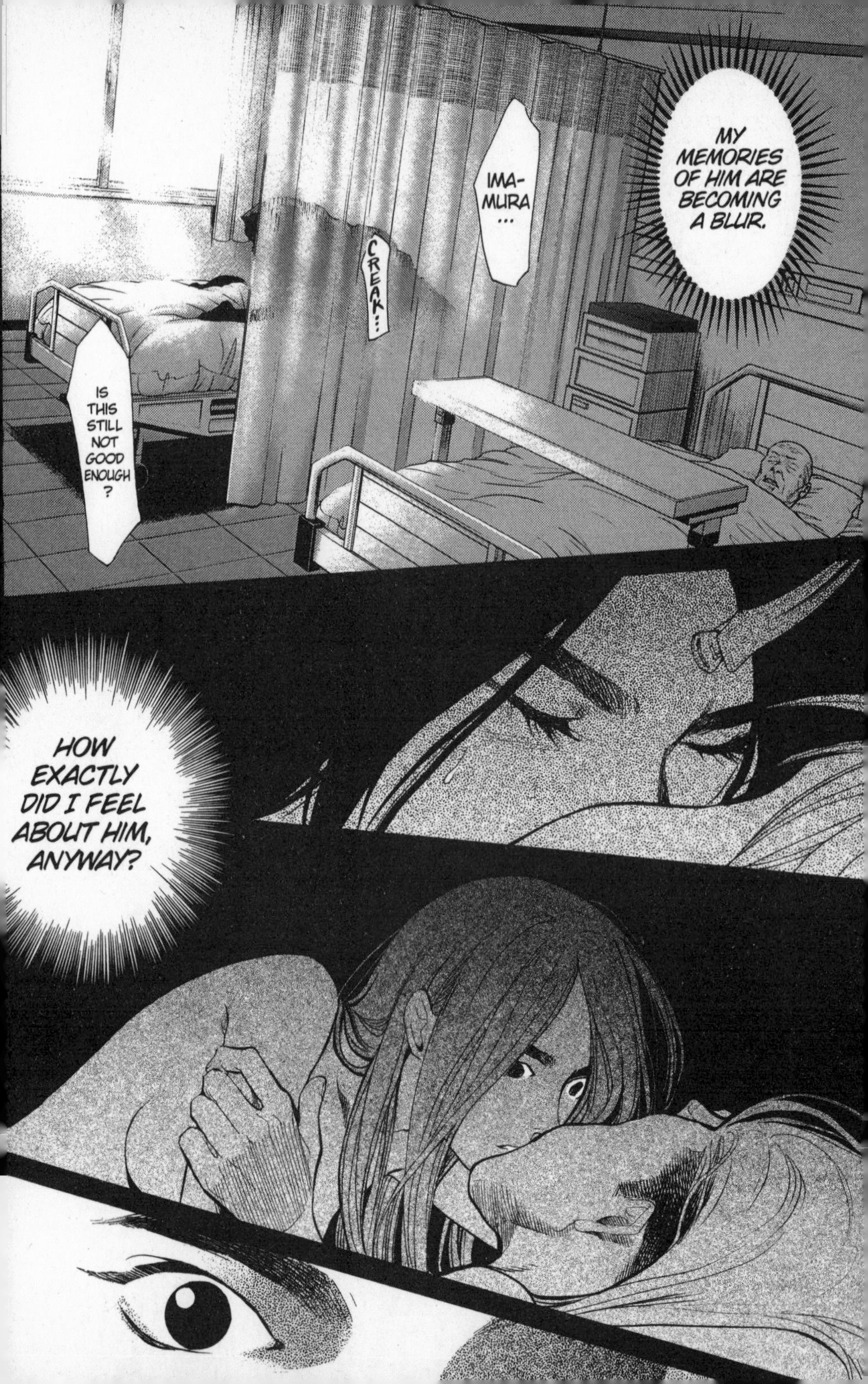
MY MEMORIES OF HIM ARE BECOMING A BLUR.
IMA-MURA...
CREAK...
IS THIS STILL NOT GOOD ENOUGH?
HOW EXACTLY DID I FEEL ABOUT HIM, ANYWAY?

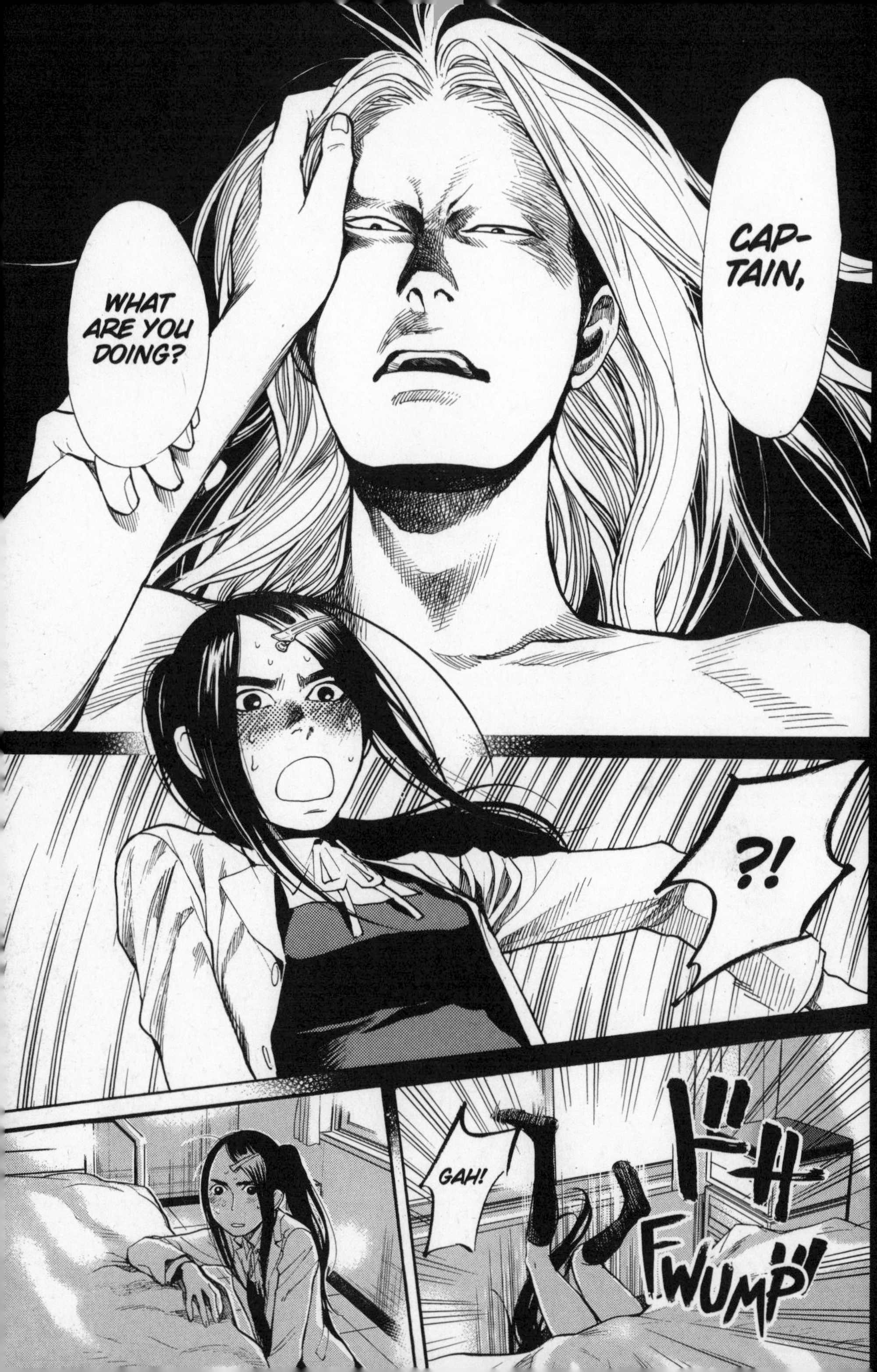
CAP-TAIN,
WHAT ARE YOU DOING?
?!
GAH!
FWUMP!!

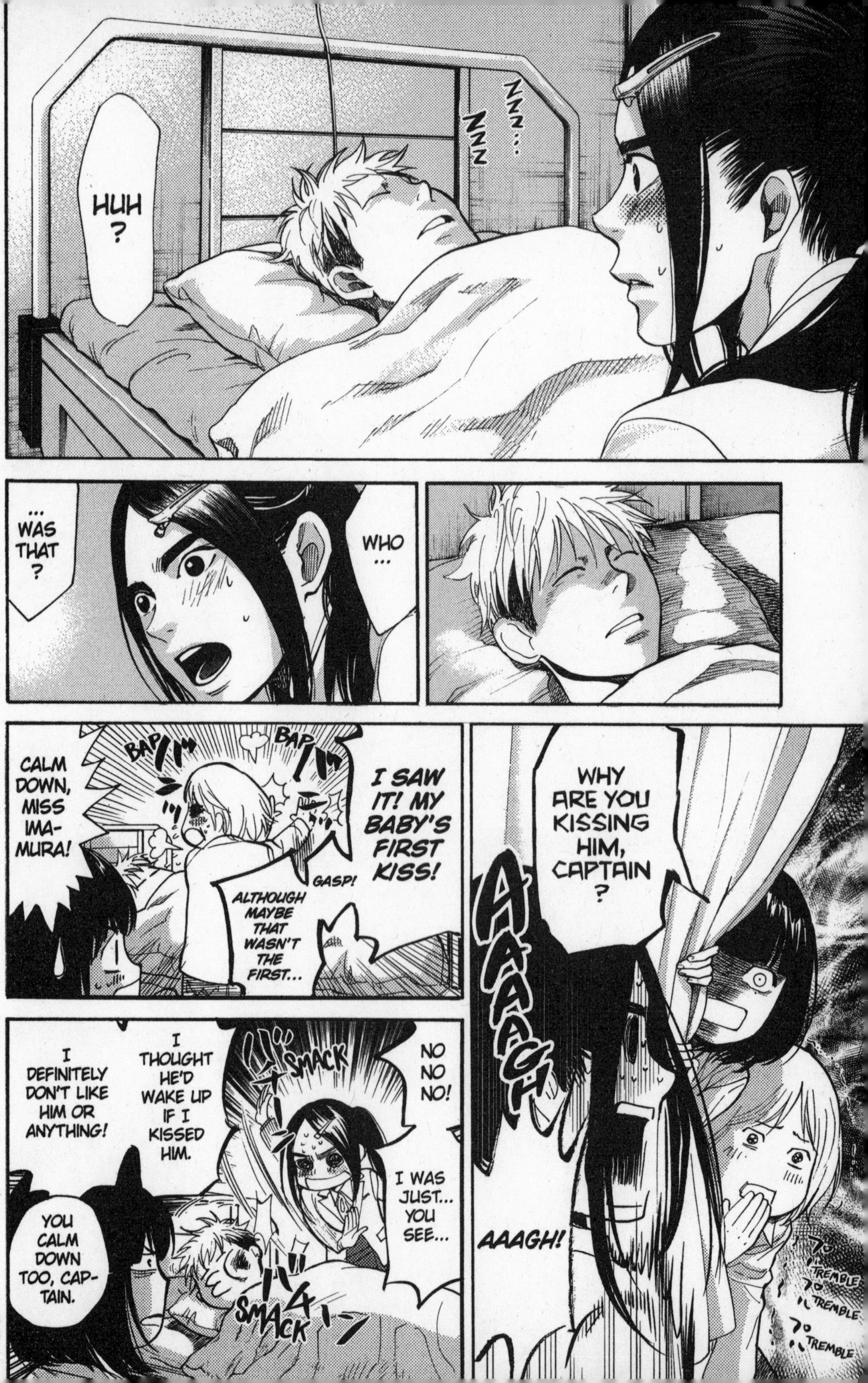
ZZZ...
ZZZ
HUH?
WHO...
...WAS THAT?
WHY ARE YOU KISSING HIM, CAPTAIN?
AAAAAGH!
AAAGH!
TREMBLE
TREMBLE
TREMBLE
I SAW IT! MY BABY'S FIRST KISS!
BAP
BAP
GASP!
ALTHOUGH MAYBE THAT WASN'T THE FIRST...
CALM DOWN, MISS IMAMURA!
NO NO NO!
SMACK
I THOUGHT HE'D WAKE UP IF I KISSED HIM.
I DEFINITELY DON'T LIKE HIM OR ANYTHING!
I WAS JUST... YOU SEE...
YOU CALM DOWN TOO, CAPTAIN.
SMACK

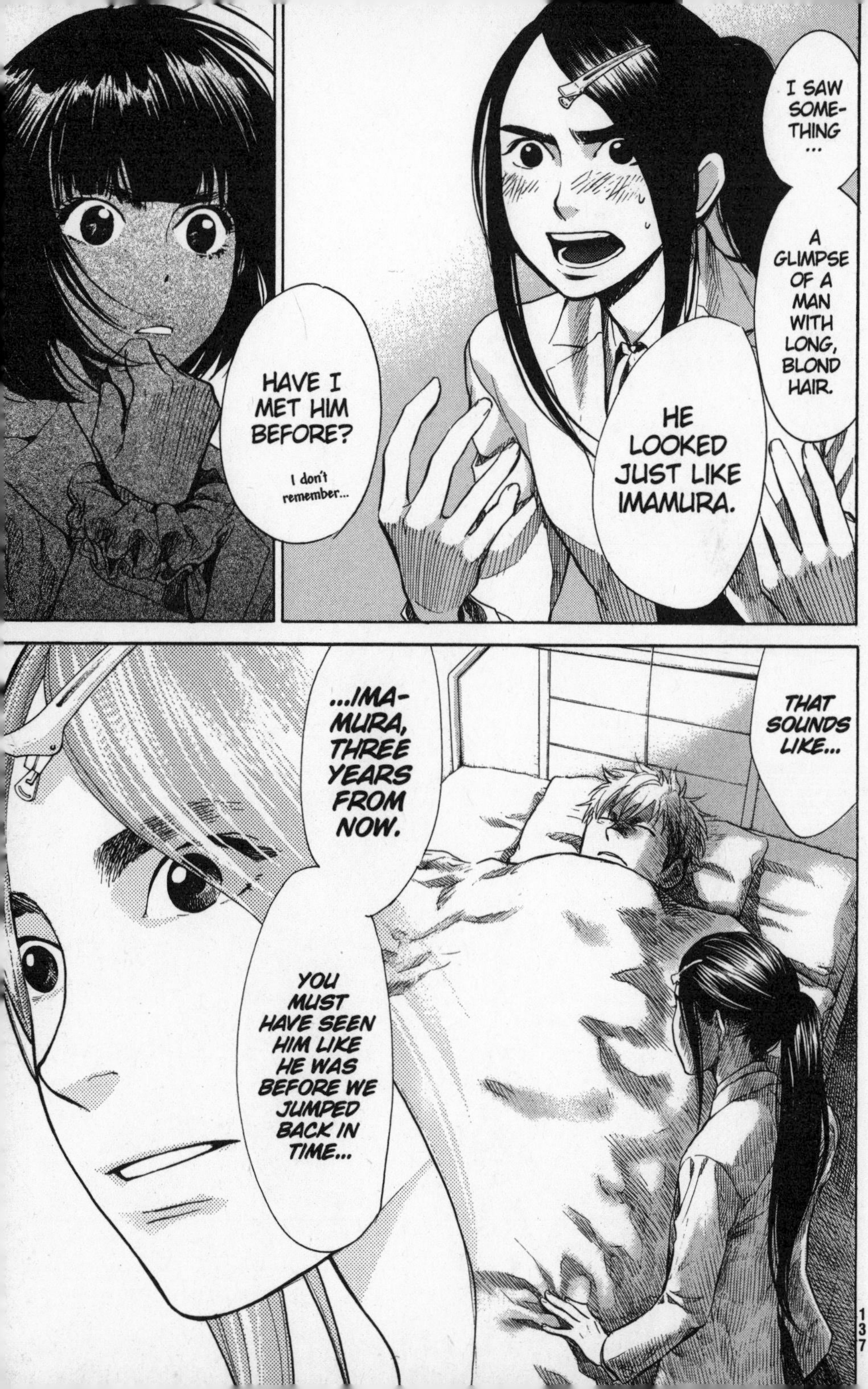
I SAW SOME-THING...
A GLIMPSE OF A MAN WITH LONG, BLOND HAIR.
HE LOOKED JUST LIKE IMAMURA.
HAVE I MET HIM BEFORE?
I don't remember...
THAT SOUNDS LIKE...
...IMA-MURA, THREE YEARS FROM NOW.
YOU MUST HAVE SEEN HIM LIKE HE WAS BEFORE WE JUMPED BACK IN TIME...

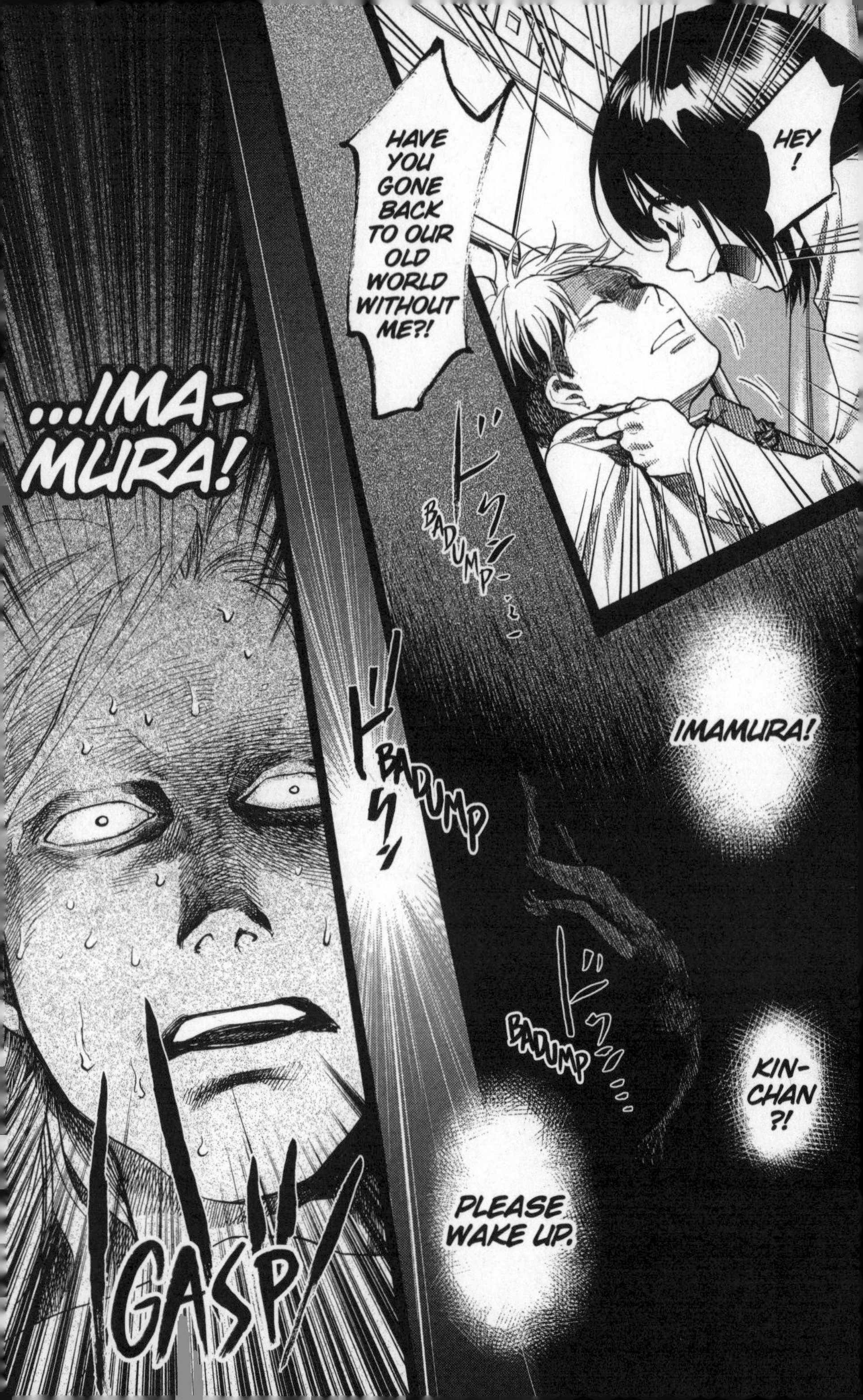
HEY!
HAVE YOU GONE BACK TO OUR OLD WORLD WITHOUT ME?!
BADUMP
IMAMURA!
KIN-CHAN?!
BADUMP
PLEASE WAKE UP.
BADUMP
...IMA-MURA!
GASP!

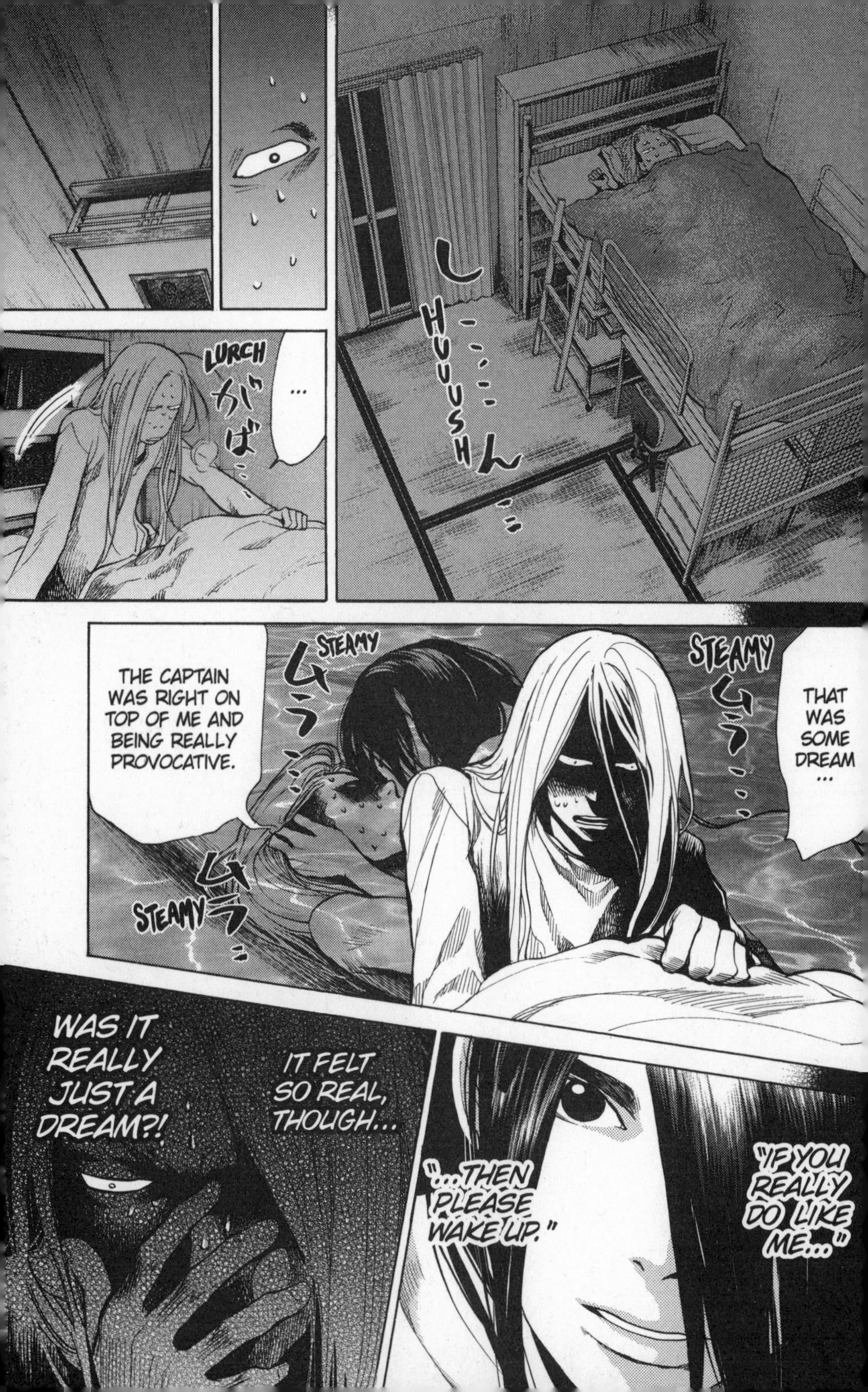

HUUUSH
しーん
LURCH
がばっ
...
THAT WAS SOME DREAM...
STEAMY
ムラ...
STEAMY
THE CAPTAIN WAS RIGHT ON TOP OF ME AND BEING REALLY PROVOCATIVE.
STEAMY
ムラ...
"IF YOU REALLY DO LIKE ME..."
"...THEN PLEASE WAKE UP."
IT FELT SO REAL, THOUGH...
WAS IT REALLY JUST A DREAM?!

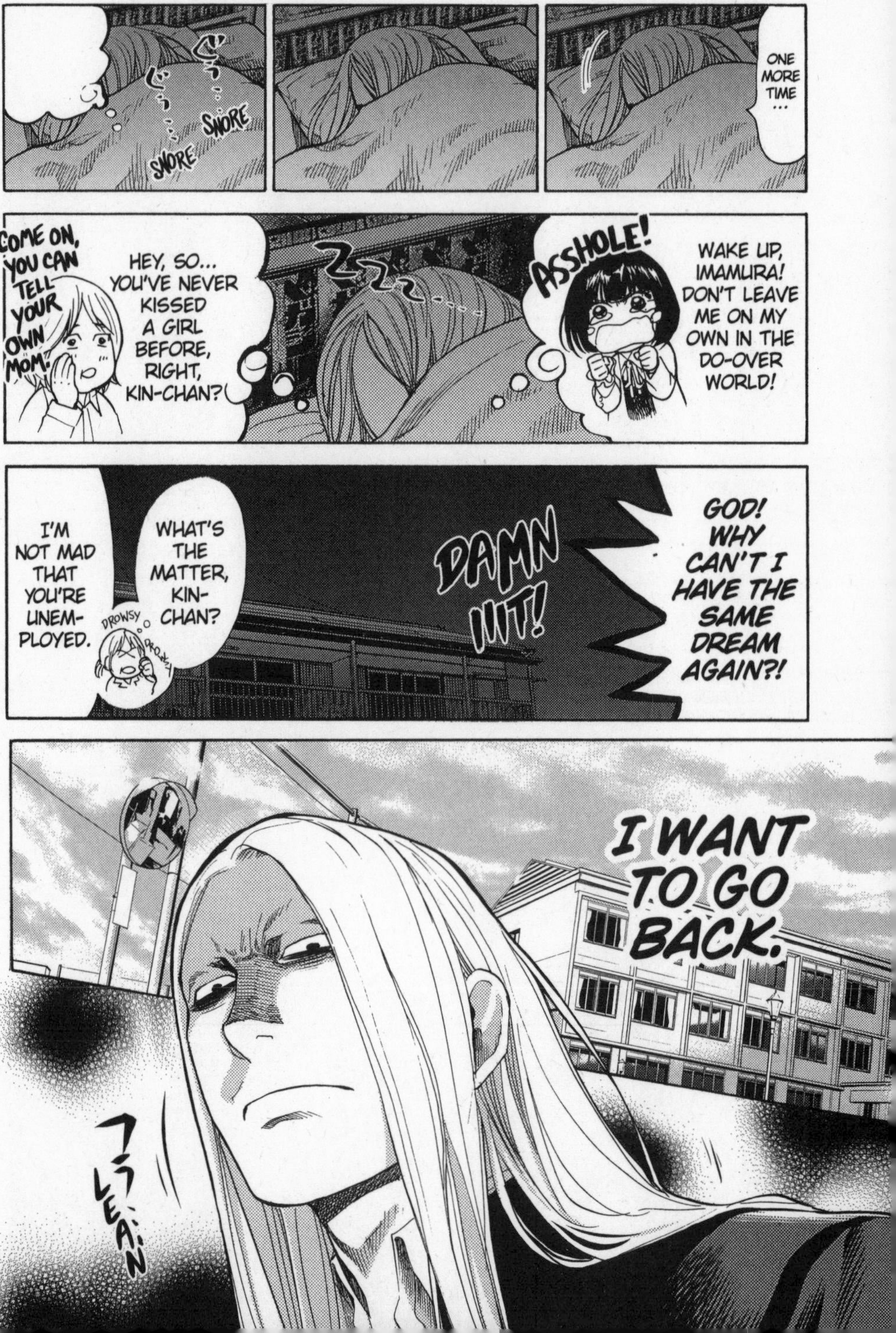
ONE MORE TIME ...
SNORE
SNORE
ASSHOLE!
WAKE UP, IMAMURA! DON'T LEAVE ME ON MY OWN IN THE DO-OVER WORLD!
HEY, SO... YOU'VE NEVER KISSED A GIRL BEFORE, RIGHT, KIN-CHAN?
COME ON, YOU CAN TELL YOUR OWN MOM.
GOD! WHY CAN'T I HAVE THE SAME DREAM AGAIN?!
DAMN IIIT!
WHAT'S THE MATTER, KIN-CHAN?
I'M NOT MAD THAT YOU'RE UNEMPLOYED.
DROWSY
I WANT TO GO BACK.
LEAN

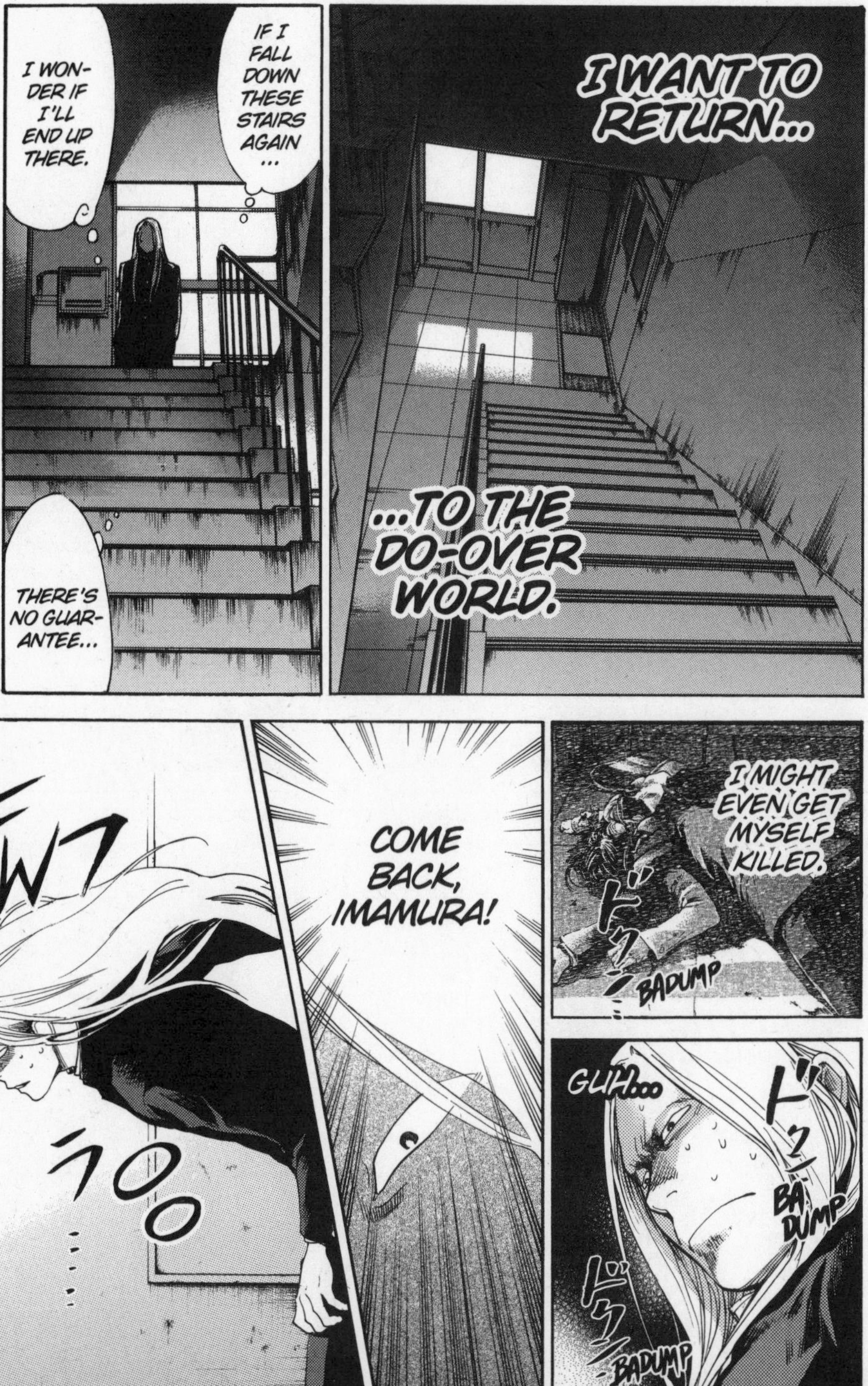
I WANT TO RETURN...
...TO THE DO-OVER WORLD.
IF I FALL DOWN THESE STAIRS AGAIN...
I WONDER IF I'LL END UP THERE.
THERE'S NO GUARANTEE...
I MIGHT EVEN GET MYSELF KILLED.
BADUMP
GULP
BA DUMP
BADUMP
COME BACK, IMAMURA!

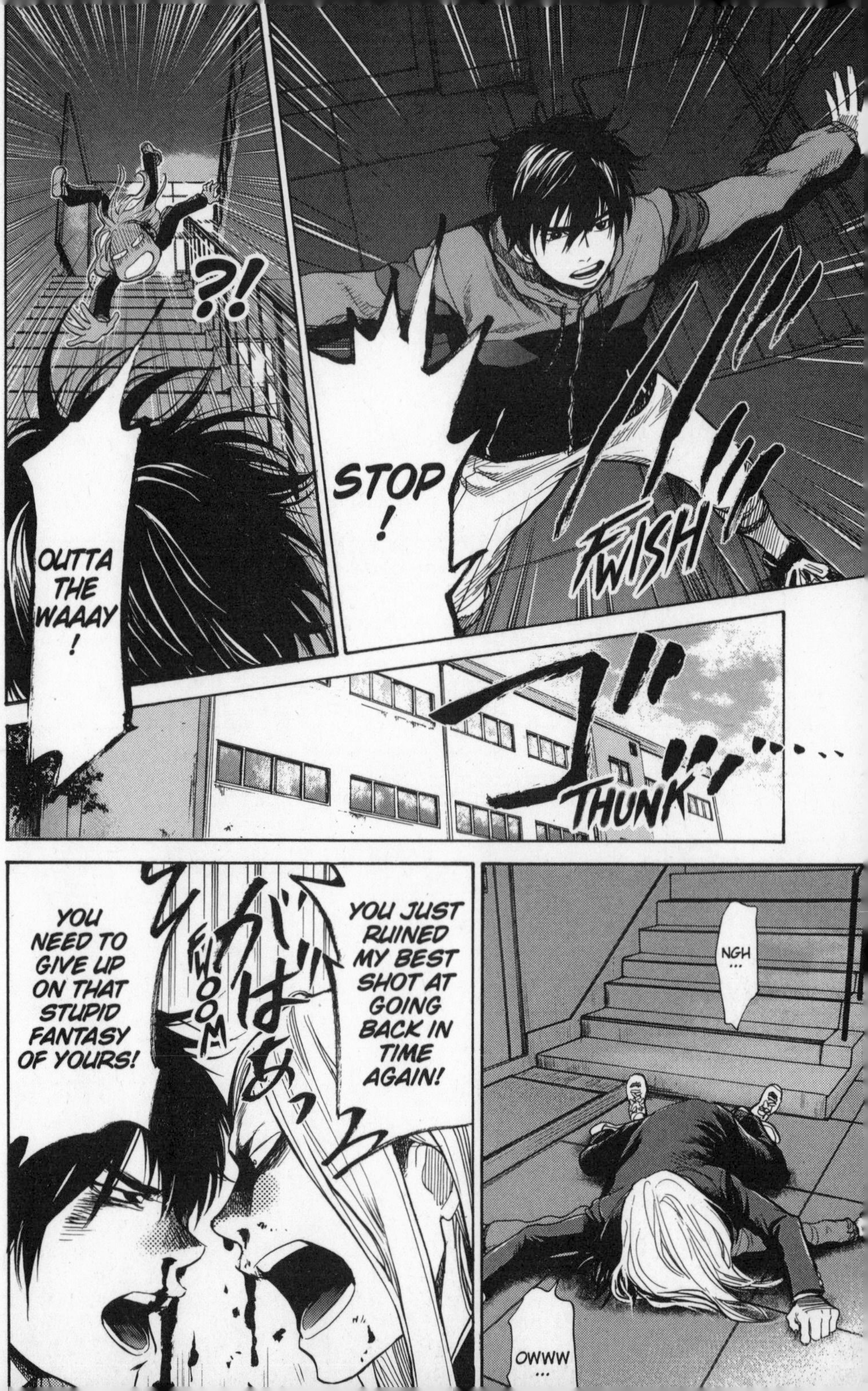
STOP!
FWISH
?!
OUTTA THE WAAAY!
THUNK
NGH...
OWWW...
YOU JUST RUINED MY BEST SHOT AT GOING BACK IN TIME AGAIN!
FWOOM
YOU NEED TO GIVE UP ON THAT STUPID FANTASY OF YOURS!

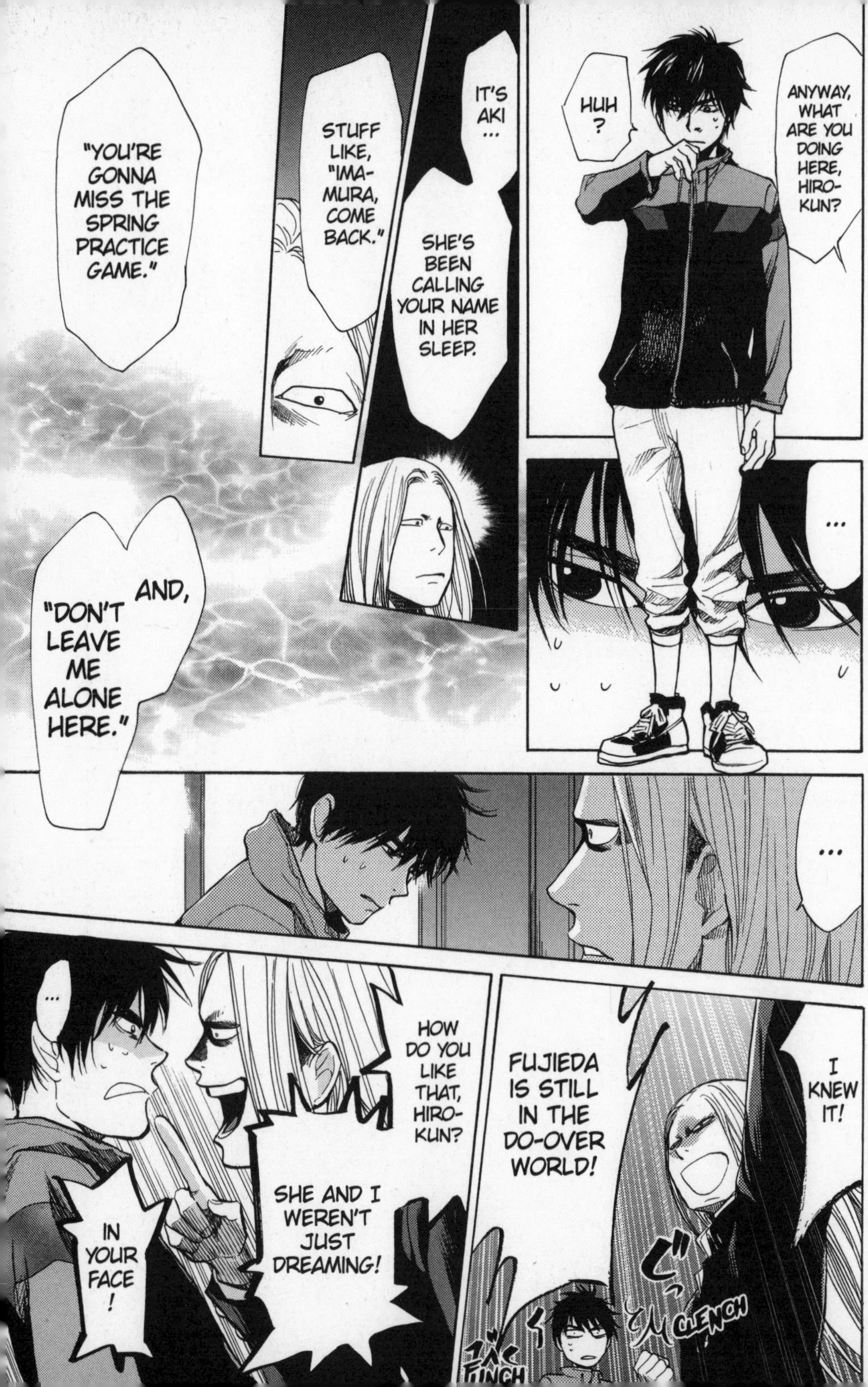
ANYWAY, WHAT ARE YOU DOING HERE, HIRO-KUN?
HUH?
IT'S AKI...
STUFF LIKE, "IMA-MURA, COME BACK."
SHE'S BEEN CALLING YOUR NAME IN HER SLEEP.
"YOU'RE GONNA MISS THE SPRING PRACTICE GAME."
AND, "DON'T LEAVE ME ALONE HERE."
...
...
I KNEW IT!
FUJIEDA IS STILL IN THE DO-OVER WORLD!
CLENCH
FLINCH
HOW DO YOU LIKE THAT, HIRO-KUN?
SHE AND I WEREN'T JUST DREAMING!
IN YOUR FACE!
...

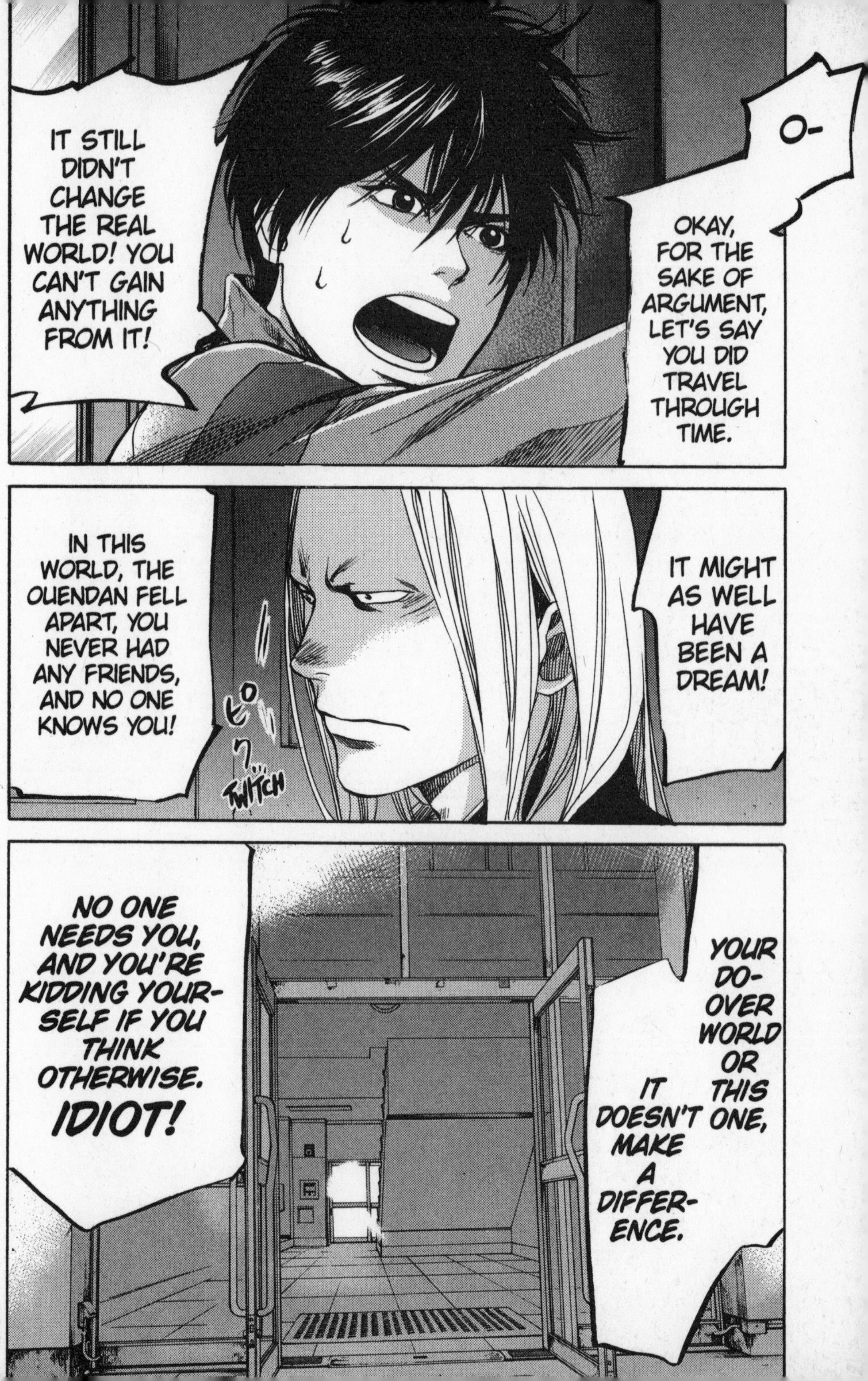
O-
OKAY, FOR THE SAKE OF ARGUMENT, LET'S SAY YOU DID TRAVEL THROUGH TIME.
IT STILL DIDN'T CHANGE THE REAL WORLD! YOU CAN'T GAIN ANYTHING FROM IT!
IT MIGHT AS WELL HAVE BEEN A DREAM!
IN THIS WORLD, THE OUENDAN FELL APART, YOU NEVER HAD ANY FRIENDS, AND NO ONE KNOWS YOU!
TWITCH
YOUR DO-OVER WORLD OR THIS ONE,
IT DOESN'T MAKE A DIFFERENCE.
NO ONE NEEDS YOU, AND YOU'RE KIDDING YOURSELF IF YOU THINK OTHERWISE.
IDIOT!

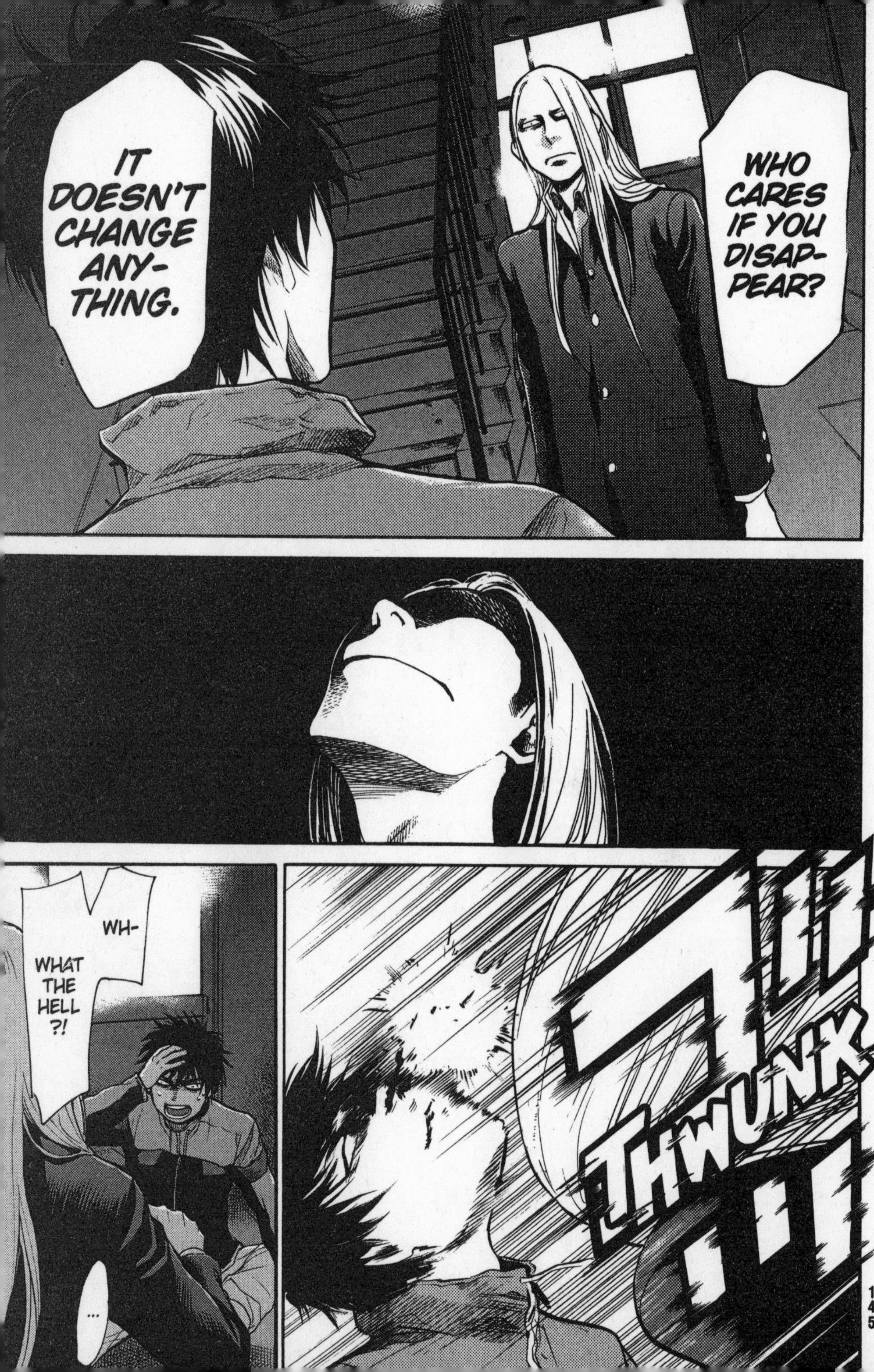
WHO CARES IF YOU DISAPPEAR?
IT DOESN'T CHANGE ANYTHING.
THWUNK
WH-
WHAT THE HELL ?!
...

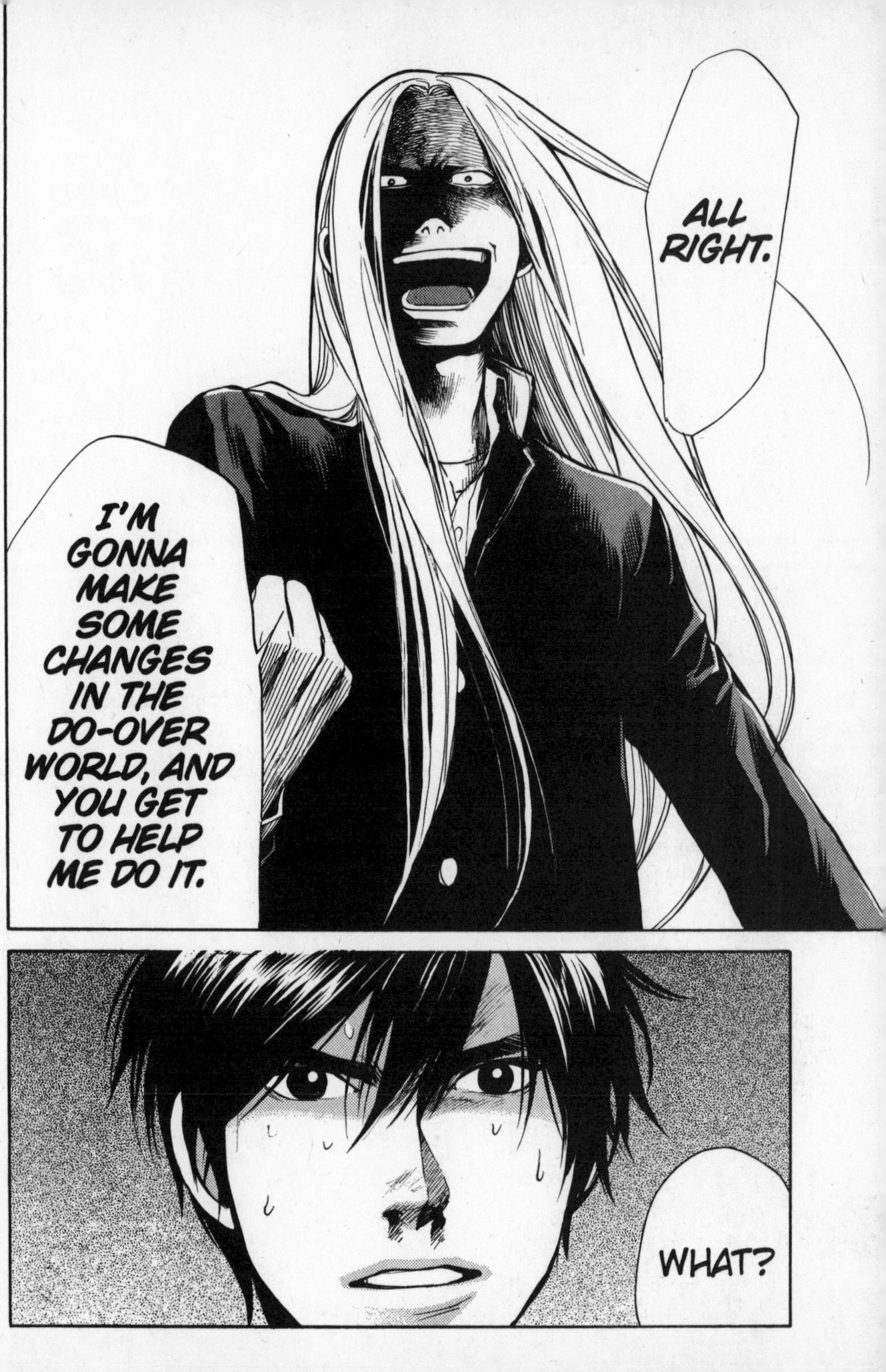
ALL RIGHT.
I'M GONNA MAKE SOME CHANGES IN THE DO-OVER WORLD, AND YOU GET TO HELP ME DO IT.
WHAT?

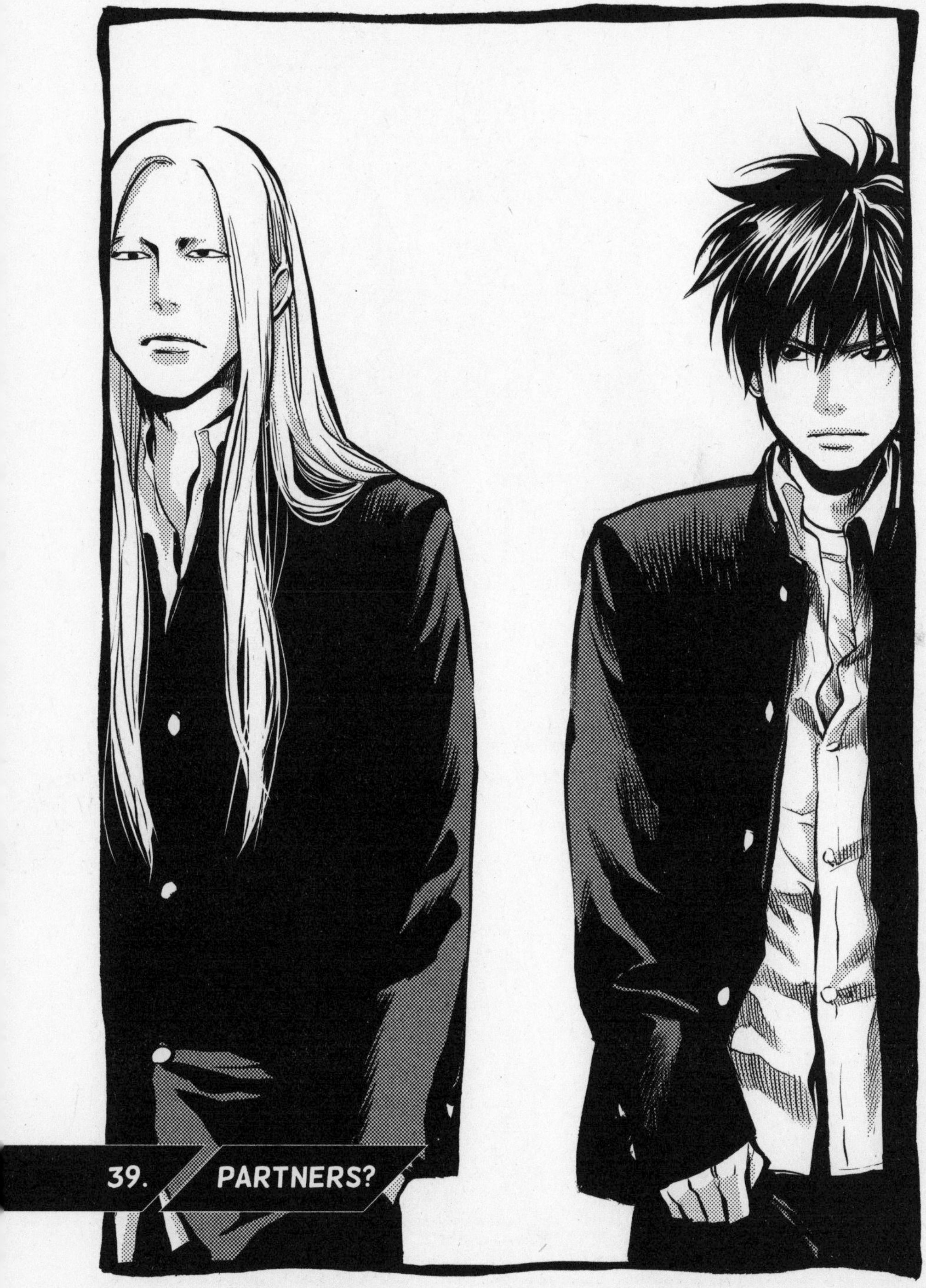

39. PARTNERS?

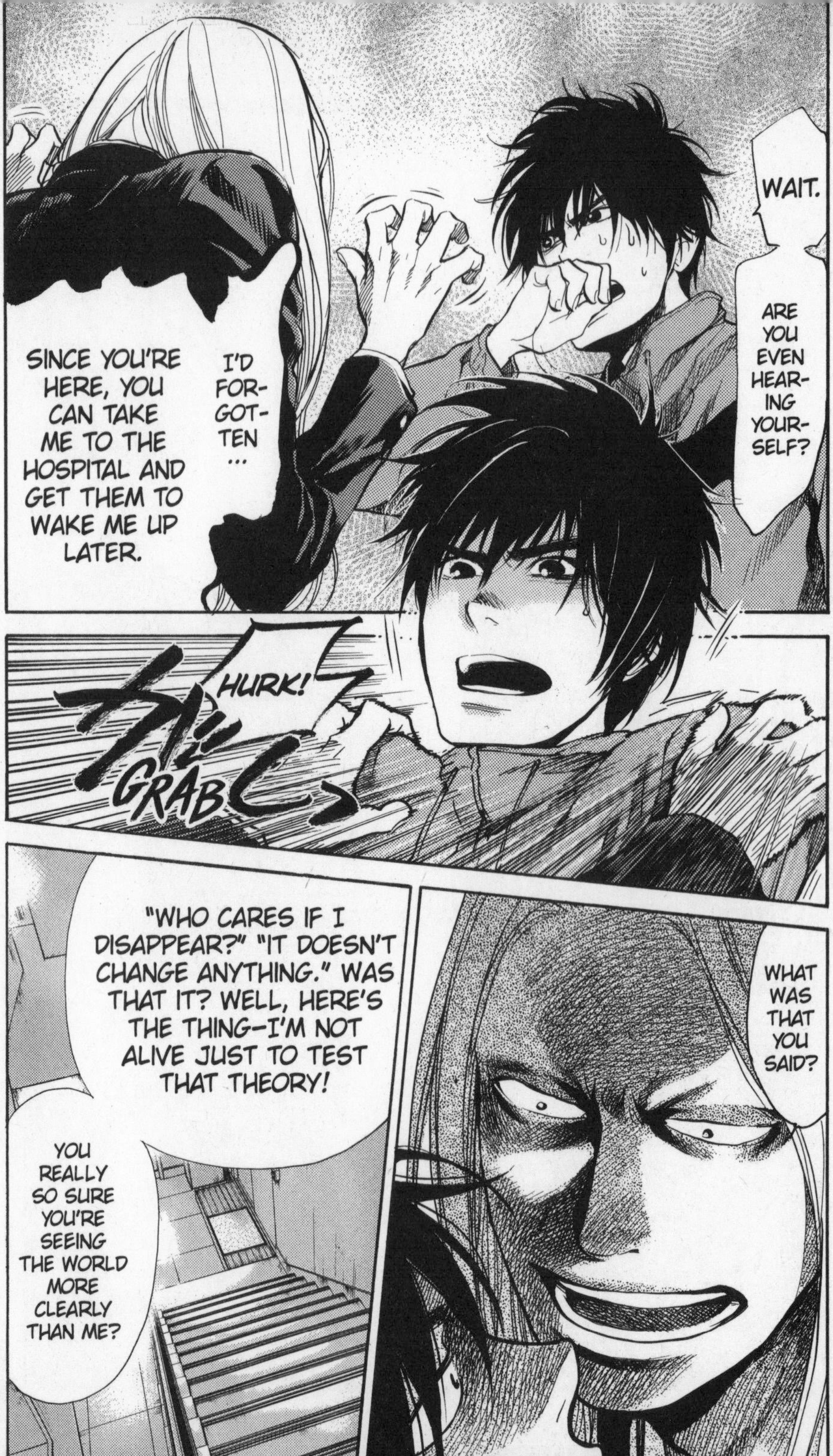
WAIT.
ARE YOU EVEN HEAR-ING YOUR-SELF?
I'D FOR-GOT-TEN ...
SINCE YOU'RE HERE, YOU CAN TAKE ME TO THE HOSPITAL AND GET THEM TO WAKE ME UP LATER.
HURK!
GRAB
WHAT WAS THAT YOU SAID?
"WHO CARES IF I DISAPPEAR?" "IT DOESN'T CHANGE ANYTHING." WAS THAT IT? WELL, HERE'S THE THING–I'M NOT ALIVE JUST TO TEST THAT THEORY!
YOU REALLY SO SURE YOU'RE SEEING THE WORLD MORE CLEARLY THAN ME?

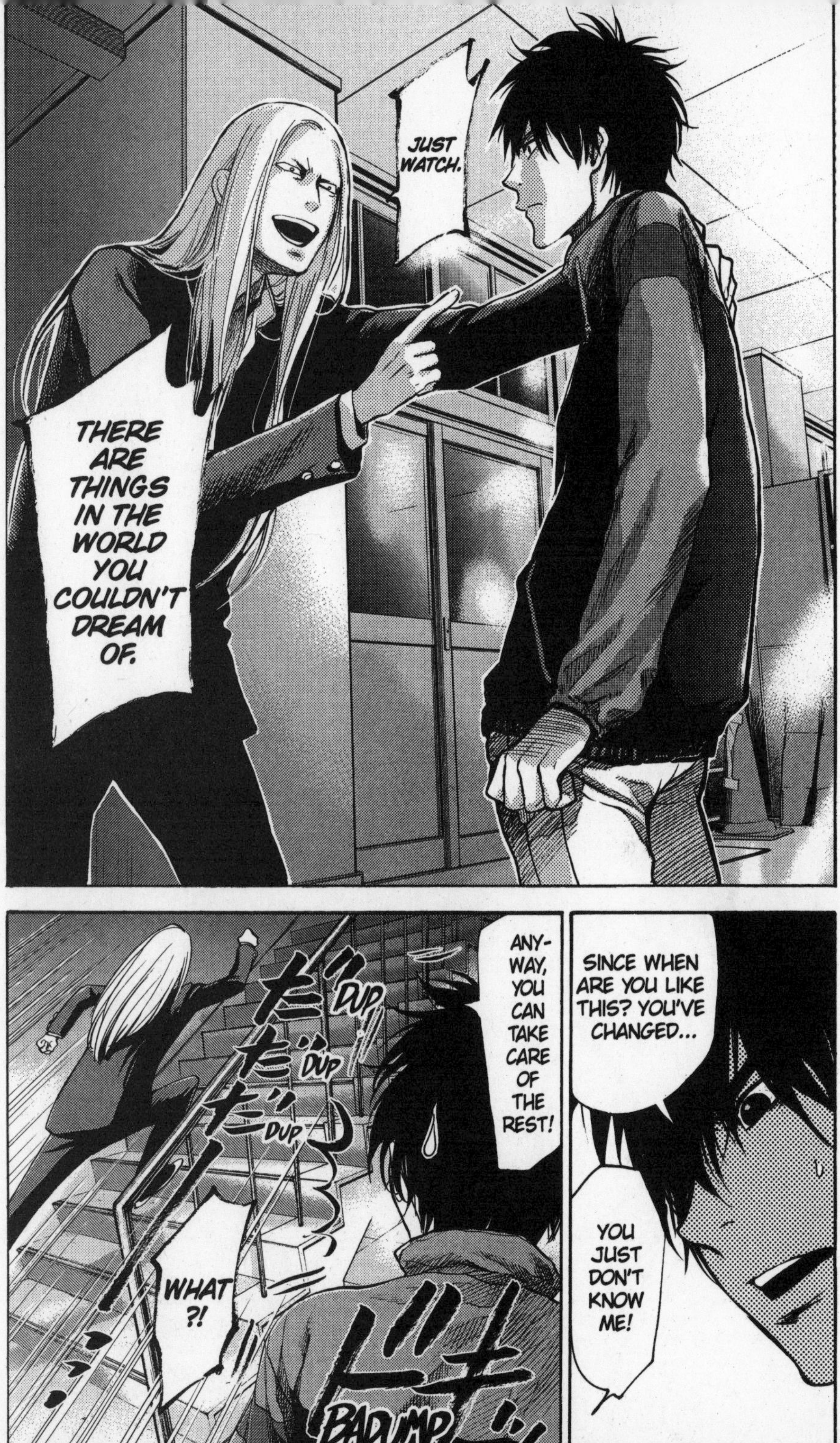
JUST WATCH.
THERE ARE THINGS IN THE WORLD YOU COULDN'T DREAM OF.
SINCE WHEN ARE YOU LIKE THIS? YOU'VE CHANGED...
YOU JUST DON'T KNOW ME!
ANY-WAY, YOU CAN TAKE CARE OF THE REST!
DUP
DUP
DUP
WHAT?!
BADUMP

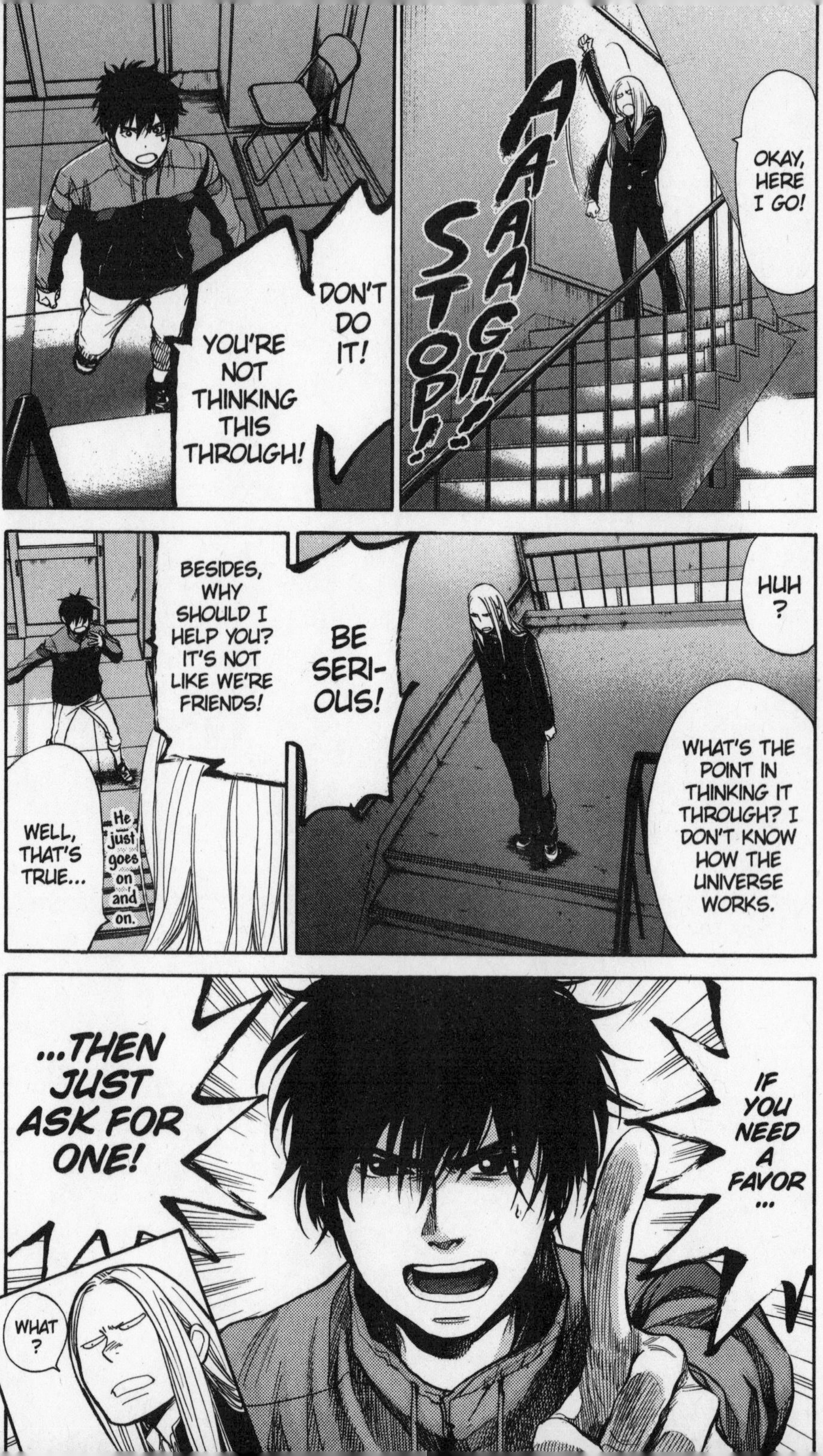
OKAY, HERE I GO!
AAAAGH!!
STOP!!
DON'T DO IT!
YOU'RE NOT THINKING THIS THROUGH!
HUH?
WHAT'S THE POINT IN THINKING IT THROUGH? I DON'T KNOW HOW THE UNIVERSE WORKS.
BE SERI-OUS!
BESIDES, WHY SHOULD I HELP YOU? IT'S NOT LIKE WE'RE FRIENDS!
WELL, THAT'S TRUE...
He just goes on and on.
IF YOU NEED A FAVOR...
...THEN JUST ASK FOR ONE!
WHAT?

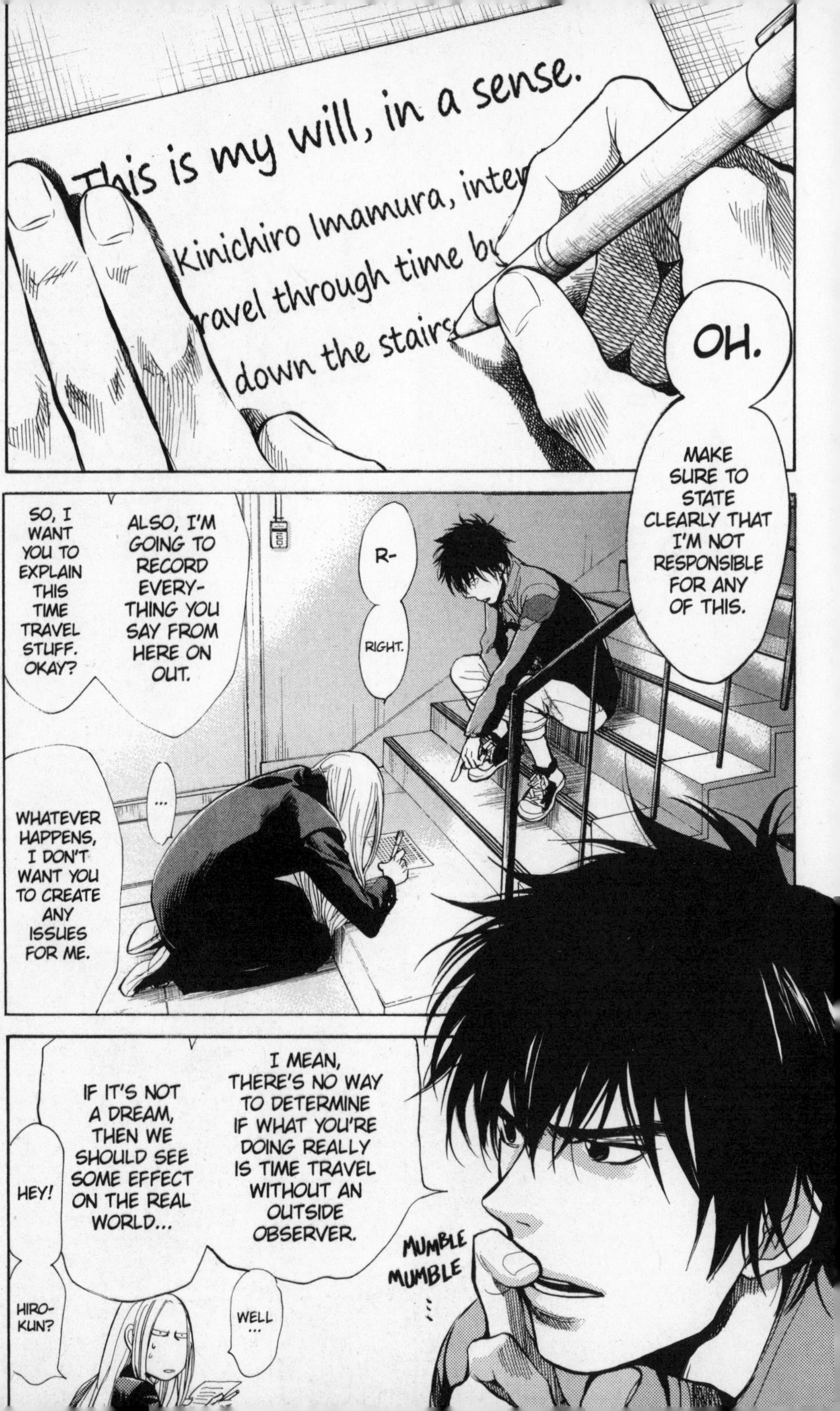

This is my will, in a sense.
Kinichiro Imamura, inte
ravel through time b
down the stairs
OH.
MAKE SURE TO STATE CLEARLY THAT I'M NOT RESPONSIBLE FOR ANY OF THIS.
SO, I WANT YOU TO EXPLAIN THIS TIME TRAVEL STUFF. OKAY?
ALSO, I'M GOING TO RECORD EVERY-THING YOU SAY FROM HERE ON OUT.
R-
RIGHT.
...
WHATEVER HAPPENS, I DON'T WANT YOU TO CREATE ANY ISSUES FOR ME.
MUMBLE MUMBLE
I MEAN, THERE'S NO WAY TO DETERMINE IF WHAT YOU'RE DOING REALLY IS TIME TRAVEL WITHOUT AN OUTSIDE OBSERVER.
IF IT'S NOT A DREAM, THEN WE SHOULD SEE SOME EFFECT ON THE REAL WORLD...
HEY!
HIRO-KUN?
WELL ...

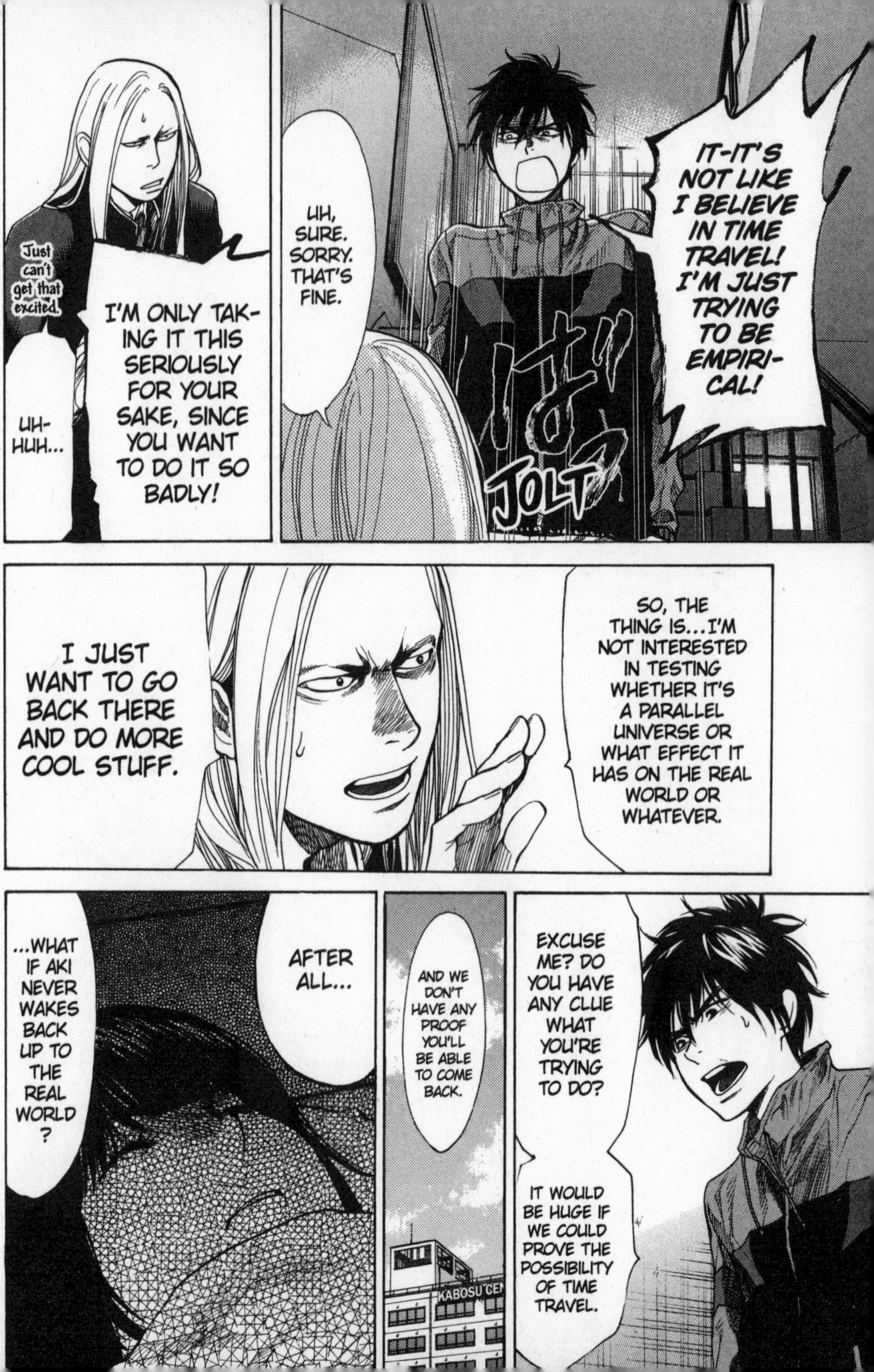
IT-IT'S NOT LIKE I BELIEVE IN TIME TRAVEL! I'M JUST TRYING TO BE EMPIRICAL!
UH, SURE. SORRY. THAT'S FINE.
JOLT
I'M ONLY TAKING IT THIS SERIOUSLY FOR YOUR SAKE, SINCE YOU WANT TO DO IT SO BADLY!
Just can't get that excited.
UH-HUH...
SO, THE THING IS...I'M NOT INTERESTED IN TESTING WHETHER IT'S A PARALLEL UNIVERSE OR WHAT EFFECT IT HAS ON THE REAL WORLD OR WHATEVER.
I JUST WANT TO GO BACK THERE AND DO MORE COOL STUFF.
EXCUSE ME? DO YOU HAVE ANY CLUE WHAT YOU'RE TRYING TO DO?
IT WOULD BE HUGE IF WE COULD PROVE THE POSSIBILITY OF TIME TRAVEL.
AND WE DON'T HAVE ANY PROOF YOU'LL BE ABLE TO COME BACK.
KABOSU CEN
AFTER ALL...
...WHAT IF AKI NEVER WAKES BACK UP TO THE REAL WORLD?

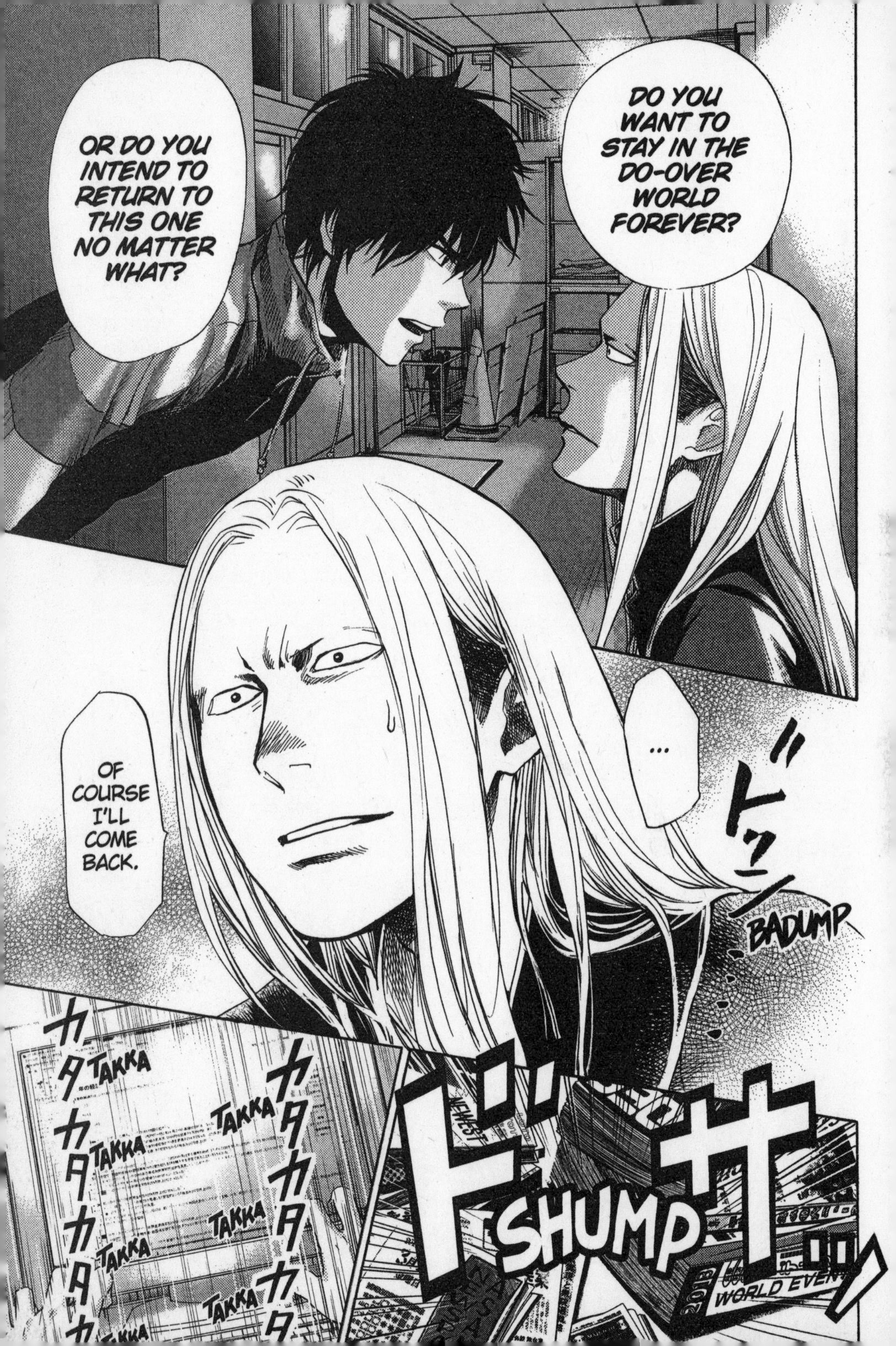
DO YOU WANT TO STAY IN THE DO-OVER WORLD FOREVER?
OR DO YOU INTEND TO RETURN TO THIS ONE NO MATTER WHAT?
...
OF COURSE I'LL COME BACK.
BADUMP
SHUMP
TAKKA
TAKKA
TAKKA
TAKKA
TAKKA
TAKKA
TAKKA

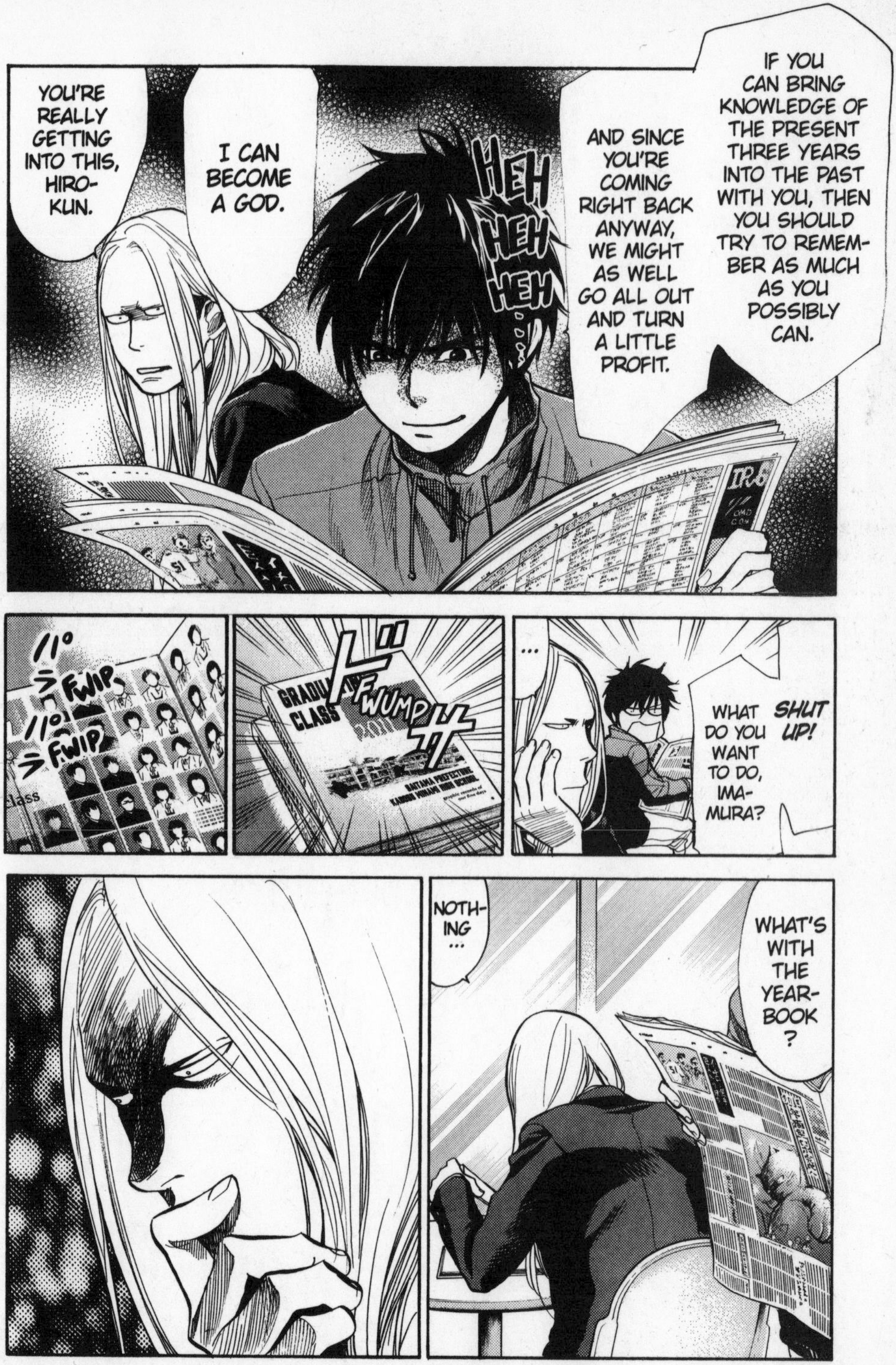

IF YOU CAN BRING KNOWLEDGE OF THE PRESENT THREE YEARS INTO THE PAST WITH YOU, THEN YOU SHOULD TRY TO REMEMBER AS MUCH AS YOU POSSIBLY CAN.
AND SINCE YOU'RE COMING RIGHT BACK ANYWAY, WE MIGHT AS WELL GO ALL OUT AND TURN A LITTLE PROFIT.
HEH HEH HEH
I CAN BECOME A GOD.
YOU'RE REALLY GETTING INTO THIS, HIRO-KUN.
SHUT UP!
WHAT DO YOU WANT TO DO, IMAMURA?
...
FWUMP
GRADU CLASS
SAITAMA PREFECTURE
FWIP
FWIP
WHAT'S WITH THE YEARBOOK?
NOTHING...

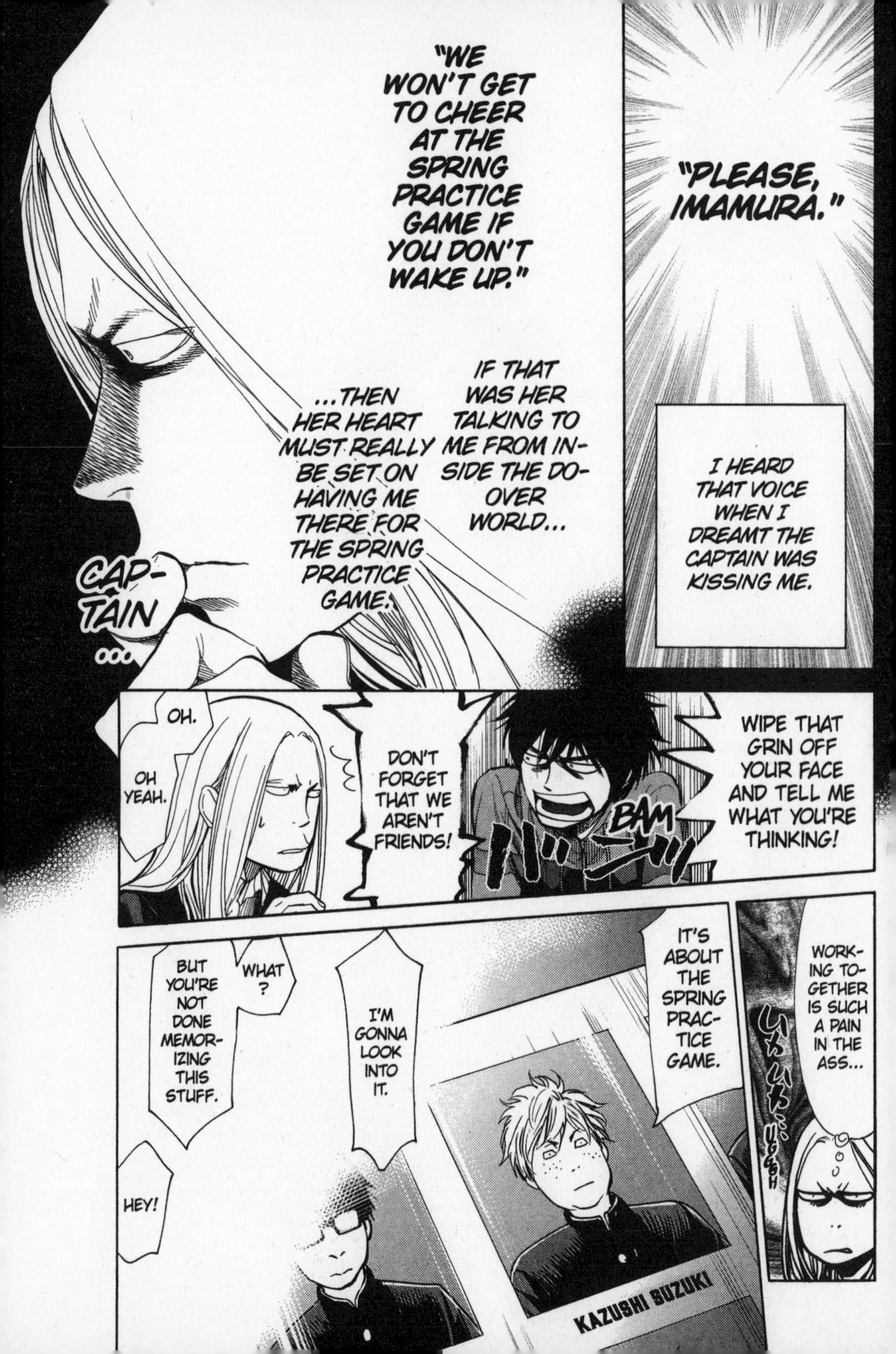
"PLEASE, IMAMURA."
I HEARD THAT VOICE WHEN I DREAMT THE CAPTAIN WAS KISSING ME.
"WE WON'T GET TO CHEER AT THE SPRING PRACTICE GAME IF YOU DON'T WAKE UP."
IF THAT WAS HER TALKING TO ME FROM INSIDE THE DO-OVER WORLD...
...THEN HER HEART MUST REALLY BE SET ON HAVING ME THERE FOR THE SPRING PRACTICE GAME.
CAPTAIN...
WIPE THAT GRIN OFF YOUR FACE AND TELL ME WHAT YOU'RE THINKING!
BAM
DON'T FORGET THAT WE AREN'T FRIENDS!
OH.
OH YEAH.
WORKING TOGETHER IS SUCH A PAIN IN THE ASS...
UGGGH
IT'S ABOUT THE SPRING PRACTICE GAME.
I'M GONNA LOOK INTO IT.
WHAT?
BUT YOU'RE NOT DONE MEMORIZING THIS STUFF.
HEY!
KAZUSHI SUZUKI

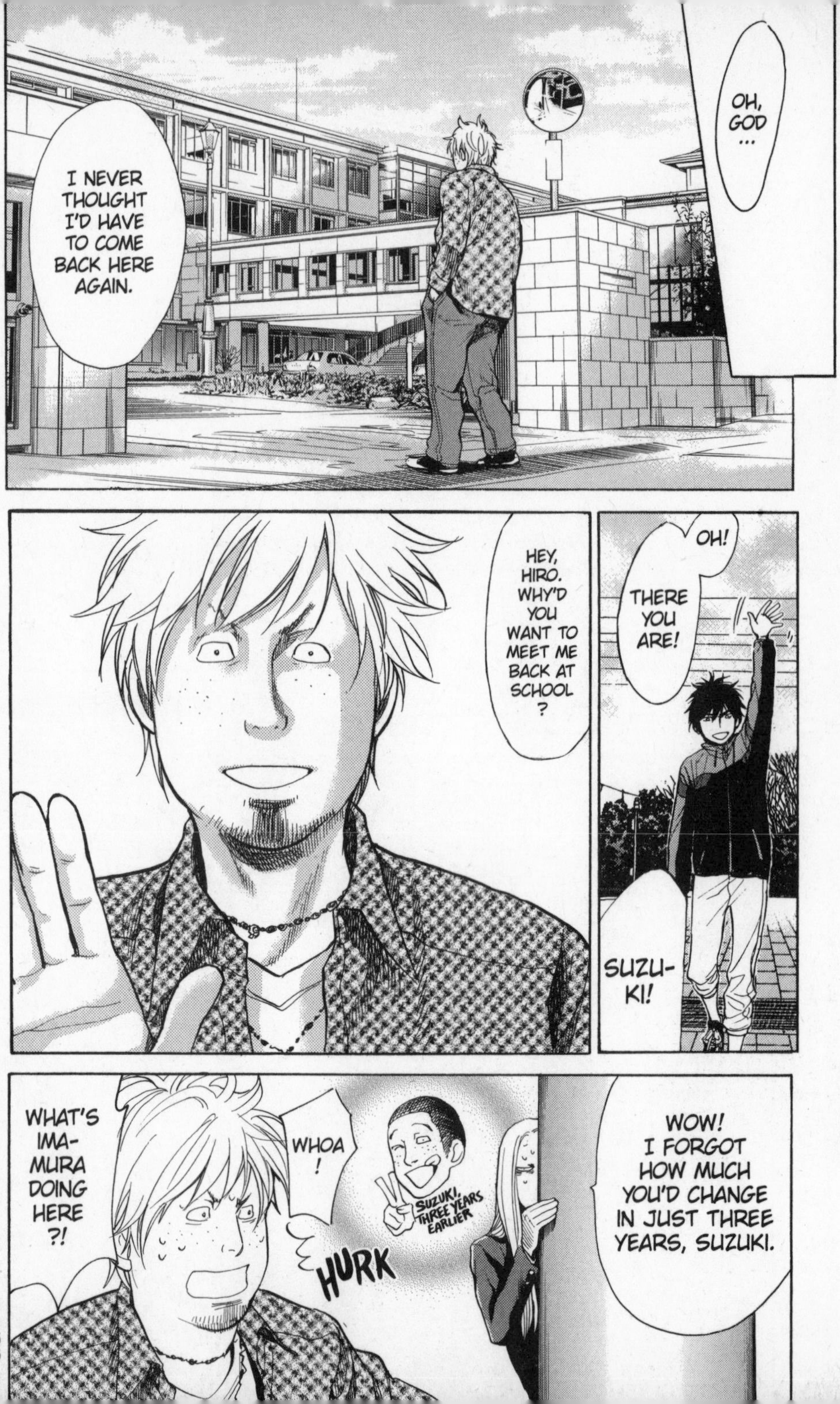

OH, GOD ...
I NEVER THOUGHT I'D HAVE TO COME BACK HERE AGAIN.
OH!
THERE YOU ARE!
SUZUKI!
HEY, HIRO. WHY'D YOU WANT TO MEET ME BACK AT SCHOOL?
WOW! I FORGOT HOW MUCH YOU'D CHANGE IN JUST THREE YEARS, SUZUKI.
WHOA!
SUZUKI, THREE YEARS EARLIER
HURK
WHAT'S IMAMURA DOING HERE?!

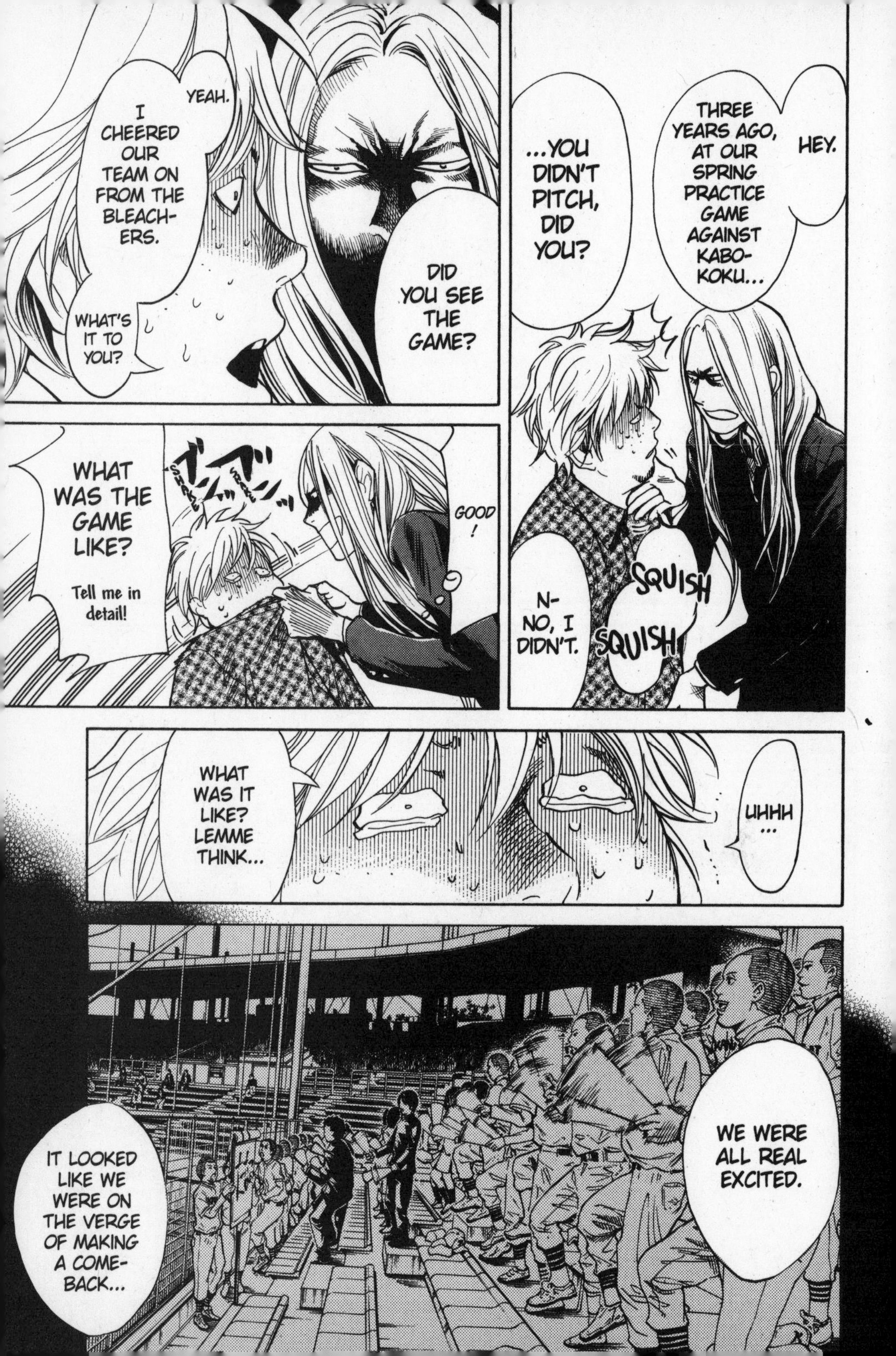
HEY.
THREE YEARS AGO, AT OUR SPRING PRACTICE GAME AGAINST KABO-KOKU...
...YOU DIDN'T PITCH, DID YOU?
SQUISH
SQUISH
N-NO, I DIDN'T.
DID YOU SEE THE GAME?
YEAH.
I CHEERED OUR TEAM ON FROM THE BLEACHERS.
WHAT'S IT TO YOU?
GOOD!
WHAT WAS THE GAME LIKE?
Tell me in detail!
UHHH...
WHAT WAS IT LIKE? LEMME THINK...
WE WERE ALL REAL EXCITED.
IT LOOKED LIKE WE WERE ON THE VERGE OF MAKING A COME-BACK...

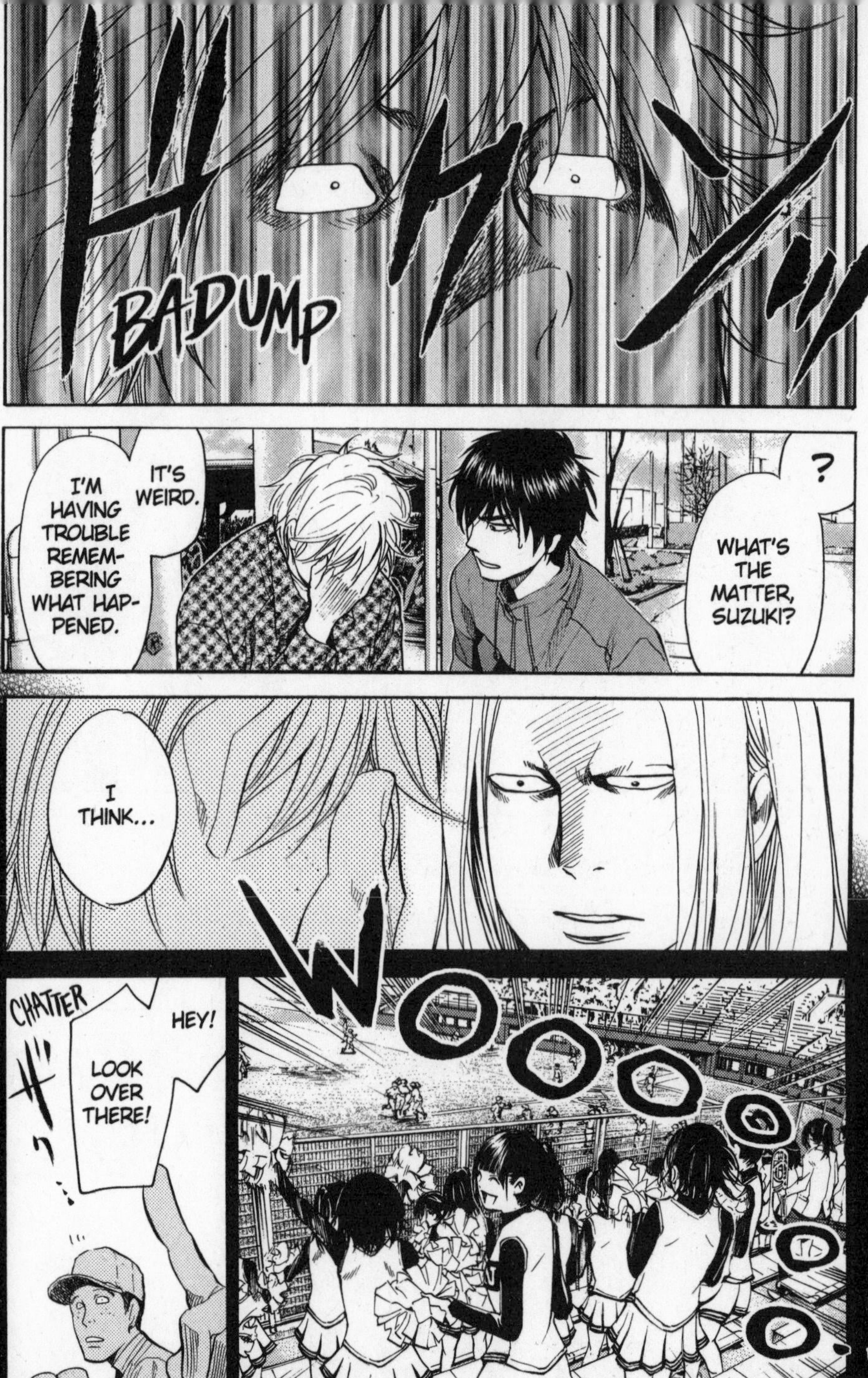
BADUMP
?
WHAT'S THE MATTER, SUZUKI?
IT'S WEIRD.
I'M HAVING TROUBLE REMEMBERING WHAT HAPPENED.
I THINK...
WOOOOO...
CHATTER
HEY!
LOOK OVER THERE!

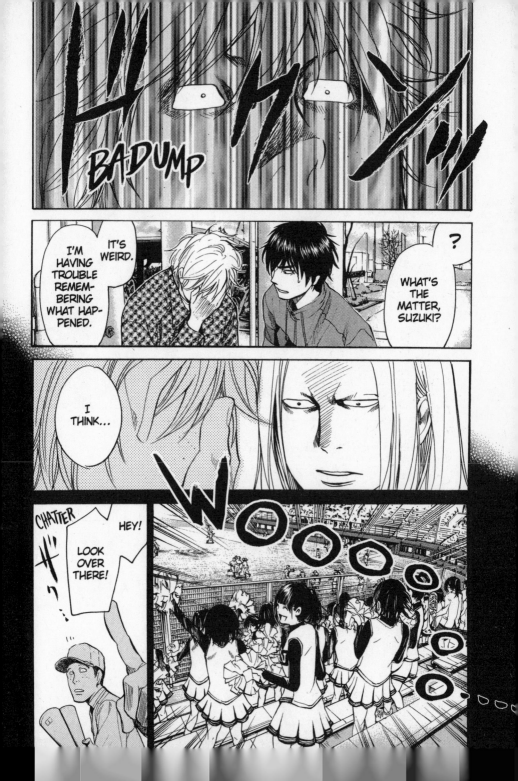

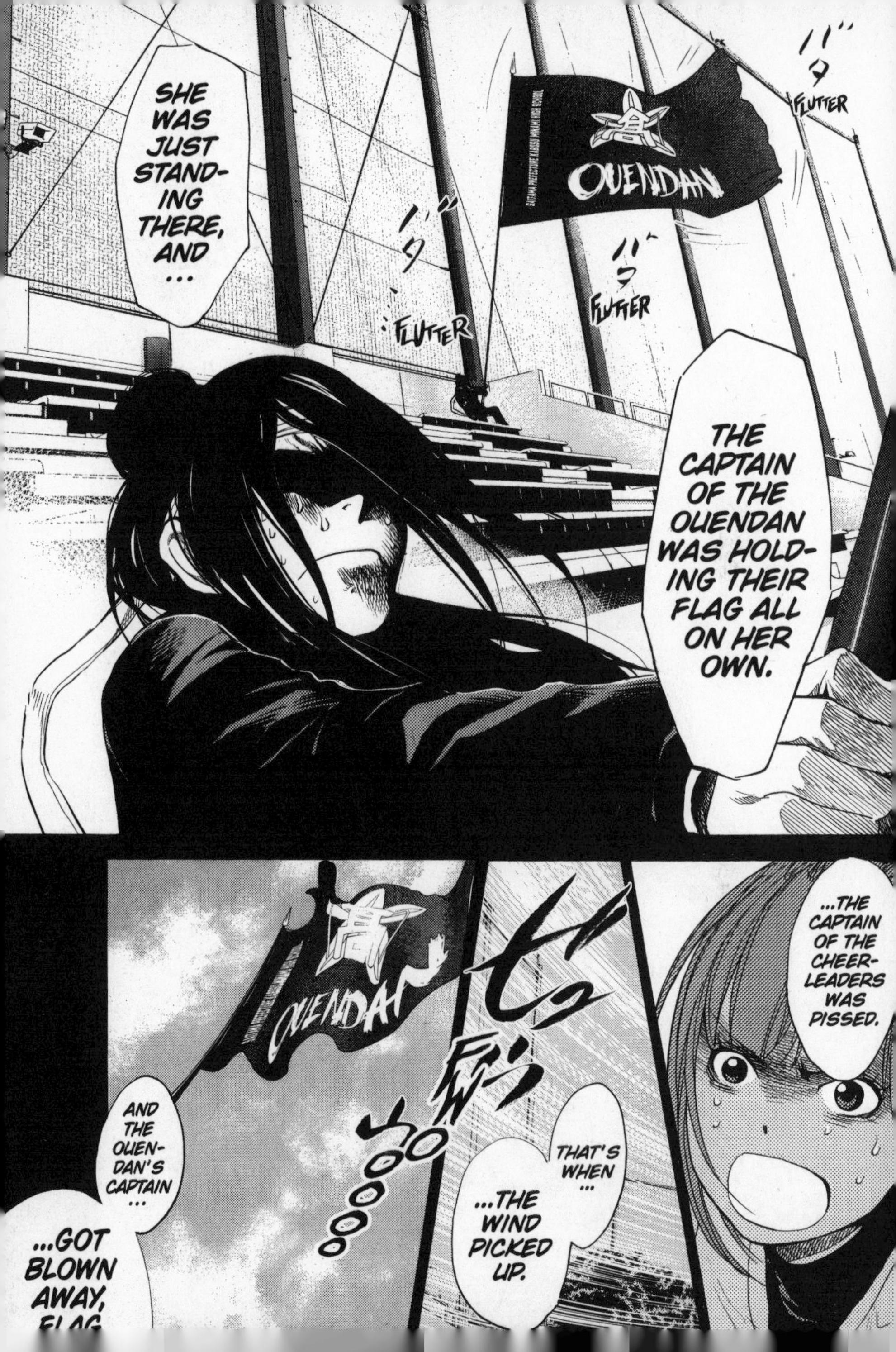
FLUTTER
THE CAPTAIN OF THE OUENDAN WAS HOLDING THEIR FLAG ALL ON HER OWN.
FLUTTER
OUENDAN
FLUTTER
SHE WAS JUST STANDING THERE, AND ...
...THE CAPTAIN OF THE CHEERLEADERS WAS PISSED.
THAT'S WHEN ...
...THE WIND PICKED UP.
OUENDAN
AND THE OUENDAN'S CAPTAIN ...
...GOT BLOWN AWAY, FLAG

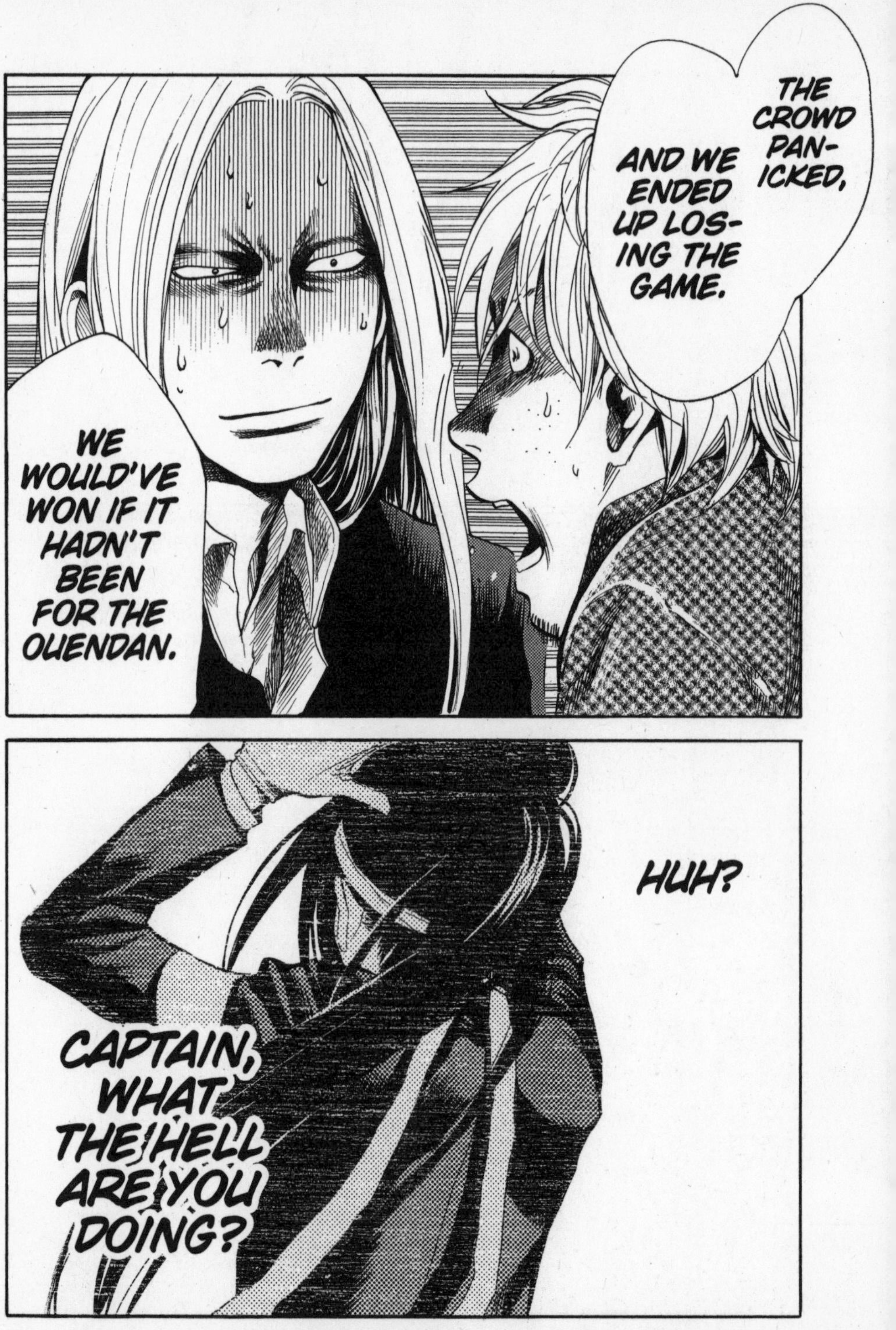
THE CROWD PANICKED,
AND WE ENDED UP LOSING THE GAME.
WE WOULD'VE WON IF IT HADN'T BEEN FOR THE OUENDAN.
HUH?
CAPTAIN, WHAT THE HELL ARE YOU DOING?

40. REUNION

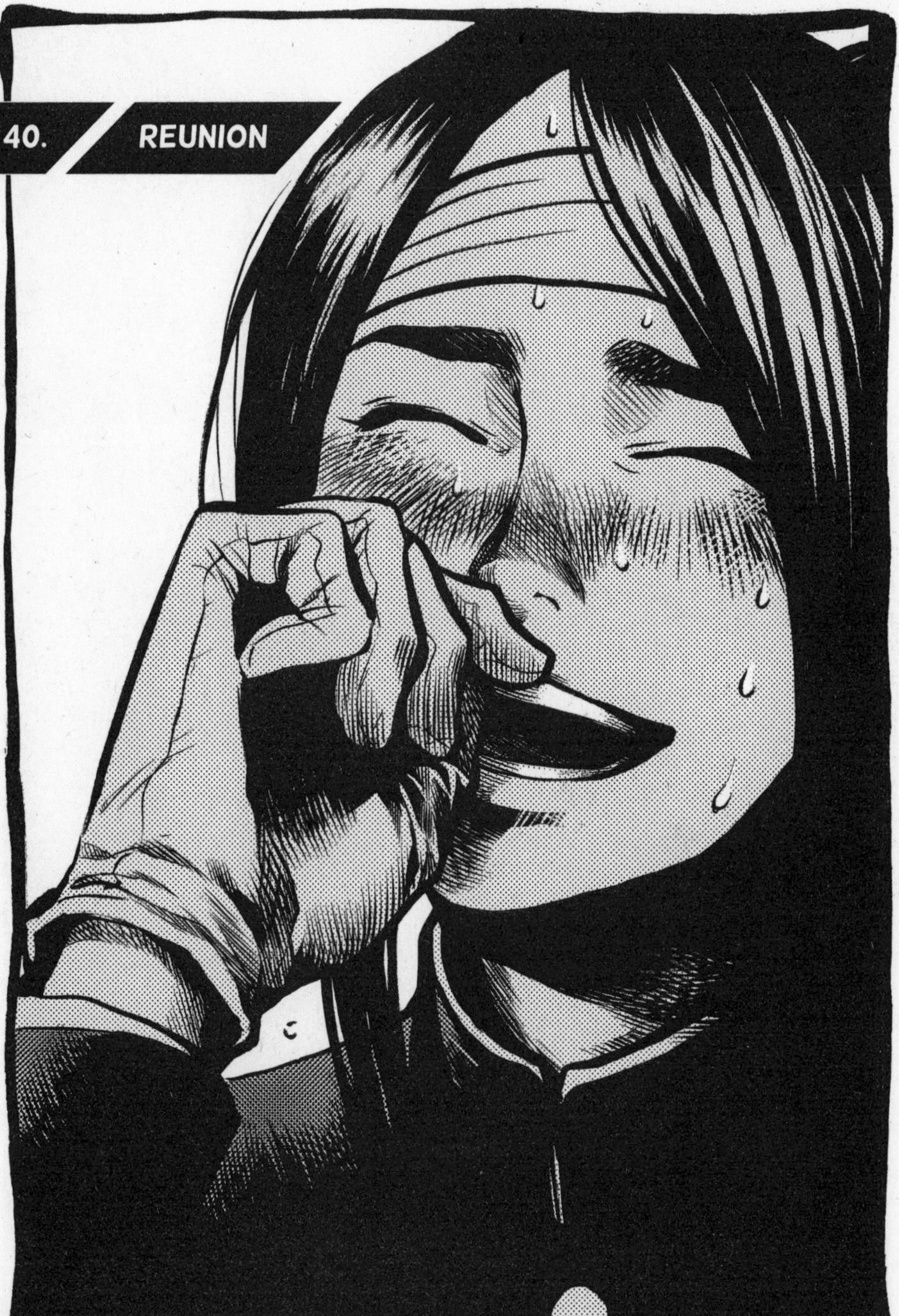

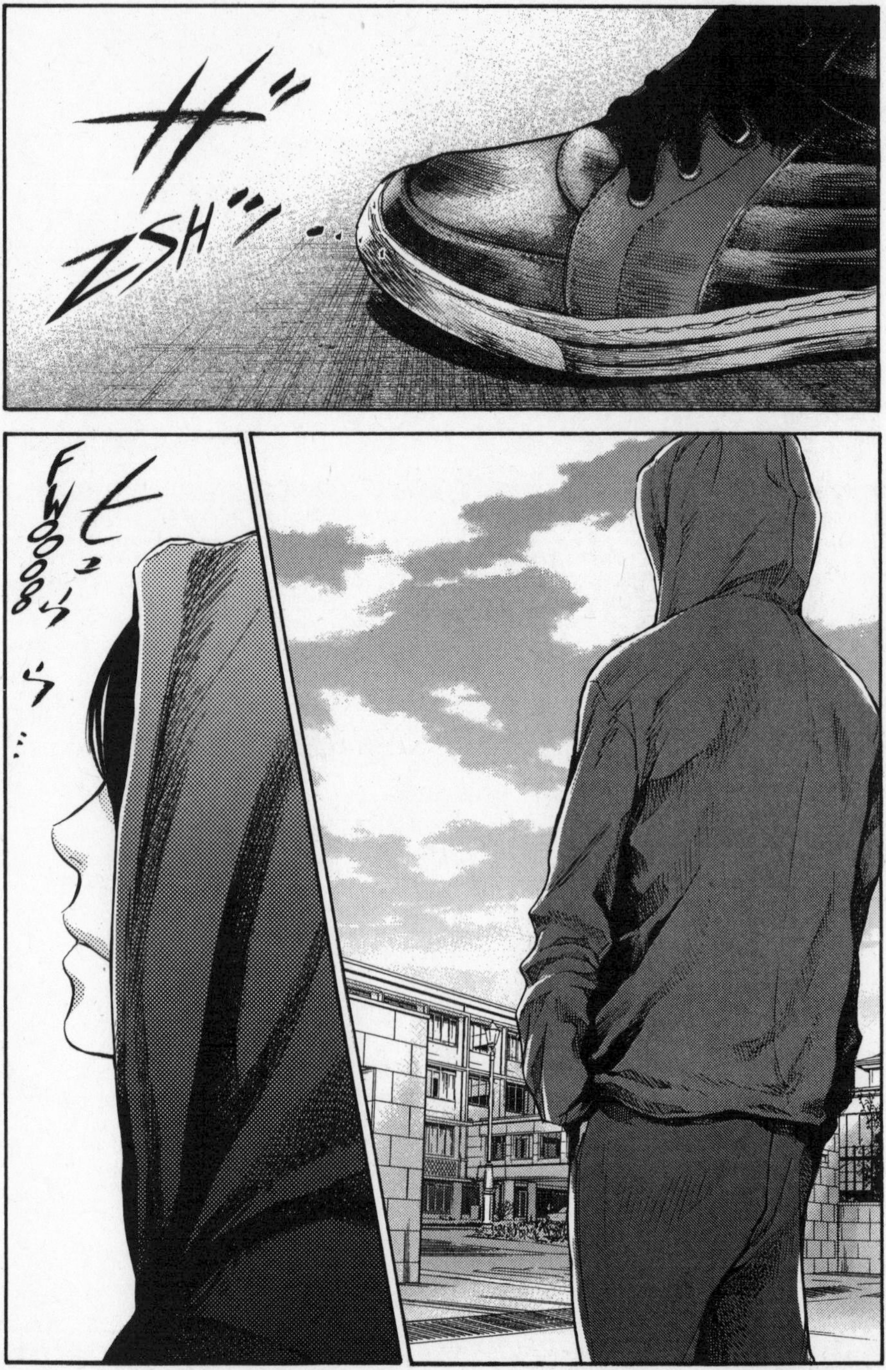
ザッ
ZSH...
ヒュゥゥ…
FWOOOS

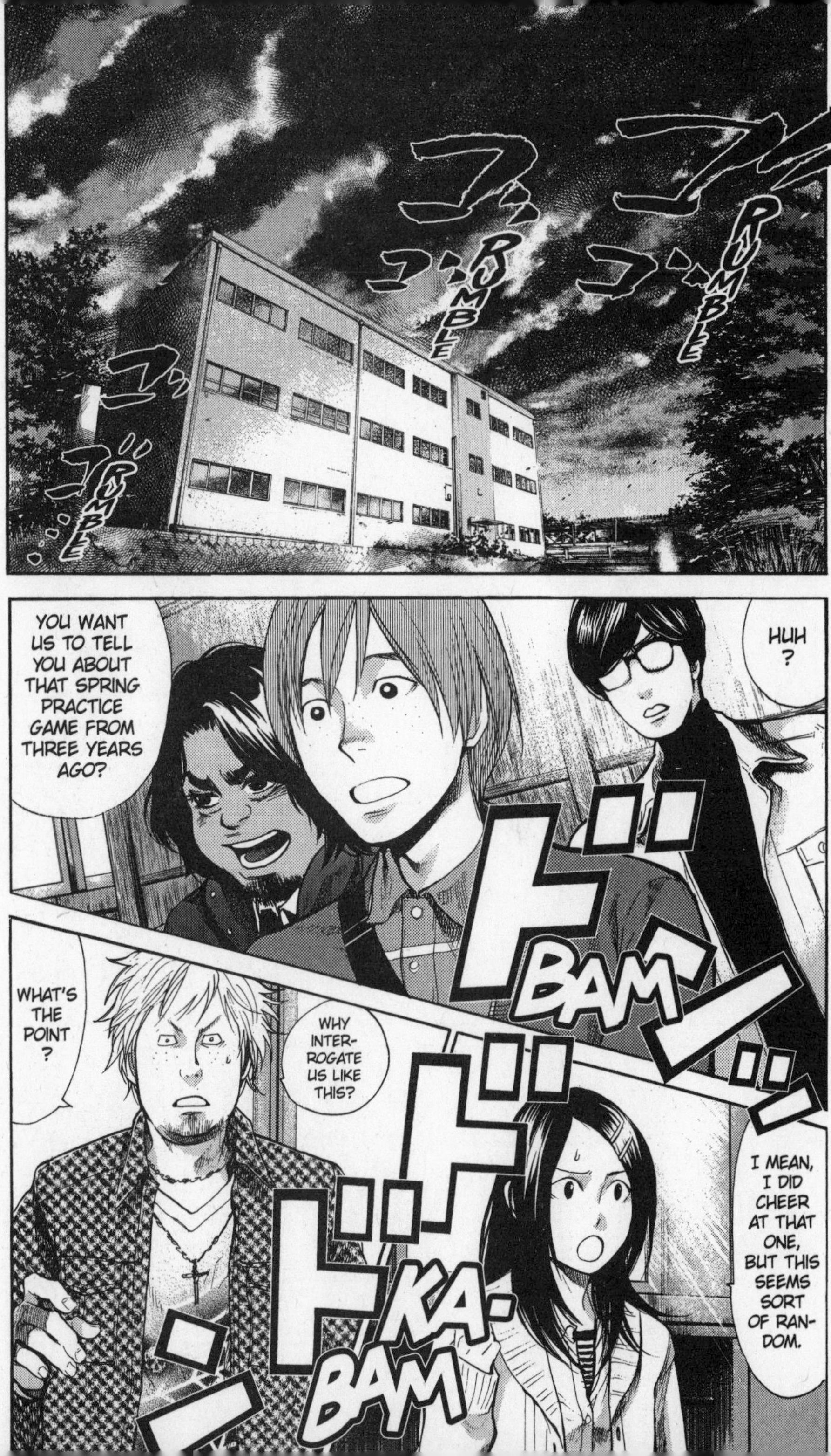

RUMBLE
RUMBLE
RUMBLE
HUH?
YOU WANT US TO TELL YOU ABOUT THAT SPRING PRACTICE GAME FROM THREE YEARS AGO?
BAM
I MEAN, I DID CHEER AT THAT ONE, BUT THIS SEEMS SORT OF RANDOM.
WHY INTERROGATE US LIKE THIS?
WHAT'S THE POINT?
KA-BAM

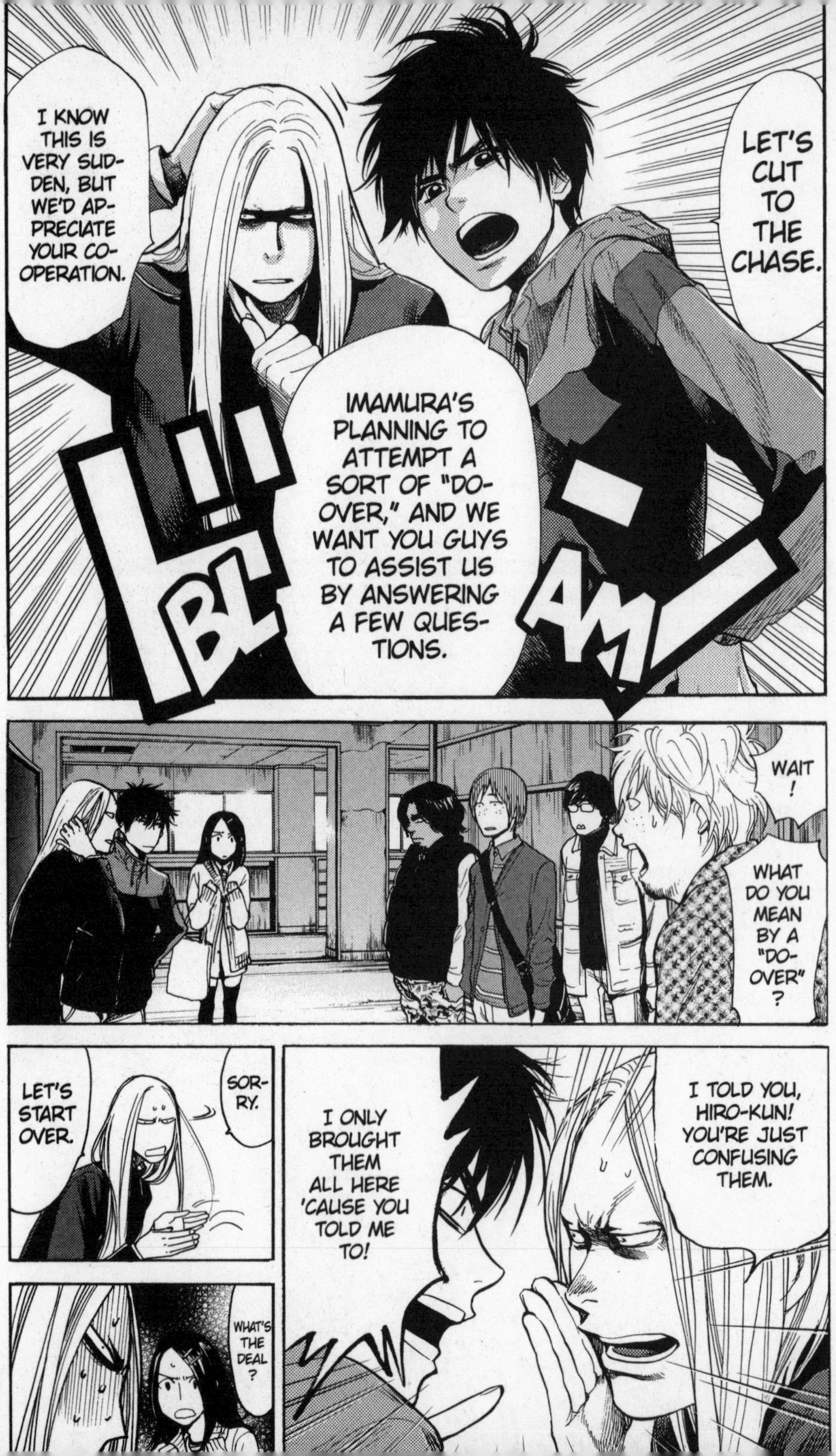
LET'S CUT TO THE CHASE.
I KNOW THIS IS VERY SUDDEN, BUT WE'D APPRECIATE YOUR CO-OPERATION.
IMAMURA'S PLANNING TO ATTEMPT A SORT OF "DO-OVER," AND WE WANT YOU GUYS TO ASSIST US BY ANSWERING A FEW QUESTIONS.
BLAM!!
WAIT!
WHAT DO YOU MEAN BY A "DO-OVER"?
I TOLD YOU, HIRO-KUN! YOU'RE JUST CONFUSING THEM.
I ONLY BROUGHT THEM ALL HERE 'CAUSE YOU TOLD ME TO!
SORRY.
LET'S START OVER.
WHAT'S THE DEAL?

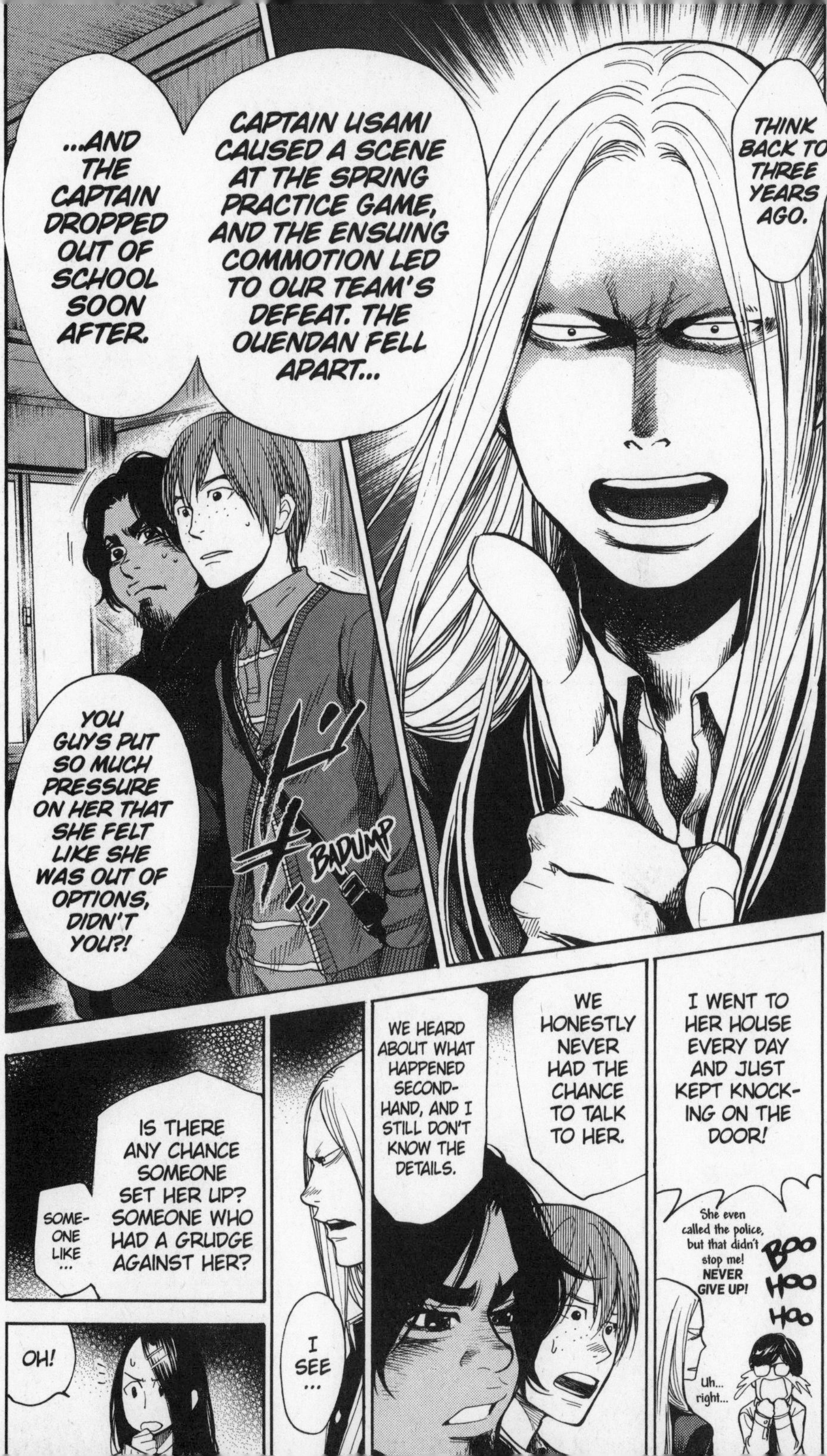
THINK BACK TO THREE YEARS AGO.
CAPTAIN USAMI CAUSED A SCENE AT THE SPRING PRACTICE GAME, AND THE ENSUING COMMOTION LED TO OUR TEAM'S DEFEAT. THE OUENDAN FELL APART...
...AND THE CAPTAIN DROPPED OUT OF SCHOOL SOON AFTER.
YOU GUYS PUT SO MUCH PRESSURE ON HER THAT SHE FELT LIKE SHE WAS OUT OF OPTIONS, DIDN'T YOU?!
BADUMP
I WENT TO HER HOUSE EVERY DAY AND JUST KEPT KNOCKING ON THE DOOR!
She even called the police, but that didn't stop me! NEVER GIVE UP!
BOO HOO HOO
Uh... right...
WE HONESTLY NEVER HAD THE CHANCE TO TALK TO HER.
WE HEARD ABOUT WHAT HAPPENED SECOND-HAND, AND I STILL DON'T KNOW THE DETAILS.
I SEE...
IS THERE ANY CHANCE SOMEONE SET HER UP? SOMEONE WHO HAD A GRUDGE AGAINST HER?
SOME-ONE LIKE...
OH!

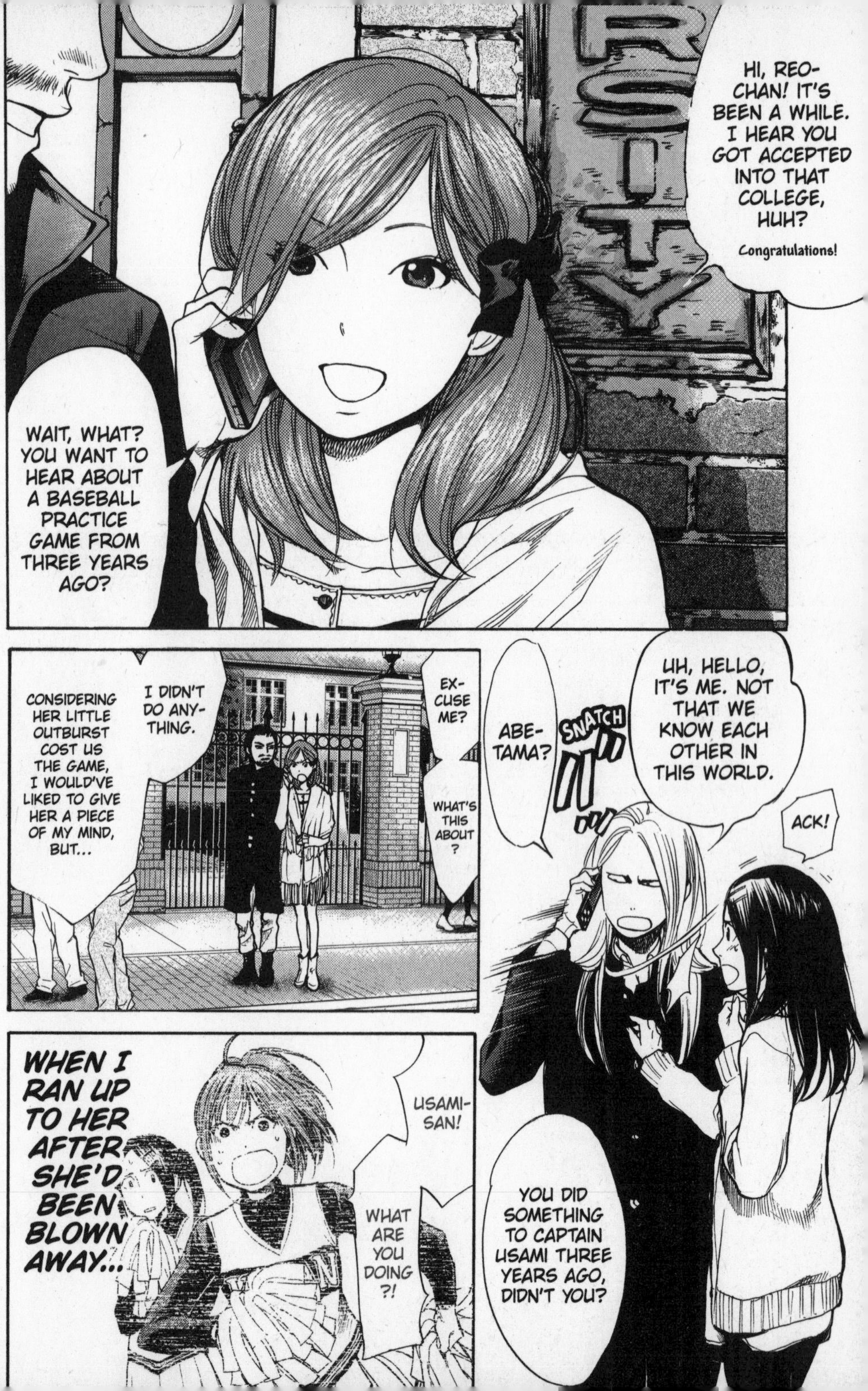
HI, REO-CHAN! IT'S BEEN A WHILE. I HEAR YOU GOT ACCEPTED INTO THAT COLLEGE, HUH?
Congratulations!
WAIT, WHAT? YOU WANT TO HEAR ABOUT A BASEBALL PRACTICE GAME FROM THREE YEARS AGO?
UH, HELLO, IT'S ME. NOT THAT WE KNOW EACH OTHER IN THIS WORLD.
ACK!
SNATCH
ABE-TAMA?
YOU DID SOMETHING TO CAPTAIN USAMI THREE YEARS AGO, DIDN'T YOU?
EX-CUSE ME?
WHAT'S THIS ABOUT?
I DIDN'T DO ANY-THING.
CONSIDERING HER LITTLE OUTBURST COST US THE GAME, I WOULD'VE LIKED TO GIVE HER A PIECE OF MY MIND, BUT...
USAMI-SAN!
WHAT ARE YOU DOING?!
WHEN I RAN UP TO HER AFTER SHE'D BEEN BLOWN AWAY...

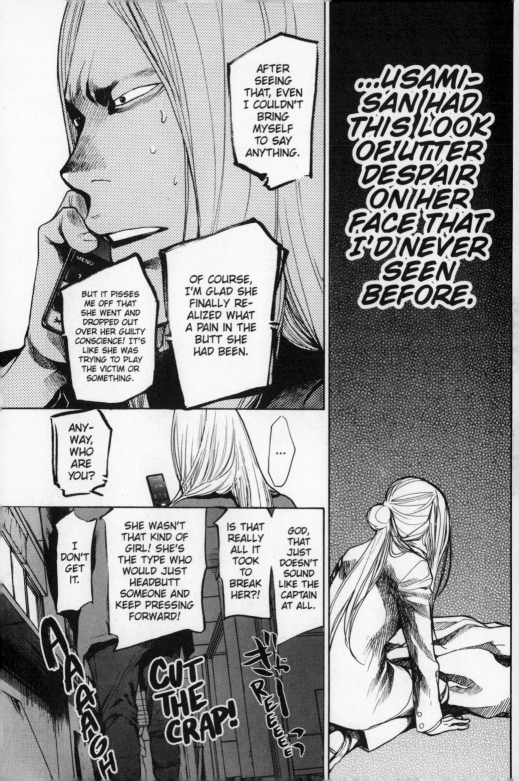

...USAMI-SAN HAD THIS LOOK OF UTTER DESPAIR ON HER FACE THAT I'D NEVER SEEN BEFORE.

AFTER SEEING THAT, EVEN I COULDN'T BRING MYSELF TO SAY ANYTHING.

OF COURSE, I'M GLAD SHE FINALLY REALIZED WHAT A PAIN IN THE BUTT SHE HAD BEEN.

BUT IT PISSES ME OFF THAT SHE WENT AND DROPPED OUT OVER HER GUILTY CONSCIENCE! IT'S LIKE SHE WAS TRYING TO PLAY THE VICTIM OR SOMETHING.

ANYWAY, WHO ARE YOU?

...

GOD, THAT JUST DOESN'T SOUND LIKE THE CAPTAIN AT ALL.

IS THAT REALLY ALL IT TOOK TO BREAK HER?!

SHE WASN'T THAT KIND OF GIRL! SHE'S THE TYPE WHO WOULD JUST HEADBUTT SOMEONE AND KEEP PRESSING FORWARD!

I DON'T GET IT.

AAAAGH

CUT THE CRAP!

REEEEE

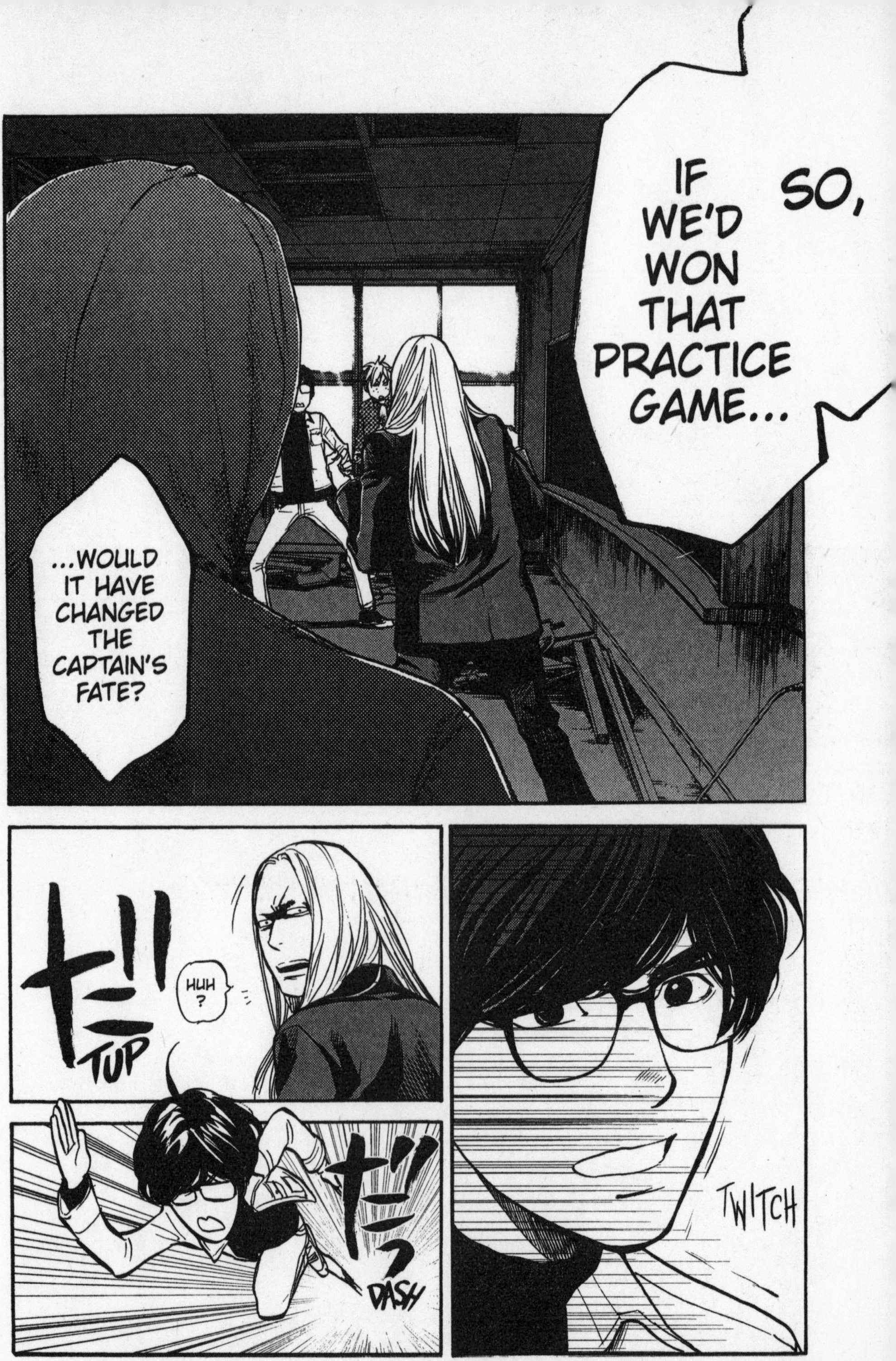
SO, IF WE'D WON THAT PRACTICE GAME...
...WOULD IT HAVE CHANGED THE CAPTAIN'S FATE?
TWITCH
HUH?
TUP
DASH

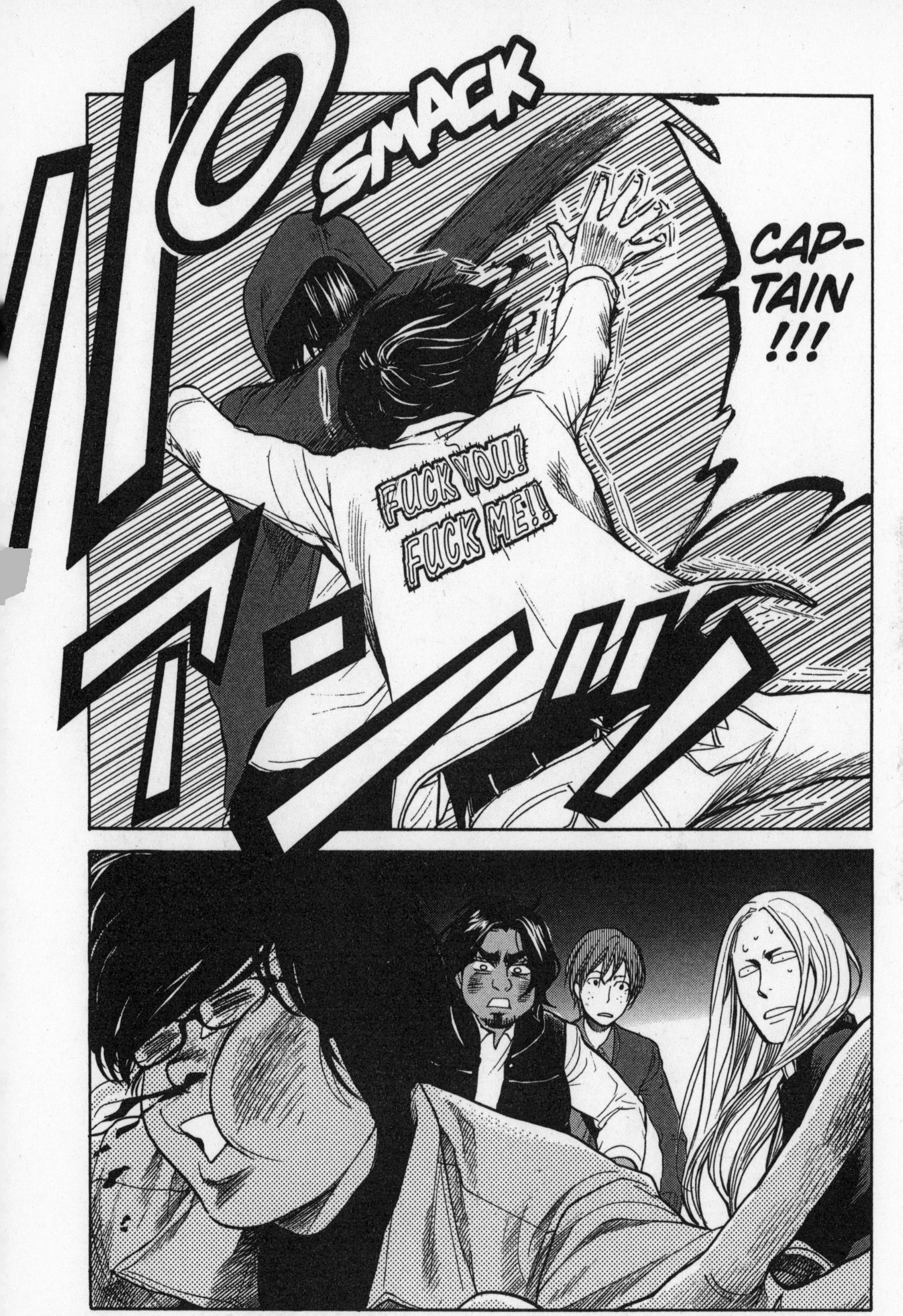
CAP-TAIN!!!
SMACK
FUCK YOU! FUCK ME!!

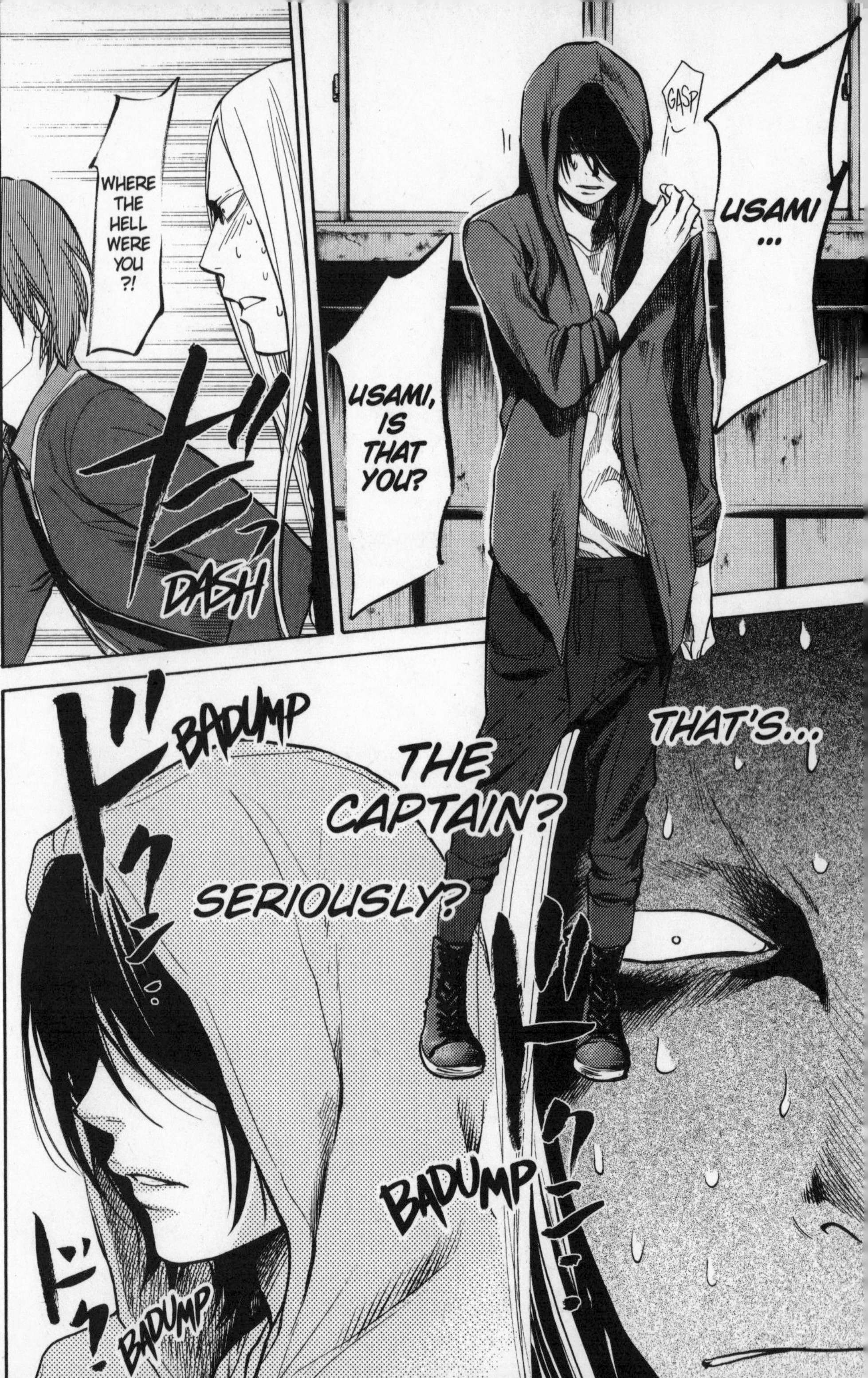
GASP
USAMI ...
USAMI, IS THAT YOU?
WHERE THE HELL WERE YOU ?!
DASH
BADUMP
THAT'S...
THE CAPTAIN?
SERIOUSLY?
BADUMP
BADUMP

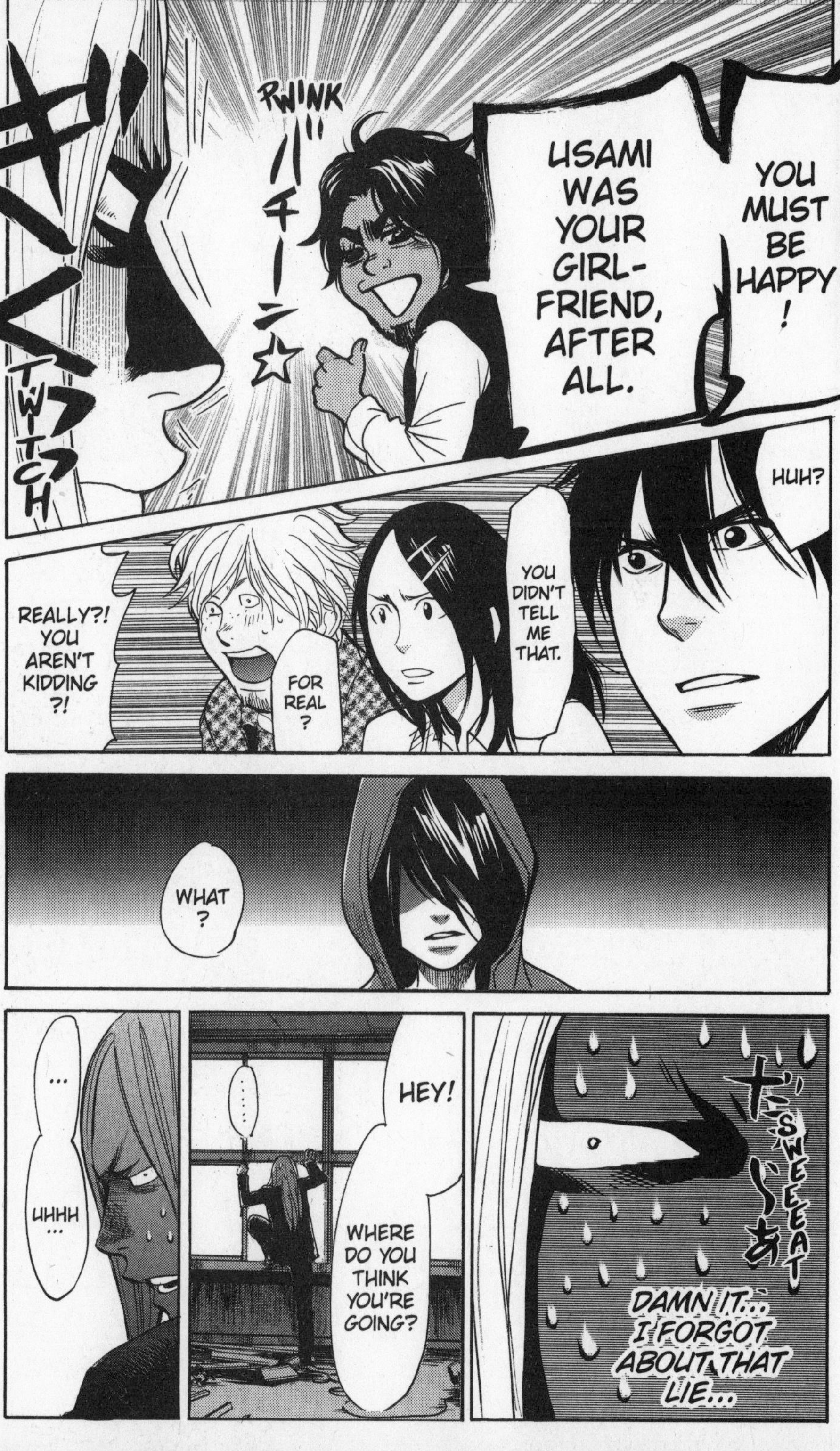
YOU MUST BE HAPPY!
USAMI WAS YOUR GIRL-FRIEND, AFTER ALL.
バチーン☆
PWINK
ぎく
TWITCH
HUH?
YOU DIDN'T TELL ME THAT.
FOR REAL?
REALLY?! YOU AREN'T KIDDING?!
WHAT?
SWEEEAT
DAMN IT... I FORGOT ABOUT THAT LIE...
HEY!
WHERE DO YOU THINK YOU'RE GOING?
......
...
UHHH...

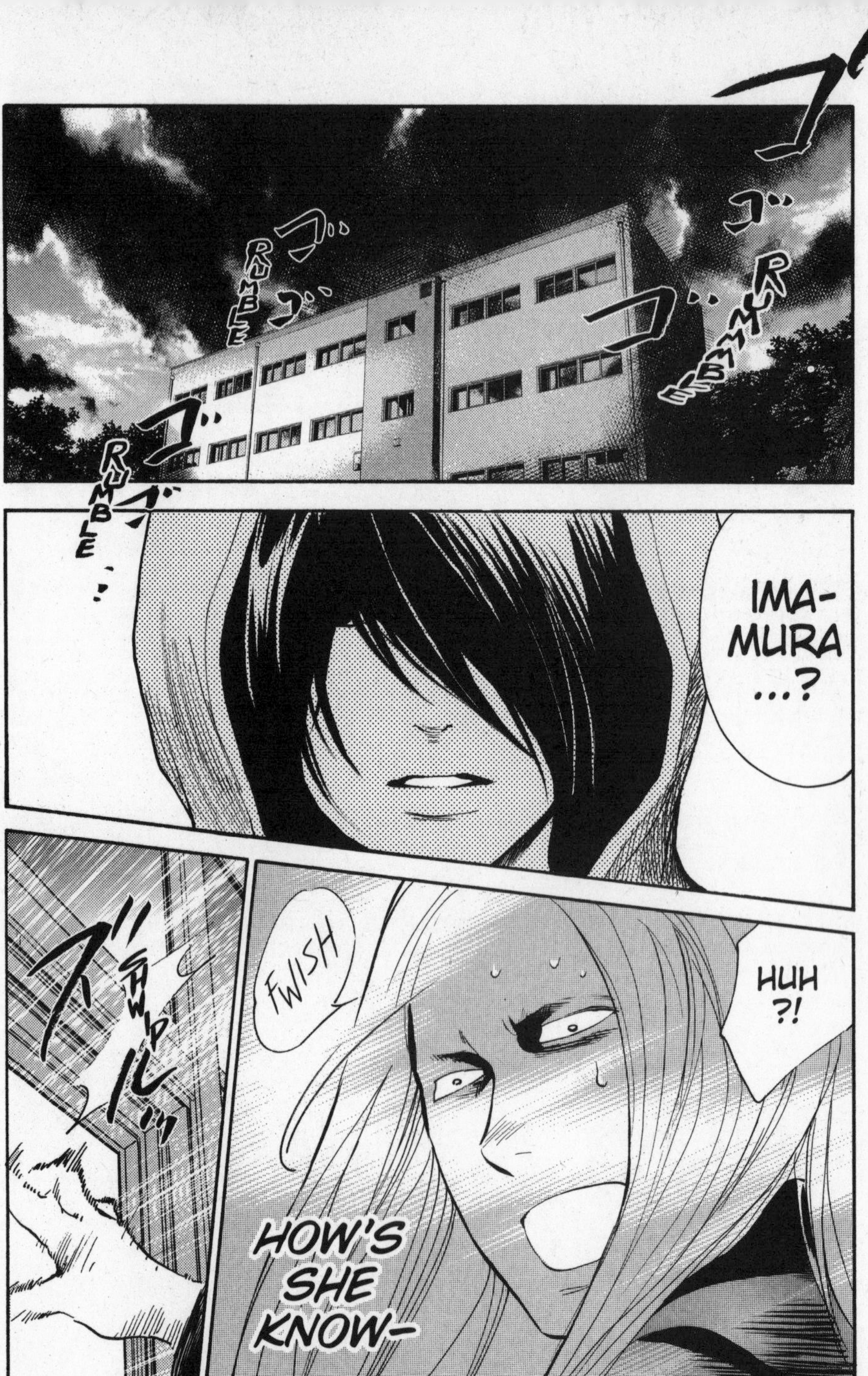
RUMBLE
RUMBLE
RUMBLE
...
IMA-MURA...?
HUH?!
FWISH
HOW'S SHE KNOW-
SHWIP

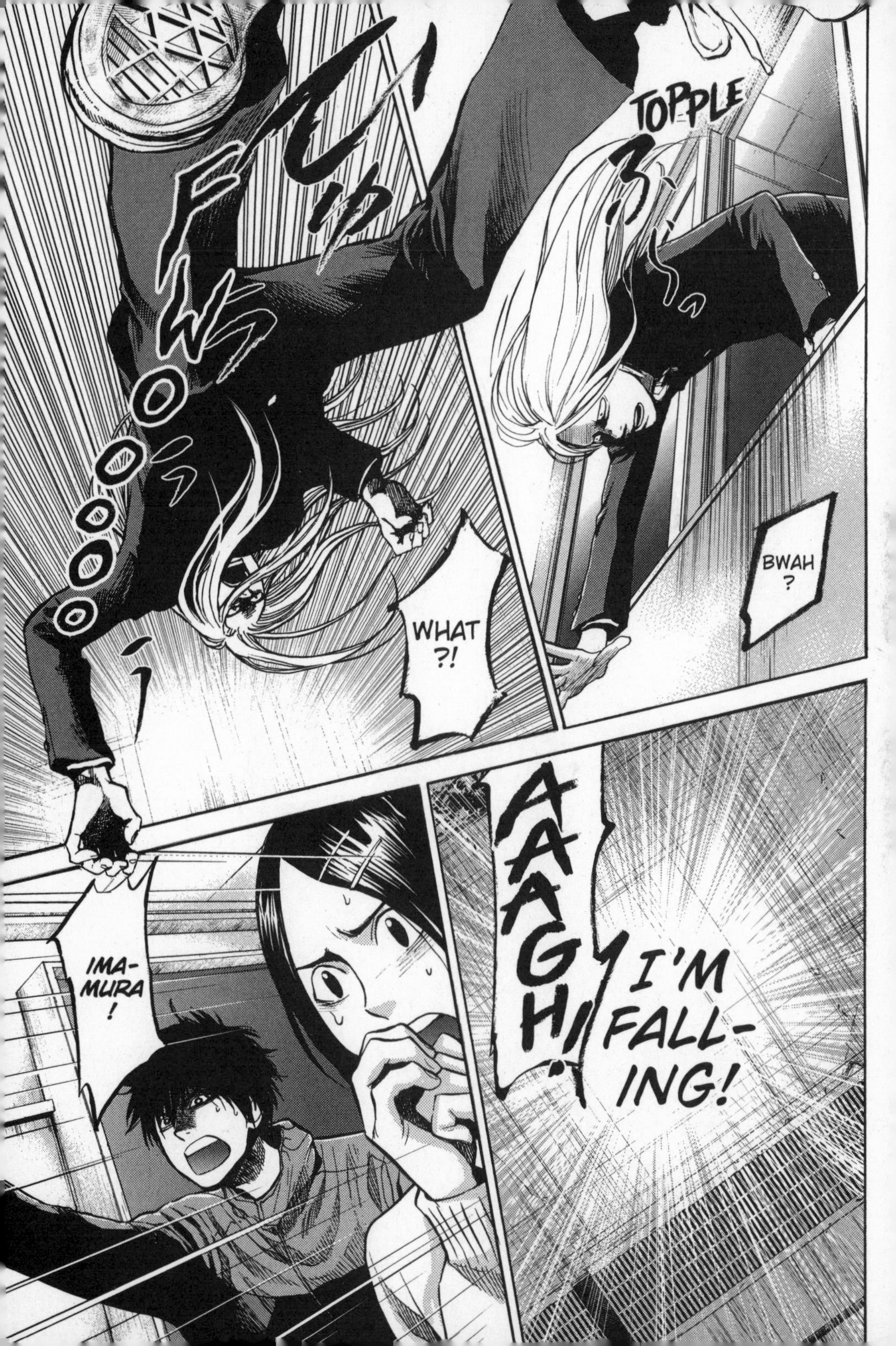
TOPPLE
BWAH?
FWOOOOOOO
WHAT?!
AAAGH!
I'M FALL-ING!
IMA-MURA!

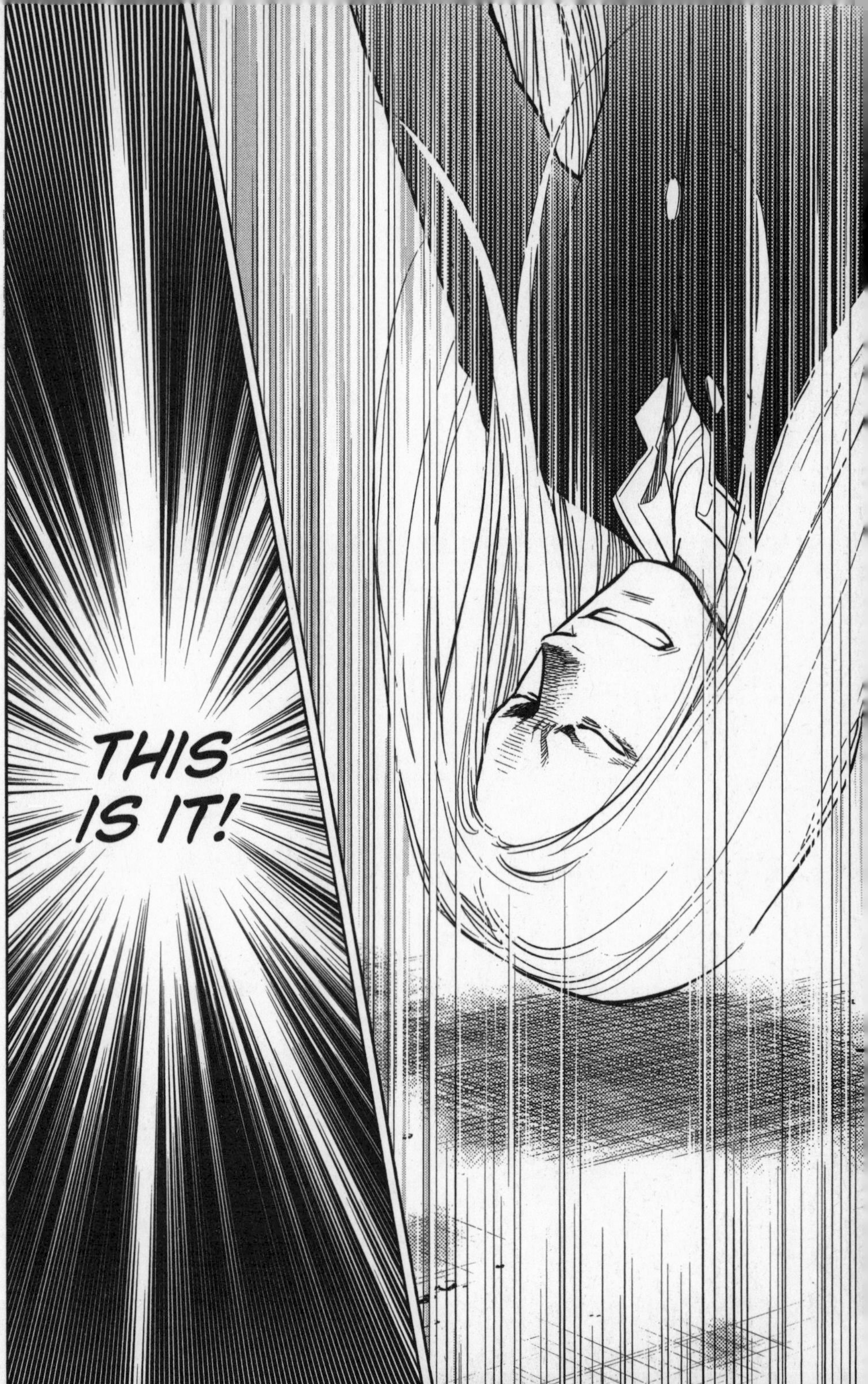
THIS IS IT!

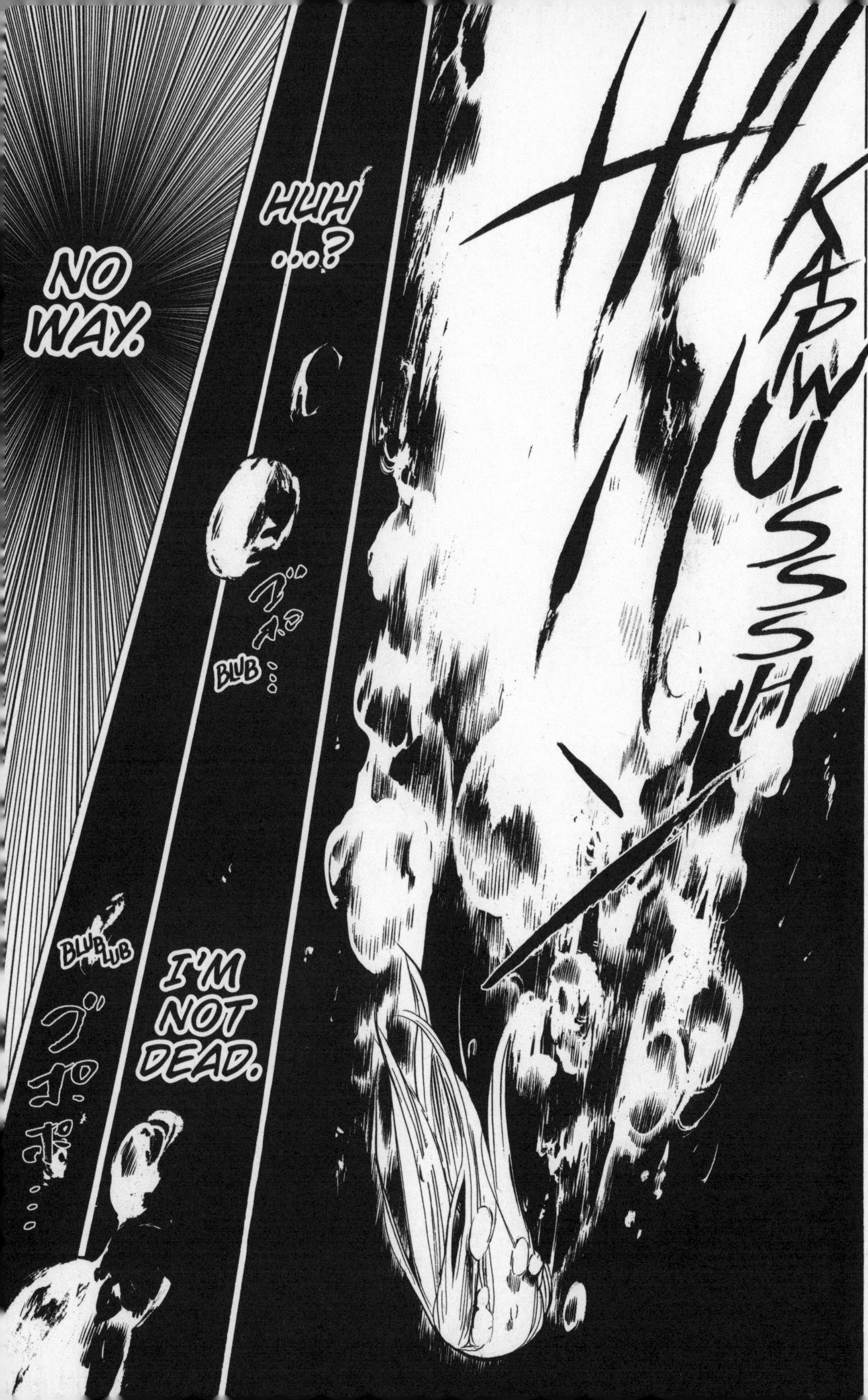
KAPWUSSSH
HUH ...?
BLUB
I'M NOT DEAD.
BLUBLUB
NO WAY.

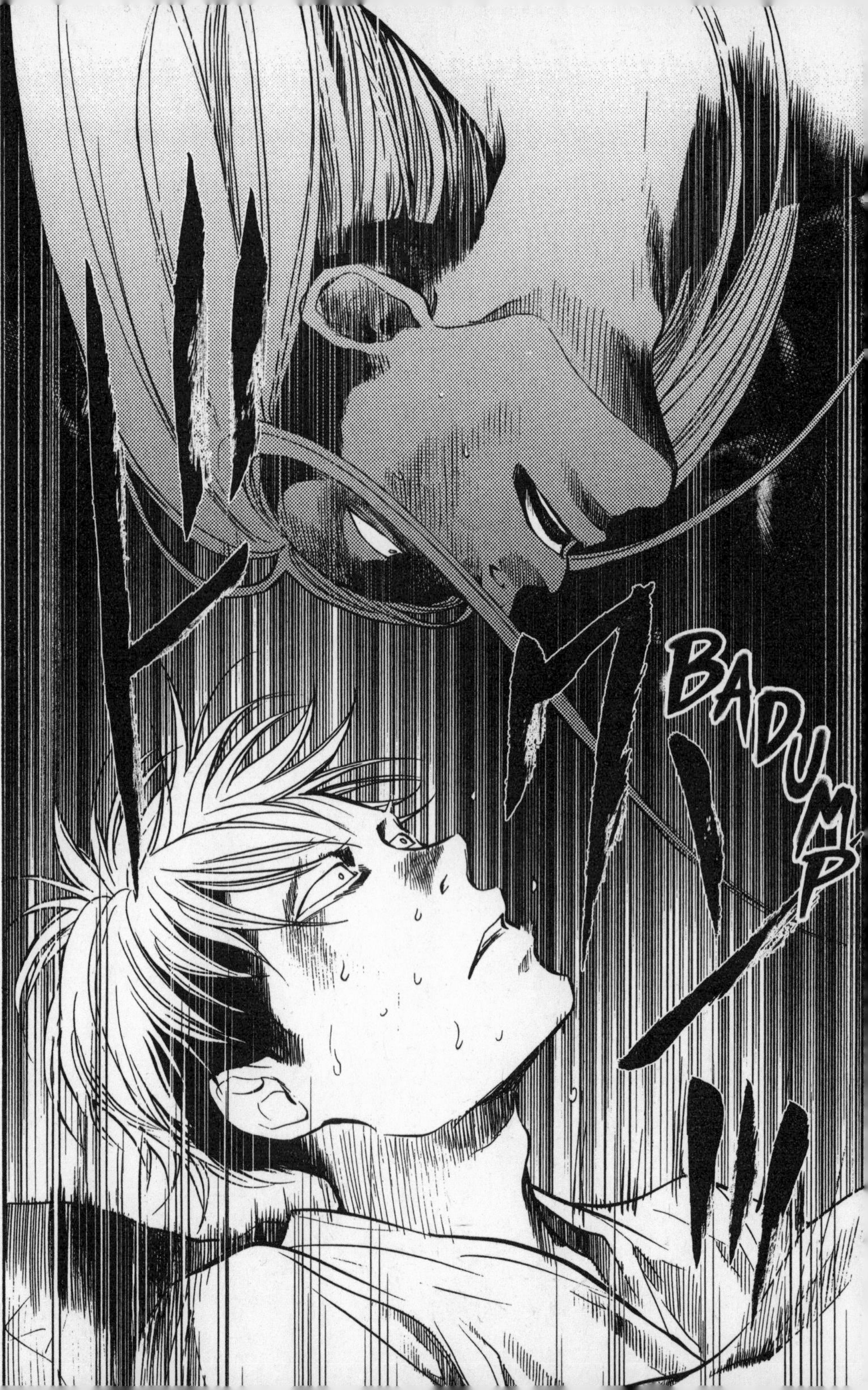
BADUMP

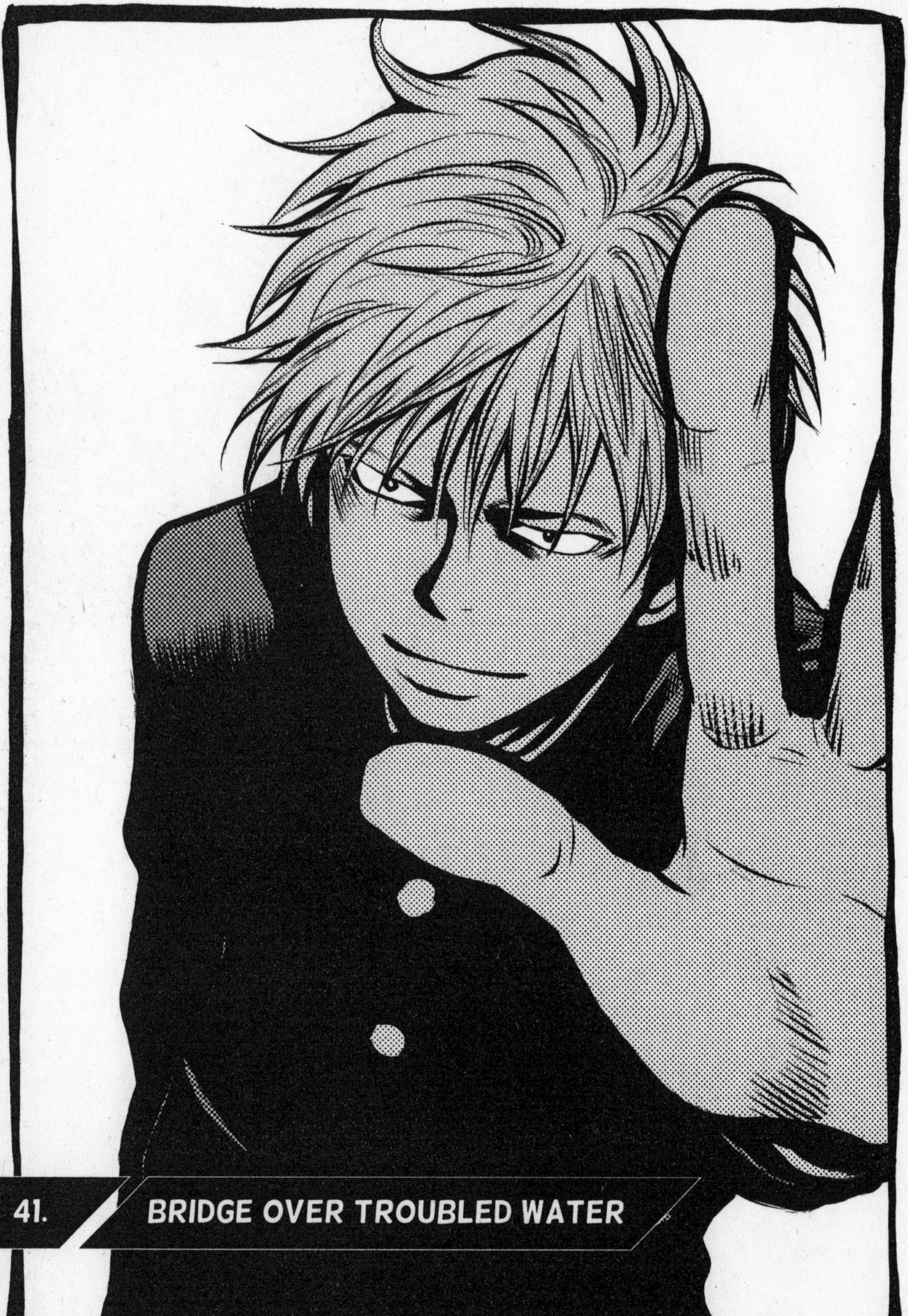

41. BRIDGE OVER TROUBLED WATER

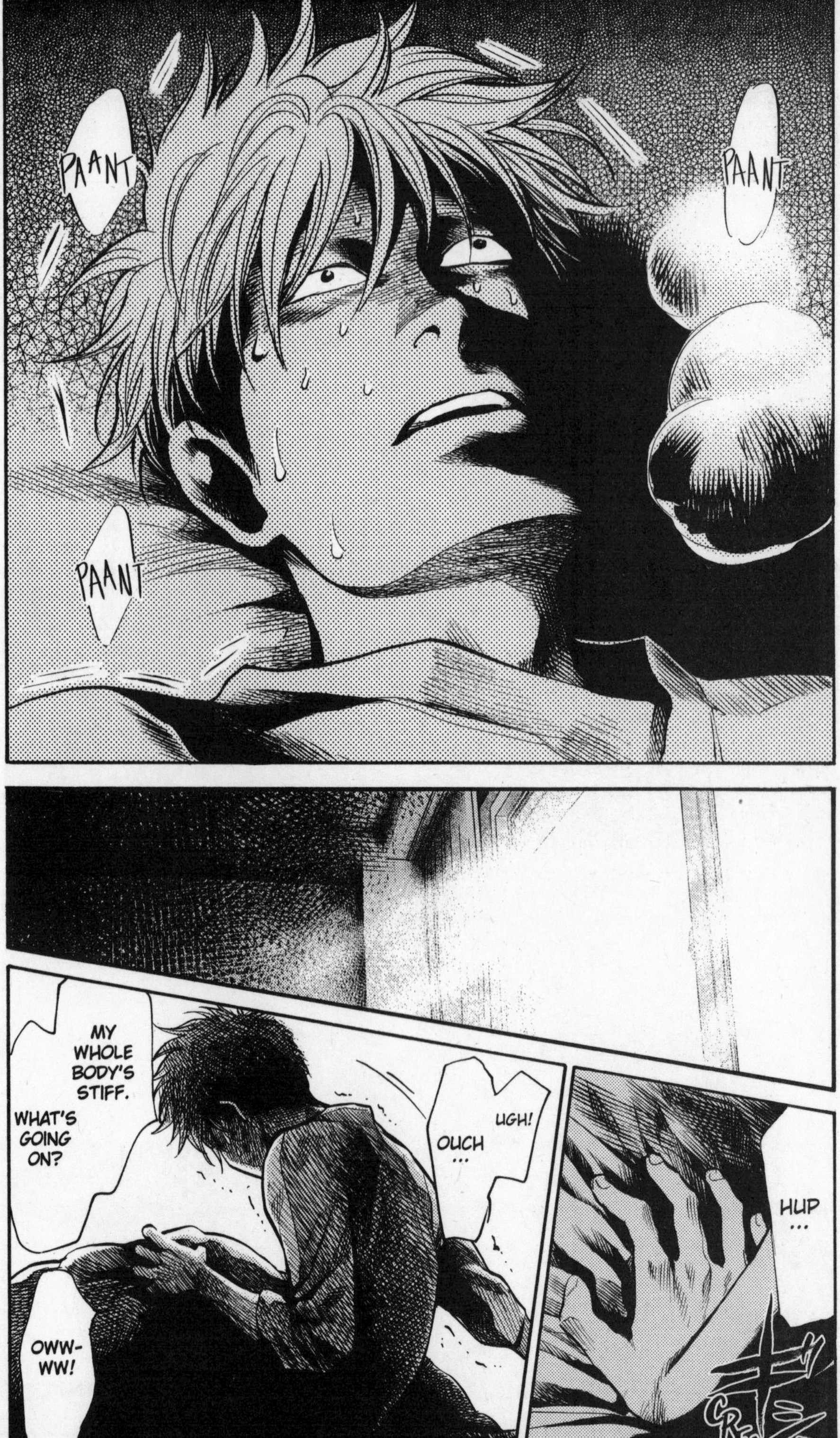
PAANT
PAANT
PAANT
HUP...
CREAK
UGH!
OUCH...
MY WHOLE BODY'S STIFF.
WHAT'S GOING ON?
OWW-WW!

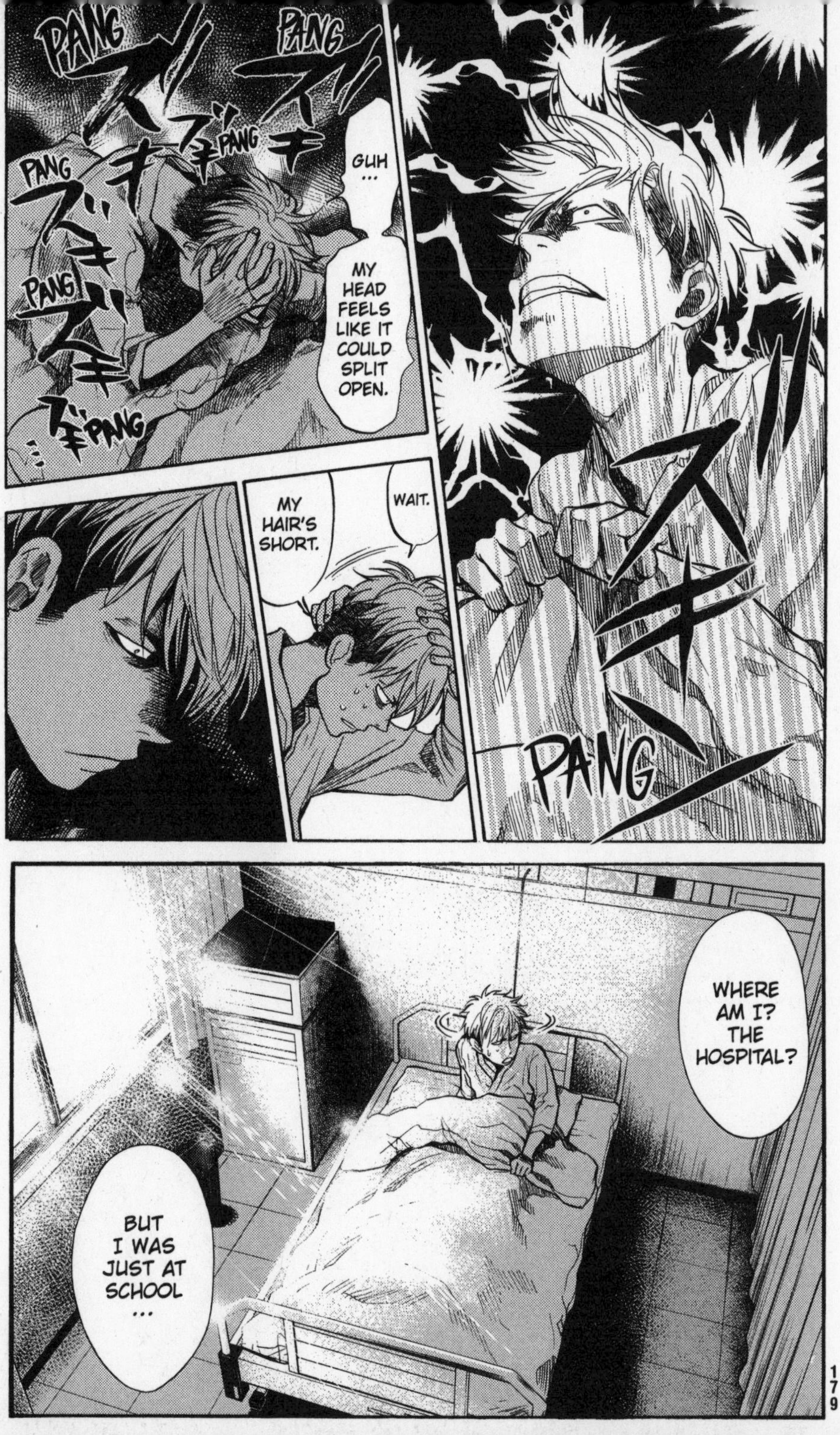
PANG
PANG
PANG
GUH ...
MY HEAD FEELS LIKE IT COULD SPLIT OPEN.
PANG
PANG
PANG
PANG
WAIT.
MY HAIR'S SHORT.
WHERE AM I? THE HOSPITAL?
BUT I WAS JUST AT SCHOOL ...

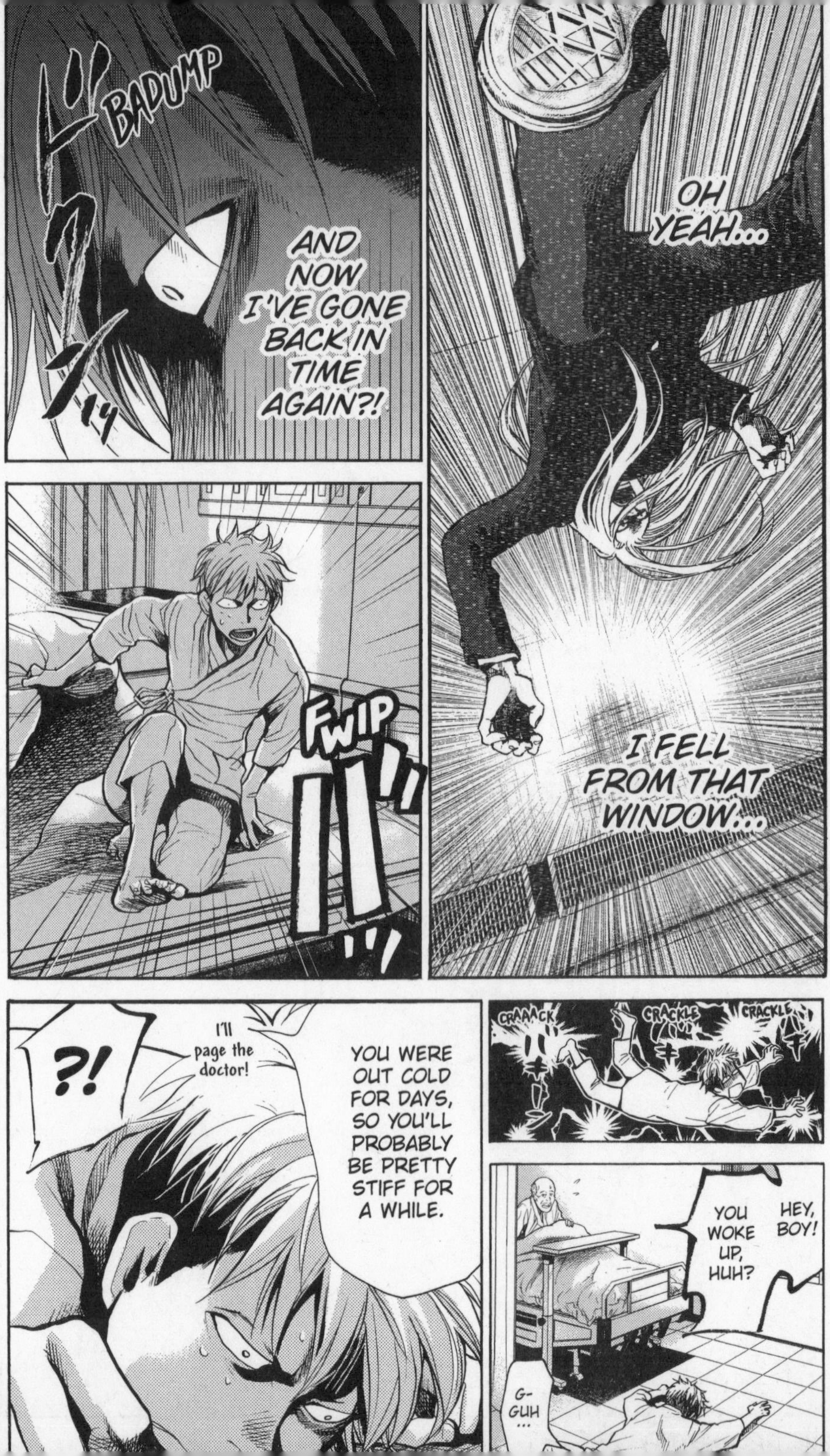
OH YEAH...
I FELL FROM THAT WINDOW...
BADUMP
AND NOW I'VE GONE BACK IN TIME AGAIN?!
FWIP
CRAAACK
CRACKLE
CRACKLE
HEY, BOY!
YOU WOKE UP, HUH?
G-GUH...
YOU WERE OUT COLD FOR DAYS, SO YOU'LL PROBABLY BE PRETTY STIFF FOR A WHILE.
I'll page the doctor!
?!

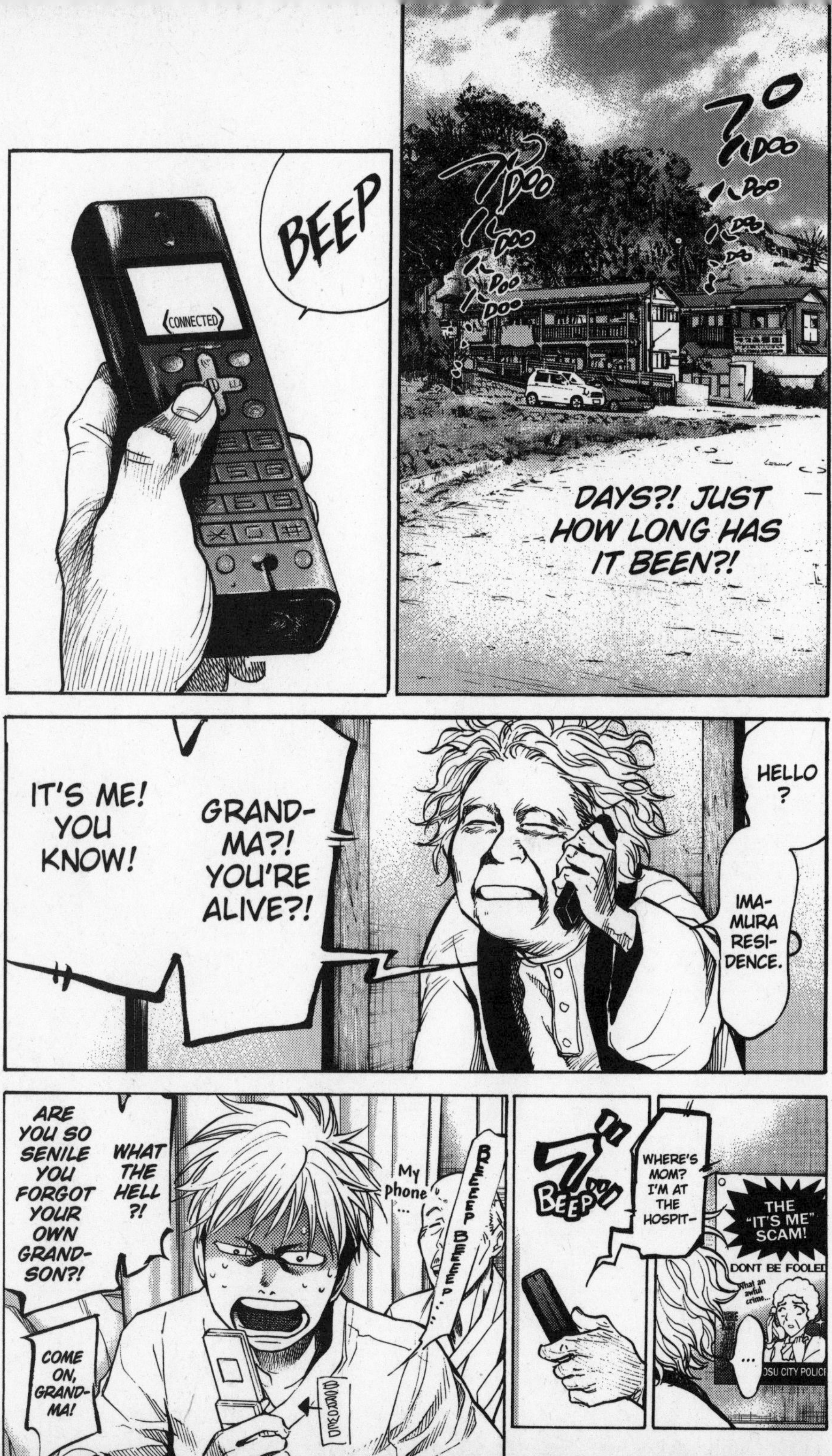

DOO
DOO
DOO
DOO
DAYS?! JUST HOW LONG HAS IT BEEN?!
BEEP
CONNECTED
HELLO?
IMAMURA RESIDENCE.
GRANDMA?! YOU'RE ALIVE?!
IT'S ME! YOU KNOW!
THE "IT'S ME" SCAM!
DONT BE FOOLED
What an awful crime...
OSU CITY POLIC
WHERE'S MOM? I'M AT THE HOSPIT-
BEEP
...
My phone ...
BEEEEP BEEEEP...
WHAT THE HELL?!
ARE YOU SO SENILE YOU FORGOT YOUR OWN GRANDSON?!
COME ON, GRANDMA!

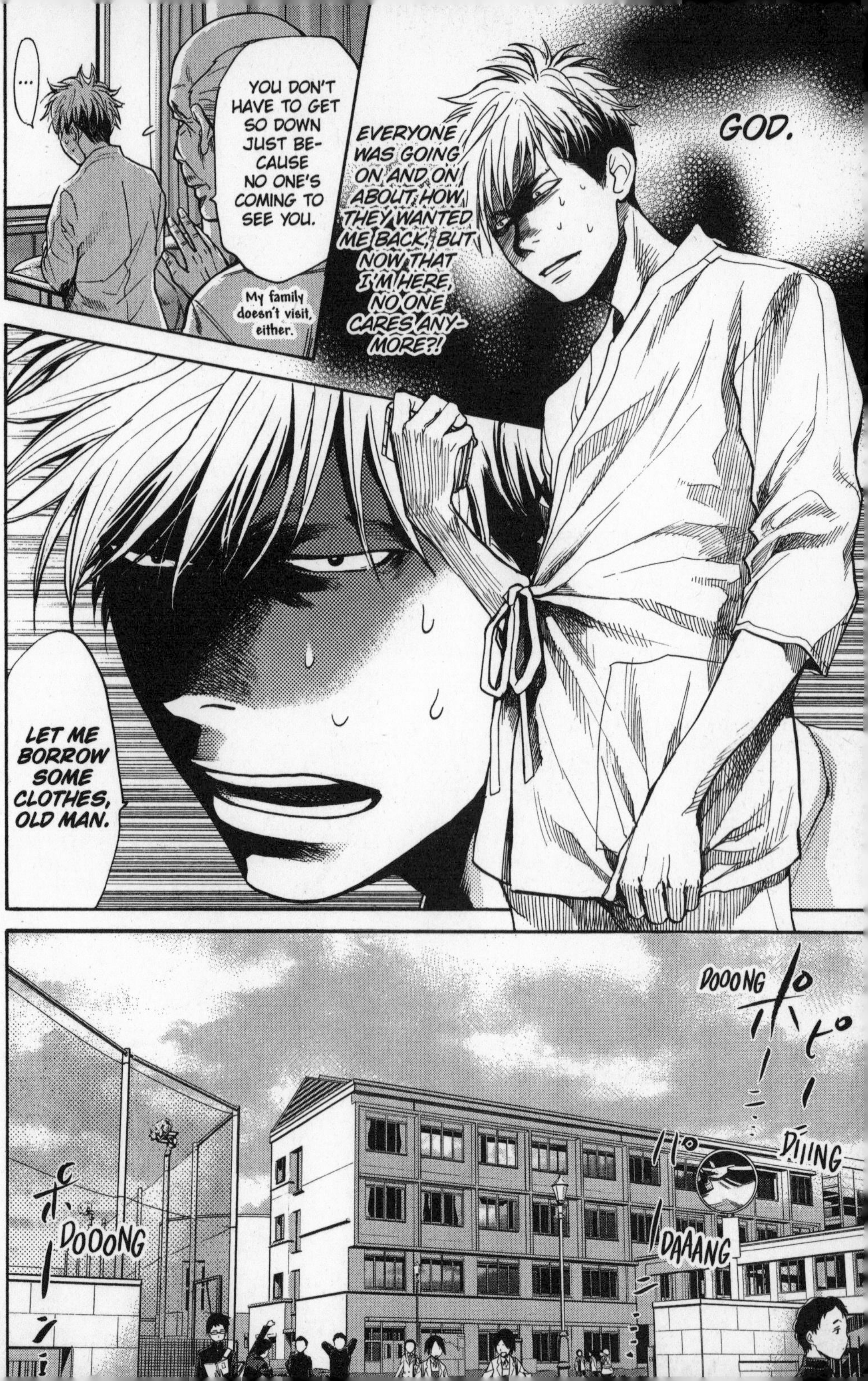

GOD.
EVERYONE WAS GOING ON AND ON ABOUT HOW THEY WANTED ME BACK, BUT NOW THAT I'M HERE, NO ONE CARES ANYMORE?!
YOU DON'T HAVE TO GET SO DOWN JUST BECAUSE NO ONE'S COMING TO SEE YOU.
My family doesn't visit, either.
...
LET ME BORROW SOME CLOTHES, OLD MAN.
DOOONG
DIIING
DAAANG
DOOONG

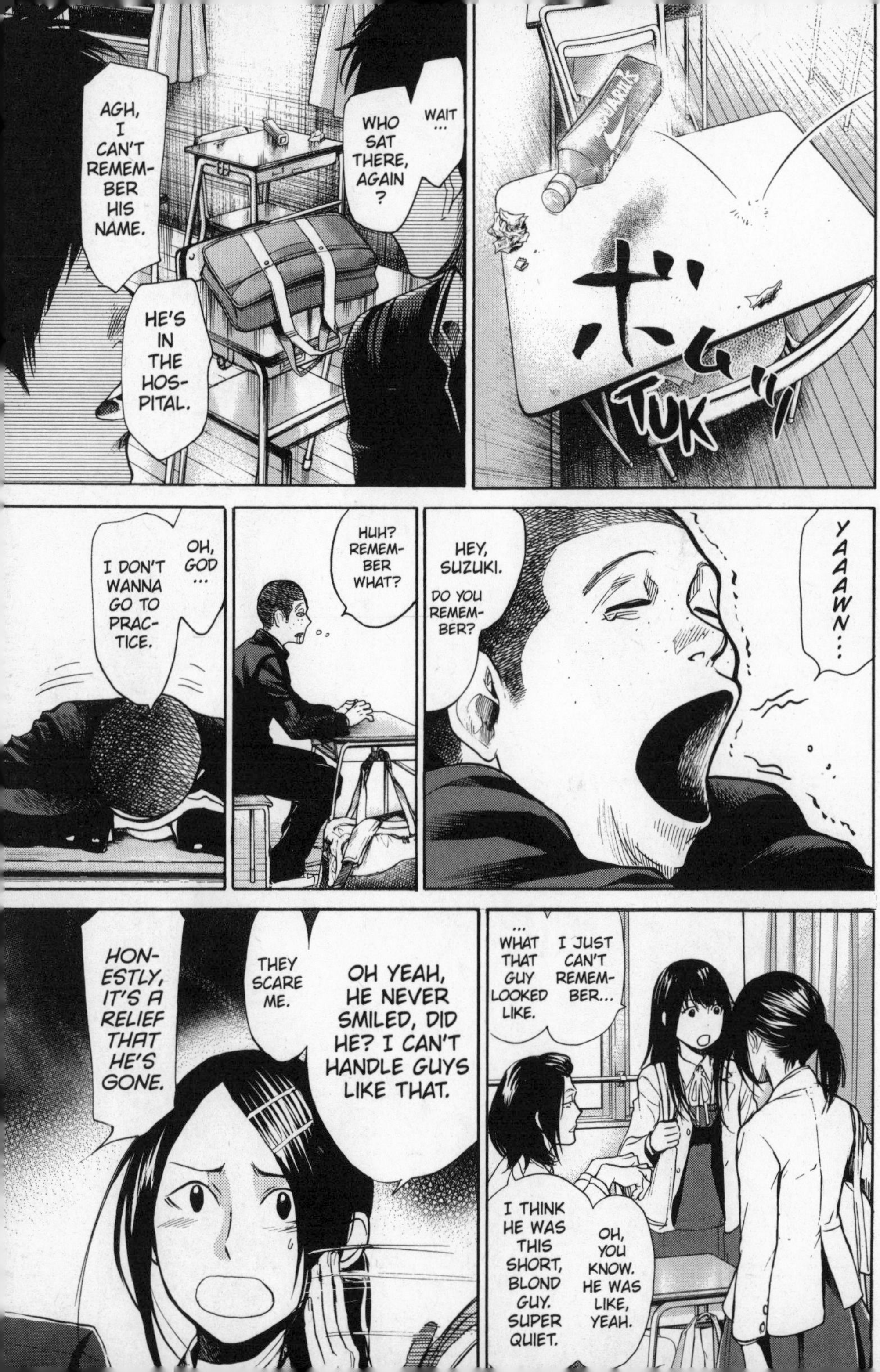
TUK
WAIT...
WHO SAT THERE, AGAIN?
AGH, I CAN'T REMEMBER HIS NAME.
HE'S IN THE HOSPITAL.
YAAAWN...
HEY, SUZUKI.
DO YOU REMEMBER?
HUH? REMEMBER WHAT?
OH, GOD...
I DON'T WANNA GO TO PRACTICE.
I JUST CAN'T REMEMBER...
...WHAT THAT GUY LOOKED LIKE.
OH, YOU KNOW. HE WAS LIKE, YEAH.
I THINK HE WAS THIS SHORT, BLOND GUY. SUPER QUIET.
OH YEAH, HE NEVER SMILED, DID HE? I CAN'T HANDLE GUYS LIKE THAT.
THEY SCARE ME.
HONESTLY, IT'S A RELIEF THAT HE'S GONE.

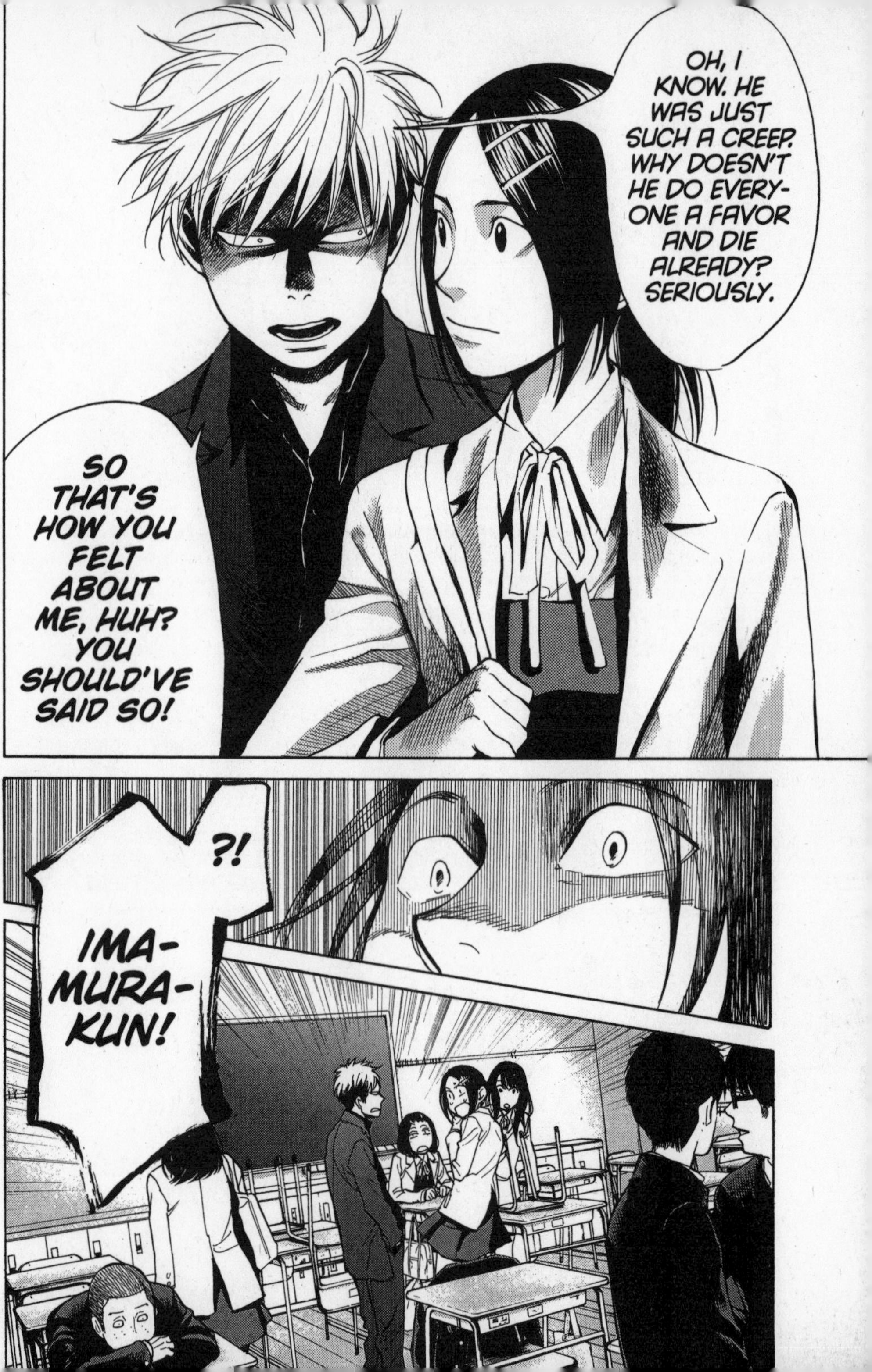
OH, I KNOW. HE WAS JUST SUCH A CREEP. WHY DOESN'T HE DO EVERY-ONE A FAVOR AND DIE ALREADY? SERIOUSLY.
SO THAT'S HOW YOU FELT ABOUT ME, HUH? YOU SHOULD'VE SAID SO!
?!
IMA-MURA-KUN!

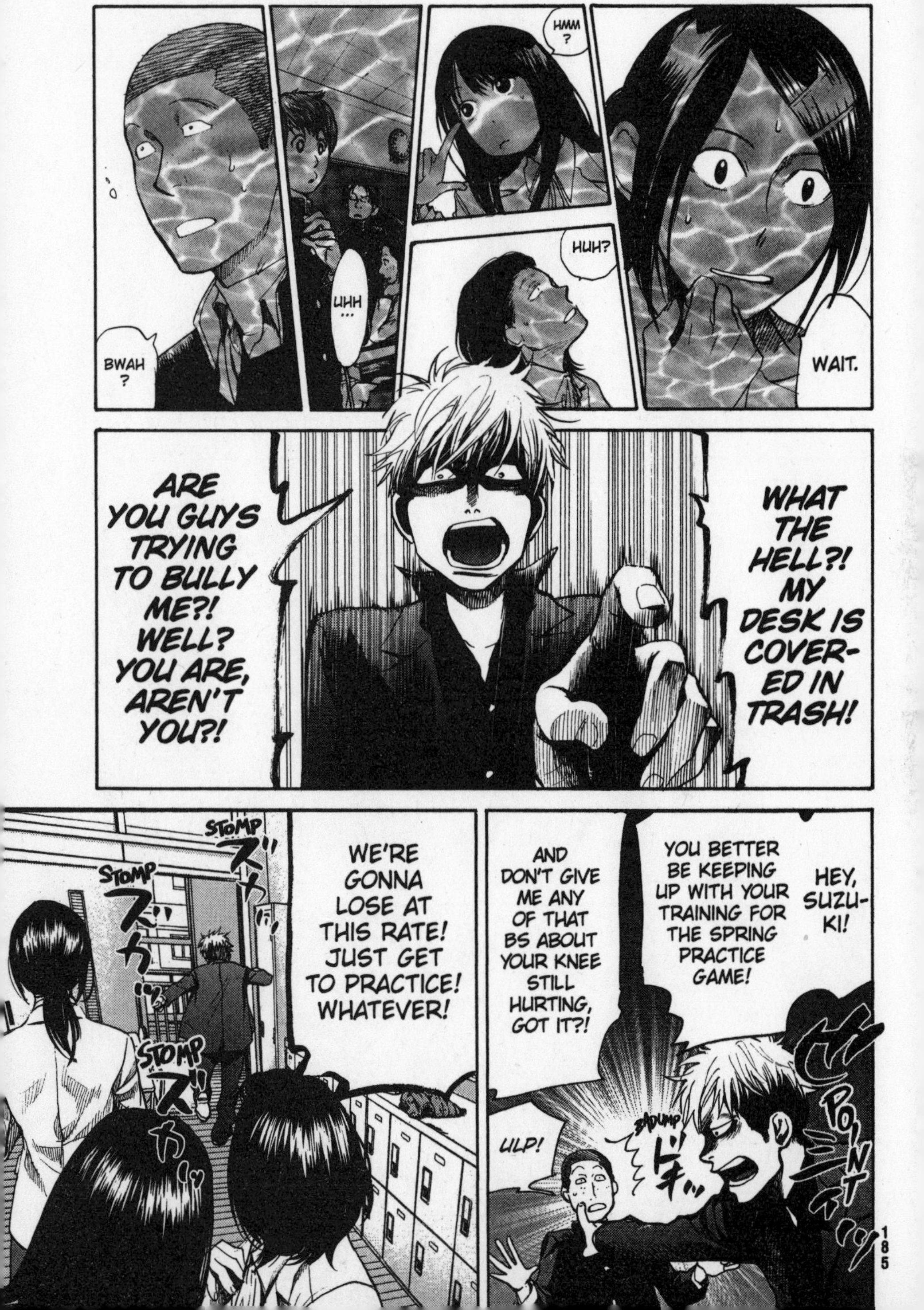

WAIT.
HMM?
HUH?
UHH...
BWAH?
WHAT THE HELL?! MY DESK IS COVERED IN TRASH!
ARE YOU GUYS TRYING TO BULLY ME?! WELL? YOU ARE, AREN'T YOU?!
HEY, SUZUKI!
YOU BETTER BE KEEPING UP WITH YOUR TRAINING FOR THE SPRING PRACTICE GAME!
POINT
AND DON'T GIVE ME ANY OF THAT BS ABOUT YOUR KNEE STILL HURTING, GOT IT?!
BADUMP
ULP!
WE'RE GONNA LOSE AT THIS RATE! JUST GET TO PRACTICE! WHATEVER!
STOMP
STOMP
STOMP

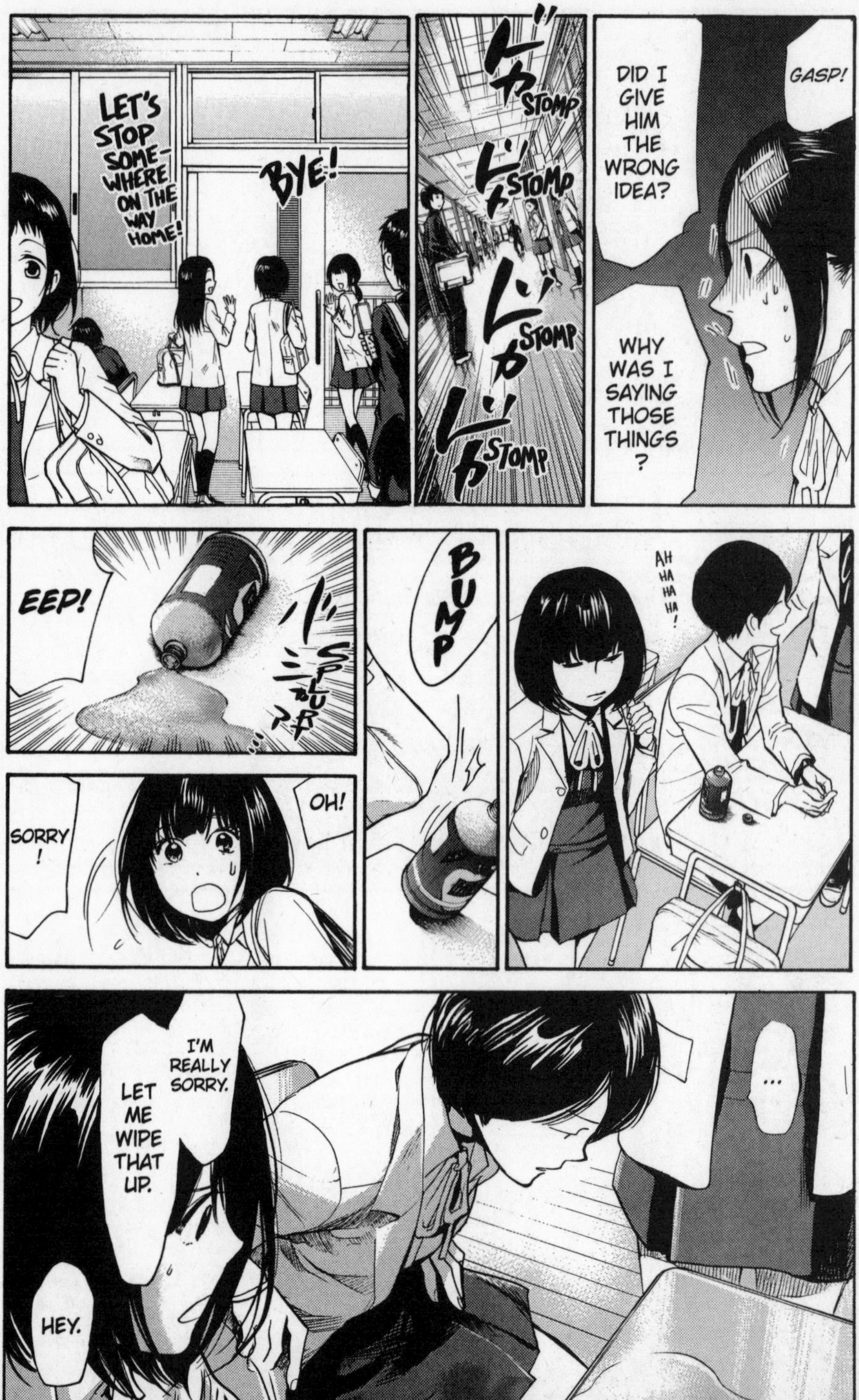
GASP!
DID I GIVE HIM THE WRONG IDEA?
WHY WAS I SAYING THOSE THINGS?
STOMP
STOMP
STOMP
STOMP
LET'S STOP SOME-WHERE ON THE WAY HOME!
BYE!
AH HA HA HA!
BUMP
EEP!
SPLURT
OH!
SORRY!
...
I'M REALLY SORRY.
LET ME WIPE THAT UP.
HEY.

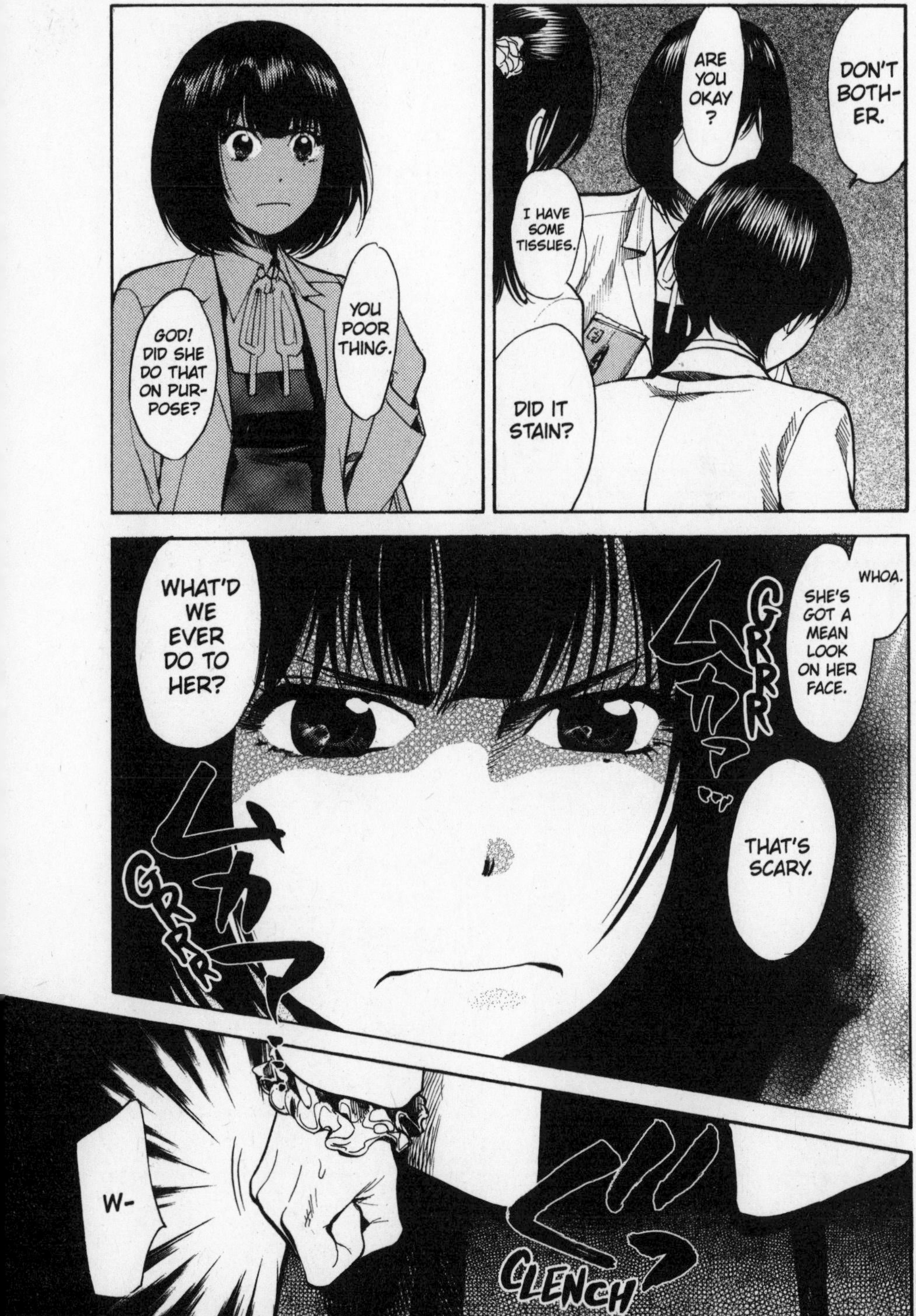
DON'T BOTH-ER.
ARE YOU OKAY ?
I HAVE SOME TISSUES.
DID IT STAIN?
YOU POOR THING.
GOD! DID SHE DO THAT ON PUR-POSE?
WHOA.
SHE'S GOT A MEAN LOOK ON HER FACE.
GRRR
THAT'S SCARY.
WHAT'D WE EVER DO TO HER?
GRRR
CLENCH
W-

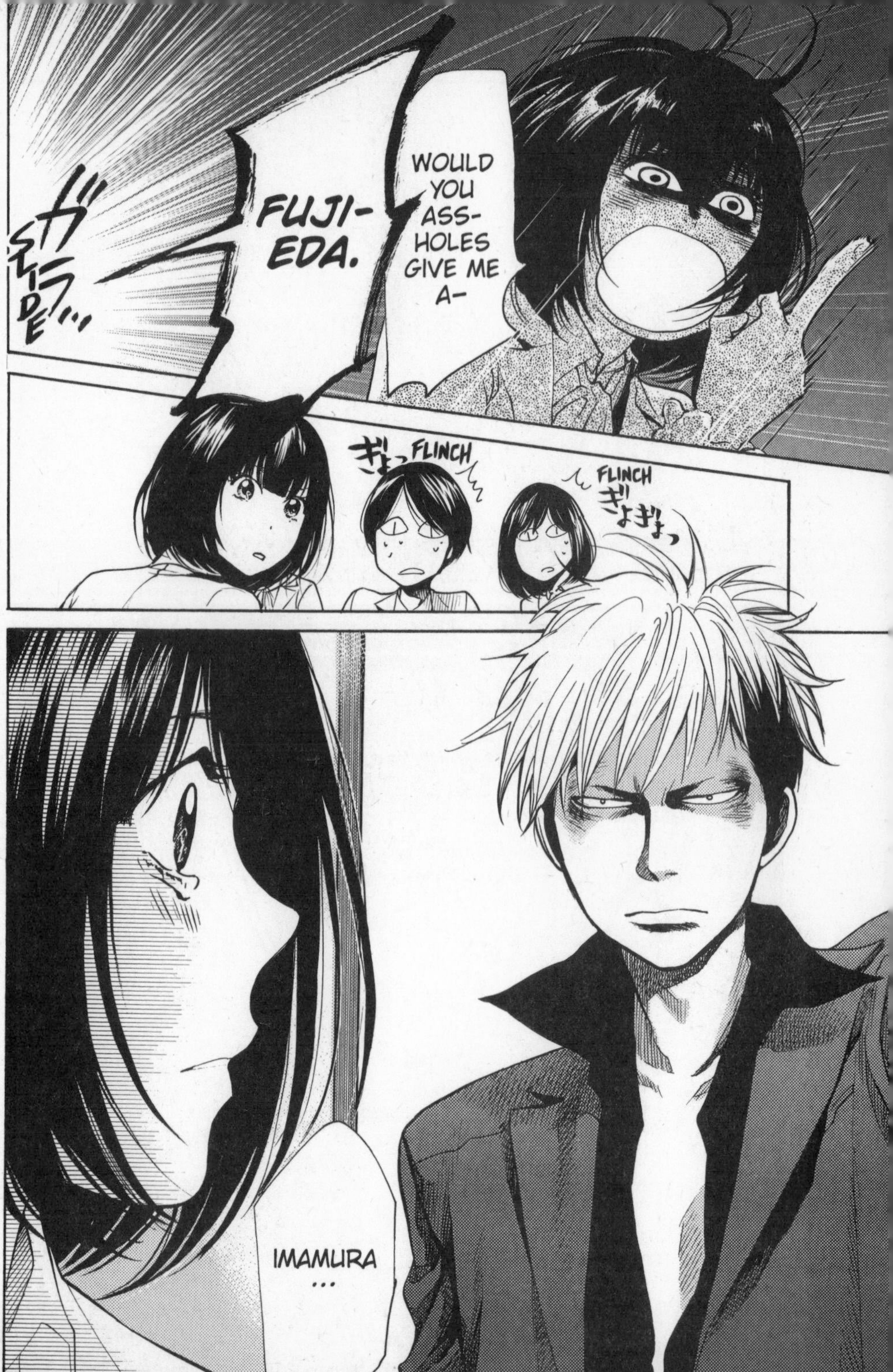
WOULD YOU ASS-HOLES GIVE ME A-
FUJI-EDA.
ガラ
SLIDE...
FLINCH
ぎょぎょっ
ぎょっ
FLINCH
IMAMURA...

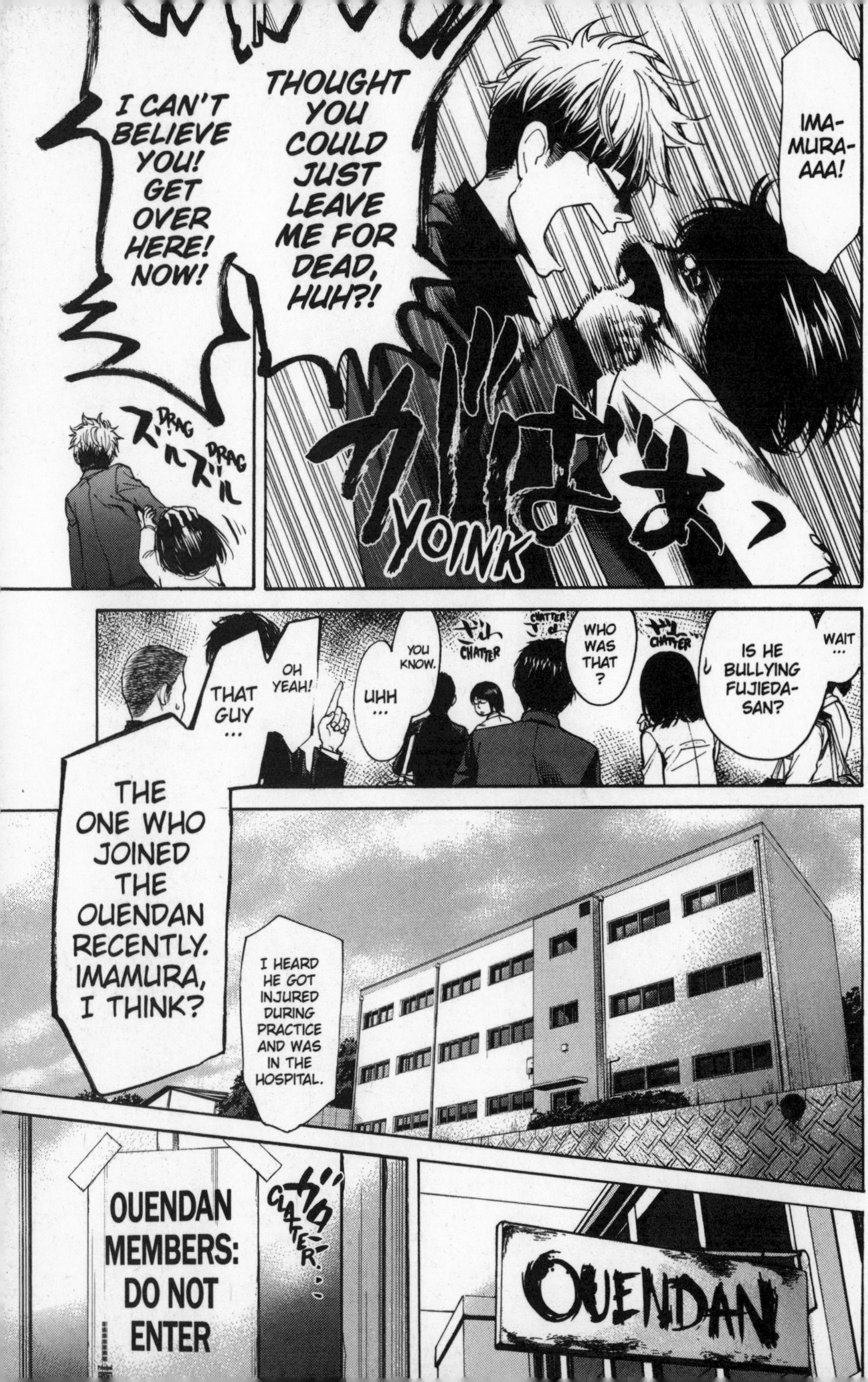
IMA-MURA-AAA!
THOUGHT YOU COULD JUST LEAVE ME FOR DEAD, HUH?!
I CAN'T BELIEVE YOU! GET OVER HERE! NOW!
YOINK
DRAG DRAG
WAIT ...
IS HE BULLYING FUJIEDA-SAN?
CHATTER
WHO WAS THAT ?
CHATTER
CHATTER
YOU KNOW.
UHH ...
OH YEAH!
THAT GUY ...
THE ONE WHO JOINED THE OUENDAN RECENTLY. IMAMURA, I THINK?
I HEARD HE GOT INJURED DURING PRACTICE AND WAS IN THE HOSPITAL.
OUENDAN
CLATTER...
OUENDAN MEMBERS: DO NOT ENTER

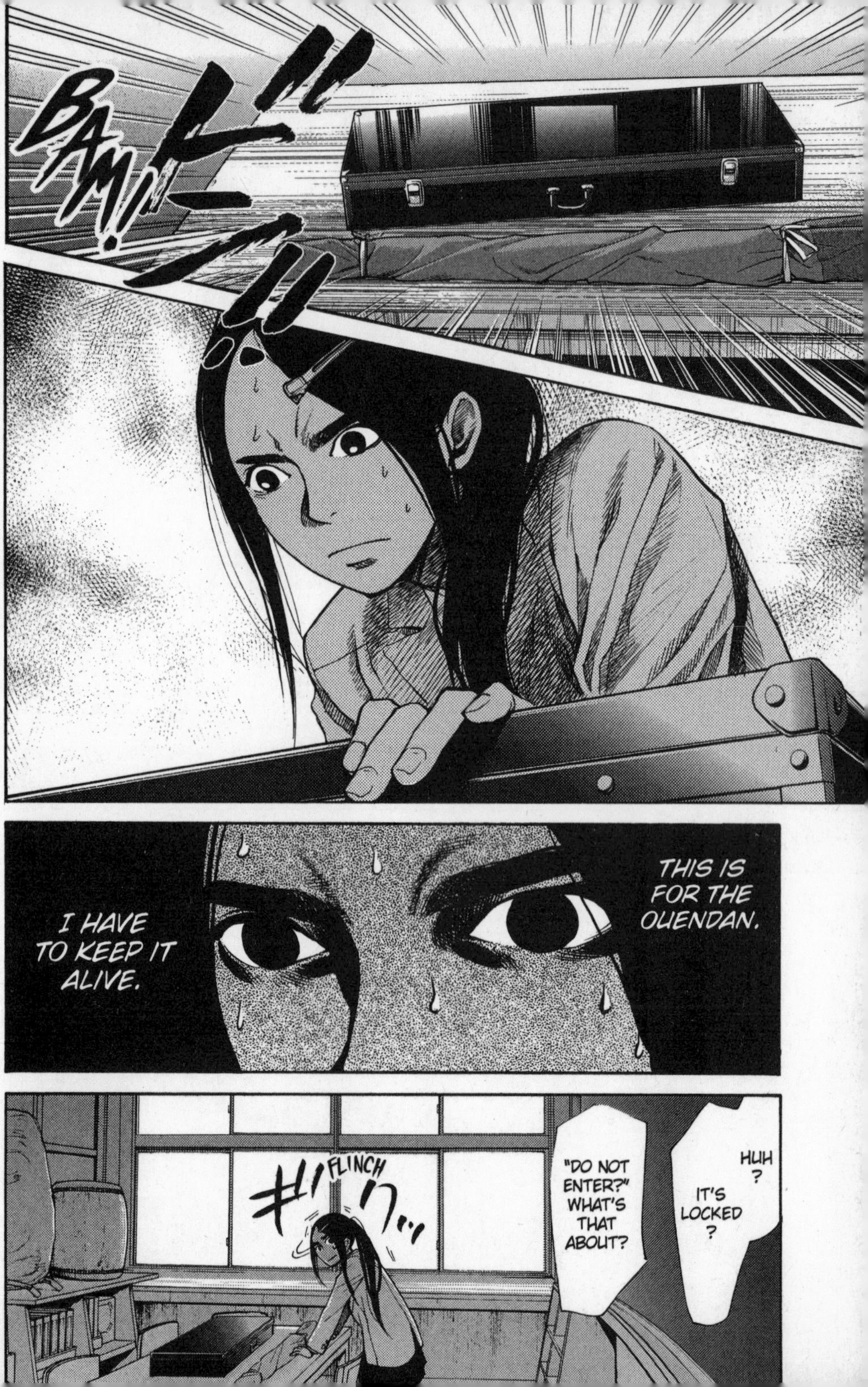
BAM!!
THIS IS FOR THE OUENDAN.
I HAVE TO KEEP IT ALIVE.
HUH?
IT'S LOCKED?
"DO NOT ENTER?" WHAT'S THAT ABOUT?
FLINCH

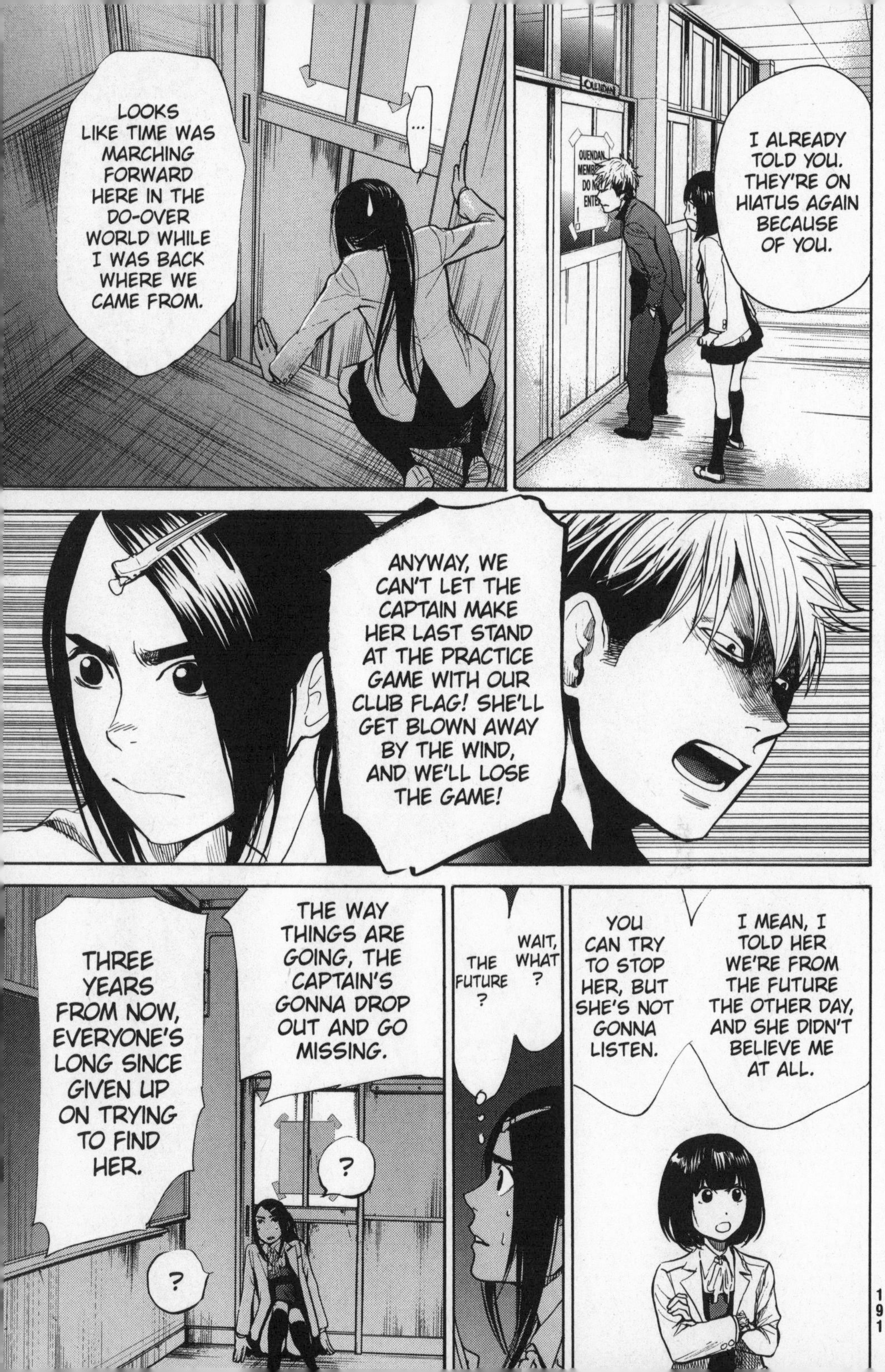
I ALREADY TOLD YOU. THEY'RE ON HIATUS AGAIN BECAUSE OF YOU.
...
LOOKS LIKE TIME WAS MARCHING FORWARD HERE IN THE DO-OVER WORLD WHILE I WAS BACK WHERE WE CAME FROM.
ANYWAY, WE CAN'T LET THE CAPTAIN MAKE HER LAST STAND AT THE PRACTICE GAME WITH OUR CLUB FLAG! SHE'LL GET BLOWN AWAY BY THE WIND, AND WE'LL LOSE THE GAME!
I MEAN, I TOLD HER WE'RE FROM THE FUTURE THE OTHER DAY, AND SHE DIDN'T BELIEVE ME AT ALL.
YOU CAN TRY TO STOP HER, BUT SHE'S NOT GONNA LISTEN.
WAIT, WHAT?
THE FUTURE?
THE WAY THINGS ARE GOING, THE CAPTAIN'S GONNA DROP OUT AND GO MISSING.
THREE YEARS FROM NOW, EVERYONE'S LONG SINCE GIVEN UP ON TRYING TO FIND HER.
?
?

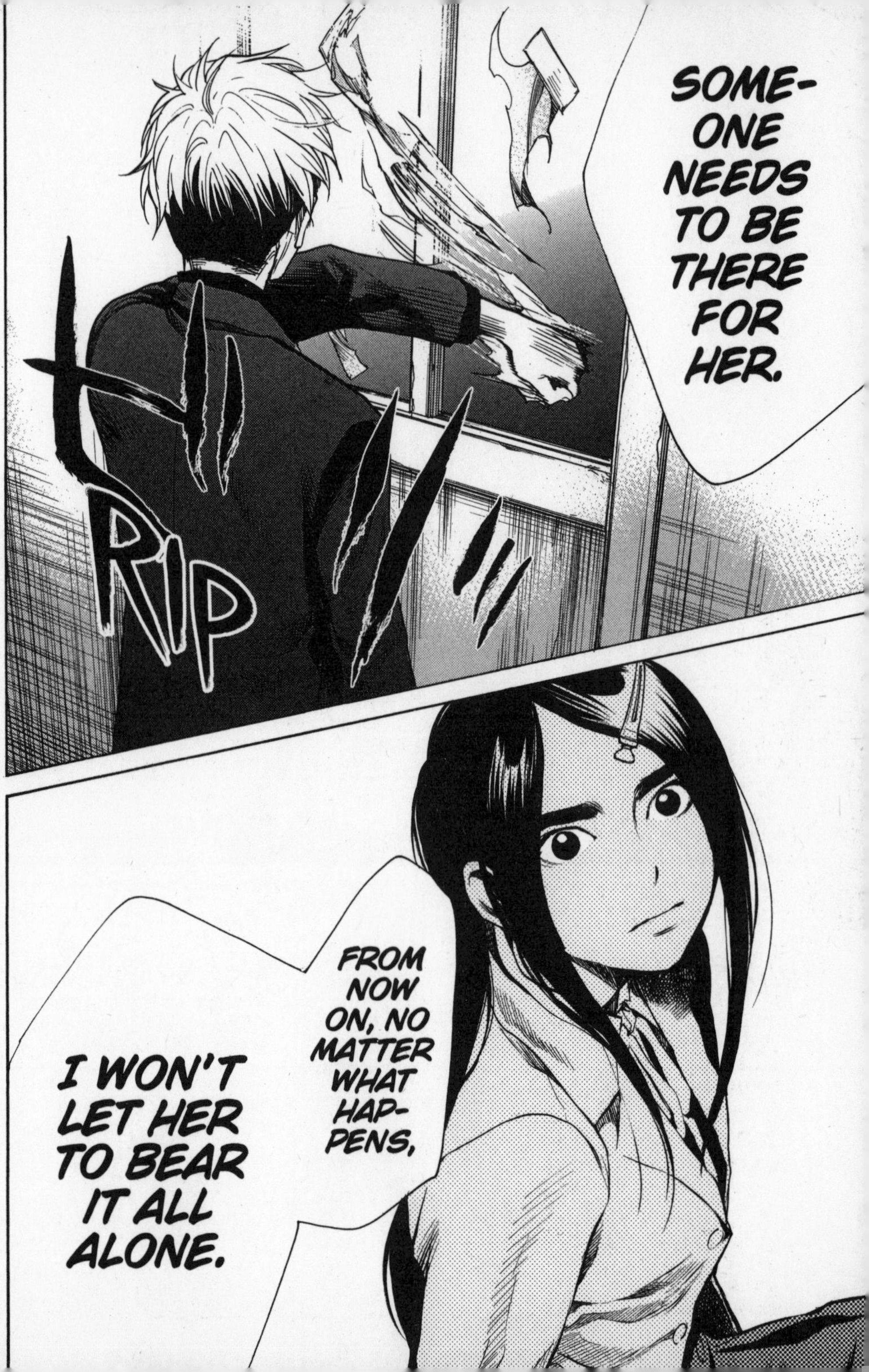

SOME-ONE NEEDS TO BE THERE FOR HER.
RIP
FROM NOW ON, NO MATTER WHAT HAP-PENS,
I WON'T LET HER TO BEAR IT ALL ALONE.

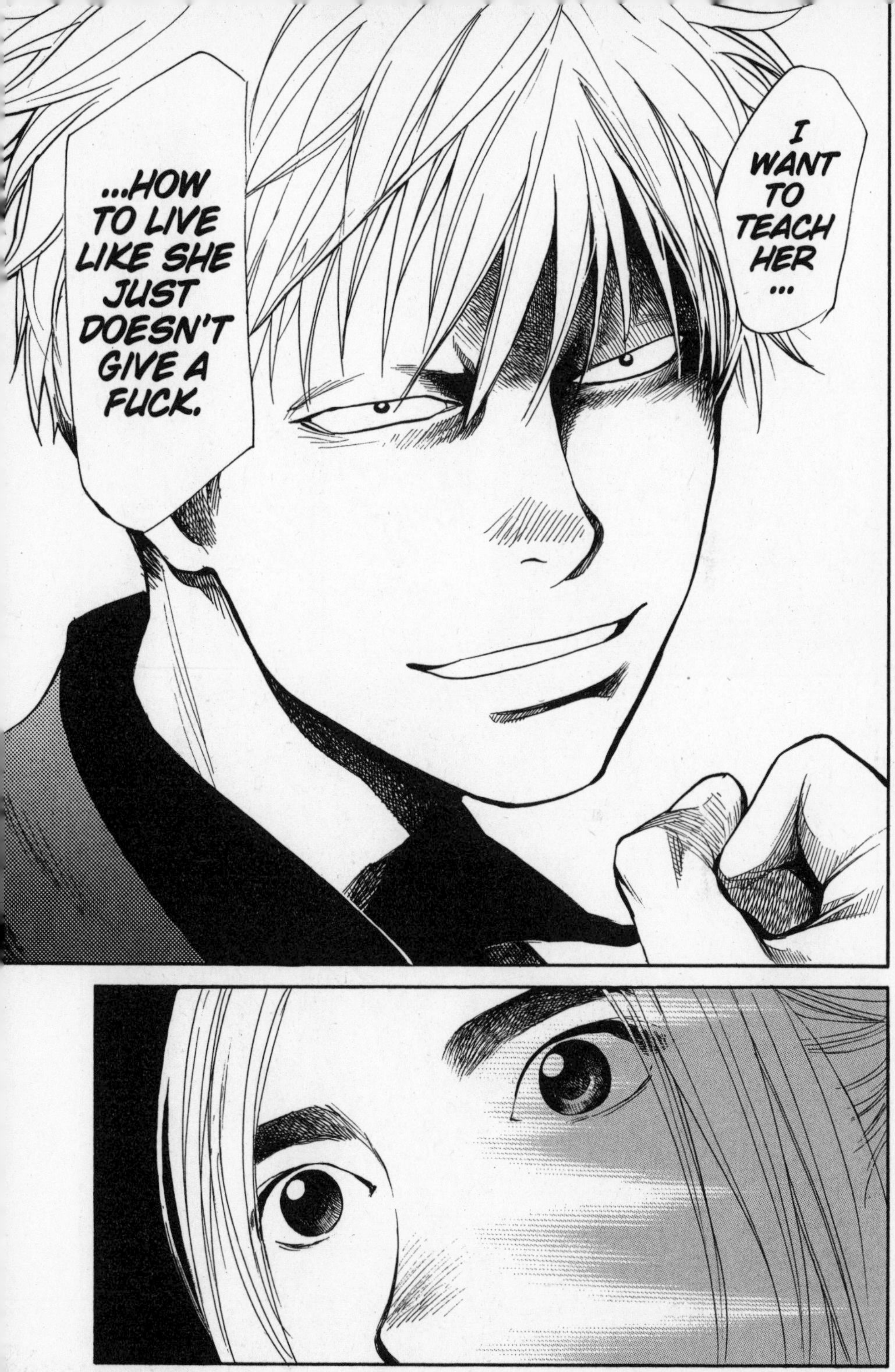
I WANT TO TEACH HER...
...HOW TO LIVE LIKE SHE JUST DOESN'T GIVE A FUCK.

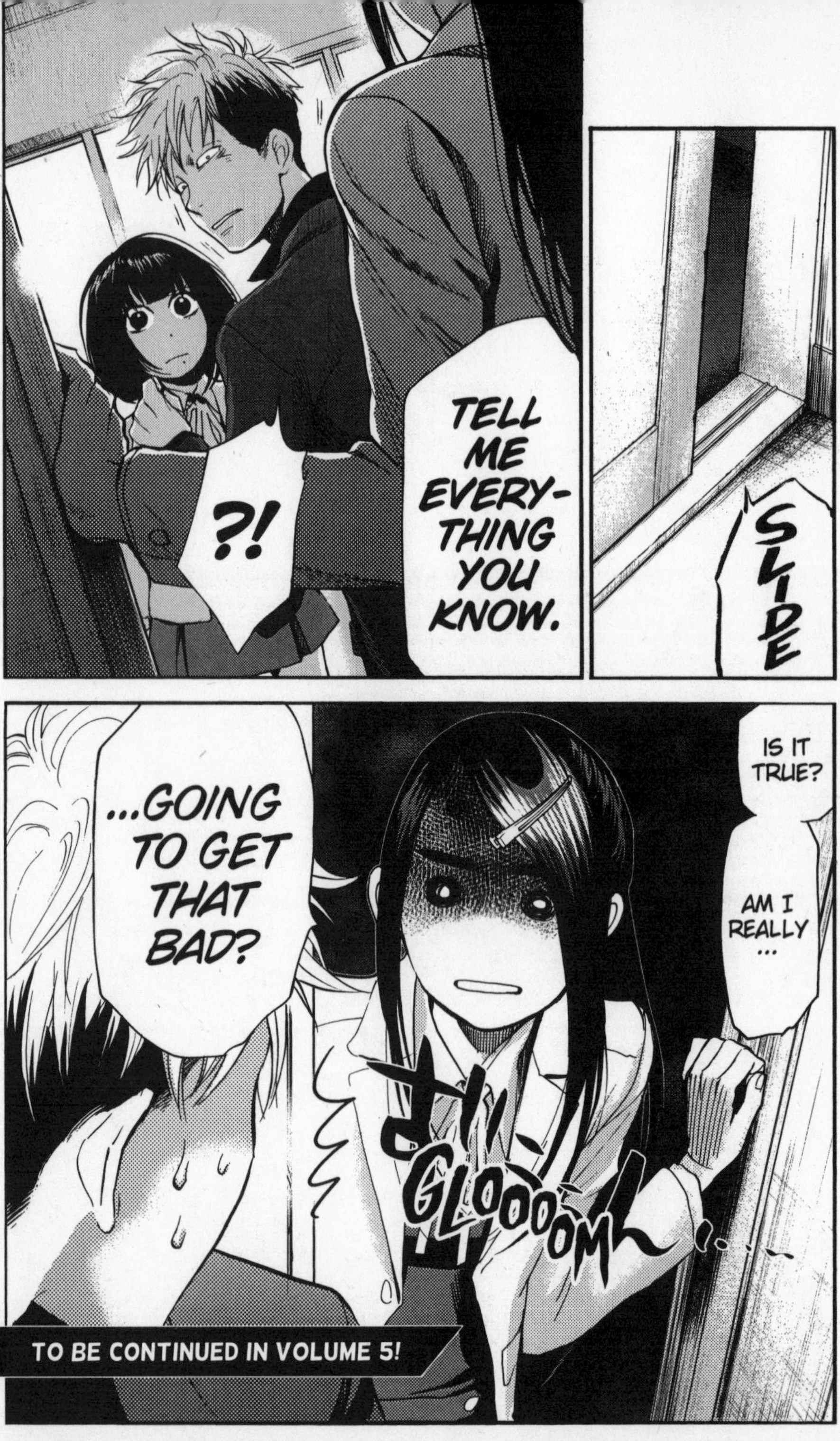
SLIDE
TELL ME EVERYTHING YOU KNOW.
?!
IS IT TRUE?
AM I REALLY ...
...GOING TO GET THAT BAD?
GLOOOOM
TO BE CONTINUED IN VOLUME 5!

Again!!

アゲイン!!

IN THE NEXT VOLUME...

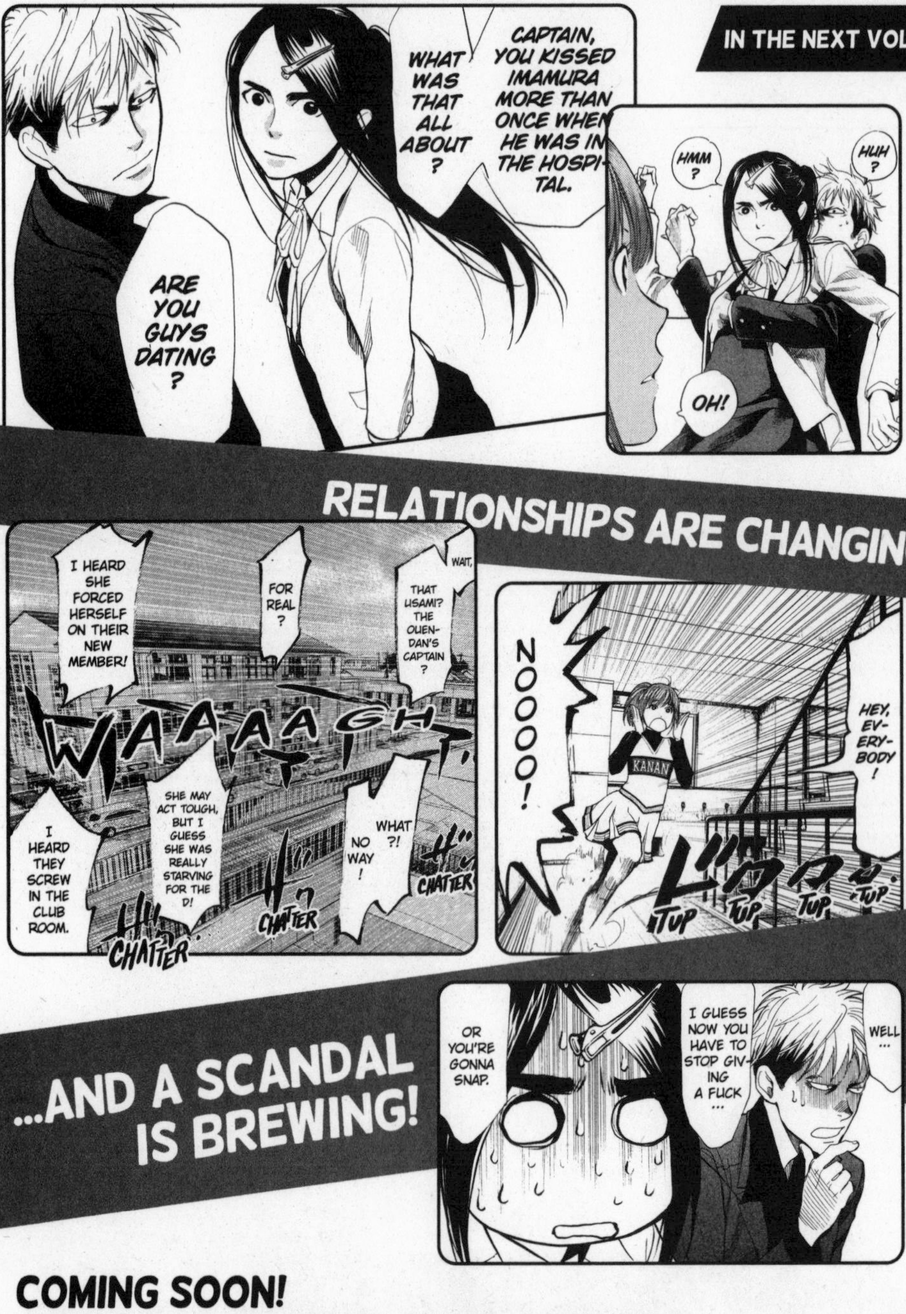
HMM ?
HUH ?
OH!
CAPTAIN, YOU KISSED IMAMURA MORE THAN ONCE WHEN HE WAS IN THE HOSPITAL.
WHAT WAS THAT ALL ABOUT ?
ARE YOU GUYS DATING ?
NOOOOO!
HEY, EVERYBODY !
KANAN
TUP TUP TUP TUP TUP
WAIT, THAT USAMI? THE OUENDAN'S CAPTAIN ?
FOR REAL ?
I HEARD SHE FORCED HERSELF ON THEIR NEW MEMBER!
WAAAAGH
WHAT ?!
NO WAY !
CHATTER
SHE MAY ACT TOUGH, BUT I GUESS SHE WAS REALLY STARVING FOR THE D!
CHATTER
I HEARD THEY SCREW IN THE CLUB ROOM.
CHATTER
WELL ...
I GUESS NOW YOU HAVE TO STOP GIVING A FUCK ...
OR YOU'RE GONNA SNAP.

RELATIONSHIPS ARE CHANGING.

...AND A SCANDAL IS BREWING!

COMING SOON!

WHAT'S NEXT FOR THIS MUCH GOSSIPED-ABOUT COUPLE?!

Again!!
アゲイン!!

Translation Notes

"Taiko no Tatsujin"
Page 30

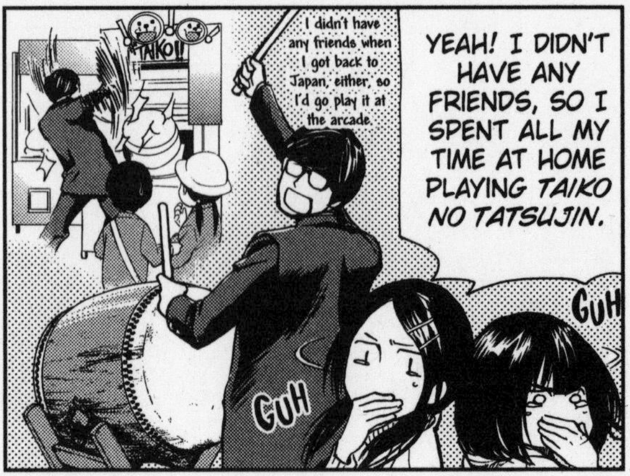

YEAH! I DIDN'T HAVE ANY FRIENDS, SO I SPENT ALL MY TIME AT HOME PLAYING *TAIKO NO TATSUJIN.*
I didn't have any friends when I got back to Japan, either, so I'd go play it at the arcade.
TAIKO!!
GUH
GUH

Taiko no Tatsujin (literally "Taiko Master") is a series of rhythm games ubiquitous in the video arcades of Japan. They feature a large drum controller and a selection of pop songs the player plays along with. Given the precision such games require, mastering the higher difficulty levels might very well have given Okuma a credible degree of drumming skill.

"It's Me Scam"
Page 181

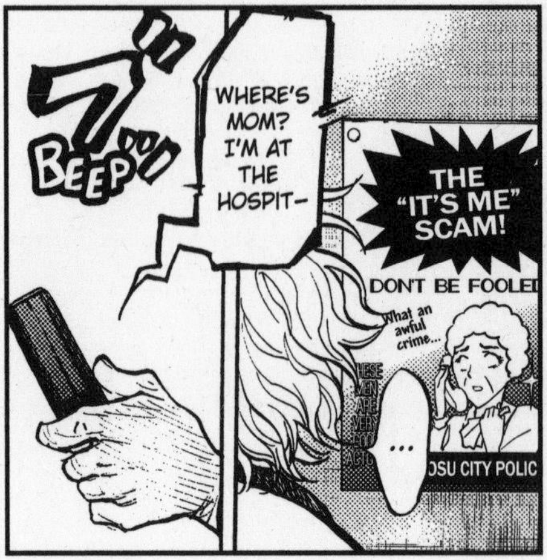

BEEP
WHERE'S MOM? I'M AT THE HOSPIT–
THE "IT'S ME" SCAM!
What an awful crime...
...

The *Ore Ore Sagi* (literally "Me Me Swindle") is a type of fraud targeted at the elderly. The perpetrator calls their target on the phone and poses as a younger relative—a grandchild or similar—in need of money: "Grandma, it's me! Don't you remember?" The scam became common enough to require public awareness campaigns, which is what Kinichiro's grandmother takes note of before she hangs up on her actual grandson.

Again!!
アゲイン!!

"Complex Age feels like an intimate look at women in fandom... I can't recommend it enough."
—*Manga Connection*

complex age

yui sakuma

26-year-old Nagisa Kataura has a secret. Transforming into her favorite anime and manga characters is her passion in life, and she's earned great respect amongst her fellow cospayers. But to the rest of society, her hobby is a silly fantasy. As demands from both her office job and cosplaying begin to increase, she may one day have to make a tough choice— what's more important to her, cosplay or being "normal"?

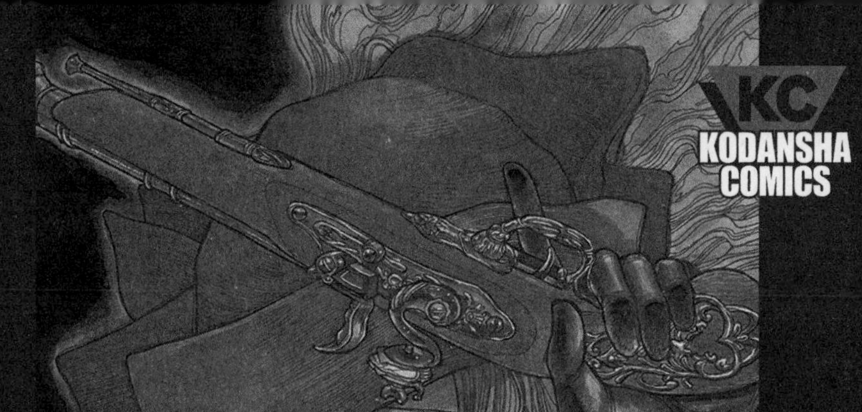

The Black Museum The Ghost and the Lady

By Kazuhiro Fujita

Deep in Scotland Yard in London sits an evidence room dedicated to the greatest mysteries of British history. In this "Black Museum" sits a misshapen hunk of lead–two bullets fused together–the key to a wartime encounter between Florence Nightingale, the mother of modern nursing, and a supernatural Man in Grey. This story is unknown to most scholars of history, but a special guest of the museum will tell the tale of The Ghost and the Lady...

Praise for Kazuhiro Fujita's *Ushio and Tora*

"A charming revival that combines a classic look with modern depth and pacing... **Essential viewing both for curmudgeons and new fans alike.**" — Anime News Network

"**GREAT!** The first episode of Ushio and Tora captures the essence of '90s anime." — IGN

HAPPINESS

ハピネス

By Shuzo Oshimi

From the creator of *The Flowers of Evil*

Nothing interesting is happening in Makoto Ozaki's first year of high school. His life is a series of quiet humiliations: low-grade bullies, unreliable friends, and the constant frustration of his adolescent lust. But one night, a pale, thin girl knocks him to the ground in an alley and offers him a choice. Now everything is different. Daylight is searingly bright. Food tastes awful. And worse than anything is the terrible, consuming thirst...

Praise for Shuzo Oshimi's *The Flowers of Evil*

"A shockingly readable story that vividly—one might even say queasily—evokes the fear and confusion of discovering one's own sexuality. Recommended." —The Manga Critic

"A page-turning tale of sordid middle school blackmail." —Otaku USA Magazine

"A stunning new horror manga." —Third Eye Comics

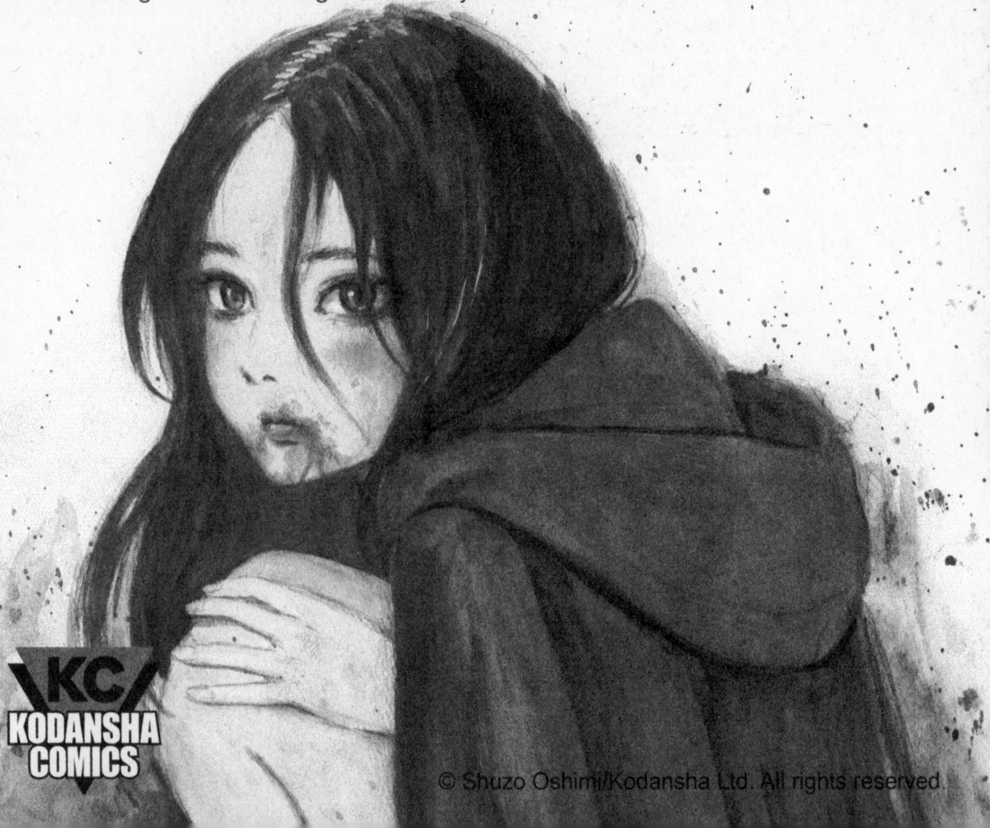

KC KODANSHA COMICS

Based on the critically acclaimed classic horror manga

The first new *Parasyte* manga in over 20 years!

NEO PARASYTE f

BY ASUMIKO NAKAMURA, EMA TOYAMA, MIKI RINNO, LALAKO KOJIMA, KAORI YUKI, BANKO KUZE, YUUKI OBATA, KASHIO, YUI KUROE, ASIA WATANABE, MIKIMAKI, HIKARU SURUGA, HAJIME SHINJO, RENJURO KINDAICHI, AND YURI NARUSHIMA

A collection of chilling new *Parasyte* stories from Japan's top shojo artists!

Parasites: shape-shifting aliens whose only purpose is to assimilate with and consume the human race... but do these monsters have a different side? A parasite becomes a prince to save his romance-obsessed female host from a dangerous stalker. Another hosts a cooking show, in which the real monsters are revealed. These and 13 more stories, from some of the greatest shojo manga artists alive today, together make up a chilling, funny, and entertaining tribute to one of manga's horror classics!

KC KODANSHA COMICS

Princess Jellyfish

Akiko Higashimura

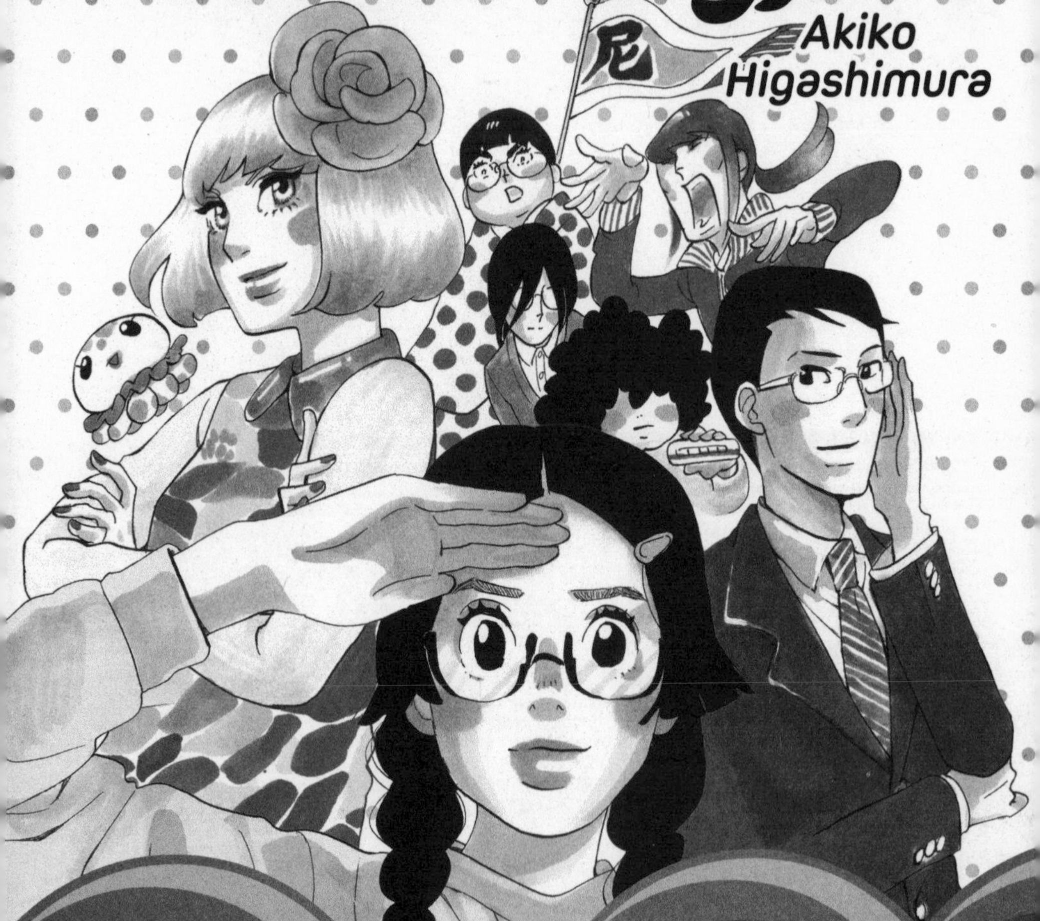

尼

ALSO AN ANIME!

"One of the best manga for beginners!"
—***Kotaku***

Tsukimi Kurashita is fascinated with jellyfish. She's loved them from a young age and has carried that love with her to her new life in the big city of Tokyo. There, she resides in Amamizukan, a safe-haven for geek girls where no boys are allowed. One day, Tsukimi crosses paths with a beautiful and fashionable woman, but there's much more to this woman than her trendy clothes...!

Having lost his wife, high school teacher Kōhei Inuzuka is doing his best to raise his young daughter Tsumugi as a single father. He's pretty bad at cooking and doesn't have a huge appetite to begin with, but chance brings his little family together with one of his students, the lonely Kotori. The three of them are anything but comfortable in the kitchen, but the healing power of home cooking might just work on their grieving hearts.

"This season's number-one feel-good anime!" —Anime News Network

"A beautifully-drawn story about comfort food and family and grief. Recommended." —Otaku USA Magazine

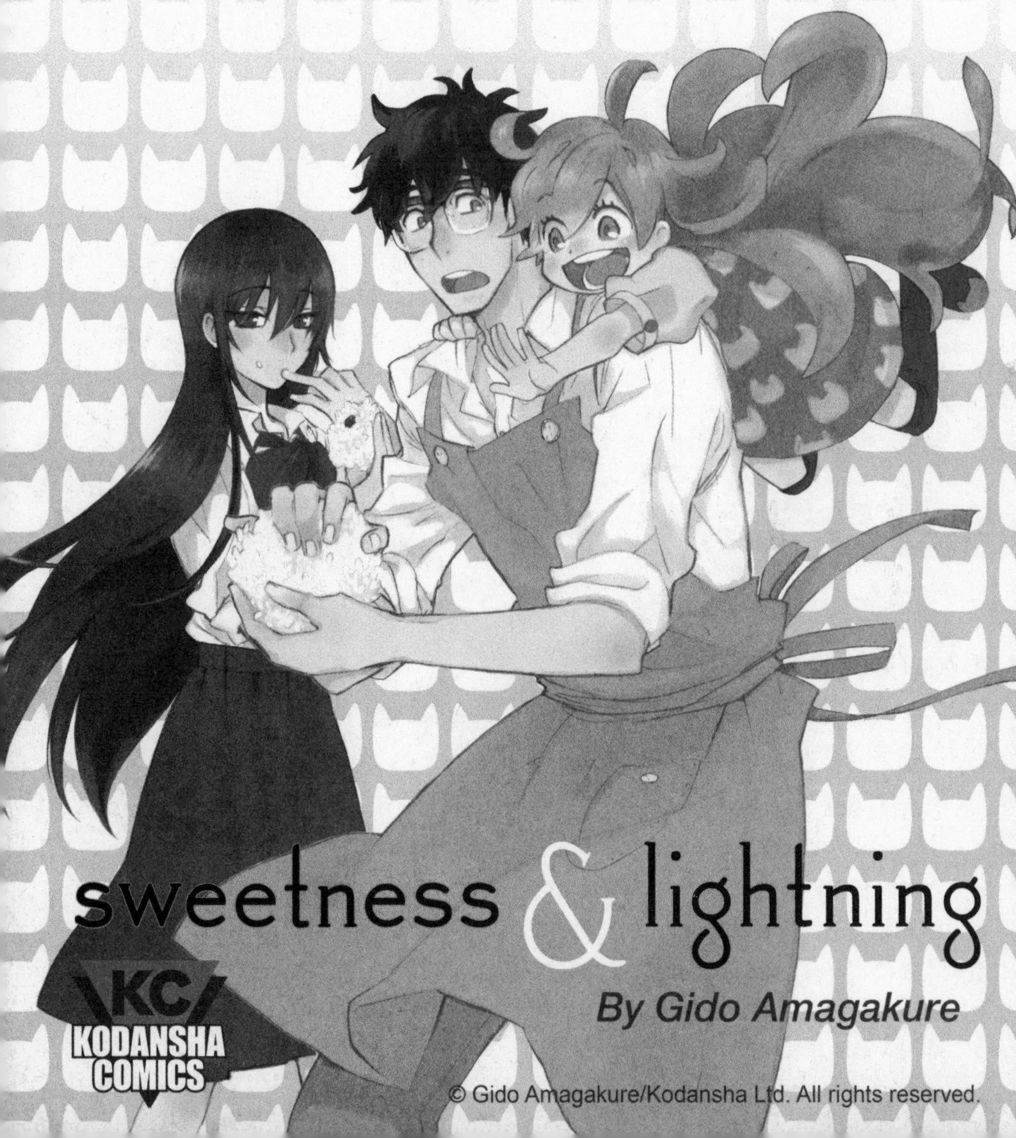

sweetness & lightning

By Gido Amagakure

KODANSHA COMICS

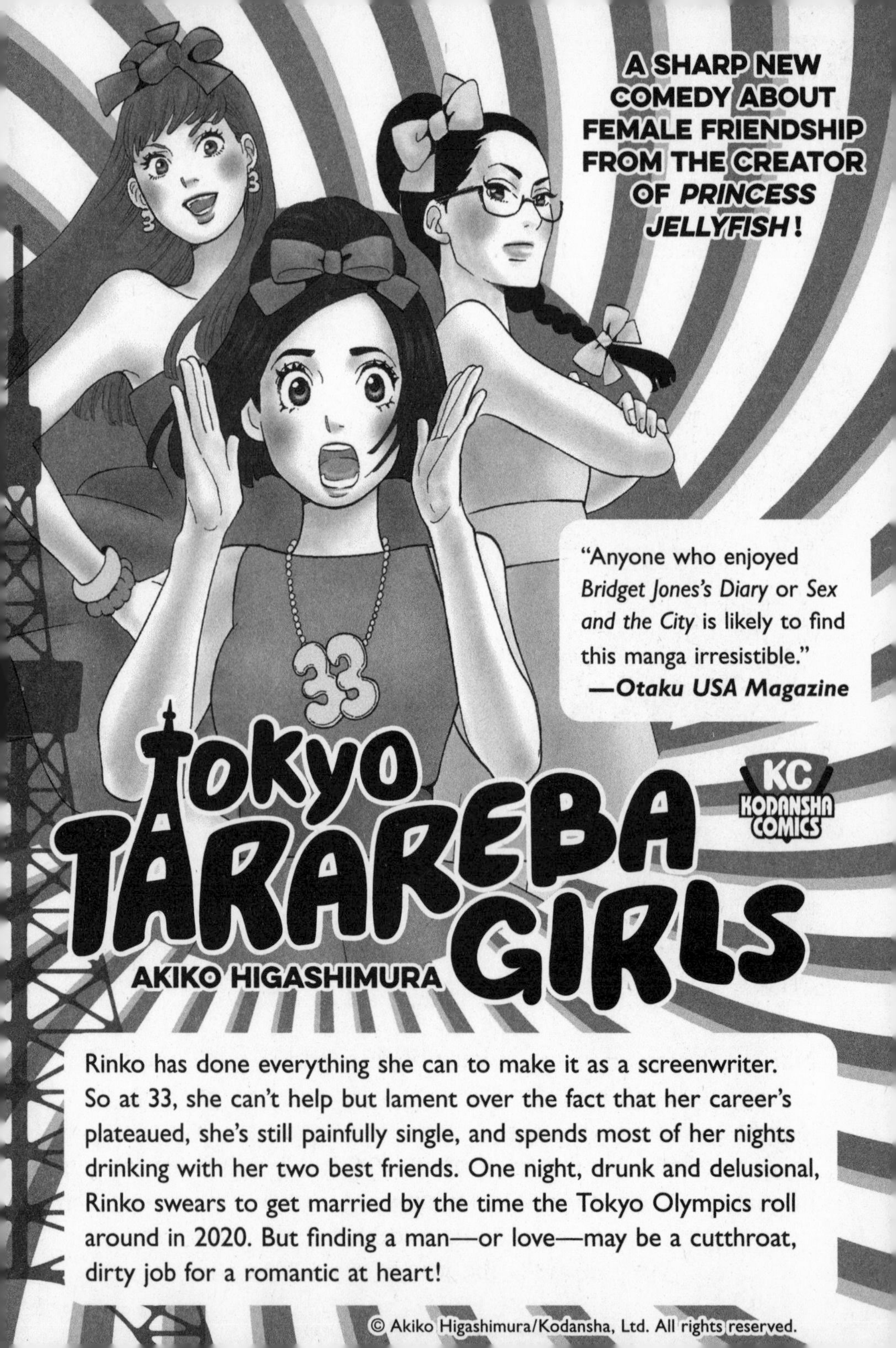
A SHARP NEW COMEDY ABOUT FEMALE FRIENDSHIP FROM THE CREATOR OF *PRINCESS JELLYFISH*!
"Anyone who enjoyed *Bridget Jones's Diary* or *Sex and the City* is likely to find this manga irresistible."
—Otaku USA Magazine
TOKYO TARAREBA GIRLS
AKIKO HIGASHIMURA
KC KODANSHA COMICS
Rinko has done everything she can to make it as a screenwriter. So at 33, she can't help but lament over the fact that her career's plateaued, she's still painfully single, and spends most of her nights drinking with her two best friends. One night, drunk and delusional, Rinko swears to get married by the time the Tokyo Olympics roll around in 2020. But finding a man—or love—may be a cutthroat, dirty job for a romantic at heart!
© Akiko Higashimura/Kodansha, Ltd. All rights reserved.

In love, there are
no save points.

KC
KODANSHA
COMICS

NOW AN
ANIME!

ヲタクに恋は難しい

WOTAKOI:
LOVE IS HARD FOR OTAKU

by FUJITA

Narumi has had it rough: Every boyfriend she's had dumped her
once they found out she was an otaku, so she's gone to great
lengths to hide it. At her new job, she bumps into Hirotaka, her
childhood friend and fellow otaku. When Hirotaka almost gets
her secret outed at work, she comes up with a plan to keep him
quiet. But he comes up with a counter-proposal:
Why doesn't she just date him instead?

A Kodansha Comics Trade Paperback Original.

Again!! volume 4 copyright © 2012 Mitsurou Kubo
English translation copyright © 2018 Mitsurou Kubo

Published in the United States by Kodansha Comics, an imprint of Kodansha USA Publishing, LLC, New York.

Publication rights for this English edition arranged through Kodansha Ltd., Tokyo.

First published in Japan in 2012 by Kodansha Ltd., Tokyo, as *Agein!!* volume 4.

ISBN 978-1-63236-648-1

Printed in the United States of America.

www.kodanshacomics.com

9 8 7 6 5 4 3 2 1

Translator: Rose Padgett
Lettering: E. K. Weaver
Editing: Paul Starr
Editorial Assistance: Tiff Ferentini
Kodansha Comics edition cover design by Phil Balsman